OPTIONS
ESSENTIAL CONCEPTS AND TRADING STRATEGIES

Edited by

The Options Institute:
The Educational Division
of the Chicago Board
Options Exchange

BUSINESS ONE IRWIN
Homewood, Illinois 60430

*This book is dedicated to revealing the best kept secret
in the securities industry . . . options.*

© The Chicago Board Options Exchange, 1990

This publication is designed to provide accurate and
authoritative information in regard to the subject matter
covered. It is sold with the understanding that neither the
author nor the publisher is engaged in rendering legal, accounting,
or other professional service. If legal advice or other expert
assistance is required, the services of a competent
professional person should be sought.

*From a Declaration of Principles jointly adopted by a Committee
of the American Bar Association and a Committee of Publishers.*

Acquisitions editor: Amy Hollands
Project editor: Susan Trentacosti
Production manager: Irene H. Sotiroff
Jacket design: Michael S. Finkelman
Compositor: Bi-Comp, Incorporated
Typeface: 11/13 Times Roman
Printer: R. R. Donnelley & Sons Company

Library of Congress Cataloging-in-Publication Data

Options : essential concepts and trading strategies / edited by the
Options Institute.
    p. cm.
  ISBN 1-55623-102-4
  1. Options (Finance) I. Options Institute (Chicago Board Options
Exchange)
HG6024.A3065 1990
332.63′228—dc20   90–2965
                                                          CIP

Printed in the United States of America

  5 6 7 8 9 0 D O 7 6 5 4 3 2

PREFACE

Option books as a rule tend to be long on theory and short on practical application. They also tend to be either too elementary, including 50 pages of definitions, or too complicated, written for a Ph.D. mathematician. This book is aimed at readers who find themselves in between these extremes and interested in a guide for practical uses of options. These readers might want the right to buy an underlying security (a *call option*) or the right to sell the security (a *put option*) at some predetermined price before the expiration date. Only they aren't sure how to proceed.

How can options improve risk management or income? When and to what extent can options be used to speculate? Written by industry practitioners, this book provides practical guidance to investors trying to find the inherently subjective answers in options applications.

After Chapter 1, which presents an entertaining and informative in-depth history of options, the book is organized into three parts: Essential Concepts, Trading Strategies, and Real Time Applications.

The Essential Concepts part begins with Fundamentals of Options and skips the mathematics that often confuse rather than clarify. Instead, the reader finds a general discussion of option pricing theory, including usable concepts regarding the change in an option's price relative to stock price movement, passage of time, and changes in implied volatility. Chapter 3, Option Strategies: Analysis and Selection, presents strategies, giving the range of considerations for selecting a strategy, such as the effect of time and the optimal price movement of the underlying security, as well as taking a look at equivalent positions.

Part 2, Trading Strategies, discusses subjective elements and practical considerations for individual investors, institutional investors, and floor traders. Individual investors can learn practical uses of equity options including the most important considerations in strategy selection and the most common pitfalls to be avoided. Institutional investors are shown how options can be used on a portfolio basis to manage risk, to increase income, and to benefit properly from leverage. In addition to exploring index option strategies, Chapter 5 covers controversial option strategies (such as selling equity puts and buying out-of-the-money calls), and it describes how they can be appropriate and profitable for the professional money manager.

Chapter 6, The Business of Market Making, gives the reader a close look at the method by which floor traders earn their living. The myths that floor trading is akin to gambling and that floor traders profit on every trade may well disappear after an examination of this low profit-per-transaction business. While not designed as a "how-to manual," this chapter does explain the trader's method of operation. Then it develops the conclusion that by providing the market with liquidity and by taking only the spread between bid and ask, the floor trader is not in competition with the off-floor trader.

Part 3, Real Time Applications, gives applications and results. Chapter 7, Using Option Market Information to Make Stock Market Decisions, takes a look at three indicators: the put-call ratio, the option premium level, and the level of implied volatility. It gives a good discussion of how this information has been used to make stock market predictions.

Chapter 8, Institutional Case Studies, presents two actual case studies in contrasting investing environments. These real situations give the reader the opportunity to apply theory to practice.

Finally, the appendix, Computer Software for the Options Investor, provides a comprehensive list of software vendors. A glossary of industry jargon is included as a reference for those interested readers.

ACKNOWLEDGMENTS

Any person even slightly close to a book-writing experience knows the many hours invested by numerous people to reach the production date. This project proved equally laborious. One person, in particular, turned the fantasy into reality. Jim Bittman's extra efforts as an author, editor, and coordinator deserve separate note. In addition, our many heartfelt thanks to our authors as well as to the following folks (listed alphabetically):

Jane E. Abe	Walter E. Auch	Fred Bruch
Robert Ackerman	James Brown	Cynthia Buciak

Alger B. Chapman
Deborah Clayworth
Nancy Crossman
Joe Doherty
Darrell Dragoo
Richard G. DuFour
Dianna Feltman
Alicia Goldberg
Bonnie Greenberg

Libby Heimark
Charles J. Henry
Alex Jacobson
Claudia Kasvin
Gary Lahey
Peter Layton
Joe Levin
Mary Lindsey
Paul Lowenstein

Donald A. Lucki, Jr.
Bob McDonald
Warren Moulds
Edward O'Connor
Nicolette Prepura
Monika Ryan
Joseph Sullivan
Fred Weintraub
Elaine E. Woerner

The Options Institute:
The Educational Division
of the Chicago Board
Options Exchange

ABOUT THE AUTHORS

Susan Abbott (Appendix, Computer Software for the Options Investor) is a Chicago-based freelance financial writer specializing in the futures and options industry. A former senior editor at *Futures* magazine, she originated the guide to software (in the appendix) while on the marketing staff of the Chicago Board Options Exchange.

Michael A. Berry (Chapter 8, Institutional Case Studies) is Assistant Professor of Business Administration at the Darden School, University of Virginia. He teaches investment management, portfolio management, and corporate finance. His research interests include the arbitrage pricing model, risk management, value investing strategies, and backtesting systems.

As president of Investment Strategy Analysts, a Charlottesville, Virginia, firm specializing in investment research and investment software development, he has research projects in progress for Citibank, Mellon Bank, and Dreman Value Management.

Berry is active in The Options Institute Institutional Investor's Program, where he leads classes using case studies on a variety of topics. He is also a frequent contributor to the *Financial Analyst's Journal* and he has written for *Institutional Investor* and other investment journals. His book, *Investment Management: A Case Approach,* has been recently published by the Dryden Press. In addition, Berry originated a new options pricing and management system in use at several banks and by several institutional investors worldwide.

James B. Bittman (Chapter 2, Fundamentals of Options, and Chapter 5, Institutional Uses of Options) has nine years experience as a floor trader—three years at the Chicago Board Options Exchange trading equity options and six years at the Chicago Board of Trade trading options on financial futures and options on agricultural futures.

As a regular instructor at The Options Institute at the Chicago Board Options Exchange, Bittman teaches options to stock brokers and professional money managers from the United States and Europe.

Bittman holds a bachelor of arts from Amherst College and a master's degree in business administration from Harvard University.

Elliot Katz (Chapter 1, History of Options, and Chapter 3, Option Strategies: Analysis and Selection) is a regular staff instructor at The Options Institute at the Chicago Board Options Exchange and is involved in teaching options to stock brokers and professional money managers from the United States and Europe.

Prior to joining The Options Institute, Katz was the Options Strategist for Tucker, Anthony and R. L. Day where he developed and recommended option strategies for retail and institutional clients.

Katz holds a bachelor of science in computer science from State University of New York at Stony Brook. He currently lives in suburban Chicago with his wife, Lori, and their son, Jonathan.

John C. Nelson (Appendix, Computer Software for the Options Investor) is the Director, Options Group, for Oster Communications, Inc. He developed the OptionSource option analysis and simulation system that is used in conjunction with the FutureSource quote system from Commodity Communications Corporation. Nelson is a contributor to *Futures* magazine and presents seminars through the Commodity Education Institute and the Chicago School of Finance.

Prior to joining Oster Communications, Inc., he was president of The Applied Research Company. In that position, he was editor of The Commodity Option Analyst newsletter and developed The Option Calculator software package.

He is a certified trading advisor and has traded options on futures at American exchanges.

Nelson holds a bachelor of science in mathematics and a master of science in statistics from Kansas State University, and a master's degree in engineering management from Northwestern University. He is a member of Who's Who in the World.

Harrison Roth (Chapter 4, Option Strategies for the Small Investor) had been involved with options for more than 10 years when the Chicago Board Options Exchange started listed options trading. During his nine years with Drexel Burnham Lambert, he wrote several options reports which became widely known and respected. These include *Trading Put Options, Trading Index Options,* and *The Future of Derivative Products.* He wrote the text for two options videotapes, *Conservative Use of Options* and *Index Options,* as well as writing the text for an audiotape on options buying and writing.

Roth, a recognized option authority, is quoted frequently in *Barron's, Forbes, Investor's Daily,* and other publications. He makes liberal use of computers and says he is most proud of his work in pioneering "custom-made" options computer programs for account executives.

Roth is now the senior options strategist at Cowen & Company. He lives in New York with his wife, the financial writer Judith McQuown, and daughter, Jessica (14 5/8).

Anthony J. Saliba (Chapter 6, The Business of Market Making) has been the managing general partner of Saliba and Company; president of the International Trading Institute; a member of the Chicago Board Options Exchange Board of Directors; and since 1979, an independent market maker on the Chicago Board Options Exchange floor.

Saliba began his career as a market maker in the Teledyne trading pit. He developed his own trading system which made him one of the most active individual pit traders on the Chicago Board Options Exchange floor. Saliba is also a member of the Chicago Board of Trade, Chicago Mercantile Exchange, New York Stock Exchange, and Midwest Stock Exchange.

Currently, Saliba is directing the International Trading Institute, which conducts high performance trading simulation for the derivative securities industry.

Saliba attended Indiana University where he received a bachelor of science in accounting in 1977.

Gary L. Trennepohl (Chapter 8, Institutional Case Studies) is professor of Finance and Chairman of the Finance Department at Texas A&M University. He leads graduate and undergraduate classes on futures, portfolio management, and corporate financial policy. In addition, he teaches options case analysis in The Options Institute Institutional Investor's Program.

A frequent seminar leader in executive development programs, Trennepohl has also taught financial concepts to business journalists during the past seven summers at the University of Missouri's Davenport Program. In addition, he has served as a financial consultant to several corporations and institutions in the areas of endowment fund management, investment policy, and employee benefit programs.

Trennepohl has written one book about corporate financial management, *An Introduction to Financial Management* (Addison-Wesley), and currently is writing a textbook about investment management and portfolio theory, *Investment Management* (Dryden Press). He has published numerous articles on investment management and portfolio strategies using options for such professional journals as the *Journal of Financial and Quantitative Analysis, Journal of Financial Research,* and *Financial Management.*

He has held leadership positions in several professional associations and currently serves as vice president for education for the Financial Management Association. He received a bachelor of science degree from the University of Tulsa in 1968 and his Ph.D. from Texas Tech University in 1976.

James W. Yates, Jr. (Chapter 7, Using Option Market Information to Make Stock Market Decisions) is president of DYR Associates of Vienna, Virginia, an investment research and consulting firm specializing in listed options. He is the creator of The Option Strategy Spectrum, a visual presentation of the relationship of option strategies.

DYR Associates provides daily option research to a number of institutions and brokerage firms. Among the products developed by DYR are The Institutional Option Writers Index, a gauge of option strategy performance, and The Option Phase Chart, a measure of volatility expectations contained in the market. DYR's philosophy is that the listed option market provides a superior risk management tool that can be of significant value when used with fundamental research.

As a consultant, Yates helped develop the Chicago Board Options Exchange's Options Institute, and he teaches at many seminars sponsored by The Institute.

CONTENTS

CHAPTER 1

HISTORY OF OPTIONS

At 10:00 A.M. EST, April 26, 1973, the investment world changed forever. On that morning, the Chicago Board Options Exchange (CBOE) began trading listed stock options in the smoker's lounge just off the main trading floor of the Chicago Board of Trade. Joseph W. Sullivan, a CBOE founder and its first president, declared on opening day that this was one baby "long overdue." Few could foresee the enormous impact this fledgling exchange was to have on the investing landscape, let alone feel confident of its success at all.

Only five years later, in *The Dow Jones-Irwin Guide to Put and Call Options,* Henry J. Clasing stated that the creation of standardized option contracts was akin to man's progressing "from out of the cave to far more protection against the storms of nature . . . ."[1] The CBOE now stands as the largest options exchange in the world. Options are also traded on other exchanges in the United States and abroad on stocks, bonds, indexes, currencies, and financial and commodity futures contracts. The investor's need to adjust risk versus reward contributes to their popularity.

Options were not a new idea when their application was extended to stocks. Whether used to protect the value of an asset or to lock in its purchase price, options have been a part of doing business since the early days of commerce.

Although the body of this book is devoted to option strategies and their development and applications, options have a long, interesting, admittedly imperfect, history. The authors would be remiss if that history were not paid its due respect. You are doing more than reading history; learning about the ancient Greek, Thales, lets you catch onto the options maneuver—easily.

1

THE HISTORICAL RECORD OF OPTIONS

The march of time has buried the physical evidence of the first option trade. It is known, however, that the Phoenicians and Romans traded contracts, with terms similar to those that make up an option, on the delivery of goods they transported on their ships.

Perhaps the earliest record of options dates back to ancient Greece and the philosopher, mathematician, and astronomer, Thales. Using his knowledge of the stars, Thales was able to forecast, during one winter, a great olive harvest for the following spring. In the winter, there was very little bidding for the use of olive presses. With competition scarce, Thales was able to negotiate bargain prices for their use come spring. His prediction was correct. The great harvest came and the demand for olive presses boomed. Thales exercised his options and rented the presses to his neighbors at a considerable profit!

Options were also used in Holland in the first half of the 17th century. During the tulip bulb craze, contracts were routinely traded for the option to buy or sell a particular type of bulb at a specific price by some future date—not unlike today's options. Dealers in tulip bulbs could buy call options to ensure they would have adequate supplies in case the price rose substantially. Tulip growers, on the other hand, could buy put options to make sure they could sell their bulbs at a set price. A secondary market blossomed in which these options were traded. Speculators stepped into the market to trade any price fluctuations. In this quintessential example of crowd behavior, the frenzy reached its peak when average citizens began mortgaging their homes and selling businesses to get the money to trade tulip bulbs.

Around 1640, the bubble burst and the Dutch economy fell into a state of disrepair, partially the result of speculators' disavowing what were now their obligations. It took decades for the economy to recover. The gravity of the situation was described by Charles Mackay in *Extraordinary Popular Delusions and the Madness of Crowds,* originally published in 1841:

> Confidence was destroyed and a universal panic seized upon the dealers. "A" had . . . to purchase ten Semper Augustines [tulip species] from "B," at four thousand florins each . . . "B" was ready with the flowers . . . but the price had fallen to three or four hundred florins, and "A" refused to pay the difference or receive the tulips.[2]

It is no wonder that options were thought of badly and carried this stigma throughout Europe.

Another mania hit Europe in the early 1700s. This time it landed in England. The South Sea Company, formed in 1711, was granted a trading monopoly in exchange for assuming some of the debt obligations of the government. The public was very eager to invest in a company that would have sole access to the lucrative trade with the South Seas.

In early 1720, shares of the company rose from £130 to £300. The company subsequently offered additional stock to the public at £300 and £400 in April. Each offering was met with increasing ardor. Then fighting erupted in Exchange Alley. The shares of the South Sea Company eventually reached £1000 in the summer. Then news leaked that the directors had sold their shares upon realizing that the company would not produce the profits necessary to maintain such a high share price. The price plummeted. By fall, the stock was at £150.

Option trading, although not responsible for the collapse, allowed the public to speculate in the South Sea Company. The greedy suffered as their Dutch counterparts had a century before. As a result, option trading was eventually declared illegal in London, although it continued clandestinely into the 1900s. The conditions of these markets were a far cry from the regulated environment in which the public invests and trades today.

Wall Street Advertises Options in 1800s

In America, stock options had existed for almost 200 years by the time the idea of an organized exchange on which to trade them was born. Options first appeared in the United States in the 1790s, not long after the historic Buttonwood Tree Agreement was signed, establishing what was to eventually become the New York Stock Exchange. In the 1800s, Wall Street was drumming up business. The gentlemen at Tumbridge & Company, 2 Wall Street, compiled a list of suggestions, included in their 1875 book. Among these were:

> If you think stocks are going down, secure a Put. If you think stocks are going up, secure a Call.[3]

It was stated unequivocally that "there is no liability, or risk beyond the amount paid for a privilege." (The word *option* was coined later.) Always mindful of the public's voracity for quick profits "we desire to be understood as saying that any person who has money which cannot be spared, had better not risk it either in speculations on margins or with privileges.''[4] As early as 1875, then, the prudent use of options was recommended! And, as early as 1875, the Tumbridge book proclaimed: ''Stock and gold privileges negotiated on responsible parties at lowest market rates.'' It sounds like these transactions were even then in the financial vocabulary.

It was also during the late 19th century that Russell Sage, one of the great railroad speculators of his day, secured his place in option history. Considered by many the grandfather of modern option trading, Sage organized a system of puts and calls and began trading them on an over-the-counter market.

He also introduced the concept of '*conversion*'. He found that calls could be changed, i.e. converted, into puts and vice versa, when he established a pricing relationship between the option price, the price of the underlying security, and the interest rate. Conversion was used by over-the-counter put-call dealers to add liquidity to the market and is just as important today. Such conversion is now called the *put-call parity equation,* and it is one of the relationships that establishes option prices. Put-call parity is discussed in detail in Chapter 2.

In 1901, *The Theory of Stock Speculation* was written by Arthur Crump, a British stock operator. In the book, he stated emphatically that, ''speculation by 'options' is of all methods of speculating the most prudent, as it is the most sensible, for all parties concerned . . . . The indefinite mischief that is caused by speculation which allows the operator to incur unlimited risk on credit is prevented by the system of options inasmuch as a fixed payment must be made by the speculator at the time the account is opened.''[5] Crump was encouraging perhaps the most knowledgeable and financially strong investors of his time—the stock market operators—to consider the risk and capital management aspects of options.

Reputation Plummets

But the infamous trading pool reached its lowest form in the 1920s. One type was the option pool. By definition, the option pool acquired much of the stock it was to hold by acquiring options directly from major stockholders, including entities such as directors, banks, and the corporation itself. The option, once secured, could be exercised at the discretion of the pool manager. If the operations of the pool could cause the stock price to rise significantly above the contract price, a substantial profit would be made. In the case of the Sinclair Consolidated Oil pool, the pool managers were able to obtain options to buy about 20 percent of the authorized stock at 30. During negotiations, the stock was trading at about 28. On the day the agreement was signed, the stock opened at 32 and closed at 35 3/4! It ran up to 37 1/4 the next day! The pool obtained the stock and sold it in the open market, netting profits in excess of $2 million. It was during this era that option dealers themselves followed the operations of regular pools:—"If you knew which pool was going to move which stock in the next two days, you could do well."[6]

Reputation Rescued

The days of the pool were numbered. In the years following the "panic" of 1929, only a handful were operating. During the congressional hearings from which the Securities and Exchange Commission was born, the options market was brought to the fore. The fate of the options business was indeed very dark in 1932.

Herbert Filer, author of the landmark book *Understanding Put and Call Options,* had been in the options business since 1919. His fellow put-call dealers felt that he was the most qualified among them to testify before Congress and to save options. This proved to be a difficult task. Filer, in his book, recalled how he was seated in the hearing room with 300 onlookers as the bill was read paragraph by paragraph. When it was declared that ". . . not knowing the difference between good and bad options, for the matter of convenience we strike them all out," the situation seemed hopeless.[7] Congress, it seems, had not made any distinction between the options used by pool operators and those publicly offered. Prejudging the entire options business, these legislators had concluded that all options were manipulative stating:

> Many of the most flagrant abuses upon stock exchanges would not be possible without the aid of options. They are an indispensable commitment of every pool operation designed to distribute stock at an increased price. Enormous profits have been made by operators who traded against options without incurring the slightest risk or obligation.[8]

Filer explained to the committee the difference between, "the options in which [put-call dealers] deal which are primarily offered and openly sold for a consideration, and the manipulative options secretly given, for no fee, but for manipulative purposes."[9]

Congressmen also questioned Filer regarding the excessive number of options that expired worthless. The committee's reasoning was that

the public was losing considerable amounts of money from option speculation. Filer responded that about 12 1/2 percent of options were exercised. The questioner continued by saying, "If only 12 1/2 percent are
exercised, then the other 87 1/2 percent of the people who bought options
have thrown their money away?" To which Filer replied, "No sir. If you
insured your house against fire and it didn't burn down you would not say
that you had thrown away your insurance premium."[10]

He also argued successfully for the economic value options add to
the securities market, citing the protective nature of options and their
ability to stabilize stock prices in certain environments. Filer's beliefs
are echoed by authors of the mid-1980s. Richard M. Bookstaber, in
Option Pricing and Investment Strategies, gives a very succinct explanation of the importance of options markets. He stated that "the ideal
market would have a range of financial instruments available to enable
investors to meet their investment objectives directly" and "would per-
mit the investor to cover any contingency in the market, to fine-tune a
portfolio to meet personal investment objectives and perceptions exactly. Options create such a market."[11] Mark Rubinstein and John Cox,
in *Options Markets,* argue convincingly in favor of Bookstaber's point
and show that an options marketplace is not only a valid securities
market, but is beneficial even to those who never trade in options. They
use matrix algebra, which is too complex for the purposes of this book.
The reader is directed to their book for the complete explanation.

Rescued—But Restricted
The options business was saved, but with certain conditions. The Investment Act of 1934, creating the Securities and Exchange Commission
(SEC), gave it the power to regulate trading in options and allowed
options to exist, "if not in contravention to the rules set down by the
SEC." The die was cast—the SEC would henceforth keep a very close
watch on the activities in the option markets. However, the SEC also
concluded that there is plenty of room for legitimate speculation and
admitted that not all options are manipulative.

This did not create an environment for growth. As recently as the
1940s, trading volume was still very small. Growth was further stunted
by World War II, which in effect closed exchanges in Europe and quieted
volume here in the United States. But the postwar environment was
friendlier. The study of economics became popular, awakening aca-
demics and lay persons to theories of investing, the stock market, and
options.

In 1959, Herbert Filer wrote his book, which was the first complete presentation of put and call options, giving strategies available and their various uses. Unfortunately, its impact was minor. It took until 1968 for annual volume to reach 300,000 option contracts, representing less than 1 percent of the volume of stock transactions. Even then, only 1 in 10,000 investors could claim any knowledge about options! Despite almost 200 years of history here, why had options trading not enjoyed more success? Reading the following sections will help answer that question.

THE OPTIONS MARKET BEFORE THE CBOE

The stock options market, until 1973 when the Chicago Board Options Exchange (CBOE) opened, was controlled by put-call dealers who traded options in an over-the-counter market. Typically, a dealer would advertise in each morning's edition of *The Wall Street Journal* some of his put and/or call offerings for that day. An individual wanting to buy or sell any of the advertised options or wishing a quotation for another option would call a dealer. Upon consummation of the trade, a physical contract was prepared with the pertinent details of the option(s) bought or sold (Figure 1–1). These included:

1. The date of the contract.
2. The name of the security on which the contract was written.
3. The price at which the security could be bought or sold.
4. The length of the contract in number of days from the date the contract was written.
5. The actual date on which the contract expired.
6. The endorsement by a member firm of the New York Stock Exchange guaranteeing the terms of the contract.

With contract in hand, the option buyer now had a legal right to buy or sell the security on which it was written.

Drawbacks

However, the existence of a physical contract with another party contained some drawbacks. If contract owners wanted to exercise their option, they were required to present the contract before the expiration time of 3:15 P.M. to the cashier of the stock exchange member firm that endorsed the contract. Filer recommended in his book that, "in order to

FIGURE 1–1   Physical Option Contracts from 1875 (top) and 1959 (bottom)

New York, March 3d, 1875.

For Value Received, The Bearer may CALL ON ME for One Hundred Shares of the Capital Stock of the Union Pacific Railroad Company, at Forty three per cent, any time in thirty days from date.

The Bearer is entitled to ALL DIVIDENDS OR EXTRA DIVIDENDS paid during the time.

Expires April 2d, 1875.

1:45 P. M.   Signed..............

Negotiated by
TUMBRIDGE & CO.
Bankers and Brokers in Stock Privileges,
P. O. Box 2282.   3 Wall St.

CALL OPTION

Copyt. 1957, Put and Call Brokers and Dealers Assn., Inc.

New York, N. Y. _____ MAY 22nd, 19 59

For Value Received, the BEARER may CALL on the endorser for ONE HUNDRED (100) shares of the ____ COMMON stock of the __ XYZ CORPORATION __ at __ Dollars ($ 70.00) per share

ANY TIME WITHIN __ NINETY __ __ SEVENTY - - __ days from date.

THIS STOCK OPTION CONTRACT MUST BE PRESENTED, AS SPECIFIED BELOW, TO THE ENDORSING FIRM BEFORE THE EXPIRATION OF THE EXACT TIME LIMIT. IT CANNOT BE EXERCISED BY TELEPHONE.

DURING THE LIFE OF THIS OPTION:

1. (a) — the contract price hereof shall be reduced by the value of any cash dividend on the day the stock goes ex-dividend; (b) — where the Option is entitled to rights and/or warranty the contract price shall be reduced by the value of same as fixed by the opening sale thereof on the day the stock sells ex-rights and/or warrants.

2. (a) — In the event of stock splits, reverse splits or other similar action by the above-mentioned corporation, this Option shall become an Option for the equivalent in new securities who duly listed for trading and the total contract price shall not be reduced; (b) — stock dividends or the equivalent due-bills shall be attached to the stock covered hereby, when and if this Option is exercised, and the total contract price shall not be reduced.

Upon presentation of this Option attached to a comparison ticket in the manner and time specified, the endorser agrees to accept notice of the Bearer's exercise by stamping the comparison, and this acknowledgment shall constitute a contract and shall be controlling with respect to delivery of the stock and settlement in accordance with New York Stock Exchange usage.

SOLD BY MEMBER
PUT & CALL
BROKERS & DEALERS
ASSOCIATION, INC.

The undersigned acts as intermediary only, without obligation other than to obtain a New York Stock Exchange firm as Endorser.

Filer Schmidt & Co.

EXPIRES __ AUGUST 20th __ 19 59
3:15 P. M.

P N° 554

NEGOTIATED BY
Filer Schmidt & Co.
ESTABLISHED 1919
Member Put and Call Brokers and Dealers Association, Inc.
PUT AND CALL OPTIONS
GUARANTEED BY MEMBERS N. Y. STOCK EXCHANGE
120 BROADWAY, N. Y. C. 5   BARCLAY 7-6100

Source: Herbert Filer, *Understanding Put and Call Options* (New York: Crown Publishers, 1959).

eliminate the chance of loss in late presentation of an option and to avoid delay when a contract is exercised, contracts should never be kept outside of New York City but should remain with your stockbroker or option-dealer for safekeeping. The maker of an option contract will not accept it if it is presented after it expires.''[12]

Option holders had a big responsibility to ensure performance of the contract. If they forgot to exercise it, the contract expired worthless regardless of the relation of the option's contract price to the stock price. In today's markets, there are provisions to ensure that certain in-the-money options are exercised automatically.

What actions prior to expiration could the option holder take? Herein lies the second drawback to over-the-counter trading. Because the contract was endorsed by a stock exchange member firm with the put-call dealer acting as intermediary, the option holder could turn only to the dealer to liquidate before the expiration date. Even though the contract was in bearer form and could be sold to another party, the holder needed the dealer's network to locate that other party.

The dealer rarely functioned as the *maker* i.e., initial buyer or seller of options. His purpose was to match both parties. He made his living on the *spread* between what the buyers wanted to pay and what the sellers wanted to receive. Theoretically, there could be no limit to the size of the spread. Filer stated,

> the option-dealer does not operate on a commission basis, but his profit is made in the difference between what he pays for an option and what he receives for it. An option-dealer having an order to buy an option for $500 will probably bid $450 to the maker of the option which he is going to sell for $500, and therefore make $50 on the transaction.[13]

If the dealer could not find a buyer and were to act as buyer from the holder, he would exercise the option for his own account and sell, for a call, or buy, for a put, the corresponding stock. The holder would receive the proceeds of the transaction minus two stock commissions and applicable taxes. With liquidity limited, holders of profitable options often had to resort to this alternative to realize their gain.

What price should option buyers pay for an option? Against what criteria could this price be measured? How could buyers be confident that they are getting the best price? These are the questions investors would need answers to before entering into an option contract. These answers were not available from the options market at that time.

Secondary offerings of options were advertised as ''Specials'' (Figure 1–2). These contracts were held by the dealer as inventory, most

FIGURE 1-2
The Advertising or Offering of Special Options

Orders for these options may be placed through your stock broker

These special options are offered for resale. Quotations for regular 60 day, 90 day or 6 month contracts can be had on request.

SPECIAL CALL OPTIONS

Special Put Options

Per 100 Shares (Plus Tax)		
Jones & Laughlin	71⅝ Aug. 21	$850.00
Union Pacific	36⅛ July 27	275.00
Philco	31⅞ Aug. 31	375.00
Raytheon	56 July 30	575.00
American Motors	37⅜ Dec. 7	625.00
Lee Rubber	26¾ Aug. 31	250.00
General Motors	52⅛ Aug. 18	275.00
Admiral	25⅛ July 20	200.00
Western Airlines	36¼ Aug. 25	200.00
Trans World Airlines	22¼ Dec. 9	375.00
Rayonier	27 Aug. 24	200.00
U. S. Rubber	65½ Sept. 4	575.00
Reynolds Tobacco	52⅝ Aug. 24	225.00
John Morrell	28 July 22	225.00
Amer. Stand. Radiator	16½ Nov. 17	237.50
Gen'l Prec. Eqpmt	38⅞ Aug. 31	325.00
Amer. Steel Fdry	64 July 27	400.00
Cudahy Packing	13¾ Nov. 30	225.00
Diners' Club	35¼ July 23	400.00
Crane Co.	44.30 Aug. 31	400.00

Subject to prior sale or price change
Ask for Booklet on How to Use Options

PER 100 SHARES			
U. S. Steel	95½	Dec. 8	$700.00
Miami Copper	45	Nov. 30	425.00
Kaiser Aluminum	51⅛	Sep. 1	375.00
International Silver	44¼	Dec. 2	425.00
N.Y. Central RR Co.	30⅛	Aug. 28	425.00
Siegler Corp.	35	Aug 31	375.00
Raytheon	56	July 30	475.00
American Motors	37⅜	Dec. 7	525.00
Chrysler	72	July 27	425.00
Chance Vought	36	July 27	425.00
Beech Aircraft	40	July 20	425.00
Sperry Rand	28⅛	Aug. 25	325.00
Boeing Airplane Co.	37⅝	Dec. 2	400.00
Revlon	58	July 23	525.00
Minneapolis Moline	25¼	Aug. 25	250.00
Great Atlantic & Pac	43¼	Dec. 2	375.00
Harris Intertype	51¼	Aug 17	600.00
Gillette	51⅞	July 20	475.00
Tri Continental wts	28⅞	Nov. 24	300.00
Anaconda	68	5/31/60	875.00

Subject to Price Change & Prior Sale
ASK FOR BOOKLET ON HOW TO USE OPTIONS

Filer, Schmidt & Co.
MEMBERS PUT & CALL BROKERS & DEALERS ASSN. INC.
120 Broadway, N. Y. 5   BA 7-8100

Filer, Schmidt & Co.
MEMBERS PUT & CALL BROKERS & DEALERS ASSN. INC.
120 Broadway, New York 5   BArclay 7-6100

These advertisements offer special options. The one on the left is from *The New York Times* and the one on the right is from *The Wall Street Journal*, both of the June 2, 1959, issues.

Source: Herbert Filer, *Understanding Put and Call Options* (New York: Crown Publishers, 1959).

likely purchased with the intention of reselling them. In this way, the dealer was functioning as a *maker* of options. If the dealer were long on a call option, he would be expecting an advance in the stock to gain a profit on the option contract. It should be no surprise that advertisements for call options appeared the day following a market advance; those for puts after a market decline.

Advantages of Listed Securities

Compare this to the listed stock market where buyers and sellers meet at a central location designated to trade a given stock. The price at which the stock trades reflects the collective total of the opinion of that stock's current value by all the buyers and sellers. Option buyers, on the other hand, had no way of knowing what the real market was. Furthermore, unlike the listed market where price is set immediately by open outcry, or in the over-the-counter equity market where quotes can be given as firm, almost all quotes for option prices were given subject to being completed. Every trade was done individually and by phone. Indeed, it was not uncommon for a dealer to make as many as 50 calls before locating the other side of a trade, a process that could take more than one trading day.

In terms of the contract itself, contract prices were mostly set "at the market." For example, a call buyer would ask for a quote on a given option. The dealer would return with a price that reflected the current price of the stock. If the buyer decided in favor of purchase, the contract price could become the price of the stock at that time. The price could be some fractional amount between round numbers. A report like the following would be given to the buyer: "Sold you call 100 XYZ at 70 5/8 for 90 days for $400 expires October 24," indicating that the buyer now owned one call option on 100 shares of XYZ with a strike price of 70 5/8, expiring 90 days from the trade date.

Expiration dates were as varied as contract prices. Although contracts would be entered into for periods of mostly 60 and 90 days, and 6 and 12 months, these dates were always calculated from the date of the initial transaction. In fact, prior to 1935, contracts were rarely longer than 30 days and were commonly traded for 15, 7, and even 2 days!

One can easily see how complex the market could become. These inconsistencies of over-the-counter options added to the difficulties of using them. It is clear that this was not an easy market in which to participate. In 1968, options were still being traded in much the same way as they had been for 350 years.

CREATION OF THE CBOE

By the late 1960s, the commodity futures markets were experiencing a drastic decline in volume. In 1968, at the Chicago Board of Trade (CBOT), only 4.7 million contracts were traded on $36 billion of commodities, a far cry from the 1966 record of 7.6 million contracts valued at $81 billion. Contracts were on agricultural products, and with volume and revenue plunging, the CBOT found it necessary to diversify.

The first attempt was the creation of a futures contract on plywood. A boom in housing construction provided the demand and price movement that are essential ingredients for success. But the real wind of change was blowing from the East.

In lower Manhattan, a bull had been unleashed on Wall Street. Still, the poor commodity traders could only watch the rising market from their quiet trading pits. In July 1968, then CBOT President Henry H. Wilson received a letter from the SEC all but ordering the Board of Trade to give up its registration as a national securities exchange. The SEC recommended that, because the CBOT had long since ceased to be an active stock market, the CBOT should relinquish the registration voluntarily, instead of having the commission take the steps necessary to terminate it.

This came as quite a surprise. In 1935, one year after the Securities Exchange Act had been passed, the CBOT received its registration as a stock exchange, but never developed one. Now the timing was perfect—the commodity markets were awful and the stock market was booming. But could the CBOT find a way to capitalize on this?

At the Board of Trade's 1969 annual membership meeting, President Wilson announced that the CBOT was studying the creation of an exchange for put and call options. Initial institutional support was expressed by Paul Haake of Continental Illinois National Bank and Trust who said, "This market the Board is proposing is an intriguing proposition and has substantial potential for us in writing options on stocks in pension funds we manage."

However, the decision to create a listed options market was not unanimous, and the approval process was not going to be quick or easy. Stock options did not have a good reputation, and the trading process was difficult. Still, options were already in existence. So the SEC, even with its regulations, gave them some legitimacy—but only after a convincing study put forth by a news reporter.

SEC Stalls

The study was led by Joseph W. Sullivan, CBOT vice president for planning. Sullivan came to the CBOT from *The Wall Street Journal* where he served as a political correspondent. Actually, his lack of formal knowledge of the securities industry was an asset. He started from ground-zero, gathering information.

With the tarnished history of options, Sullivan correctly understood that his first goal was simply to convince the SEC to allow the exchange to exist.

The Wall Street Journal reported that SEC officials, while neither expressing approval nor disapproval, said, "we have some questions we want to explore further with them,"[14] a clear indication that the SEC intended to be intimately involved with the formation of the exchange. Clearly, the SEC was serious. One of the "final"proposals submitted to the SEC came back accompanied by 200 questions.

Sullivan's second goal was to create the environment for a liquid secondary market. Without one, options trading would be no better than it was currently. By observing problems with the over-the-counter options market, Sullivan discovered that there were two essential traits missing. They were so important, in fact, that adding them could be the difference between success and failure.

CBOT Pushes for Liquid Market

The big leaps forward that the CBOT was proposing were to: (1) standardize the options contract, and (2) guarantee its performance via an intermediary—the Options Clearing Corporation (OCC). Prior to the creation of the CBOE, options contracts were traded in an over-the-counter market where contracts were negotiated and entered into between the buyer and the seller with the put-call dealer acting as intermediary. Furthermore, contract prices and expiration dates were variable. Standardization would eliminate these problems by reducing the variables to one—the premium.

The Saturday following the third Friday of the month was set as the standard expiration date. A cycle of quarterly expiration dates was devised to allow options to be selected over time. For example, a cycle of expiration dates in the months of January, April, July, and October was made available with only three consecutive three-month options trading at any given time. In response to the demand for near-term options, this concept has evolved into a cycle of the current and following months and two longer-term options expiring up to, but not limited to, five and eight months (Figure 1–3).

To standardize contract prices, *strike prices* were created with regular intervals of 5 and 10 points. It was determined later that strike prices of 5 points were too great in percentage terms for stocks trading at prices below $25 per share. A system of 2 1/2 point strike prices was set for these stocks.

The Options Clearing Corporation (OCC) was established to issue the options contracts and to guarantee clearance, settlement, and performance. With centralized clearing, buyers who wanted to exercise could

FIGURE 1–3

Option Quotation Page from *The Wall Street Journal*

LISTED OPTIONS QUOTATIONS

Tuesday, January 23, 1990

Options closing prices. Sales unit usually is 100 shares. Stock close is New York or American exchange final price.

CHICAGO BOARD

Option & NY Close	Strike Price	Calls–Last Feb	Calls–Last Mar	Calls–Last Apr	Puts–Last Feb	Puts–Last Mar	Puts–Last Apr
Alcoa	60	3 1/2	r	4 7/8	1 3/8	2	2
63 1/2	65	1	1 1/2	2 1/2	r	4 5/8	4 5/8
63 1/2	70	3/16	1/2	7/8	8 1/4	r	8 3/4
63 1/2	75	1/8	s	1/2	14 1/2	s	r
63 1/2	80	1/16	s	1/4	19 1/2	s	r
AmGenl	35	r	r	1/8	r	r	r
AGreet	35	r	r	1	r	r	r
AmStr	60	r	2 1/4	3 1/4	r	r	r
AT&T	35	s	s	6	s	s	5/16
40 7/8	40	1 7/8	2 5/8	2 7/8	5/8	1 3/8	1 5/16
40 7/8	45	1/4	1/2	13/16	4	r	4 3/8
40 7/8	50	1/16	r	1/4	r	r	9
Amrtch	55	3 3/8	r	4 1/2	5/8	3/4	1
59 1/4	60	3/4	1 3/4	2 3/4	r	r	r
59 1/4	65	r	r	3/4	r	r	r
59 1/4	70	r	s	1/4	r	s	r
Atl R	100	s	s	9	s	s	1 5/8
107 5/8	105	3 5/8	4 7/8	r	r	r	2 7/8
107 5/8	110	1 1/8	2	3	4 1/4	r	5 1/4
107 5/8	115	3/16	9/16	1 1/2	r	r	r
Avon	30	2 1/2	2 7/8	3 3/4	1 1/4	r	2 1/8
31 1/4	35	1/2	1	1 1/2	4 1/4	r	4 1/2
31 1/4	40	1/8	1/4	5/8	r	r	r
B A T	12 1/2	s	s	1	s	s	s
BankAm	25	1 3/4	r	2 1/2	11/16	r	1 1/4
26	30	1/8	5/16	5/8	4	r	4 3/8
26	35	s	s	1/8	s	s	8 3/4
BankNY	35	2 1/2	r	r	3/8	r	r
37 1/2	40	r	r	r	3 1/8	r	r
BattlM	15	r	r	3 3/8	r	r	r
18	17 1/2	15/16	1 1/8	1 5/8	3/8	r	13/16
18	20	3/16	r	11/16	r	r	2 7/16
BearSt	15	r	r	1/4	r	r	r
Beckin	20	r	r	3/16	r	r	r
BellAtl	90	s	s	r	s	s	1 1/2
95 3/4	95	2 5/8	r	4 1/2	1 7/8	r	4 3/8
95 3/4	100	1	r	2 7/8	r	r	r
95 3/4	105	r	r	1 1/4	r	r	r
95 3/4	110	r	s	5/8	r	s	r
Beth S	15	r	r	r	1/4	r	5/8
16 3/4	17 1/2	5/8	3/4	1 3/8	1 1/8	1 1/2	1 1/2
16 3/4	20	1/4	r	5/8	r	r	r
16 3/4	22 1/2	s	s	3/8	s	s	r
Biogen	15	r	2 3/8	r	3/16	r	r

Option & NY Close	Strike Price	Calls–Last Feb	Calls–Last Mar	Calls–Last Apr	Puts–Last Feb	Puts–Last Mar	Puts–Last Apr
348 3/4	360	3 5/8	r	10 3/8	15 5/8	r	23 5/8
348 3/4	370	2	s	5 1/2	r	s	r
348 3/4	380	s	s	4	s	s	r
348 3/4	390	s	s	1 1/2	s	s	r
Tex In	30	3 3/4	r	r	3/8	r	15/16
33 1/4	35	9/16	r	1 1/2	2 1/8	r	3
33 1/4	40	r	r	1/2	6 1/4	r	r
33 1/4	45	s	s	3/16	s	s	r
Upjohn	30	r	r	6 1/2	r	r	1/2
35 1/4	35	1 7/16	r	2 7/16	1	r	1 7/8
35 1/4	40	1/8	r	13/16	5	r	5
35 1/4	45	r	r	5/16	r	r	r
Weyerh	22 1/2	r	r	2 1/8	r	r	r
24 1/8	25	5/16	r	3/4	1 1/4	r	r
24 1/8	30	1/16	r	3/16	r	r	r
24 1/8	35	s	s	1/16	s	s	r
Xerox	50	r	r	6	1/4	r	9/16
54 3/4	55	1 3/8	r	2 1/8	1 3/8	r	2 1/8
54 3/4	60	1/8	r	9/16	5 3/8	r	4 3/4
		Feb	**Mar**	**May**	**Feb**	**Mar**	**May**
AlexAl	25	r	r	r	5/16	9/16	r
27	30	r	r	r	3	r	r
Amdahl	12 1/2	2 1/4	r	r	r	r	r
14 1/2	15	1/2	7/8	1 3/8	13/16	r	r
14 1/2	17 1/2	1/16	r	5/8	r	r	r
A E P	30	1 1/8	r	r	r	r	11/16
AInGrp	80	r	s	s	1/2	s	s
93 3/4	85	r	s	s	1	s	s
93 3/4	90	r	r	r	1 3/8	2	3 7/8
93 3/4	95	3 1/4	3 7/8	6 1/4	4	5	r
93 3/4	100	7/8	2 1/8	r	6 1/2	r	r
93 3/4	105	1/2	s	2	r	s	r
93 3/4	110	r	s	1 5/8	r	s	r
93 3/4	115	1/4	s	r	r	s	r
Amoco	45	6 1/2	r	6 3/8	r	1/4	r
50 1/2	50	1 3/4	2	3 3/8	1	r	2 1/4
50 1/2	55	1/8	r	1 1/4	r	r	r
50 1/2	60	1/8	s	r	r	s	r
A M P	40	4 1/4	r	5 1/4	1/8	r	r
44	45	5/8	1 1/4	2	r	r	r
44	50	1/8	r	r	r	r	6 3/8
Anadrk	30	r	r	r	r	r	11/16
33 7/8	35	r	r	2 1/8	1 1/2	r	r
33 7/8	40	r	r	5/8	r	r	r

MOST ACTIVE OPTIONS

CHICAGO BOARD

		Sales	Last	Chg.	N.Y. Close
CALLS					
SP100	Feb320	28020	2 1/2	– 1	311.81
SP100	Feb315	21196	4 1/2	– 1	311.81
SP100	Feb325	19972	1 5-16	– 9-16	311.81
SP100	Feb310	15157	6 7/8	– 1 1/4	311.81
SP100	Feb330	14520	3/4	– 1/4	311.81
PUTS					
SP100	Feb310	30145	8 1/4	+ 1/4	311.81
SP100	Feb305	20095	6 7/8	+ 5/8	311.81
SP100	Feb300	17480	5	+ 1/4	311.81
SP100	Feb290	15731	2 3/4	– 1/8	311.81
SP100	Feb315	15238	10 3/4	+ 3/8	311.81

AMERICAN

		Sales	Last	Chg.	N.Y. Close
CALLS					
Rorer	Feb60	2763	4	– 5/8	61 1/2
Rorer	Feb65	2702	7/8	– 1/8	61 1/2
MMIdx	Mar585	2581	5/8	– 5/8	526.21
Disney	Apr110	2331	5 1/4	– 3/4	104 7/8
PhilPt	May30	1969	3/8	....	23 1/8
PUTS					
F N M	Feb35	1426	1 5/8	....	34 1/2
BkBost	Feb15	1346	1 13-16	+ 7/8	14 1/8
F N M	Feb30	1279	1/4	....	34 1/2
AirPd	Mar45	1130	1/2	– 3/8	47 1/4
LinB	Feb105	1045	3 3/4	+ 1 3/8	107 3/4

PACIFIC

		Sales	Last	Chg.	N.Y. Close
CALLS					
Compaq	Feb85	1555	1 13-16	+ 1/8	81 3/8
CirCty	Feb20	1504	7/8	+ 1/8	19 1/4
Hilton	Feb75	1418	1 3/4	– 2 7/8	66
Hilton	Feb70	1362	3 1/8	– 4 3/8	66
RynMtl	Feb55	1212	3/8	+ 1/8	50 1/4
PUTS					
CirCty	Feb20	1621	1 3/8	+ 3/8	19 1/4
Compaq	Feb75	1203	1 5-16	– 3/8	81 3/8
Compaq	Feb80	1173	2 5/8	– 5/8	81 3/8
Hilton	Feb75	866	10	+ 5 1/2	66
Hilton	Feb70	708	7	+ 4 1/2	66

NEW YORK

Option & NY Close	Strike Price	Calls–Last Feb	Calls–Last Mar	Calls–Last Jun	Puts–Last Feb	Puts–Last Mar	Puts–Last Jun
Ford	40	3 7/8	4 1/8	4 5/8	1/4	1/2	1 1/8
44	45	3/8	15/16	1 3/4	2 1/8	2 1/8	3 1/4
44	50	r	1/16	7/16	r	6 5/8	6 7/8
44	55	s	1/16	r	s	11 3/4	r
FundAm	30	r	r	r	r	r	3/4
Fuqua	25	r	r	r	1 3/4	r	2 3/8
Gap	45	r	r	r	3/4	1 1/4	r
49 1/4	50	1 1/4	2	r	2 3/4	3 1/4	4 1/2
49 1/4	55	r	r	2 1/4	6 3/8	7	8 1/4
Gen El	50	s	r	r	s	3/16	3/8
63 3/8	55	s	9 1/4	r	s	3/8	7/8
63 3/8	60	3 7/8	4 3/4	6 1/8	1/2	7/8	2
63 3/8	65	7/8	1 5/8	3 3/8	2 1/4	3 1/4	4
63 3/8	70	1/8	3/8	1 1/2	r	r	7 1/2
G M	40	1 3/4	2 3/8	3	13/16	1 1/4	2 1/8
41 3/8	45	1/16	5/16	1	4 3/8	4 1/2	5
41 3/8	50	r	1/16	3/8	r	9 1/4	r
GtLCh	40	r	r	r	r	r	1 3/4
42	45	r	r	r	3 1/8	r	r
42	50	r	3/8	1 1/8	r	r	r
Handlm	20	r	r	r	1/2	3/4	r
Hanson	17 1/2	r	1 1/4	r	r	r	r
18 1/2	20	1/16	3/16	r	r	1 3/8	r
18 1/2	22 1/2	r	r	1/8	r	r	r
Heinz	27 1/2	s	r	s	s	3/16	s
31	30	1 13/16	2	r	1/2	3/4	1 1/8
31	32 1/2	s	r	2 1/8	s	1 13/16	r
31	35	r	3/8	7/8	r	3 3/4	r
I T T	50	5	r	6 1/2	r	r	r
54 3/4	55	1 1/4	2	3 3/8	1 5/8	r	2 1/4
54 3/4	60	r	9/16	1 3/8	r	r	r
54 3/4	65	r	1/4	5/8	r	r	r
K mart	30	3 5/8	4 3/8	r	r	3/8	3/4
33 7/8	35	1/2	7/8	1 11/16	r	1 3/4	2 1/4
33 7/8	40	r	3/16	1/2	r	r	6 1/8
33 7/8	45	s	1/8	s	s	r	s
LandsE	17 1/2	7/8	1 7/16	r	r	r	r
18 1/8	20	r	1/2	r	r	2 1/2	r
Litton	70	r	r	r	r	r	1 7/8
75 1/8	75	2 1/4	r	r	r	3	r
75 1/8	80	7/8	1 7/8	r	r	r	r
75 1/8	85	5/16	r	r	r	r	r
Loews	105	5 1/4	r	r	1 3/4	r	4 3/4

now rely on the OCC to faithfully match and execute their requests. The OCC also made it possible for buyers or sellers to close their positions with an offsetting transaction in the open market with a party different from the one in the initial trade. In the over-the-counter market, these transactions had to go back through the put-call dealers and their network.

Once the powerful combination of these two innovations instantly made a liquid secondary market possible, the way the CBOT structured how options were to be traded made that market a reality. A new system of market makers required individuals to respond with a two-sided market, i.e., bid and offer, for an option on demand. Natural competition among many market makers to make the best one and the support of the capital of many participants created a market in which the public could trade with more confidence. Other characteristics such as certificate-less trading and one-day settlement all added up to one thing—options could now be traded cost-effectively on a level playing field!

While the major drawbacks to over-the-counter options trading had been overcome an even larger question still remained unanswered—"WOULD LISTED OPTIONS SUCCEED?"

WHAT DO A BUNCH OF GRAIN TRADERS IN CHICAGO KNOW ABOUT STOCKS AND OPTIONS?

The idea for a listed stock options market may have been born during a bull market, but its realization, after four years of hard work, came at a less propitious time. In 1973, the U.S. economy was in bad shape, and the stock market was in one of its worst declines in history. In New York, the reception for a new exchange was cool, and CBOT leader Joe Sullivan quickly found out that this was not the best moment to sell the Wall Street community on the idea. Exchange memberships for $10,000 apiece weren't an easy sell.

One common retort was, "What do a bunch of grain traders in Chicago know about stocks and options?" Besides, the idea was coming from the wrong side of the Hudson River. *The Wall Street Journal,* in March of 1973 just before the Exchange opened, described puts and calls as "among the most esoteric of stock instruments." In the face of all this skepticism, the CBOT stood strong—the investing public would have the final word.

The new exchange—called the Chicago Board Options Exchange—

began trading on April 26, 1973, as an SEC "pilot program" with call options on 16 stocks. The SEC, which regulated the CBOE (making it independent of the CBOT), had made it clear early-on that it intended to maintain flexibility in regulating this new type of exchange market. Commission leaders contended that it could pose complex problems and special risks to investors and for the marketplace.

Those Chicago Grain Traders Knew Plenty

First-day volume was 911 contracts, but by mid-1974, just after celebrating its first anniversary, the CBOE was already trading an average of 20,000 options daily. The exchange had also, by this time, doubled the number of underlying stocks to 32. This success did not go unnoticed. Membership also doubled to 567 from the 284 who had bravely invested $10,000 apiece for the first seats. The market received a major vote of confidence when authorities relaxed regulations barring the use of options by bank trust departments and insurance companies.

The skeptics were now quiet. At the exchange's first birthday party, New Jersey Senator Harrison A. Williams, chairman of the Senate Banking Committee's Securities Subcommittee, proclaimed that, "This is not just a new exchange, but a vigorous and important experiment in a new way of trading a new kind of security. We are here to celebrate the spectacular start of a bold new idea, responsibly implemented."

The CBOE had originally paid for a daily, one-column advertisement in *The Wall Street Journal* to let the outside world know the exchange existed. But now daily option prices were being carried by 150 newspapers across the country.

Two Professors Narrow Spreads, Giving Impetus to New Exchange

We must now take a small step backward in time for a moment. It is mysterious how seemingly unrelated events converge at a point in history and create something much greater than either one alone could have produced. The letter from the SEC to the CBOT about the CBOT's registration as a national securities exchange converged with the search for new products, and such was the case with the creation of the CBOE and the research of two University of Chicago professors—Fischer Black and Myron Scholes.

In the 1973 issue of the university's *Journal of Political Economy,* an article entitled "The Pricing of Options and Corporate Liabilities" appeared.[15] Written by Black and Scholes, it contained a revolutionary idea—a mathematical formula that could derive the price of an option, a warrant, or perhaps any time-bounded contingent claim. The formula was immediately embraced by the option trading community. Why?

Prior to 1973, in the over-the-counter market, the forces of supply and demand aside, there was no accepted convention regarding what an option should be worth. The large variance of prices and wide bid-asked spreads made options expensive to trade—one cause of their illiquidity. The formula put forth by Black and Scholes captured and quantified the effects of the variables that were known intuitively to impact option pricing—variables such as time decay and volatility, mentioned earlier by Filer in his 1959 book.

Time decay had always been accepted as a factor in the pricing of options. As time passes, the underlying security has less time to change price. Hence, it is expected that an option with more time before expiration would be worth more than an option with less time.

Volatility, the variability of price, impacts the value of an option because it reflects the range of prices within which the stock is expected to move. As such, a stock known to trade wildly deserves a higher premium, because there is more uncertainty.

The system of competing market makers helps make prices fair, but an accepted pricing convention provides market participants with a way to judge the price relationships among different options on the same underlying security. The Black-Scholes model added another source of liquidity and bid-asked spreads narrowed as traders began to compete for "mispriced" options. For details on the important arbitrage implications of the Black-Scholes formula, turn to Chapter 6. Despite discussions and suggested modifications regarding the model, it remains, for the most part, widely accepted to this day.

Growing Pains

With volume expanding geometrically, the CBOE experienced its first growing pains. Plans were made for a new trading floor. Logistically it was a nightmare. How could a new floor be constructed in the vicinity of an active commodity futures exchange? Officials decided that the new facility could be built over the existing trading floor at night and on weekends, so as not to disturb the daily operation of the Board of Trade.

On December 2, 1974, less than two years after the first opening bell had rung in that smoker's lounge, the CBOE moved into its new home—a 20,000 square-foot trading floor within the CBOT, uniquely constructed and immediately recognizable by the noticeable absence of structural columns. The floor size was determined from a forecast that had called for 200 options classes and an average daily volume of 200,000 contracts. The new facility permitted the stock list to be more than doubled again. This time the total was 67 stocks.

CBOE Not the Only One Growing
In 1975, the American Stock Exchange and what is now the Philadelphia Stock Exchange began to trade listed stock options. This was also the year that the CBOE commissioned and issued a study done by the economic consulting firm, Robert A. Nathan and Associates, covering the first nine months of listed options trading. The study found that options had no discernable impact on the underlying stocks on which they were traded, and concluded that

> during a period of great uncertainty in the capital markets generally, the CBOE has attracted a number of investors to return to equity-type risks through risk redistribution, risk limitation, and various hedging strategies it makes possible. We believe this has helped improve the efficiency and fairness of the stock market itself.[16]

With the results of the study in hand and having done much to quell the fears of investors and regulators that stock prices could be manipulated by options trading, the CBOE formally filed with the SEC to list and trade put options. Despite support from the investment and academic community, the SEC, continuing its policy of careful monitoring, announced that it would defer a decision on the petition until 1977.

THE LATE 1970S—OPTIONS GO INTERNATIONAL

Delay by the SEC proved to be a minor setback. Call option volume continued to surge. In 1976, the Pacific Stock Exchange opened for options trading. Local markets opened in Montreal, Toronto, Sydney, and in 1978, London, as foreign stock markets began to acknowledge the growth and acceptance of listed options in the United States.

The evolution of financial products was not limited to the options market by any means. October of 1975 marked another milestone when the first futures contracts on a financial instrument, Government National Mortgage Association (GNMA or Ginnie Mae) pass-through certificates, began trading at the Chicago Board of Trade. In August 1977, futures on U.S. Treasury bonds were introduced.

All in all, the period from the late 1970s to the present will be remembered as a time of great creativity in the financial markets. The development and success of the listed options market is but one of many manifestations of the strong desire to manage risk that has dominated this period.

SEC's Moratorium

In 1976, it seemed as though 1977 was a lifetime away. Its eventual arrival proved to be a mixed blessing. Put trading did finally begin, but on only five stocks. Acceptance by investors was immediate. Unfortunately, the optimism at the exchange created by the quick endorsement of puts was short-lived. Only four months after the first puts were traded, the SEC declared a moratorium on additional options listings and expansion plans. The commission planned to conduct a complete review of the structure and regulatory procedures of every options exchange. There was some talk that one result of this review would be a recommendation to establish a central marketplace for options trading. CBOE President Joe Sullivan put the moratorium into perspective in a speech before the New York Society of Securities Analysts:

> I believe the single, most salient measure of the utility of our market is simply the fact that investors have determined to use it in ever growing numbers and with an ever growing diversity of objectives.[17]

Putting expansion plans on hold did not retard volume growth. By the end of 1977, annual volume had reached 25 million contracts, evidence that the concept of the listed option was succeeding. Investors were beginning to understand the flexibility options could provide. Common stock ownership was no longer two-dimensional. Investors could better manage the risks of owning common stocks and prepare their portfolios for market uncertainties. As the Stanford Research Institute, in its "Outlook for the U.S. Securities Industry—1981," reported:

> From the investor's standpoint, the function that options perform is the generation of new possibilities for the allocation of risk and reward. . . . They (options) give the investor more freedom of choice in shaping the

expected return of his portfolio in a manner consistent with his risk tolerance, and this added freedom contributed by options can only make the
investor better off.[18]

The institutional side of the business was also growing. A 1976
Harris Poll had shown that the vast majority of the institutions polled
concluded that options could help reduce the risk of owning stocks and
agreed that options broaden the field of investment opportunities in
stocks.

Stepping Beyond Stock; Options on Other Securities

Off the trading floor, a more important concept was taking shape. In June
of 1977, the CBOE filed with the SEC a series of rule changes to enable
trading of non-stock options. Although proposed with the intention of
using the changes to trade options on government securities, the future
implications of the eventual acceptance of these recommendations
would be felt worldwide and lead to the creation of cash-settled index
options.

During 1979, two major barriers to the institutional use of options
fell. The U.S. Labor Department ruled that use of options was not a
breach of fiduciary responsibility for pension fund managers, and the
federal Comptroller of the Currency expanded a 1974 decision by easing
restrictions on bank trust departments.

On March 26, 1980, the SEC lifted the moratorium, expressing
satisfaction with the improvement of regulatory procedures adopted by
various exchanges. To this day, the CBOE continues to invest in the
development and implementation of systems and procedures to improve
the marketplace for the investing public, placing as much importance on
the protection of investors as it does on their participation in the marketplace.

THE 1980S—NEW PRODUCTS FOR UNCERTAIN TIMES

By 1980, the CBOE had already outgrown its first home and was rapidly
approaching the limits of its second. Annual volume in the fiscal years
1977, 1978, and 1979 was 24.8 million, 34.3 million, and 35.4 million
contracts, respectively. It was clear that with the explosive growth of

listed stock options and new products yet to come, the trading facilities in the old Board of Trade building were no longer sufficient. Indeed, the CBOE was old enough and big enough to leave home.

But the CBOE decided to stay in the neighborhood and erect its own self-contained building (right across the street from the CBOT) on the site of the old LaSalle Street Station. It took until 1984 to complete. And when it opened, on schedule, the CBOE had built the largest trading floor in the world. Any doubts as to whether the new construction embodied too much optimism about the continued growth of options faded in the coming years.

The early 1980s signaled the end of one of the most turbulent times in the economic history of the United States. Rampant inflation and repeated recessions of the late 70s reached their crescendo when the prime rate hit 21.5 percent in late 1980. The stinging, swift recession that followed sent the stock market into a decline that would eventually sink the Dow Jones Industrial Average to 776.92 on August 12, 1982, some 250 points below its April 27, 1981, peak of 1,024.05. The CBOE's 1983 annual report reflected on the impact of this period on the financial services industry:

> The same market forces that made us more sophisticated consumers simultaneously reshaped the entire [industry]. Years of inflation and volatility demanded new investment alternatives. Surviving in an increasingly complex financial environment now requires more flexibility, more control.[19]

Pioneers T-Bond Options

In response to these forces, the CBOE was ready to act on its 1977 petition to trade options on securities other than stocks. By February of 1981, everything was in place for trading of the first non-equity based option—a contract on Ginnie Mae pass-through certificates.

The scheduled opening day in October was preempted by litigation challenging the SEC's jurisdiction over an option on an instrument already trading futures—Ginnie Mae futures had been trading on the Chicago Board of Trade since 1975. In December, in the midst of that heated debate, the SEC approved the CBOE's proposal to trade options on U.S. Treasury bonds. In March of 1982, the regulatory feud was settled, giving the SEC the power over options on debt instruments. Deciding that the GNMA options could be difficult to understand and to trade, the new exchange did not introduce the product, but rather began trading options on U.S. Treasury bonds in October.

Jumping on the Bandwagon

The momentum of this creative energy was not limited to the listed options market. The Chicago Mercantile Exchange became the first exchange to trade cash-settled financial futures in 1981 when it introduced futures contracts on Eurodollars. Within a short time, other exchanges applied the concept to stock indexes. The Kansas City Board of Trade began trading futures contracts on the Value Line Composite Average in February of 1982. The Chicago Mercantile Exchange followed in April with a futures contract based on the widely followed Standard & Poor's 500 Stock Index. Not to be left out, the New York Futures Exchange, a unit of the New York Stock Exchange, introduced futures on the NYSE Composite Index in May.

It was also in May that the CBOE announced that it had created the CBOE 100 Index and would trade cash-settled options on the index shortly. This index of the 100 companies with the highest capitalization (of all stocks trading options on the CBOE), opened for trading on March 11, 1983, with a respectable volume of 4,827 contracts.

Although stock index futures enjoyed strong initial growth, the system of adjustments to a position's value (based on the daily movement of the contract) could become difficult for the average investor to manage. An option, on the other hand, could be purchased with no need for additional capital should the market move against the investor's position.

Cash settlement, common to the index futures contract and the index option, provides a simple way to realize profit or loss. The value of a call option on the CBOE 100 Index, for example, at expiration is the difference of the value of the index on expiration and the strike price of the call (not less than zero) times the multiplier. However, a futures contract is valued at 500 times its numerical value, so a 1-point move in the futures contract represents a $500 profit or loss. For the public investor, this could be a large amount, the initial margin requirement to establish a futures position notwithstanding. The CBOE decided to value its contract at 100 times the index. This also made the premiums of OEX options consistent with the premiums of equity options which represent 100 shares of the underlying stock.

The combination of cash settlement, limited risk to option holders, and more reasonable index valuation became a watershed. Acceptance by the public and professional investing communities was immediate. The CBOE 100, renamed the Standard & Poor's (S&P) 100 Stock Index in June, quickly established itself as the most popular option with volume increasing from 10.5 million contracts in 1983 to 64.3 million in 1984.

The OEX, as it is known by its trading symbol, was called "the most significant new financial product since the introduction of the listed option" by Macon Brewer, then chief of options at Dean Witter Reynolds, Inc.[20] In 1987, annual contract volume would reach 108 million in the OEX alone. (See Figure 1–4.)

FIGURE 1–4
CBOE Annual Volume (in millions)

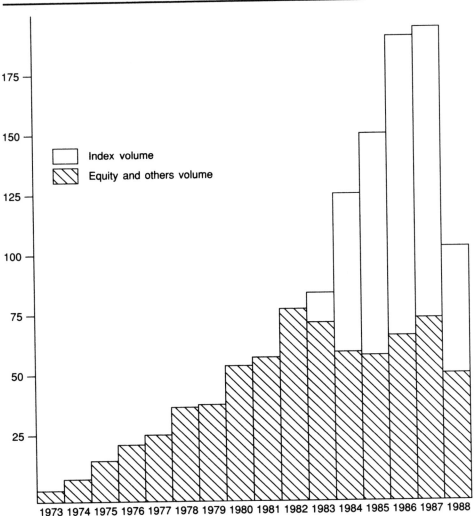

Other index options have since been created: the Major Market Index (XMI) of the American Stock Exchange, the New York Stock Exchange Composite (NYA), and the S&P 500 (SPX), to name a few. Options on foreign currencies are traded at the Philadelphia Stock Exchange.

THE FUTURE

The financial landscape and economic climate are constantly changing. Technological developments are transforming the financial markets' scope, speed, size, and complexity. Because of technical advances in electronic communications, investors and traders around the world are instantly informed about conditions on any exchange in any city. Computer technology has given exchanges the ability to handle many more times the volume than they had carried only a decade before. Investment firms now perform complex financial analyses that could not have even been conceived in the past. Market participants use trading strategies such as stock index arbitrage and portfolio trading that were previously difficult, if not impossible, to execute.

Global Marketplace

The late 1980s will be remembered as the time when the 24-hour global marketplace became a reality. Trading "books" are now passed from time zone to time zone. Formerly obscure exchanges have become sources of investment opportunity. New futures and options markets have opened or are scheduled to open in many cities around the world.

From humble beginnings in 1969 (when the Chicago Board of Trade diversified from grain futures) and from an opening day volume of 911 contracts in 1973, America's listed options markets now trade, on the average, more than 2,000 contracts per minute! Total volume in all derivative financial products is even greater.

As the world marketplace grows, so will the options markets. Product innovations will not stop with index options. The "risk management" business is still in its infancy. The CBOE, in one of its annual reports, conveyed the intelligence, creativity, and pragmatism underlying the options markets' continuing progress:

To become a working idea, theory must be transformed by risk into innovation. The listed option is grounded in history, polished by investment performance and proven in the trading process. Growth will continue because the option concept works![21]

NOTES

1. Henry J. Clasing, *Dow Jones-Irwin Guide to Put and Call Options* (Homewood, Ill.: Dow Jones-Irwin, 1978).
2. Charles Mackay, L. L. D., *Extraordinary Popular Delusions and the Madness of Crowds,* first published in 1841, Farrar, Straus and Giroux (1932), p. 95.
3. Herbert J. Filer, *Understanding Put and Call Options* (New York: Crown Publishers, 1959), p. 92.
4. Ibid., p. 98.
5. Arthur C. Crump, *The Theory of Stock Speculation* (New York: S. A. Nelson, 1901). Reprint, Burlington, Vt.: Fraser Publishing, 1983, p. 32.
6. Filer, *Understanding Put and Call Options,* p. 82.
7. Ibid., p. 78.
8. Congressional report of 1934, as cited in *Options,* Martin Torosian, (MTA Financial Service Corporation, 1986), p. 3.
9. Filer, *Understanding Put and Call Options,* p. 79.
10. Ibid.
11. Richard M. Bookstaber, *Option Pricing and Investment Strategies* (Chicago: Probus, 1985), p. 8.
12. Filer, *Understanding Put and Call Options,* p. 36.
13. Ibid., p. 59.
14. *The Wall Street Journal,* February 19, 1969.
15. Fischer Black and Myron Scholes, "The Pricing of Options and Corporate Liabilities," *Journal of Political Economy* (May–June 1973), pp. 637–54.
16. Excerpt of report by Robert A. Nathan and Associates, as reprinted in CBOE *Annual Report,* 1978, p. 35.
17. *Annual Report* of the CBOE, 1978, p. 30.
18. Excerpt from "Outlook for the U.S. Securities Industry—1981," by the Stanford Research Institute, as reprinted in the CBOE *Annual Report,* 1978, p. 33.
19. Annual Report from the CBOE, 1983, p. 1.
20. Ibid., p. 9.
21. Ibid., p. 1.

PART 1

ESSENTIAL CONCEPTS

CHAPTER 2

FUNDAMENTALS OF OPTIONS

Options are derivative instruments. This means that an option's value and its trading characteristics are tied to the asset on which that option trades. It is this essential defining characteristic that makes options valuable to the knowledgeable investor. One major advantage of options is their versatility. They can be used in accordance with a wide variety of investment strategies. In most situations, understanding options arms the investor with a choice of ways in which to invest. As a result, any investor who understands when and how to use options in pursuit of his or her individual financial objectives can enjoy a clear advantage. Finally, the astute will have an effective means of managing the risk inherent in any investment program.

The asset on which the option is traded might be a stock, an equity index, a futures contract, a Treasury security, or another type of security. Although this chapter centers on stock options, the concepts and pricing theories also apply to other kinds of underlying assets.

Whatever the underlying asset, the pricing of an option is commonly thought to be an esoteric and difficult task, certainly not something to be attempted by the mathematically unsophisticated. At one level, this perception is true—advanced mathematics for the pricing of options has been used in the past and continues to be utilized. The Black-Scholes option-pricing model, for example, was first developed with stochastic calculus and partial differential equations. What these techniques are need not concern you here. The important point is that option pricing can generally be explained using a conceptual approach, rather than a highly technical mathematical approach. The discussion of options pricing that follows is directed toward the investor who seeks an explanation in accessible terms at the intermediate level.

This chapter explains option pricing theory in four steps. First, puts, calls, and related terms are defined. Second, the five elements of an option's theoretical value are covered in a general fashion. Third, each of these elements are examined in greater depth. Fourth, and finally, the concept of put-call parity ties together many of this chapter's concepts and demonstrates how the options markets actually function and increase overall market liquidity.

SOME DEFINITIONS

Option

An *option* on an underlying asset is either the right to buy the asset (a *call* option), or the right to sell the asset (a *put* option) at some predetermined price and within some predetermined time period. The price and other terms are written in the option contract.

The key feature here is that an option owner has a right, not an obligation. If the owner does not exercise his or her right prior to the predetermined time, the option and the opportunity to exercise it cease to exist.

The seller is obligated to fulfill the requirements of the option if it is exercised. In the case of a call option on stock, the seller has sold the right to buy that stock. The seller of the call option is therefore obligated to sell the stock to the call option owner if the option is exercised. In the case of a put option on a stock, the seller of the put option has sold the right to sell that stock. This seller is therefore obligated to buy the stock from the put option buyer if the option is exercised.

Strike Price and Expiration Date

The "predetermined price" of the option is known as its *strike price*. When an option is exercised, the holder pays (or receives) the amount of the strike price in exchange for receiving (or delivering) the underlying asset. The "predetermined time" in the future is called the *expiration date*. For example, the XYZ Sep 50 call option is the right to buy the stock XYZ at the price of $50 per share until the expiration date in September.

Listed options have clearly defined rules establishing strike prices, contract sizes, and expiration dates. Although rules can vary slightly from exchange to exchange, listed stock options generally have strike prices at intervals of $2.50 (on a stock price of $10 to $25). Between stock prices of $25 to $200, option strike prices are generally set at intervals of $5. Above stock prices of $200, strike intervals are $10.

Stock options in the United States are denominated in quantities of 100 shares each or one round lot of stock. If that XYZ Sep 50 call option was quoted at $3, its actual cost would be $300. This is because the $3 quoted price represents the cost for one share, but the call option contract covers 100 shares. Thus, 100 shares times $3 per share equals the cost of $300.

Expiration Rules

Listed stock options in this country technically expire on the Saturday following the third Friday of the expiration month. Exceptions are made when legal holidays fall on the Friday or Saturday in question. Saturday expiration, however, is irrelevant to nonexchange members. The Saturday expiration exists so that brokerage houses and exchange members can have the morning after the last trading day to resolve any errors.

Customers of brokerage firms must concern themselves with two procedures in regard to expiration. First, the customer must be aware of the rules for automatic exercise. For example, most brokerage firms may automatically exercise a call option if the stock closes 75 cents or more above the strike price unless specifically instructed by the customer not to exercise. Second, the client must be aware of his brokerage firm's specific rules regarding the notification deadline for exercise. Many brokerage houses have a final notification deadline of 4:00 P.M., EST, on the expiration Friday, but this rule varies from firm to firm.

While listed stock options have fairly consistent specifications, listed futures options differ considerably in contract specifications, strike prices, expiration dates, and unit value of price movements. This occurs because the specifications of futures contracts themselves vary. While stock prices are dollar-denominated in 100 share lots and stock option prices move accordingly, a futures contract on corn at the Chicago Board of Trade covers 5,000 bushels and a futures contract on No. 2 heating oil at the New York Mercantile Exchange covers 42,000 gallons. Even futures contracts on the same underlying asset can vary: The Japanese yen futures contract at the Chicago Mercantile Exchange covers 12,500,000 yen and the contract at the MidAmerica Commodity Exchange covers 6,250,000 yen. As a result of these differences, the trader must be familiar with all the terms of a contract before trading. One who does not do this first usually learns very fast, but, unfortunately, it can be an expensive process.

American Call Option

An *American* call option is the right (but not the obligation) to purchase the underlying asset at some predetermined price at any time until the expiration date.

European Call Option

A *European* call option is the right (but not the obligation) to purchase the underlying asset at some predetermined price only on the expiration date of the option.

The difference between European and American options has nothing to do with geography. Instead, the distinguishing feature is the right of early exercise that exists with American options, but does not exist with European options. Until the Chicago Board Options Exchange (CBOE) introduced European options on the S&P 500 Index on July 1, 1983, the distinction was not particularly important to investors in U.S. markets since only American options had been listed; since then, several European options have been listed.

For the purpose of this discussion, the early exercise feature of American options as it relates to pricing theory need not be considered in detail. It is sufficient to point out that the early exercise privilege of American options is a feature that sometimes has value and never has cost. As a result, American options sometimes have a higher theoretical value than do European ones. With this one distinction, the following discussion of option pricing theory applies to both types of options.

ELEMENTS OF AN OPTION'S VALUE

The five components of an option's *theoretical value* are:
1. The price of the underlying asset.
2. The strike price of the option.
3. The time remaining until the expiration date.
4. The prevailing interest rates.
5. The expected volatility of the underlying asset.

As a reminder, the following discussion centers on stock options, but the concepts apply to all types of options.

Price and Strike Price

The relationship of the stock's price to the option's strike price determines whether the option is called *in-the-money, at-the-money,* or *out-of-the-money.*

A call option is in-the-money when the stock price is above the strike price. A call option is at-the-money when the stock price is at the strike price. And a call option is out-of-the-money when the stock price is below the strike price. Figure 2–1 depicts the general relationship between a call option's price and the underlying stock's price as the stock moves from below to above the strike price.

As Figure 2–1 illustrates, when the stock price is significantly below the option's strike price, the call option's value approaches zero. As the stock price rises, the call option's value also rises.

FIGURE 2–1
Depiction of Theoretical Call Option Value

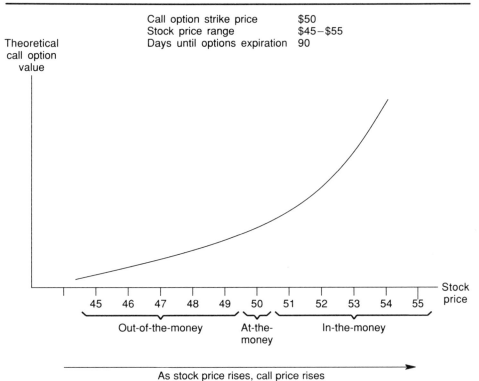

Call option strike price	$50
Stock price range	$45–$55
Days until options expiration	90

Theoretical call option value

Out-of-the-money

At-the-money

In-the-money

Stock price

As stock price rises, call price rises

At first, the option price rise is only a small fraction of the stock price rise. This fraction increases as the stock price rises. When the stock price is significantly above the strike price, the option price movement approaches 100 percent of the stock price movement. The fractional price movement of the option for a $1 price move in the stock is called the option's *delta*. This is discussed in greater depth later in this chapter.

For a put option, the in-the-money, at-the-money, and out-of-the-money designations are opposite those of call options because put options increase in price as the price of the underlying stock decreases.

A put option is in-the-money when the stock price is below the strike price. A put option is at-the-money when the stock price is at the strike price, and a put option is out-of-the-money when the stock price is above the strike price. Figure 2–2 depicts the general relationship be-

FIGURE 2–2
Depiction of Theoretical Put Option Value

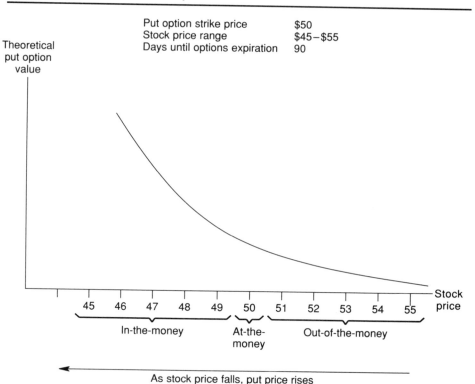

Put option strike price	$50
Stock price range	$45–$55
Days until options expiration	90

As stock price falls, put price rises

tween a put option's price and the underlying stock's price as the stock moves from above to below the strike price.

Time

Options, of course, have an expiration date. The amount of time remaining until expiration has a great impact on their value. There are two ways to demonstrate the effect of time graphically. First, Figure 2–3, option price versus stock price, shows the effect of time at three different points—at 90 days, at 45 days, and at expiration.

The second graphical method of depicting the effect of time on an option's price is to assume that the stock price remains constant and to graph the option's theoretical price versus the number of days remaining until expiration. This is called the *time decay line* and is illustrated in Figure 2–4.

As is apparent from Figure 2–4, option values do not decay in a straight line. The relationship is related to the square root of time. Although this sounds esoteric, the relationship is quite simple. If a 30-day out-of-the-money option has a value of $1, the 60-day option (having approximately twice as much time until expiration) has a value of approximately $1 \times \sqrt{2}$ or $1 \times 1.414 = 1.414$. One can expand this simple concept into the following:

If the 30-day option $= \$1$, then the 60-day option $\approx 1 \times \sqrt{2} = 1.414$
If the 30-day option $= \$1$, then the 90-day option $\approx 1 \times \sqrt{3} = 1.734$
If the 30-day option $= \$1$, then the 120-day option $\approx 1 \times \sqrt{4} = 2.000$
If the 30-day option $= \$1$, then the 150-day option $\approx 1 \times \sqrt{5} = 2.235$
If the 30-day option $= \$1$, then the 180-day option $\approx 1 \times \sqrt{6} = 2.450$

This list demonstrates that during the first half of an option's life it loses less than one third of its value from time decay. Certainly this should give pause to those option traders who resolutely believe in buying only front-month options. Considering time decay alone, option buyers should prefer to buy longer-term options. After all, it is cheaper to buy one 6-month option for $2.45 than it is to buy 6 one-month options at $1 each. Conversely, with all else equal, option sellers should have a preference to sell shorter-term options since there is more profit to be made by selling 6 one-month options than one 6-month option.

FIGURE 2–3

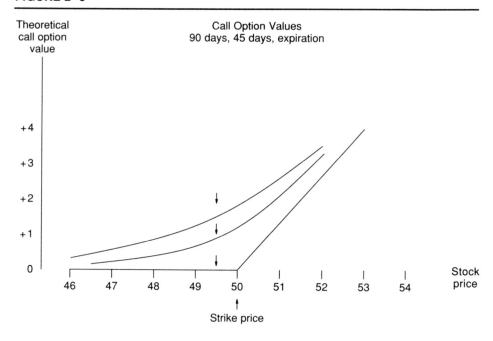

Theoretical call option value

Call Option Values
90 days, 45 days, expiration

Stock price

Strike price

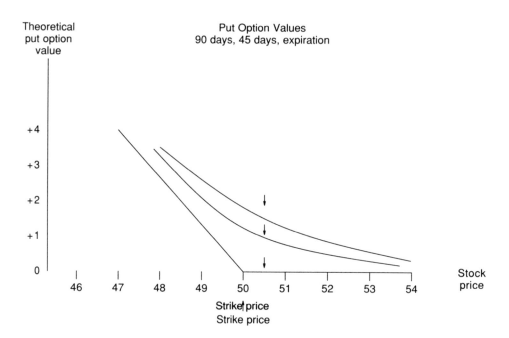

Theoretical put option value

Put Option Values
90 days, 45 days, expiration

Stock price

Strike price
Strike price

FIGURE 2–4
The Time Decay Line (effect of time to expiration on call and put prices)

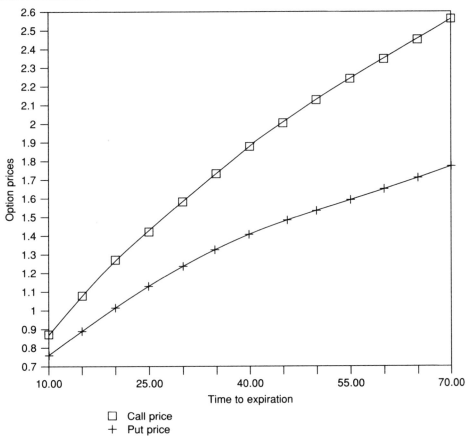

□   Call price
+   Put price

Note: Figures 2–4, 2–5, 2–9, and 2–12 through 2–17 were produced using The Options Analyst, a set of Lotus 1-2-3 spreadsheets produced by FinCalc, Inc. Based on the Black-Scholes option pricing model, The Options Analyst calculates theoretical values for options, spreads, and positions including an underlying stock. The "what if?" capability enables the user to analyze the effect of a change in one or more of the inputs to the pricing model.

Interest Rates

Understanding the effect of changes in interest rates is most easily understood after having read the section of this chapter on put-call parity, where the arbitrage relationship between options and stock is explained. At this point, it is sufficient to be aware of two points that are illustrated in Figure 2–5.

The first point revealed, which is surprising to many traders, is that

FIGURE 2–5
Effect of Interest Rate on Call and Put Prices

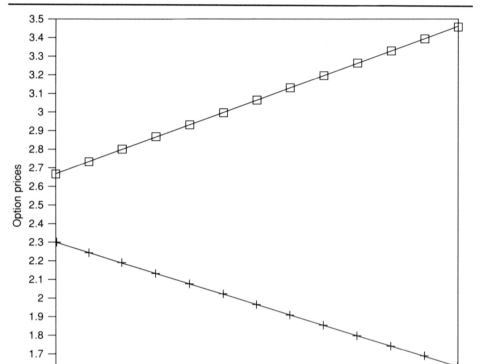

rising interest rates boost call prices and depress put prices. The second point is that the effect of changes in interest rates is small. This figure shows that a rise in interest rates from 3 to 15 percent causes call prices to rise from $2.67 to $3.44 and put prices to decline from $2.30 to $1.64.

Volatility

Mathematically, volatility is a measure of stock price fluctuation without regard to direction. Specifically, *volatility* is the annualized standard deviation of daily percentage changes in a stock's price. Since the mathematics of this definition is beyond the scope of this book, the following discussion presents volatility in a nontechnical way as a concept that is essential to the understanding of options. For an extensive mathematical treatment of volatility, there are a number of references available; for example, books on options by John C. Cox and Mark Rubinstein, Robert A. Jarrow and Andrew Rudd, and Sheldon Natenburg.

Most people intuitively understand that volatility relates to price movement, and this intuition is correct. It can be said that a stock that had a 12-month high of $120 and a 12-month low of $80 is more volatile than one that traded between $95 and $105. Over a shorter term, it can be said that a stock with an average daily trading range (high to low price) of $5 is more volatile than one that has an average daily trading range of $2 (assuming the average underlying price of both stocks is the same).

Observation of historical price movements shows that individual stocks go through periods of high and low volatility. There are many possible explanations for these variations. One explanation might be general economic factors affecting an industry group of stocks; another might be specific developments for the specific stock. A third possibility could be the psychological state of investors. Regardless of the cause, investors must be aware that the volatility characteristics of a stock can change dramatically at any point in the future.

But what is the concept of volatility relevant to the option user?

Figure 2–6 depicts the price movement of the S&P 500 beginning October 1, 1986 and ending September 30, 1987. During this year, some months appear to have more volatility than others, but how can the differences be measured? More important, how can the level at any time be defined? Figure 2–6 does not answer these questions.

Since volatility is nondirectional, it is more helpful to look specifically at the daily price changes, rather than at the total price itself.

Figure 2–7 shows the daily price changes of the S&P 500 during the same year covered in Figure 2–6. Although Figure 2–7 gives a better view of daily price changes—i.e., volatility—there are several unanswered questions. For example: Given these daily price changes, how can volatility be measured? And, what does this tell about future price fluctuations?

To answer these and other questions, one must rank the daily price changes by frequency of occurrence. From Figure 2–7 it appears that small price changes occur more frequently than large ones, but to what extent is this true? Figure 2–8 presents the ranking of daily price changes by frequency of occurrence, and this takes us one step closer to understanding volatility. In this figure, daily price changes between −.5 and +.5 are grouped together in the bar at the center of the graph over the number 0. Price changes of −.5 to −1.5 are represented by the bar over

FIGURE 2–6
S&P 500 Index (10/01/86–9/30/87)

FIGURE 2–7
S&P 500 Daily Point Change (10/01/86–10/01/87)

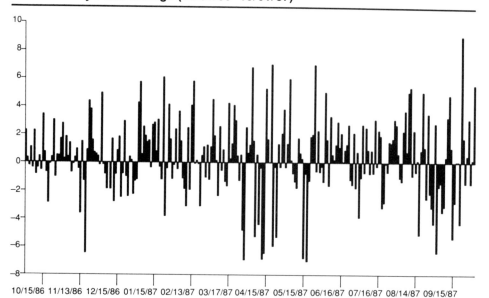

FIGURE 2–8
Distribution of S&P 500 Daily Point Changes (10/01/86–9/30/87)

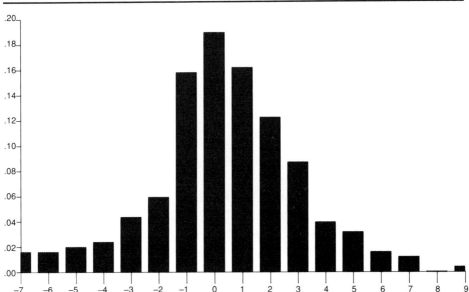

the number −1, and changes of +.5 to +1.5 are represented by the bar over the number 1. The vertical axis at the left indicates the percentage of times that a daily price change in each group occurred. For example, a price change of between −.5 and +.5 occurred 19 percent of the time during the year graphed. Daily price changes of −.5 to −1.5 occurred about 16 percent of the time, and a movement of +2.5 to +3.5 occurred about 9 percent of the time.

Figure 2–8 shows a one-year historical distribution of daily price changes for the S&P 500. From this distribution, the annualized standard deviation can be calculated. This number is the volatility. Although the mathematics is beyond the scope of this discussion, there is value in knowing the result of this calculation. First, the derived volatility permits calculation of an option price. Second, it tells something important about the distribution of price movements themselves.

VOLATILITY AND AVERAGE PRICE MOVEMENTS

A *standard deviation* is a measure of the probability of a random event occurring. Probability tables exist so that if a standard deviation is known (or assumed), the likelihood or probability of an event occurring within a specific range can be determined. Although these probabilities can be calculated exactly, the following approximations are sufficient for traders of options:

- Approximately 2 out of 3 outcomes will occur within one standard deviation of the mean.
- Approximately 19 out of 20 outcomes will occur within two standard deviations of the mean.
- Approximately 369 out of 370 outcomes will occur within three standard deviations of the mean.

This concept is related to price movement of stock prices in the following manner: The volatility percentage for a given stock price represents one standard deviation of price movement for a one-year period. For example, if the stock price is $50 and the volatility is 10 percent, a price change of one standard deviation during a one-year period is $5 (10% × $50). Consequently, in one year it is probable that in two out of three cases, the stock would be trading between $45 ($50 − $5) and $55 ($50 + $5). Similarly, in 19 out of 20 cases, the stock would be trading between $40 [$50 − (2 × $5)] and $60 [$50 + (2 × $5)]. Also, in 369 out of 370 cases, the contract would be trading between $35 [$50 − (3 × $5)] and $65 [$50 + (3 × $5)].

Because a one-year period is not useful for options traders, the following formula can be used to calculate a price change of one standard deviation over a period of time:

Volatility percentage divided by the square root of the time period times the stock price.

Example

If a stock is trading at $50 with a volatility of 25 percent, the daily standard deviation of price change is

$$(25\% \div \sqrt{252}) \times \$50 \approx (.25 \div 16) \times \$50 \approx .79 \approx 79 \text{ cents}$$

There are approximately 252 trading days in a year, the square root of which is 15.82. In calculating the weekly standard deviation, the number to use is the square root of 52 or approximately 7.2. For a 90-day option, which has a life of one fourth of a year, the volatility percentage is divided by the square root of 4, or 2. Consequently, for the sample $50 stock with a volatility of 25 percent, a move of one standard deviation for 90 days is:

$$(25\% \div \sqrt{4}) \times \$50 \approx (.25 \div 2) \times \$50 \approx \$6.25$$

This means it is probable that in two out of three cases the sample stock, which started at $50, will be trading between $43.75 and $56.25 in 90 days. In 19 out of 20 cases, it is probable that this stock will be trading between $37.50 and $62.50 in 90 days. And in 369 out of 370 cases, it is probable that in 90 days this stock will be trading between $31.25 and $68.75.

Option Prices and Volatility

The relationship between volatility and option prices is a direct one–as the volatility percentage increases, so do option prices. A higher standard deviation means that greater movement is likely, and greater movement justifies higher option prices.

Figure 2–9 shows that the relationship between volatility changes and options prices is nearly linear, but that it is a different line for in-the-money, at-the-money, and out-of-the-money options.

It must be remembered that option prices are based on the expected volatility of the underlying stock. Mathematically, volatility is non-directional. If the market expects greater fluctuation in a stock's price, the fluctuation could be up or down. Consequently, when higher volatility is expected, both call and put prices rise.

With an increase in expected volatility, at-the-money options increase in price more than out-of-the-money options do because of how price movements are distributed according to *probability theory*. Mathematically, a $50 stock always has a greater probability of moving $1 than of moving $6. This explains why at-the-money options have higher prices than out-of-the-money options. Also, according to probability theory, an increase in the level of volatility increases the likelihood of a $1 move more than the likelihood of a $6 move. This explains why at-the-money options increase more in price than out-of-the-money options when the expected volatility increases.

Implied Volatility

Until now, the focus of this volatility discussion has been on actual daily price changes. From these actual numbers, a volatility percentage is calculated. This number, of course, is based on historical data. However, the *theoretical value* of an option depends on *future volatility* of the stock, which cannot be precisely known. (Theoretical value means an estimated fair value of an option, derived from a mathematical model.) Consequently, the price at which an option is trading tells what volatility level in the stock is implied by the option price.

Implied volatility is the volatility percentage that justifies an option's price. For the professional floor trader who trades large numbers of options and who manages large open positions, differences between actual stock price volatility and implied volatility of options can have a significant impact. For the off-floor user of options, however, differences in implied volatility and recent actual volatility rarely are significant. For them, other factors such as stock selection, timing of price movements, and desired rates of return are the most important considerations.

FIGURE 2–9
Effect of Volatility on Call and Put Prices

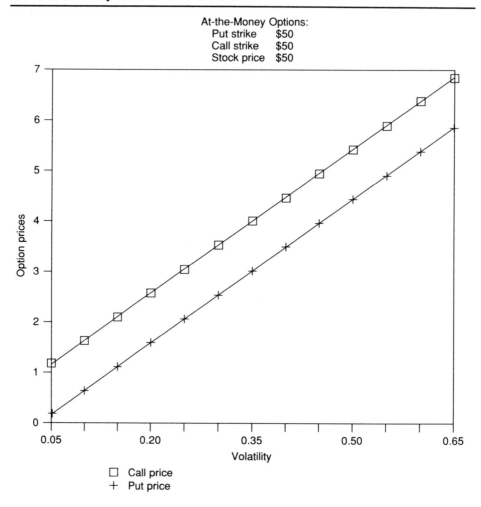

FIGURE 2–9
(continued)

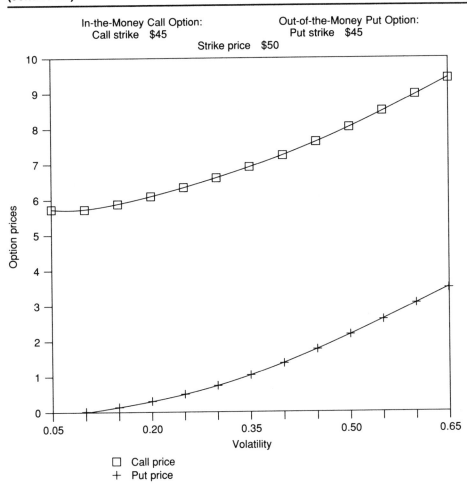

Volatility—The Unknown Factor

Of the five components of an option's theoretical value, the stock price, strike price, time until expiration, and prevailing interest rates are readily observable. Only the expected volatility of the underlying stock is unknown.

Thus you can conclude that an option's theoretical value is ultimately subjective because the selection of a volatility estimate is sub-

FIGURE 2–9
(concluded)

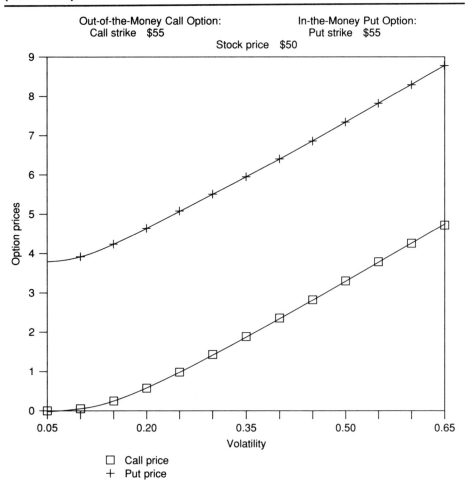

Out-of-the-Money Call Option:
Call strike $55

In-the-Money Put Option:
Put strike $55

Stock price $50

☐ Call price
+ Put price

jective. After all, it is the future volatility of a stock that determines an option's true value and the future volatility, of course, cannot be known.

While forecasting volatility seems an insurmountable task to the average person, it is a subjective process. Such forecasting is analogous to forecasting the weather: Even though technology has been developed and refined, weather predictions involve judgment and are not always accurate.

In forecasting volatility, you can turn on the computer and get the historical view for 30 days or 60 days. For those without a computer, there are daily, weekly, and monthly option services available that include volatility estimates. This expert view can be complemented by the consensus view of current option prices (the implied volatility level). But ultimately you must make a subjective decision about volatility. Both experience with a particular stock and keeping up with the latest market conditions can help.

INTRINSIC VALUE AND TIME VALUE

The price of an option can consist of intrinsic value, time value, or a combination of both. *Intrinsic value* is the in-the-money portion of an option's price. *Time value* is the portion of an option's price that is in excess of the intrinsic value.

If the stock price is above the strike price of a call option, the stock price minus the strike price represents the intrinsic value of the call option. For example, if the stock price is $54, the $50 call option has an intrinsic value of $4. Any value above $4 that the market places on this option is time value. It exists because the market realizes that the stock can decline below $50, and the stock owner can suffer a loss greater than $4—possibly as much as $54. Because this risk exists, the call option purchaser should be willing to pay more than $4 for the $50 call option because he does not have the same risk if the stock price declines below $50. The call option buyer's risk is limited to the premium paid for the option. The premium paid above $4 for the option—the time value— measures in some sense the market's estimate of the likelihood that the stock price will decline below $50. The call buyer who pays $5 for the $50 call option is paying an extra $1 to protect himself against the stock price declining below $50. If the stock price rises, he participates in the price rise. The $1 time value he paid for the option is the price of his "insurance policy" against losing money beyond a stock price decline below $50.

For put options, intrinsic value equals strike price minus stock price because put options are in-the-money when the stock price is below the strike price.

Example

If the stock price is $54, the $55 put option has an intrinsic value of the $1. Any value above $1 that the market places on this put option is time value.

FIGURE 2–10
Intrinsic Value and Time Value

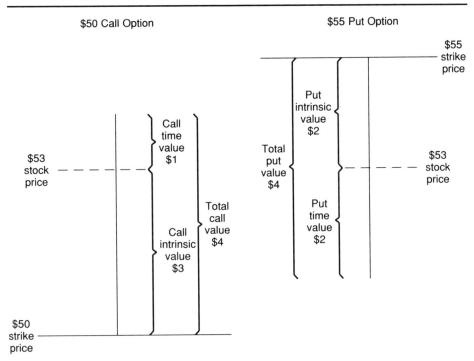

An out-of-the-money option consists entirely of time value. By definition, the price of an out-of-the-money option has no in-the-money portion; consequently, it has no intrinsic value.

The concepts of intrinsic and extrinsic value for call and put options are illustrated in Figure 2–10.

PARITY

An option is trading at *parity* with the stock if it is in-the-money and has no time value. This situation exists when the stock price minus the strike price equals the option price. For example, if the $50 call option were trading at $4 when the stock was at $54, it would be *trading at parity*. In-the-money options, especially deep-in-the-money options, tend to trade at parity when only a few days remain until expiration. This happens when the market perceives that the option is almost certain to be exercised. The logic for this is simple. Since it is only a matter of time until the option is exercised and becomes stock, the option price trades in step with the stock price until such exercise occurs.

THE SECOND LEVEL OF UNDERSTANDING

Now that the five elements of theoretical value have been introduced, the second step is to understand how a change in each element affects the theoretical value of an option. The questions to be addressed are these:

- How much will the option price change for a $1 move in stock price?
- How is time versus option price decay quantified?
- How will a 1 percent change in volatility affect an option's value?

Typically, this is the point where advanced mathematics takes the forefront. This discussion, however, continues to emphasize concepts. Successful users of options should be aware of the components of option price change, just as they should be aware of the five elements of value, but a detailed knowledge of the mathematics is not required.

DELTA: THE EFFECT OF STOCK PRICE CHANGE

During the discussion of stock price and strike price earlier in this chapter, it was stated that:

> As the stock price rises, the call option price also rises. At first, the option price rise is only a small fraction of the stock price rise. This fraction increases as the stock price rises. When the stock price is significantly above the strike price, then the option price movement approaches 100 percent of the stock price movement.

It is this "fraction of the stock price movement" that is known as the *delta*.

As an example, assume that the underlying stock rises $1 and the option price rises 25 cents. In this case, the delta of the option is .25—the option moved 25 percent of the stock price movement.

Delta, however, is not static. The delta changes as the option goes from being an out-of-the-money to an in-the-money option. The price of an out-of-the-money option changes by a small percentage of the stock price change. By contrast, the price of an at-the-money option changes by approximately 50 percent of the stock price change. As an option becomes more and more in-the-money, its delta rises and gradually approaches 1.00 or 100 percent. This means that the price of a deep-in-the-money option moves dollar for dollar with the stock price movement. The concept of delta is demonstrated in Table 2–1. Although this table highlights a line where the delta equals exactly the option price change for a $1 price rise or fall in the stock, any reader with a calculator can quickly ascertain that the other lines on the table are not as exact. This situation occurs because the delta is a theoretical measure designed for a very small stock price movement, not a full dollar move. For the mathematically sophisticated, there are many books that go into this concept in depth.

A graphical representation of how deltas change with stock price changes is presented in Figure 2–11. As the top half illustrates, call option deltas are positive and increase as the stock price rises. This is consistent with Table 2–1.

Put options, however, have negative deltas because they increase in value as stock prices decline. This is represented by the bottom half of Figure 2–11. Referring back to Figure 2–2, the $50 put option increases in price at an increasing rate as the stock price moves from $55 down to $45. Consequently, when the stock moves from $55 to $54, the put option

TABLE 2–1
Delta of Call Option

Stock Price	$50 call option Volatility: 35% Theoretical Value	Days to expiration: 90 Delta	
$56	7 1/4	.78	
55	6 1/2	.75	←——— The .75 delta
54	5 3/4	.71	implies a .75
53	5 1/8	.68	value change if
52	4 1/2	.64	the stock price
51	3 7/8	.60	rises or falls by
50	3 1/4	.54	$1.
49	2 3/4	.50	
48	2 3/8	.46	
47	2 3/16	.41	
46	1 7/8	.36	
45	1 7/16	.32	
44	1 3/16	.27	

FIGURE 2–11
Delta: Change in Option Price per 1 Unit Change in Stock

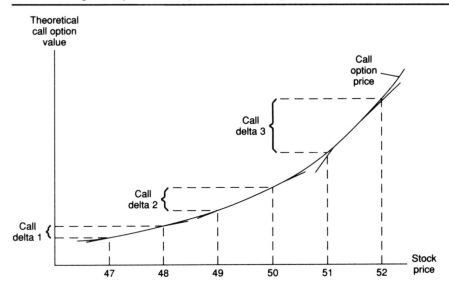

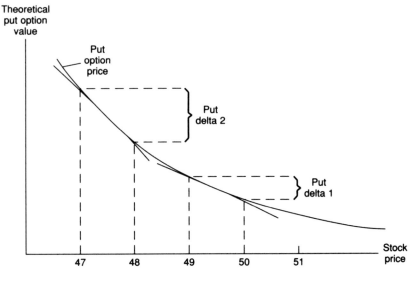

increases only slightly in price and at this point has a small negative delta. Subsequently, when the stock price moves from $46 to $45, the option price change is a much larger percentage of the $1 price change in the stock. At this point, the put option has a much larger negative delta.

Another method of illustrating the concept of how delta changes with stock price change is in Figure 2–12.

This shows delta on the vertical axis and stock price on the horizontal axis. Call deltas are shown on the top half of the graph, and put deltas are shown on the bottom. The concept is the same as that in Figure 2–11: As stock prices rise, call deltas rise from 0 to 1.00 and put deltas fall from −1.00 to 0.

The delta is important to the user of options because it gives a current estimate of the expected value of an option price change. *Current* is the key word. Too often, traders think only of what will happen on the date of expiration. Such focus, however, is limiting.

FIGURE 2–12
Effect of Stock Price on Call and Put Deltas

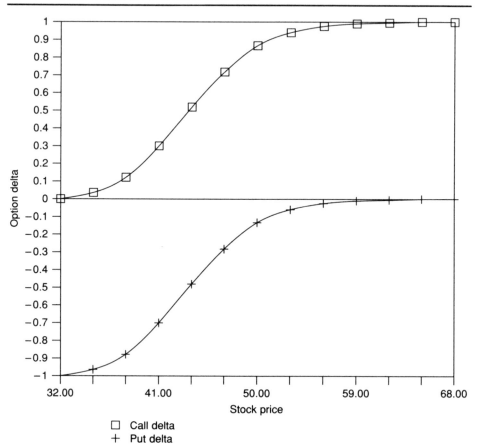

As an example, assume that you expect XYZ, which is currently at $50, to rally when company earnings are released next week. Rather than buy the stock, you buy the $50 call option to limit your risk in the event the earnings report is unfavorable. For this example, assume that the $50 call option is trading at $2, its delta is .50, and that the stock moves up $1. With a delta of .50 and a stock move of $1, the option can be expected to move by .50 to $2.50, for a profit of 50 cents. At expiration, however, the results are completely different. With the stock at $51 on the date of expiration, the $50 call option is worth $1. Since the option was purchased for $2, the result is a loss of $1. This is quite different than the profit of 50 cents realized on the movement of the stock and the option at the time of the earnings release.

Your trading time frame determines which analysis is correct for you. Was it your intention to sell the option immediately after the earnings report for a quick profit? Or was it your intention to hold the option until the expiration date with the desire of exercising the option and purchasing the stock if the option was in-the-money?

In the first situation, the trader was counting on short-term volatility with a positive expectation. The call purchase limited the downside risk, and a 50 cent profit was realized when the option was sold on the move after the earnings report. In the second situation, the call purchaser wanted to buy the stock, but was using the option as a limited risk alternative during the option's life. Had this purchaser been wrong about the stock and had it dropped sharply in price during this period, his or her loss would have been limited to the $2 paid for the option.

The Rate of Change in Delta—Gamma

As can be seen from Table 2–1, the delta not only changes with price changes of the underlying stock, it also changes at different rates if the option is in-the-money, at-the-money, or out-of-the-money. For example, when the stock moved from a price of $50 to $51, the delta of the option changed from .54 to .60—a .06 change. However, when the stock rose from $55 to $56, the delta rose from .75 to .78–a .03 change. These rates of change in delta are called *gamma*. By adding a column to Table 2–1, as in Table 2–2, you can see the gamma and how it changes.

In order to demonstrate the concept of gamma clearly, it is necessary to go out several decimal points. Another way to illustrate how gamma changes is in Figure 2–13.

TABLE 2–2
Gamma: Rate of Change in Delta

Stock Price	Theoretical Value	Delta	Gamma
56	7 1/4	.78	.03
55	6 1/2	.75	.03
54	5 3/4	.71	.04
53	5 1/8	.68	.03
52	4 1/2	.64	.04
51	3 7/8	.60	.04
50	3 1/4	.54	.06
49	2 3/4	.50	.04
48	2 3/8	.46	.04
47	2 3/16	.41	.05
46	1 7/8	.36	.05
45	1 7/16	.32	.04
44	1 3/16	.27	.05

FIGURE 2–13
Effect of Stock Price on Call Gammas

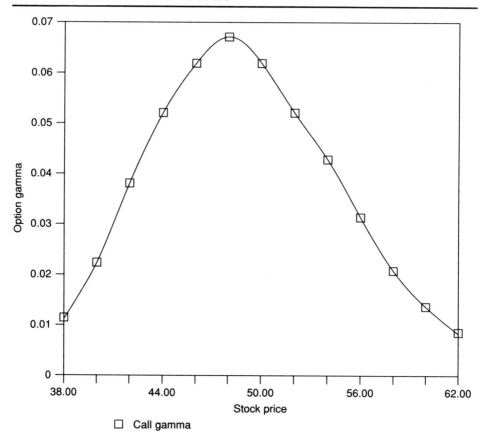

This shows that gammas are greatest when options are at-the-money and smaller when options are in-the-money, or out-of-the-money.

Gamma is a sophisticated concept (the second derivative of the price line). It has little importance to the nonprofessional or nonmarket maker who does not carry large and frequently changing option positions. Gamma is used in determining the rate at which an option position changes. Professional traders with large option positions (several hundred long and short options and thousands of shares of stock—long or short) frequently try to balance their long options against their short options with a goal of being *delta neutral*. This means that their long deltas equal their short deltas. The gamma of the position tells the professional trader how quickly the total position becomes long or short—how fast his long deltas get longer versus his short deltas getting shorter. This concept is explained further in Chapter 6.

How Deltas Change with Time

As time progresses toward the expiration date, the delta of an option changes differently, depending on whether an option is at-the-money, in-the-money, or out-of-the-money.

In-the-money options are exercised at expiration. This means that over the time period approaching expiration, the delta of an in-the-money option gradually increases to 1.00 (positive 1.00 for calls and negative 1.00 for puts). Figure 2–14 shows how, with the stock price at $50, the $45 call option delta rises to 1.00 and how the $55 put option delta declines to −1.00.

At the other extreme of delta behavior, the delta of an out-of-the-money option gradually approaches 0 because out-of-the-money options expire worthless. Figure 2–15 illustrates how, with the stock price at $50, the $55 call option delta and the $45 put option delta both gradually decrease to 0.

The delta for an at-the-money option presents an interesting theoretical discussion. The discussion is theoretical because, in reality, rarely is an option exactly "at-the-money." That is, a stock price is rarely exactly at a strike price. Normally a stock price is at least slightly above or below a strike price, thus making either the call or put in-the-money and the other out-of-the-money.

Assume, however, that a stock price is exactly at the strike. Then, as time progresses toward expiration, the delta for both the put and the call remain very close to .50 (positive 50 for calls and negative 50 for

FIGURE 2–14
Delta's Change over Time for In-the-Money Options

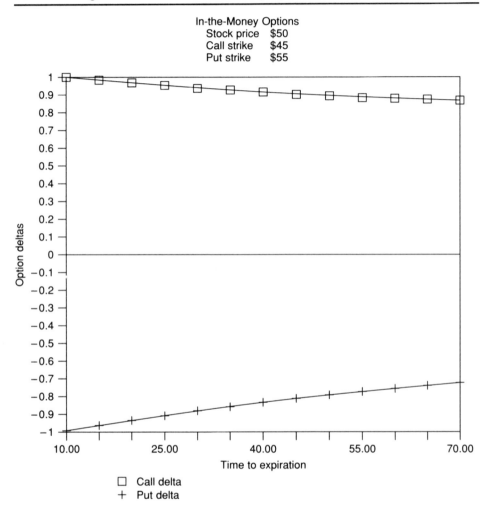

In-the-Money Options
Stock price $50
Call strike $45
Put strike $55

□ Call delta
+ Put delta

puts). While this, at first, can be difficult to comprehend, it is important to separate in one's mind the effect of time on total option price and the effect of time on delta. The total option price gradually decreases over time, but regardless of the total option price, a 1 unit change in the underlying security will cause about a 1/2 unit change in the at-the-money option. This remains true at any time right up to the point of the option's expiration. At the instant of expiration, with the stock price

FIGURE 2–15
Delta's Change over Time for Out-of-the-Money Options

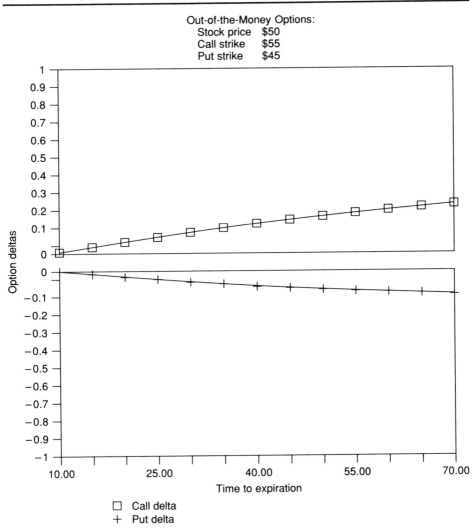

Out-of-the-Money Options:
Stock price $50
Call strike $55
Put strike $45

Option deltas

Time to expiration

☐ Call delta
+ Put delta

exactly at the strike, then the delta instantly drops to zero as the option expires worthless. But, in theory, even one second before expiration, the option has a delta of .50.

The delta hovering near .50 for at-the-money puts and calls is illustrated in Figure 2–16.

Delta's change over time is important primarily to the professional trader. An in-depth examination is not within the scope of this book.

FIGURE 2–16
Delta's Change over Time for At-the-Money Options

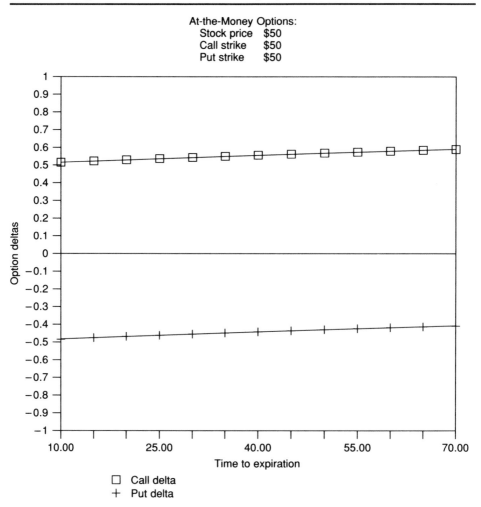

At-the-Money Options:
Stock price $50
Call strike $50
Put strike $50

□ Call delta
+ Put delta

THETA: TIME DECAY

Theta is the rate at which an option price erodes per unit of time. As seen in Figure 2–4, the price of an option decays at an increasing rate. During the first 90 of an option's life of 180 days, the time value erodes due to passage of time by less than 33 percent. The concept of theta is illustrated in Figure 2–17.

Although theta is a sophisticated mathematical concept (it is the first derivative [slope] of the time line in Figure 2–4), it is valuable to all users of options.

For speculators, theta is useful in planning the duration of trades. If a speculator plans to trade out of a purchased option before expiration, knowledge of time decay helps in deciding when to sell an option. The trader would balance time decay against the delta effect on the option from expected movements in the underlying stock price.

FIGURE 2–17
Theta: Decrease in Option Price per Unit of Time

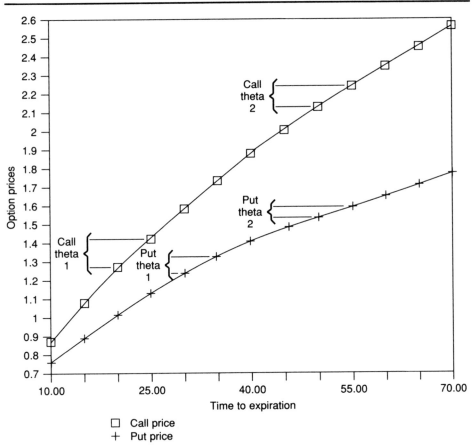

Professional traders use the theta as another balancing tool to manage large positions of long options and short options. An explanation of how some professional traders use theta is presented in Chapter 6.

VEGA: THE EFFECT OF IMPLIED VOLATILITY CHANGE

The *vega* of an option is the change in an option's value that results from a change in volatility. Vegas are expressed in dollar terms. For example, if a 1 percent change in implied volatility causes a 25 cent change in the option's value, the option is said to have a vega of .25.

Mathematically, the vega is similar to the delta and theta in that it is a first derivative. As can be seen from Figure 2–9, the relationship of volatility to option price is nearly linear. However, the linear relationship for in-the-money, at-the-money, and out-of-the-money options is different for each. The implication for vegas is that they do not change much unless the stock moves considerably in relation to the option's strike price. Again, this is a concept that is most relevant to the professional trader.

THE PUT-CALL PARITY RELATIONSHIP

We have completed a discussion of the theoretical elements of option value and how changes in each element affect that value. Now discussion will shift focus—from theory to the marketplace.

Users of options need some assurance that they are, in some sense, paying a "fair" price. Traders of stock have the same concern so they use fundamental or technical analysis as a tool. In the options market, "fair" prices are the result of an interplay of participants and a concept known as put-call parity. As will be demonstrated, an exact relationship exists between the prices of calls and puts with the same strike price and expiration, and the underlying stock.

Put-call parity is the pricing relationship concept that keeps option prices in line with each other and the underlying stock. It can be explained in four steps. First, the maximum risk of a simple stock and option position is defined. Second, it is demonstrated how the use of a second option can eliminate this risk. Third, the role that arbitrage plays in making markets function is discussed. Fourth, real world factors such as dividends, cost of money, and time are factored into the put-call parity relationship.

Step 1: Maximum Risk of a Simple Stock and Option Position

Consider the following stock and option position:

	Per Share	Total
Long 100 shares XYZ	Cost $52	$5,200
Long 1 $50 XYZ put	Cost 3	300

Question: What is the maximum risk of this combined position? (Assume no dividends and no cost of money.)

To answer this question, consider what would happen at various stock prices on the date of option expiration. At a stock price of $49, for example, the put option will be exercised and the stock will be sold at $50 for a $2 loss per share, making a total loss on the stock of $200. Adding the $300 cost of the put option to the $200 loss on the stock results in a combined loss of $500. Similarly, at any stock price from $50 down to $0, a $500 loss would result.

If the stock were to close between $50 and $52 on the option expiration date, the put option would expire worthless for a loss of $300. The per share loss on the stock, however, would be less than $2, thus making the entire loss less than $500. At $52, of course, the stock position would break even and the total loss would equal $300—the cost of the put option.

At prices above $52, the stock position would show a profit, but that profit would be reduced by the cost of the put option. The break-even stock price on this combined position would be $55, which is where a $300 profit on the long stock would equal the $300 cost of the put option. Above $55, the combined position shows a total profit because the profit on the long stock exceeds the cost of the put option.

Figure 2–18 illustrates the range of profit and loss outcomes at various stock prices at the time of option expiration.

From the preceding discussion and Figure 2–18, it is clear that the maximum possible loss from the combined position of long stock and long put described is $500.

FIGURE 2–18
Long Stock and Long Put

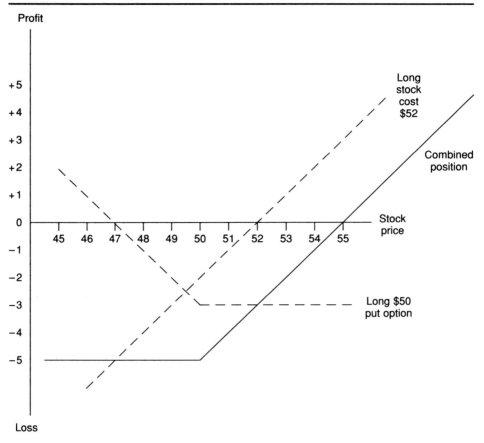

Step 2: Eliminate the Risk of the Long Stock and Long Put Position

A second option position—writing a $50 XYZ call at $500—is now added to the original combined position. The new position is as follows:

	Per Share		Total
Short 1 $50 XYZ call	Price	$ 5	$ 500
Long 100 XYZ	Cost	52	5,200
Long 1 $50 XYZ put	Cost	3	300

What is the maximum risk of this position?

Again, consider the outcome at various stock prices on the date of option expiration. At $50 or below, the $500 loss on the long stock and long put position is offset by the $500 received from selling the call option. The result is exactly break-even.

At any price above $50, the put will expire worthless for a $300 loss, but the long stock and short call combination will result in a $300 profit. This is so because at a stock price above $50, the call will be exercised and the stock will be sold at $50 for a $200 loss. The $500 received for selling the call, however, is kept. Thus, the $500 profit on the call is reduced by the $200 loss on the stock for a total net profit of $300. This, again, exactly equals the cost of the put option which expired worthless with the stock price above $50.

Net result: At any stock price, the three-way call option–put option–stock position just described achieves break-even, and this is illustrated by Figure 2–19.

Step 3: Arbitrage

The three-sided option-stock combination just described is the basis for how professional traders operate in the marketplace to provide liquidity to other participants. Professional traders, called *arbitrageurs,* are constantly active in the stock and options markets looking for opportunities to buy stock, buy puts, and sell calls. Their goal, of course, is to make a profit, not to break even as described in the previous example. There, with the stock at $52, the $50 call at $5, and the $50 put at $3, the market is said to be *in line* or *at parity*. Professional traders are constantly seeking opportunities where they can sell the call option above $5, or buy the put option below $3. This guarantees all market participants a "fair" price for the securities they are seeking to buy or sell.

The price is "fair" because the process of arbitrage keeps all prices in line with each other, thus maintaining market equilibrium or parity between calls, puts, and stocks.

For example, if an imbalance of call buying orders raised call prices, professional traders would rush to increase their bids for put options. Bidding higher for puts would presumably entice more put sellers into the market. With the increased availability of puts (at the higher prices), the arbitrageurs would be able to buy puts, buy stock, and thus sell the calls at a higher price.

After this series of transactions, both put and call prices would be higher than previously, but still "fair." The new prices would be "fair"

FIGURE 2–19
Long Stock, Long Put, Short Call

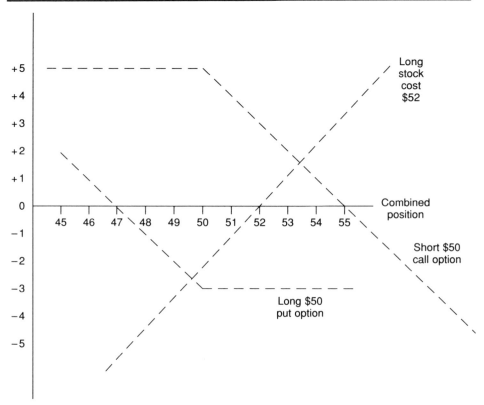

because they would be in line with each other under the new market conditions.

Similarly, in another example, if a large order to sell puts at lower prices entered the market, traders would compete against one another to offer call options at lower prices so that they could complete the three-sided option-stock position profitably. After these transactions, both puts and calls would be less expensive. Nevertheless, the prices would still be in line or at parity with each other under the new market conditions.

It should be clear from the preceding discussion that competition between professional traders causes put and call prices to rise and fall together. This concept should put to rest some misconceptions expressed in typical statements such as, "Calls are overpriced" or "Puts are cheap.'' Because of put-call parity, both puts and calls can be at a relatively high price level, or they can both be at a relatively low price level. But, barring transitory distortions, it is impossible for one to be ''overpriced'' or ''expensive'' relative to the other.

Step 4: Influence of Real-World Factors

In that simple three-way example, it is assumed that there are no dividends, no cost of money, and no early exercise. But these factors certainly affect option prices.

Dividends

Reviewing the basic three-way position of long stock, long put, and short call, we now ask this question. How would this position be affected if the stock paid a $1 dividend?

Without the dividend, the position at the stated prices broke even. The presence of a $1 dividend, therefore, implies a $1 profit. But what would competitors in the marketplace do when they saw the opportunity to make a $1 profit? Some professional traders or arbitrageurs would be willing to settle for an even smaller profit, say 75 cents. Consequently, they would be willing to pay 25 cents more for the put or the stock or sell the call for 25 cents less. Other professional traders would be satisfied with only a 40-cent profit and their bidding and offering would raise put prices and lower call prices still further.

Such competition would thus raise put prices or lower call prices (or a combination of both) until the basic three-sided stock and option position was back to breakeven. The conclusion to be drawn is that the presence of dividends has the effect of raising put prices and lowering call prices relative to each other.

Cost of Money

The cost of money is an important consideration for all investors, because investment performance is measured against a benchmark riskless investment—typically the short-term Treasury bill. It is no different for the professional trader who must borrow money to finance large stock and option holdings and who seeks a return to cover those costs and earn a profit.

To illustrate how the cost of money affects option prices, consider the following example and ask this question: At what price must the $50 call option be sold to make this position break even?

	Per Share		Total
Short 1 $50 call option	Price	?	?
Long 100 XYZ	Cost	$50	$5,000
Long 1 $50 put option	Cost	3	300
9 percent prevailing cost of money			
90 days until option expiration			

The answer to this question is reasoned as follows. In 90 days, this three-way position will turn into $50 cash per share because either the stock will be above $50 and the call will be assigned, or the stock will be below $50 and the put will be exercised. In either case, the stock is sold and $50 cash for each share is received. Thus, the question becomes: How much should be invested today to earn 9 percent (annually) if $50 per share will be received in 90 days? Since 90 days is one fourth of a year, you expect to earn $9\% \times 1/4 = 2.25\%$ on this three-sided position. Consequently, you must invest $50 \times (1 - .0225) = 48.875$ or $48 7/8 per share. Therefore, the call should be sold for $1 1/8 more than the put, or $4 1/8, and the final position looks like this:

	Per Share		Total
Short 1 $50 call option	Price	$ 4 1/8	$ 412.50
Long 100 XYZ	Cost	50	5,000.00
Long 1 $50 put option	Cost	3	300.00
Total invested		$48 7/8	$4,887.50

$48 7/8 + ($48 7/8 \times 9\% \times [1/4 \text{ of } 1 \text{ year}]) = $50 on option expiration

Interest Rates
From this example, if interest rates rise while the stock price, put price, and days until option expiration remain constant, the call price must rise by the amount of the increased interest cost. This is the necessary result because the cost of carrying the position increases and the call must be sold for a greater amount to cover that increased cost.

The effect of interest rates on put prices is exactly opposite: As interest rates rise, put prices decline. This can be demonstrated by thinking through what must happen to put prices when interest rates rise, but the other elements (stock price, call price, and days until expiration) remain constant.

Rising interest rates result in an increased cost of carry. To compensate for the higher cost, either the revenue of the position must increase, or the cost of the position must decrease. Because the call price (the revenue side) is assumed to be unchanged, then the cost of the position must be reduced. Since the stock price is assumed to be constant, then only the put price is left to be reduced to compensate for the increase in cost of carry.

CHAPTER 3

OPTION STRATEGIES: ANALYSIS AND SELECTION

The investor who adds options to the list of investment products he uses to achieve his financial goals gains a unique advantage. They increase the number of ways this investor can manage his financial assets by giving him or her the power to create positions that precisely reflect his expectations of the underlying security and, at the same time, balance his risk-reward tolerance.

This means that options increase control over financial assets by providing alternatives that were unavailable in the past. Prior to the establishment of listed options markets, there was no effective way to hedge without disrupting the allocation of assets in the portfolio. In the past, there were only two choices—Buy 'em when you like 'em, sell 'em when you don't. Today, investors discover that they can, for example, sell calls or buy puts to establish a hedge; they reserve selling for the time they no longer desire any involvement with the underlying asset. These investors also discover that options give them more control over the speculative side of their investing; they can select from strategies that run the gamut from limited to unlimited risk and from small to large capital requirements.

Many options investors spend a lot of time acquiring technical knowledge of pricing behavior. This is a worthy goal, but above all, remember that options are derivative instruments. Options cannot exist without an underlying asset. As such, there are only two important factors that direct the investor to the proper strategy. The first and foremost is the investor's opinion of the underlying security. There are strategies to take advantage of a bullish, bearish, neutral, or uncertain opinion. Any decision made without a specific opinion of the potential movement of the underlying security is unsubstantiated and has a high probability of failure. The second factor concerns the profits the investor desires if his opinion is correct and his willingness to accept any losses that accompany his strategy if his opinion is wrong.

From speculation to hedging, options can be used to construct scenarios that maximize payoff for outcomes the investor considers most likely, while controlling exposure to losses from those outcomes he considers less likely. There are ways to express the degree of one's opinion, each with its own particular risk-reward profile. One can buy calls outright to get a leveraged bullish position, or use strategies that require a smaller cash outlay, but have less profit potential. This requires understanding the trade-offs that go with every decision and the motivation one brings to strategy selection.

Options are often thought of as merely speculative instruments. This is not true. An option strategy by itself is neither speculative nor conservative. The investor using options must also understand that it is the way a strategy is selected, managed, and capitalized that determines its "personality." The goal of this and following chapters is to help the investor gain such understanding so as to use options to their fullest.

This chapter describes essential options strategies in words and illustrations. The pictures show how each strategy evolves from the day it is established until the options' expiration date. The discussion that accompanies each diagram explains how the strategy works, why an investor might select the strategy, and how to evaluate a particular risk-reward profile. The reader is encouraged to refer to this chapter periodically for review, especially if he has formulated his opinion on the underlying security and is ready to enter the options market, but remains unclear about the risk-reward profiles of the strategies being considered.

Description of Diagrams

Each strategy diagram is constructed using the following conventions:

1. The horizontal axis represents the price of the underlying security advancing from lower prices at the left to higher prices towards the right.
2. The vertical axis represents profit/loss; profit is in the area above the horizontal axis, loss below.
3. To emphasize the importance of the effects of time decay, arrows point in the direction of decreasing time until expiration. The last, straight-segment line represents the profit/loss of the strategy at options' expiration.

4. Strike prices of options used in the strategy are indicated by numbers; lower strikes by lower numbers and vice versa.
5. A break-even point is always located at any point where the position plot crosses the horizontal axis.

CALL BUYING

Without question, call buying is the most popular option strategy. It is a way to put a bullish opinion into action. If the price of the underlying security advances enough, the long-call buyer can have profits many times his initial investment of the option premium. The potential to reap such large profits is what attracts investors. It is an attraction that often results in frustrating and disappointing experiences. A better understanding of the ways call buying should be used will go a long way towards lessening the possibility of disappointment from the start.

Call buyers must know from the outset what they want from their position. If they don't, they can get results very different from what's expected. For instance, if they do not want a speculative position, yet unknowingly use the reasoning of the speculative buyer, they expose themselves to much greater risks than acceptable. If the underlying security moves in their favor, their profits are much greater than they expected, and this result usually leads to the investors' thinking they chose wisely. They are then apt to continue buying calls in a speculative manner only to be extremely dissatisfied when their forecast for the behavior of the underlying is wrong. The problem is that they did not start with an honest appraisal of their motives.

This section is divided into segments that discuss the motives, expectations, and concerns that accompany speculative and nonspeculative call buying decisions. You will soon discover why it is important to know the difference.

Expected Behavior

A call buyer is subject to profits and losses outlined in the summary and Figure 3–1, all at expiration. Throughout this section, a $50 strike price call option on XYZ stock is used as a model. As an example, start with

FIGURE 3–1
Long Call

Description: Buy call option with strike price I.

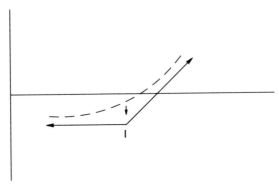

Opinion: Bullish—buy calls when you expect an advance in the price of
                   the underlying security.
Selection: Higher strike prices reflect more bullish opinion.
Profit: Profits are unlimited as long as the underlying security continues
                   to advance.
Loss: Limited to premium paid for option.
Break-even: Strike price of option I + Premium paid.
Time: Negative—decay of premium accelerates as expiration nears.
Comments: Speculative buyer looks for leverage, emphasizing quantity of
                   options he can buy. Insurance buyer counts number of shares
                   represented by options.
Equivalencies: Buy underlying security, buy put I.

XYZ at $50 per share and the 90-day call at $3. Given this option price, you can calculate the break-even points and maximum profit and loss at expiration as follows:

Break-even: $53   = Strike price ($50) + Premium ($3).

Maximum loss: $300 = The premium paid if XYZ is below $50
                           at expiration.

Maximum profit: Unlimited given by (Price of XYZ − $50 − $3).

At-expiration analysis, however, does not provide insight into what happens to a call option before the expiration date. Take a look at the expected effects of time and price movement on the $50 call option in Table 3–1.

TABLE 3–1
Expected Price Variation of $50 Strike Call

Price of XYZ	Days to Expiration					
	90	75	60	45	30	15
$56	7 1/2	7 1/4	7	6 5/8	6 3/8	6 1/8
54	5 3/4	5 1/2	5 1/4	4 7/8	4 1/2	4 1/4
52	4 1/4	4	3 5/8	3 1/4	2 15/16	2 7/16
50	3	2 11/16	2 3/8	2	1 9/16	1 1/16
48	1 15/16	1 5/8	1 3/8	1 1/16	3/4	5/16
46	1 1/8	15/16	11/16	1/2	1/4	1/16
44	5/8	7/16	5/16	3/16	1/16	1/16

The Break-Even Point

You can see that, regardless of when the option is purchased, the underlying security must be above its current price for a long call to break even. This is, after all, a bullish strategy, and one expects the price to rise. However, the break-even price (strike price plus premium) at expiration is simply the highest price the underlying needs to reach for the position to break even. Before expiration, the break-even point is lower. For example, if XYZ is $48 and you buy the $50 call for $1 15/16 with 90 days left before expiration, the option can still break even at $50 per share after 45 days. In contrast, the break-even at expiration is approximately $52 per share.

The Speculative Call Buyer

The speculative call buyer uses options for their leverage. He is attracted to the percentage gains he can achieve on his investment from a rise in the price of the underlying. He also understands that if the underlying does not make the move he needs, he can lose most, if not all, of the investment. His goal is to select calls that balance his desire for profits with the possibility of the option's expiring worthless.

To achieve this balance, the speculative call buyer must address the issues of intrinsic value, i.e., out-of-the-money or in-the-money, time decay, and delta.

In-the-Money versus Out-of-the-Money

If XYZ is $48 per share, the 90-day, $50 call is out-of-the-money. The option has a premium of $1 15/16 and an expiration break-even price of about $52, 4 points above the current price. If XYZ is $52, the call is in-the-money. The option has a premium of $4 1/4 and a break-even price of $54 1/4, only 2 1/4 points above the current price.

Because the out-of-the-money call needs a larger advance in XYZ to reach the break-even point, buying it is more bullish than the purchase of in-the-money calls. A more bullish position is riskier. For accepting more risk, the speculative buyer of out-of-the-money calls should have better results if the stock behaves as expected. This is exactly what happens. First, the cost of the out-of-the-money option is lower, $1 15/16 versus $4 1/4 for the other kind. For equivalent dollar amounts, he could buy more out-of-the-money options. This is a key to understanding the thinking of the speculative call buyer. The desire for big profits leads to an emphasis on the quantity purchased. Second, an out-of-the-money call performs relatively better if XYZ moves higher in price shortly after the option is purchased. After 15 days, the out-of-the-money call can double in price, to $4, if XYZ rises from $48 to $52. For the in-the-money option to double, i.e., trade from $4 1/4 to $8 1/2 in 15 days, XYZ would have to trade up to $57 1/2. The emphasis on quantity validates the percentage comparisons the speculative option buyer uses.

This does not mean that the out-of-the-money call is better. As time passes, the break-even point approaches the price at expiration. The prospective out-of-the-money call buyer should be aware that a decline in XYZ makes it difficult for the call to break even, even if the stock rallies. Track the call price through the following path:

1. When XYZ is $48, buy the 90-day call for $1 15/16.
2. After 30 days, XYZ is $46; the call is trading at $11/16.
3. By the end of the next 30 days, XYZ must rally to $50 3/4, or 10 percent, for the call to break even.

Out-of-the-money calls are on their own if the underlying makes this kind of a move; they have no intrinsic value and can lose 100 percent of their premium. In-the-money calls start with the support of their intrinsic value. The next segment addresses the trade-offs between time decay and intrinsic value.

Time Decay and Intrinsic Value

For the speculative call buyer, the advantages of buying at-the-money or out-of-the-money calls are balanced by the premium decay they experience. These types of call options lose 100 percent of their premium if the price of the underlying is not above the option's strike price at expiration. On the other hand, for in-the-money options to lose all of their premium, the underlying must have declined to the strike price at expiration. The difference is the intrinsic value carried by the in-the-money options and the impact its presence has on the decay of the total premium.

Go back to the table and concentrate on the price changes of the $50 call option if the price of XYZ were to remain at $46, 4 points out-of-the-money, for the entire 90 days until expiration. The option has no intrinsic value and this call is trading at only $1 1/8. The premium drops to $11/16 ($68.75) after 30 days. This is a loss of about 40 percent of the initial premium. Over the next 30 days, the decay is even greater. The option decays to $1/4, a further decline of 65 percent.

In-the-money call options also experience premium decay over time, but less than 100 percent of the total option premium. This is because these options have intrinsic value. Only time premium can decay; intrinsic value cannot. Going back to the price table, with XYZ at $54, the $50 call is $5 3/4. If the stock is $54 at expiration, the call will be worth its intrinsic value of $4. This limits the loss to $1 3/4, or 30 percent of the original premium.

Given equivalent dollar amounts, a call option position becomes less speculative the farther the call is in-the-money. The $5 3/4 premium of the in-the-money one is almost twice that of the at-the-money. The dollar profit of the in-the-money option from an advance in XYZ is closer to the profit from owning the stock, but when compared to the number of at- or out-of-the-money calls that can be purchased, this gain is made on half as many options. The smaller quantity and the smaller likelihood of the option's expiring worthless makes a position in in-the-money calls less speculative.

Delta and the Speculative Call Buyer

The delta of an option is defined as a local measure of the rate of change in an option's theoretical value for a change in the price of the underlying security. Delta underlies the speculative call buyer's emphasis on quantity. Table 3–2 shows the deltas of the $50 call for various prices of XYZ.

TABLE 3–2
Deltas

Price of XYZ	Price of 90-Day Call	Option Delta
$54	$5 3/4	.80
52	4 1/4	.70
50	3	.59
48	1 15/16	.46
46	1 1/8	.33
44	5/8	.21

As a call goes deeper in-the-money, it becomes more sensitive to price changes in XYZ. At $54 per share, the $50 call can be expected to change about 80 cents for every point change in XYZ. At $50, the sensitivity is 59 cents. If the speculative buyer has $600, he can buy two at-the-money calls or one in-the-money call. The at-the-money position has a delta of 1.20 (2 × .60). The in-the-money call has a delta of .80. Furthermore, the delta of the at-the-money calls can go from .59 to 1.00. The delta of the in-the-money can also go to 1.00, but it will do so starting from .80. This exemplifies the leverage the speculative buyer gets when buying more options for the same amount of money.

Conclusions about Speculative Call Buying
Speculative buyers have to balance many aspects of call behavior to create the right position. Most important of all is for investors to recognize that they are using calls speculatively. If they are concerned about how time decay, intrinsic value, and delta impact the performance of their investment, there is a good chance that they are speculative buyers. If they compare the number of options of different strike prices they can buy with a fixed number of dollars, they are definitely speculative buyers.

The Insurance Value of Calls

However, the investor who stands ready to buy 1,000 shares of XYZ at $50—but instead spends $3,000 for 10 at-the-money calls—is not speculating. He is making an investment decision to use the call options to protect a possible $50,000 commitment.

Why can call options be described as a kind of insurance? The upcoming section on put buying presents evidence that a long put plus long stock is equivalent to a call option. The protection provided by the put option is easy to comprehend: Puts increase in value as the underlying security falls farther below the strike price, protecting against part of the loss in the long position in the underlying. The insurance analogy, however, is sometimes more difficult to grasp when applied to calls. The following excerpt by Herbert Filer may bring the point home:

> It happened in November 1957, after the market had had a severe break. A man with a southern drawl and wearing a big ten-gallon hat, walked into our office and wanted to speak to the "boss." "You know," he said, "I bought a lot of your Calls and I tore them up—lost my money." I thought maybe he was going to pull a gun on me . . . he said, "Don't worry—how lucky it was that I bought Calls instead of stock. If I had bought the stocks way up there I would have gone broke!"[1]

Indeed, calls resemble insurance, too. The buyer wants to protect the cash he would have used to buy the underlying security and preserve the opportunity to profit from an advance. Nor is insurance free. A premium must be paid.

The "insurance investor" has a view of call options that is different from the speculative buyer's. To the "insurance buyer," the premium of a call option is the cost of wanting insurance on his capital. He understands that the seller of a call option says, in effect, to the buyer, "If, for the next three months you don't want to lose money from a direct investment in this stock should it go down, and still participate if it goes up, you are going to have to compensate me for assuming this risk instead of you." Part of that compensation is a risk premium measured by the expected volatility of the stock in exchange for the ability to let the call expire worthless. The rest is an interest payment to the seller.

In-the-Money or Out-of-the-Money?

The investor who uses call options as insurance sees out-of-the-money and in-the-money options as different types of insurance policies. In contrast, the speculator sees out-of-the-money calls as an opportunity to gain more leverage by buying increasing quantities of less expensive options. The insurance buyer of an out-of-the-money call sees it as a cheap policy with a large deductible. The deductible is the amount the underlying must move for the option to be worth anything at expiration. It is the amount of the increase in the price of the underlying the investor is willing to give up. By contrast, the in-the-money call is like an expensive policy with no deductible. It is already worth its intrinsic value and lets the investor participate now. A wise insurance buyer always balances the deductible with the premium he pays.

The Real Difference
The biggest difference between the speculative and the insurance buyer is that the insurance buyer does not count the number of options he can buy. Because he is protecting a capital commitment to a predetermined number of shares, he counts the round lots of stock the options represent at expiration. He buys the same quantity, no matter which strike price he selects. The investor using calls this way has no need for leverage.

Which Approach?

Neither approach to call buying is more correct than the other. There is room in the option market for speculative and insurance call buyers. The most important thing is to understand which one you are at any given time. If you do that, you will make better decisions and will have better experiences with this strategy.

PUT BUYING

A long put position by itself expresses bearishness. The underlying security must go down in price for this position to be profitable. The investor who buys puts in expectation of a decline in the underlying security is attracted by the potential for a very large percentage gain on the premium he pays. This is the speculative approach to buying puts. However, a put option can be used conservatively. Puts can be very effective as "term insurance policies" to protect the value of an investment in the underlying security. Speculative and insurance buyers view put options differently. We'll explore different ways to use put buying, motives behind their use, and expected results in this section.

General Behavior

At expiration, the put buyer is subject to profits and losses as outlined in the summary and Figure 3–2. We'll use the $50 strike price put option on XYZ stock as an example, and start with XYZ at $50 per share and the

FIGURE 3–2
Long Put

Description: Buy put option with strike price I.

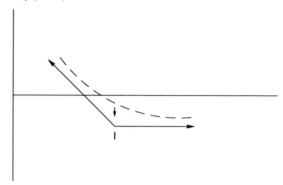

Opinion: Bearish—buy puts when you expect a decline in the price of the underlying security.
Selection: Lower strike prices reflect more bearish opinion.
Profit: Profits increase as the underlying security declines in price. Only limited by underlying security's going to $0.
Loss: Limited to premium paid for option.
Break-even: Strike price of option I − premium paid.
Time: Negative—decay of premium accelerates as expiration nears.
Comments: Speculative buyers look for leverage, emphasize quantity of options they can buy. Insurance buyers count number of shares represented by options or look to protect long position in underlying security through expiration.
Equivalencies: Short underlying, buy call option I.

90-day put at $2. Given this option price, you can calculate the break-even points, and maximum profit and loss at expiration as follows:

Break-even: $48 = Strike price ($50) − Premium ($2).
Maximum loss: $200 = The premium paid for the option.
Maximum profit: Profits are limited only by the underlying's going to $0, minus the $2 premium paid.

To get a better feel for how put options behave over time, refer to Table 3–3, summarizing the expected effects of price and time on the premium of the $50 put.

Many investors believe that put options behave exactly like calls, but in the opposite direction. This is an incorrect assumption. There are

TABLE 3–3
Expected Price Variation of $50 Strike Price Put Option

	Days to Expiration					
Price of XYZ	90	75	60	45	30	15
$54	13/16	9/16	1/2	3/8	1/4	1/16
52	1 1/4	1 1/8	1	13/16	9/16	5/16
50	2	1 7/8	1 11/16	1 1/2	1 1/4	15/16
48	2 15/16	2 13/16	2 11/16	2 9/16	2 3/8	2 3/16
46	4 1/4	4 1/8	4	4	4	4
44	6	6	6	6	6	6

differences. Lack of awareness of these differences can lead to unrealistic expectations or mismanagement of put option positions.

The most obvious difference is that at-the-money calls and puts do not have the same price. The effect of dividends notwithstanding, at-the-money calls will be priced higher than at-the-money puts. The put-call parity equation shows why this is true. In the example given, XYZ does not pay a dividend, the risk-free rate is 8 percent, and the expected annual volatility is 25 percent. Based on these conditions, the 90-day at-the-money call is $3 and the put is $2.

Time Decay

The astute investor can draw some interesting conclusions regarding the behavior of put options from the pricing table. First of all, puts decay slower than calls do. In 45 days, if XYZ remains at $50 per share, the $50 put loses 1/2 point of time premium and is worth $1 1/2. The $50 call, which starts with a premium of $3, loses 1 point. The put declines 25 percent; the call declines 33 percent. Over the next 30 days, the call loses an additional $15/16 or 47 percent. The put only loses $7/16 or 30 percent. This should give some solace to the out-of-the-money put buyer, but don't get too comfortable. The erosion of the premium eventually attacks the put as well. There is no escape!

In another observation, as puts go farther in-the-money, they lose their time premium faster than calls do. At $44, the $50 put, with 75 days left, has a value of $6. If XYZ were $56, the $50 call, also 6 points in-the-money, has a value of $7 1/8. The call retains 1 1/8 points of time premium.

Out-of-the-Money versus In-the-Money Puts

To the speculative buyer, the bearishness of a long put position is directly related to the amount a put is out-of-the-money. The underlying has to decline farther for an out-of-the-money put to break even at expiration than for an in-the-money put to break even. The price table shows that if you buy the $50 put when XYZ is $52, the break-even is $48 3/4. If you buy the same put when XYZ is $48, the break-even is $47. XYZ must decline $3 1/4 for the out-of-the-money, but only $1 for the in-the-money to break even.

There is always balance in the options market. The advantage the speculator gets for buying out-of-the-money puts is the potential for large percentage gains. For example, XYZ is $46 per share at expiration; the $50 put is priced at $4. The investor who went long on this put 90 days prior when XYZ was $54, paid $13/16 for the option. The increase of $3 3/16 in the price of the put is 392 percent of the original premium. By contrast, the investor who waited 15 days and went long on the same put when XYZ had already dropped to $50, paid $1 7/8. The put now gains $2 1/8 from its purchase price, or 113 percent of the starting premium. A speculative buyer can make this percentage comparison because his or her tendency is to maximize the number of options purchased with a given amount of premium dollars to spend. Given the relationship of the premiums in the above example, the investor can purchase 23 out-of-the-money puts for every 10 at-the-money puts.

The speculative buyer making this comparison to maximize the leverage of his position must be aware that the chance of losing the entire premium increases with the distance the puts are out-of-the-money. In-the-money puts provide less leverage; they are more expensive, so the speculative buyer cannot buy so many. However, they have a greater chance of providing some profit and a smaller chance of expiring worthless. This is the omnipresent trade-off between in-the-money and out-of-the-money options with which the speculative buyer must contend.

A Strategic Application

We observed that put options go to parity more quickly than calls. This makes in-the-money put options an attractive strategic alternative to the short sale of stock. If XYZ were $46 with 90 days before expiration, the $50 put would not have much time premium remaining. Buying the put at $4 1/4 is similar to being short the stock—the option is very sensitive to price changes in XYZ. This position has advantages over a short sale. First, no stock needs to be borrowed and no margin balance is created. Second, should XYZ rally, the risk of the put is limited to the premium paid. A short sale of XYZ is exposed to unlimited losses.

Term Insurance

The other major use for put options is like insurance. An investor who owns XYZ stock is concerned that there can be a drop in the stock's price over the next 90 days. This conclusion may be the result of technical or fundamental analysis on the stock or on the market. Whatever the reasoning, this investor needs to protect his investment over the time period in question, but he does not want to sell the stock and give up further profits if his forecast is wrong. This investor can purchase a "term insurance" policy on XYZ for the next 90 days by buying the $50 put option for $2 in the same quantity as the number of round lots he owns.

The $50 put allows the holder to sell the stock at $50 per share anytime between the day the option is bought and expiration. The out-of-the-money, $45 put, which allows him to sell the stock 5 points lower, is less valuable because the investor is leaving his stock open to more of a decline. The $45 put is $1/2. The in-the-money put, which allows him to sell the stock at $55 is more valuable. The investor is not picking up any part of a decline. And the $55 put is $5.

This does not mean that the $45 put is an inferior choice. If the owner of XYZ wants very low-cost insurance and is willing to accept $5 more of the risk of XYZ himself, the out-of-the-money put might be the better choice. Here is where the real decision is made. If you want more protection, you also have to give up more of the upside. The $50 put is $2. So the investor gives up the first 2 points of any rally in the stock in exchange for being able to sell the stock at $50. The $45 put has only a 50 cent upside opportunity cost.

Difference between Speculation and Insurance
The motivation of the investor using puts like insurance is different from that of the investor using puts to profit from a forecasted decline in the underlying security. The speculative put buyer has to balance the characteristics of put option behavior, time decay, intrinsic value, and delta, to come up with the proper position. The insurance buyer only needs to address the deductibility he is willing to accept, given the costs of the

FIGURE 3–3
Buy Stock, Buy Put

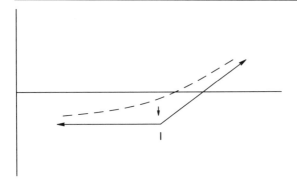

insurance. Furthermore, buying a put as insurance on a stock is certainly not bearish. The insurance buyer would much rather see his stock rally substantially than have to use the policy. If this investor were truly bearish, he would be wise to simply sell the stock.

An Interesting Equivalence

The reader with more options experience may have noticed that the purchase of a put, while holding a long position in the stock, is a strategy with a limited loss and (after subtracting the put premium) unlimited profit. Figure 3–3 is the profit/loss diagram of the result of owning XYZ at $50 and a $50 put bought for $2 at expiration. It looks exactly like the diagram of a call option at expiration. Indeed, a long put, long stock position is the same as a long call option position. When a put is bought on a stock as insurance, it turns that stock into a call for the life of the option.

CALL SELLING

Call selling achieves its maximum profit if the price of the underlying security is below the call's strike price at expiration. However, call selling is not necessarily a bearish posture. The sold call only needs to expire worthless for the investor to realize his maximum profit, and the underlying may not have to decline to satisfy this criterion. In fact, call selling can be very successful when used as a neutral strategy. Remember that, in the options market, the opposite of a bullish strategy is not a bearish strategy. Instead, it is a "*not* bullish" strategy! To illustrate, call selling is a "not bullish" strategy. (The method discussed here does not involve ownership of the underlying security. This strategy, named *covered call selling,* is discussed under its own heading.)

Still using the XYZ, 90-day, $50 strike price, at-the-money call option with a $3 premium, the seller is taking a position that has the following characteristics at expiration:

Break-even: $53 = Strike price ($50) + Premium ($3).

Maximum profit: $300 = The premium received for the option.

Maximum loss: Unlimited.

Option selling techniques are limited profit strategies. Regardless of how far below $50 the price of XYZ goes, the $3 is as good as it's going to get. The call cannot do any better for the seller than expire worthless. This is why the payoff diagram of call selling becomes horizontal as the price of XYZ declines below the strike price of the call (Figure 3–4).

FIGURE 3–4
Short Call

Description: Sell call option with strike price I without ownership of underlying security.

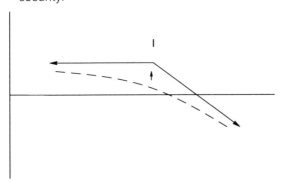

Opinion: Not bullish—underlying security will not be above break-even point at expiration.
Selection: Lower strike prices reflect increasing bearishness.
Profit: Limited to premium received from option I.
Loss: Potentially unlimited; increases as underlying security advances.
Break-even: Strike price of option sold I + Premium received.
Time: Positive—premium decay accelerates as expiration nears.
Comments: Expect narrow or down moves in the underlying security. Very large losses on big advances and takeovers. Selling in-the-money calls is very aggressive. One of the riskiest strategies if supported by too little capital.
Equivalencies: Short underlying and short put I.

TABLE 3–4
Expiration Prices of Various Call Options

Option Strike Price	Closing Price of XYZ at Expiration				
	45	49	53	57	61
$45	0	4	8	12	16
50	0	0	3	7	11
55	0	0	0	2	6

Furthermore, a short call position is exposed to large losses if the underlying advances far beyond the strike price of the option. Examine Table 3–4 of expiration values of various call options over a range of closing prices for XYZ at expiration. One can see that the call option seller cannot be bullish!

Motivation of the Call Seller

It seems that call selling is a strategy with very high risk for a small potential return. How, then, can the call seller justify using this technique? The answer is twofold. First, he is agreeing with the option market's estimate of the potential movement of the underlying. (The call buyer is the one looking for a greater move.) You have seen that expected volatility, or price movement, has a large influence on an option's premium. The call seller believes that the potential price movement of the underlying will not be greater than that implied by the premium. If he thought that it could be greater, he would do something else!

Second, the seller is acutely aware of the negative effect of passing time on option premiums. Unlike the call buyer, the call seller eagerly awaits the last weeks prior to expiration when premium decay accelerates. In Table 3–5, here's what happens to an at-the-money call.

TABLE 3–5
Expected Price of $50 Strike Call

Price of XYZ	Days to Expiration					
	90	75	60	45	30	15
$50	3	2 11/16	2 3/8	2	1 9/16	1 1/16

In-the-Money, At-the-Money, and Out-of-the-Money

The call seller must consider the relationship of the price of the underlying to the strike price of the option sold. The at-the-money call, because the strike price is close to the current price of the underlying, makes its maximum profit if the underlying stays where it is, i.e., at about the strike price, and can make some profit even if the underlying advances slightly. This is because the break-even point is above the current price. The sale of an at-the-money call happens to be a neutral strategy that is also profitable if the underlying drops in price.

Out-of-the-money calls have the greatest probability of expiring worthless. Their premiums are lower, resulting in less potential profit, but the seller of out-of-the-money calls gets a cushion against a rise in the price of the underlying. It can be very enticing to sell cheap, out-of-the-money calls continually and watch them expire. The trouble is that they do not always expire worthless.

Consider the following. XYZ has traded at around $52 1/2 per share for the last 120 days. During this time, an investor sold the $55 calls twice, i.e., over two expirations, for a total of $275. Both times, the options expired worthless and the $275 was kept as profit.

Recently, the investor has sold another $55 call with 45 days before expiration for $1 1/4 ($125). The stock is at $53 1/2. Prior to the next morning's opening, favorable news has come out on the stock. It could be a new "buy" recommendation or, even worse for the naked short call, a takeover bid. The stock finally opens at $57 1/4 and the $55 calls are $4 1/8 ($412.50). Buying the short option back at $4 1/8 creates a net loss for the investor after four months!

In-the-money calls have higher premiums than at- or out-of-the-money options. The sale of such an option is more bearish than the sale of either of the other two types because the strike price of an in-the-money call is lower than the current price of the underlying. The underlying must decline in price for a short, in-the-money call to reach its maximum profit. The break-even point is usually not much higher than the current price of the underlying, and it is lower than the break-even point of the at-the-money call.

Sale of an in-the-money call is an aggressive strategy that can lose quite a bit of money very quickly if the underlying begins to move higher. In-the-money calls have less time premium than at-the-money calls. If the $50 call is trading at $3, the $45 call is about $6 3/8. This in-the-money call does have a high dollar premium, but it has only $1 3/8 of time premium and a break-even of $51 3/8. There is not much room for error.

Another difficulty with in-the-money calls is they become less sensitive to declines in the price of the underlying. This is because the delta of a call option decreases if the price of the underlying goes down; the in-the-money call starts to look more and more like an at-the-money call. The option will continue to drop in price but will lose less on each subsequent drop. Table 3–6 shows the prices and deltas of the $45 call with 75 days left before expiration. If the investor is truly bearish, there is a better strategy to express that opinion.

It should be of more than passing interest that this discussion of the differences between the three types of call options has shown that the aspects of call behavior that hurt buyers will help sellers (and vice versa).

How Much Premium Is Enough?

It would seem that it is always best for the seller of naked calls to collect as much premium as possible. This could not be farther from the truth. Do not be enticed by large premiums. Higher call option premiums (the effect of interest rates notwithstanding), as a percent of the price of the underlying security, come from an expectation of higher volatility. This, in turn, implies an expectation of greater price movement. There are many investors who consistently sell calls for high premiums. They are also the ones who consistently buy back in-the-money calls for *even greater* premiums. At no time should an investor put premium level above break-even analysis. The call seller must always ask this question, "Do I think the underlying will be below the break-even price of the call option I am going to sell at expiration?" If the answer is an unequivocal, "Yes," then, and only then should a call be sold.

TABLE 3–6
How Delta Changes

XYZ Price	Option Price	Option Delta
$49	$5 1/4	.83
48	4 1/2	.78
47	3 3/4	.72
46	3	.65
45	2 7/16	.58

Capital Commitment and Risk

It is important to note that naked call selling is a capital intensive strategy. Without a position in the underlying, short calls are considered *naked*. Most firms require that a high minimum amount of equity be present in the account before allowing naked call selling to begin. There is also a margin requirement for each short call in the account, which could increase as the underlying increases.

The amount of capital used to support call selling determines the risk of the strategy. Investors who get into trouble with call selling usually do so because they short more options than they are willing to be short stock. If there is a big rise in the price of the underlying, the investor, who initially sold as many calls as his capital allowed, might be unable to support the now in-the-money calls.

PUT SELLING

A short put position is profitable if the underlying security closes above the break-even point (i.e., strike price minus premium) at option expiration. The maximum profit is limited to the premium received and is achieved when the price of the underlying is above the strike price at expiration (horizontal line in payoff diagram, Figure 3–5).

Assuming the $50 strike price put with 90 days to expiration is $2, the short put has these characteristics at expiration:

Break-even:	$48 = Strike price ($50) − Premium ($2)
Maximum profit:	$2 ($200 per option) at prices above $50
Maximum loss:	Unlimited

Put Selling and Insurance

Put selling can be compared to the activity of insurance underwriting. Insurance companies receive premiums from those they insure and, in return, accept certain risks. The insurance could be on a person's home, car, or life. Businesses insure inventories, plants, and equipment. Should the policyholder suffer a loss, he can make a claim and collect from the insurance company. If he never makes a claim, the insurance company keeps the premium. This is the essence of put selling. In

FIGURE 3–5
Short Put

Description: Sell put option with strike price I.

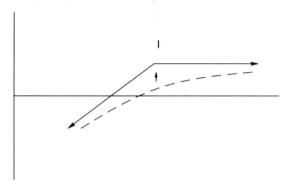

Opinion: Not bearish—underlying security will not be below break-even
price at expiration.
Selection: Higher strike prices reflect more bullish opinion.
Profit: Limited to premium received from sale of option if price of
underlying security is above strike price at expiration.
Loss: Continues to grow as underlying security declines in price.
Break-even: Strike price of option I − Premium received.
Time: Positive—decay of premium accelerates as expiration nears.
Comments: Put seller underwrites risk of underlying security in exchange for
premium. Can get put underlying. Selling puts that represent
more shares than one is willing to own is speculating.
Recommended to support strategy with enough cash to buy
underlying security.
Equivalencies: Long underlying, sell call option I.

exchange for the put option premium, the seller accepts the downside
risk of the underlying security.

Insurance companies spend a lot of time and money to determine
how much risk is in a policy. Their goal is to charge a premium that
accurately reflects the probability that the policy will be paid off. This is
no different from the options market. When an investor sells a put
option, he has entered into a position that requires him to pay off the
buyer of the put by accepting the stock at the strike price. The premium
he receives is the option market's assessment of the potential price
movement of the underlying for the time remaining to expiration of the
option.

Motivation to Sell Puts

One goal of an investor who chooses to sell puts might be to act as an underwriter and collect option premiums. He makes money if the underlying is above the break-even point at expiration; however, he must be ready to accept substantial losses if the underlying declines far below the strike price. If XYZ is below $50 at expiration, the short put is worth the difference between the final price of XYZ and the $50 strike price. Except for the $2 premium received, the put seller has assumed the risk of the stock's price falling below the strike price.

Another goal could be to acquire stock. A short put position can result in assignment, requiring the purchase of the underlying security at the strike price. Let's say a short XYZ $50 strike put option results in the purchase of 100 shares of XYZ stock at $50 per share. The $2 premium received from selling the put lowers the purchase price of the XYZ stock to $48. Assignment of a short put always results in the purchase of stock at a net price that is the break-even point! Should XYZ move beyond $50 at expiration, the put will expire worthless and the $2 premium is kept as a consolation profit.

Regardless of his motives for selling puts, it is imperative that the put seller not be bearish. No investor wants to buy a stock he doesn't like.

The Lost Opportunity

There is a break-even price on the upside for the put seller. From our example, the upside break-even point is $52. A position in XYZ or the short put has a $2 profit if XYZ is $52 per share at expiration. Above $52,

TABLE 3–7
Expiration Profit/Loss of Short Put

XYZ at Expiration	Value of $50 Put	Profit/ (Loss)
$50	$ 0	$ 200
47	300	(100)
44	600	(400)
41	900	(700)
35	1,500	(1,300)

a long position in XYZ stock continues to earn profits. The put profit of the short put is limited to the $2 premium.

There is no financial loss above the upside break-even price; but there is an opportunity loss. The upside break-even price is the figure beyond which a long position in the underlying does better than the short put. The investor who wants to benefit from an increase in the price of the underlying above the upside break-even price may not find put selling the proper strategy. As for any option selling strategy, the expiration price range defined by the financial and opportunity break-even prices should match or encompass the investor's expectations.

Speculative or Conservative?

The investor who stands ready to purchase the underlying security is not speculating. This investor has the capital necessary to establish a long position in the underlying security. The assignment making him long the stock may not be his goal, but it is not a cataclysm either.

Put selling becomes speculative when the investor sells puts that represent more shares than he is willing to own. He can do this because there is only an initial margin requirement for each short put. (For margin purposes, a short put is considered uncovered regardless of the amount of capital supporting the activity.) This investor has the possibility of a bigger loss than he is prepared to accept. That is speculation.

COVERED CALL SELLING

A covered call combines a short call with a long position in the underlying security. The two covered call strategies—covered writing and over-writing—are explained here. Covered call selling, whether via buy-writes or overwrites, allows an investor to profit from a correct forecast of the limit of price performance of the underlying.

In exchange for receiving the option premium, the covered call seller has limited the profit he can realize from a gain in the price of the security on which he has sold the call. The call buyer can take possession of the underlying at the strike price via exercise, so a covered call seller makes his maximum profit if the underlying security is above the call's strike price at expiration. The profit is the option premium received plus the gain from the advance, if any, of the price of the underlying up to the strike price. If the sold call is in-the-money, the loss from selling the underlying below its purchase price must be subtracted. The option premium also provides a partial hedge against a decline in the price of the underlying (Figure 3–6).

Covered Writing

When an investor buys stock and sells call options simultaneously, the strategy is called *covered writing* or *buy-writing*. Say that an investor buys 500 shares of XYZ stock at $40 per share and at the same time sells five of the 90-day $40 calls for $2 1/4 each. The total premium, excluding commissions, is $1,125. The cost of the stock, also excluding commis-

FIGURE 3–6
Covered Call

Description:	Buy or already own underlying security; sell call option with strike price I.

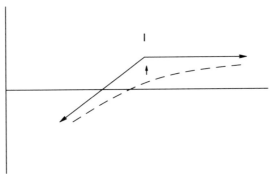

Opinion:	Not bearish—covered writer is willing to sell stock at strike price of sold call in exchange for option premium income.
Selection:	At-the-money option is most often used to maximize income. Use out-of-the-money options for potential of more capital gain from stock, but you get lower option premium income.
Profit:	Limited to premium received for option I + (Strike price I − Price paid for underlying).
Loss:	Price paid for underlying security − Premium received.
Break-even:	Price paid for underlying security − Premium received.
Time:	Positive—value of sold option decreases over time.
Comments:	Very common strategy; used by pension plans, fiduciaries. Works very well in neutral market—options expire worthless and underlying security changes little. Expect ordinary moves in underlying security, and give up large profits if big move up.
Equivalencies:	Short put.

TABLE 3–8
Profit/Loss

Price of XYZ	Value of $40 Call	Profit/(Loss) on Calls	Profit/(Loss) on Stock	Total Profit/(Loss)
$30	$ 0	$1,125	$(5,000)	$(3,875)
35	0	1,125	(2,500)	(1,375)
39	0	1,125	(500)	625
40	0	1,125	0	1,125
41	1	625	500	1,125
45	5	(1,375)	2,500	1,125
50	10	(3,875)	5,000	1,125

sions, is $20,000. At expiration, his profit/loss can be seen in Table 3–8. Above $40, at expiration, the profit of the covered write is limited to the premium received for the options. Below $40, the position loses $1,225 less than the stock investment. Whenever the call is assigned, the covered writer sells XYZ at $40 and realizes the maximum profit of $1,125.

Profits or Protection?
Like any other option strategy, the covered write can be used to express varying degrees of one's opinion. At-the-money buy-writes are neutral. They realize most, if not all, of their profit from the option premium.

Out-of-the-money buy-writes are bullish. Say, for example, that the stock was purchased at $37 1/2 and the option sold for about $1 1/8. The option premium is lower because the call is out-of-the-money. However, the position has greater potential profit than the at-the-money buy-write because there is profit to be made on the advance of XYZ to the strike price. The maximum profit on this buy-write, for 500 shares, is $1,812.50. The option premium provides $562.50; the stock, $1,250. In the first example, the stock provided no additional profit.

Another difference in the two positions is that the out-of-the-money provides less protection against a decline ($1 1/8 per share versus the at-the-money's $2 1/4 per share). This is always the trade-off in selecting a covered write in a stock. The potential for larger profits is balanced by the smaller premium.

How Much Premium?
High premiums alone do not make a good covered write. Option premium levels and risk, as defined by volatility, are directly related. If there

are two $25 stocks, HIV (high volatility) and LOV (low volatility), their respective 120-day call premiums might be $2 1/8 and $1 1/2, representing 9 1/2 and 6 percent of the stock price. The covered write on HIV is not necessarily the superior one. Its possible return is higher, but it comes with the additional risk of owning a stock that could have a wider range of price movement than LOV.

Your main criterion should be your opinion of the underlying. If you do not want to own the underlying if it is not called away, you should not purchase it for the sole purpose of collecting high option premiums.

Overwriting

The other type of covered call selling is *overwriting*. In this strategy, the investor already owns the underlying security and now sells call options. He or she may have bought the security yesterday, six months ago, or six years ago.

The investor now feels that the probability of a move in the price of the underlying is small. Without options, this investor can take only one of two possible actions—sell it or hold it. Only selling allows him to extract any money from his holding.

Overwriting provides a third alternative of selling call options. This investor can select among expirations to balance the premium received, the selling price *if called,* and the timeframe over which he expects the underlying to underperform. There can be 50-, 80-, and 140-day call options available with strike prices 2 points and 7 points out-of-the-money. For a stock at $53 per share, the following call options and prices might exist:

Option Strike Price	50-Day Call	80-Day Call	140-Day Call
$55	1 3/16	1 3/4	2 3/4
60	1/4	9/16	1 7/16

Whichever option he chooses, the overwriter must be aware that, in exchange for the premium received, he has *sold* the right of ownership of his stock at the strike price to *someone else!* He has capped the appreciation of the stock at the strike price. The premium is not ''free money.'' It comes with an opportunity cost that prevents additional profits above the strike price plus premium and a financial cost of providing only as much protection as the premium. The overwriter concludes that the financial and opportunity break-even prices given by the call he sells limit the range of prices he expects.

Covered or Naked?

Addition of a long position in the underlying security makes the covered call seller very different from the naked call seller. That is, the investor who sells naked calls has a position with limited profit if the underlying is below the strike price and unlimited risk if it rallies substantially. He is neutral with a bearish bias. The covered call writer has limited profit if the underlying is above the strike price and risk if the underlying declines substantially. He is neutral with a bullish bias.

The difference is the price range over which the investor wants to take his risk. It is very important that an investor with a neutral opinion also consider on which side of the market he is willing to take risk if he is wrong.

Covered Writing and Put Selling

Compare the expiration profit/loss diagrams of covered call selling and put selling. They have the exact same shape! This can come as a surprise to many investors who feel that any option selling strategy is extremely risky.

If covered call writing is the equivalent strategy, it should have the same characteristics as put selling:

1. The covered call seller is willing to forgo any additional profits from the stock on movements beyond the strike price. So is the put seller.
2. The put seller underwrites the risk of the stock through expiration. In covered call selling, in exchange for the premium of the call option, the investor maintains the risk of the underlying.
3. The break-even point of both strategies is lower than the current price of the underlying.

BULL SPREADS

A *bull call spread* is created by purchasing one call option and simultaneously selling another call option with a higher strike price, as in the following example (XYZ at 80 3/4).

> Buy 1 XYZ 90-day $80 call $5 1/4
> Sell 1 XYZ 90-day $85 call   − 2 7/8
> Net cost of bull call spread $2 3/8

A bull call spread is a combination of two options—one long, one short. The result is a position that has limited risk and profit. The limited risk is the net premium paid for the spread. If XYZ is below $80 at expiration, both call options will expire worthless and the investor will lose the $2 3/8 he paid for the spread. The profit from the spread is limited because the short $85 call has value if XYZ is above $85 at expiration. This value erases any additional profits gained from the long $80 call. In Table 3–9, you can see what the $80 to $85 bull call spread looks like at expiration. This example demonstrates that a spread can only be worth as much as the difference between the strike prices of the options! For prices of XYZ between $80 and $85, the $80 call advances without any offsetting effect from the $85 call. Above $85, this effect limits the spread's value.

Table 3–9 shows the expiration points of maximum profit, and break-even. The maximum profit is $2 5/8 ($262.50) per spread—the maximum value of the spread, $500, minus the initial cost of $237.50. Maximum profit is realized at every price of XYZ above $85 at expiration. The break-even point is $82 3/8. At $82 3/8, the long $80 call is worth $2 3/8, and the short $85 is worth nothing. The break-even point of a bullish call spread is the strike price of the long call plus the net premium paid for the spread. The bull call spread strategy is drawn in Figure 3–7, showing the limited loss, limited profit characteristics.

TABLE 3–9
Bull Spread

Price of XYZ	Value of Long $80 Call	Value of Short $85 Call	Value of Spread
$75	$ 0	0	$ 0
80	0	0	0
81	100	0	100
82	200	0	200
83	300	0	300
84	400	0	400
85	500	0	500
90	1,000	($500)	500
95	1,500	($1,000)	500

FIGURE 3–7
Bull Spread

Description:	Buy call with strike price I; sell call with strike price II.

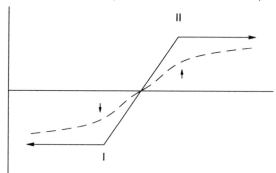

Opinion:	Bullish—expecting underlying security to advance.
Selection:	More bullish; spread strikes farther apart and/or move options toward out-of-the-money. Less bullish; set strikes closer together and move options toward in-the-money.
Profit:	Limited to difference in strike prices (II − I) minus (Premium paid for option I − Premium received from option II) when underlying security is above strike II at expiration.
Loss:	Limited to premium paid for option I − Premium received from option II, i.e., difference in premiums.
Break-even:	Lower strike price I + Difference in premiums.
Time:	Mixed—helps as underlying security approaches strike price II; hurts if closer to strike price I.
Comments:	Hedged position with lower cost than outright call; give up unlimited profit potential of long call.
Equivalencies:	Long put with strike price I, short put with strike price II done for initial credit. Credit is profit if underlying is above strike price II at expiration.

Motivation of the Bull Spreader

The bull spread can be used by the bullish investor who may not be entirely comfortable with a long call position. He may not be bullish enough to warrant the purchase of a call option straight out. He may have a target price limit (thus being willing to forgo additional profits from any advance beyond that target) or he may be uncertain as to the size of the advance, hesitating to ''pay'' to profit from every price of XYZ above the break-even point of a long call. Given these opinions, a hedged strategy is appropriate. The bull call spread is the particular hedged option position that satisfies this investor.

Many investors with bullish opinions delay buying calls when premiums seem a little too rich for them. The decision to wait can result in a lost opportunity. The bull spread lets these investors establish a bullish position now. Later on, naked long calls can be purchased. There's nothing wrong with starting with a hedged position.

The Trade-Offs of Spreading

The major trade-off of spreading is the elimination of the unlimited profit potential that goes with a long option position. In the example, the cost of the spread versus the long $80 call option is lowered because of the premium received from the short $85 call option. Therefore, the call spread has less risk, on a dollar-for-dollar basis, than the long call. For this lower cost, the buyer of the spread gives up additional profits from every price of XYZ above $85 per share at expiration.

There is another important trade-off besides the limitation of profits. It is the time trade-off. Here is Table 3–10, summarizing the performance of the $80 to $85 spread over different prices and time. If XYZ advanced to $90 per share in 15 days (75 days to expiration), the spread is worth about $3 7/8 and the investor has to wait 75 days for the remaining $1 1/8. The $80 call, on the other hand, is trading at 11 7/8! The spreader trades in immediate performance for a lower cost of entry.

Types of Bull Call Spreads

Some bull call spreads are more bullish than others. Bullishness is determined by the strike price of the short call. This determines how much the underlying has to move for the spread to achieve its maximum value. For

TABLE 3–10
Expected Value of $80–$85 Call Spread

Price of XYZ	Days to Expiration				
	75	60	45	30	15
$78	1 1/16	1 9/16	1 7/16	1 3/16	13/16
82	2 1/2	2 1/2	2 1/2	2 7/16	2 3/8
86	3 5/16	3 3/8	3 1/2	3 5/8	3 15/16
90	3 15/16	4 1/16	4 1/4	4 7/16	4 3/4

example, the $85 to $90 call spread is more bullish than the $80 to $85 call spread. The more bullish spread is more likely to expire worthless, but it can be more profitable. The $85 to $90 call spread costs only $1 7/16 and has a maximum profit of $3 9/16.

The name *bull spread* can be somewhat inaccurate. Returning to XYZ at $80 3/4, the $75 call option is $8 1/2. The bull spread of a long $75 call and a short $80 call will cost $3 1/4 ($8 1/2 − $5 1/4). This 5-point spread has a maximum profit of $1 3/4 (5 − 3 1/4) if XYZ is at least $80 at expiration. The stock is currently $80 3/4. This is a bull spread that is profitable, even if XYZ does not move! The spread works because the time premium in the short option is greater than that in the long option. The time premium, however, makes the spread a position that does not reach its maximum profit if the underlying advances quickly. The full advantage of selling more time premium than is bought is not gained until the expiration date is very close.

But the *spread* between the options' strike prices can be larger than 5 points (for stocks with fractional strike prices, spreads less than 5 points can be possible). A $75 to $85 call spread costs $5 5/8 ($8 1/2 − $2 7/8). Break even is $80 5/8. The distance between the strikes is 10 points and, therefore, the maximum profit is $4 3/8 if XYZ is above $85 at expiration ($10 −$5 5/8).

The break-even point of this spread is very close to the current price of the stock—$80 3/4. At expiration, the spread has the same results as the stock between $75 and $85. Below $75, the spread is worthless and the loss is $562.50; the owner of XYZ stock continues to suffer losses. Above $85, the spread is worth $10 and the profit is limited to $437.50. The owner of XYZ stock continues to profit. This spread might be suitable for an investor who wants to profit from a rally in the stock to at least $85 over the next 90 days, but who does not want to be subject to additional losses if XYZ drops below $75. Figure 3–8 compares the spread to owning the stock or the $75 call.

The Bullish Put Spread

In the put market, the bull call spread has an equivalent—sell the higher strike put and buy the lower strike put. This would create a net credit because the premium of the sold put is higher than the one of the purchased put. The maximum profit of this position is the credit. If the price of the underlying is above the strike price of the short put at expiration, both options expire worthless. On the risk side, if the price of

FIGURE 3–8
Comparison of Spread, Long Call, and Long Stock

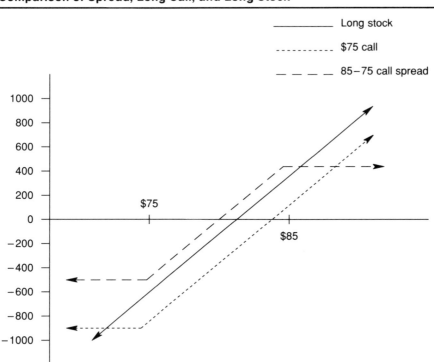

the underlying is below the lower strike price at expiration, the seller of this spread can lose the difference in the strike prices minus that initial credit.

Selling the $85 put and buying the $80 put is a *bullish put spread*. With XYZ still at $80 3/4, the prices of 90-day puts would be $5 3/8 and $2 7/8, respectively. The "sale" of the put spread creates an inflow of $2 1/2 ($250) per spread. If XYZ is above $85 at expiration, both options are worthless and the investor retains the $250 as profit. Below $80, the $85 put is always worth 5 points more than the $80 put. The 5 point maximum value of the spread results in the maximum loss of $2 1/2. Recall that the call spread cost $2 3/8 and had a maximum profit of $2 5/8.

The two positions are equivalent! The reason for the smaller profit in the put spread is explained in the discussion of the box spread arbitrage in Chapter 6.

The bullish *short put* spread can have a distinct advantage over the bullish *long call* spread. Because the long call spread results in an initial debit, it must be paid for in full when it is established. The short put spread results in an initial credit. Under current margin rules, it is only necessary for the risk of the spread, i.e., the credit received minus its maximum value, to be available in the account. There need not be an initial cash outlay if the margin account has excess equity.

Two Special Risks of Early Assignment

Dividends concern the call spreader. If the options of a call spread are far enough in-the-money the day before the ex-dividend date of the stock, the short call can be assigned. There is no stock risk because the long option can be exercised the next day. However, the stock that is delivered against the assignment is delivered cum-dividend, i.e., with the dividend. The stock that is purchased via exercise is purchased ex-dividend. The risk to the investor in this situation is the dividend. This is a sudden additional cost that lowers his profit in the position.

The second special situation that a spreader should be aware of involves spreads of American index options (see Chapter 2). If the short option in an index spread of this type is assigned early, the cash settlement mechanism of index options creates a debit in the account for the amount that the short option is in-the-money at the end of that business day, adjusted by the multiplier of the index. When the long option is exercised, the amount credited to the account will be determined by the settlement value of the index on the DAY it is exercised. There is a full one day's risk if the long option is not sold at some time during the next trading day!

BEAR SPREADS

The *bear spread* is commonly established with puts. It is a hedged strategy consisting of a long put and a short put with the short put having the lower strike price. The cost of the spread is the difference between the premium paid for the long option and the premium received for the short option:

Buy 1 XYZ 90-day $80 put	$2 1/2
Sell 1 XYZ 90-day $75 put	− 1
Net cost of bear put spread	$1 1/2

Like the bull call spread, the bear put spread is a position that has limited risk and limited profit (Figure 3–9). Risk is limited to the net premium

FIGURE 3–9
Bear Spread

Description: Buy put with strike price II; sell put with strike price I.

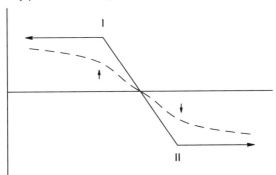

Opinion: Bearish—expecting underlying security to decline.
Selection: More bearish, spread strikes farther apart and/or move strikes
                toward out-of-the-money. Less bearish, set strikes closer
                together and/or move options toward in-the-money.
Profit: Limited to difference in strike prices (II − I) minus (Premium
                paid for option II − Premium received from option I) when
                underlying security is below strike I at expiration.
Loss: Limited to premium paid for option II − Premium received for
                option I, i.e., net premium paid.
Break-even: Higher strike price II − Net premium paid.
Time: Mixed—helps position as underlying security approaches I;
                hurts if closer to II.
Comment: Hedged position with lower cost than outright put purchase.
                Give up large profit potential of long put.
Equivalencies: Long call with strike price II; short call with strike price I done
                for initial credit, which makes a profit if underlying security is
                below strike price I at expiration.

paid for the spread. If XYZ is above $80 at expiration, both put options expire worthless, and the investor loses the $1 1/2 he paid for the spread. The profit from the spread is also limited because the short $75 put has value if XYZ is below $75 at expiration. This value erases any additional profits gained from the long $80 put. The $80 to $75 bear put spread, in Table 3–11, looks like this at expiration.

The value of the spread at expiration, and hence, its profit, is limited at prices of XYZ below $75. The value of the $80 put is unaffected by the $75 put until the latter is in-the-money. The spread is worthless for prices above $80. Table 3–11 also shows that the break-even point for a bear put spread is the strike price of the long put minus the net premium paid to

TABLE 3–11
Bear Spread

Price of XYZ	Value of Long $80	Value of Short $75	Value of Spread	Profit/(Loss) in Spread
$85	$ 0	0	$ 0	($150)
80	0	0	0	($150)
79	100	0	100	(50)
78	200	0	200	50
77	300	0	300	150
76	400	0	400	250
75	500	0	500	350
70	1,000	($500)	500	350
65	1,500	($1,000)	500	350

establish the spread. In this example, the break-even price, at expiration, is $78 1/2.

Motivation of the Bear Spreader

The rationale for using the bear spread is similar to that for the bull spread. Investors feel the cost of entry into a long put position is too high, but they want to establish a position now. Investors who may have a price target on the underlying, are willing to give up the unlimited profits that accompany a long option position. The difference is that these investors select a bear spread when they expect the underlying to decline.

Trade-Offs of Bear Spreading

Besides limited profits, there is a performance trade-off because of time. Before expiration, the time premium remaining in the options prevents the spread from reaching its full value if the underlying declines soon after the spread is purchased. When choosing a spread over a naked long position, the spread needs to be held. Table 3–12 shows the value of the $80 to $75 put spread for various prices of XYZ in 15 day intervals.

If XYZ were to decline to $74 with 60 days remaining to expiration, the $80 put would be worth $6 1/8 and the $75 put, $2 15/16. The spread would be worth $3 3/16. It takes the entire 60 days for the spread to gain the remaining $1 13/16. The spreader trades in immediate performance for a lower cost of entry into a position!

TABLE 3–12
Bear Spread

Price of XYZ	Days to Option Expiration				
	75	60	45	30	15
$82	1 3/8	1 5/16	1 3/16	1	11/16
80	1 3/4	1 3/4	1 11/16	1 9/16	1 5/16
78	2 3/16	2 3/16	2 3/16	2 3/16	2 3/16
76	2 5/8	2 11/16	2 3/4	2 7/8	3 1/8
74	3 1/16	3 3/16	3 5/16	3 5/8	4 1/16

Types of Bear Put Spreads

A bear spread is not limited to 5 points. The $85 to $75 put spread costs about $4 1/2. The break-even price for this position at expiration is $80 1/2, i.e., strike price $85 minus $4 1/2. If XYZ is below $75 at expiration, the spread is worth 10 points. It is worth comparing this spread to the $80 to $75 spread in which both options are out-of-the-money. The profit of each spread is truncated at $75 at expiration. The out-of-the-money spread has a maximum value of $5 and a maximum profit of $3 1/2. The $85 to $75 spread has a maximum value of $10 and a maximum profit of $5 1/2.

Spreads can be used speculatively. For example, if the investor places similar dollar amounts into each spread, the $80 to $75 spread in which both options are out-of-the-money is a more speculative position and should have a greater potential return. This out-of-the-money spread can have a 233 percent profit ($3 1/2 on $1 1/2). The spread is worthless if XYZ is above $80 at expiration. The 10-point spread can have a 122 percent profit ($5 1/2 on $4 1/2), breaks even at $80 1/2, and only expires worthless if XYZ is above $85 at expiration.

Taking the comparison one step farther, the $85 to $80 put spread costs $2 5/8. The break-even point of this spread is $82 3/8, and the maximum profit is 90 percent ($2 3/8 on $2 5/8). However, the stock is only $3/4 above the price at which the spread achieves its maximum value of 5. As a position that is less bearish than either the $80 to $75 or the $85 to $75, this spread should have less potential than either, and it does. The three positions are compared in Figure 3–10.

The bearishness of a put spread is determined by the strike price of the short option. The farther out-of-the-money that put is, the farther the

FIGURE 3–10
Comparison of Three Put Spreads

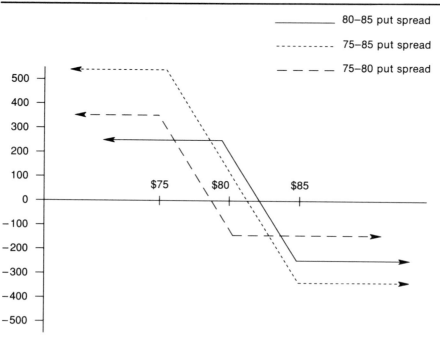

underlying must drop to bring the spread to its maximum value. The most aggressive spreads have both options out-of-the-money and a small difference in their strike prices. The least aggressive spreads have both options in-the-money and a small difference in their strike prices.

The Bearish Call Spread

Calls can be used to establish *bear spreads* just as puts can be used to create bull spreads. Let's go back to the $75 to $80 bull call spread from the previous section. The $80 call was $5 1/4 and the $75 call was $8 1/2. The bear call spread is the result of selling the $75 call and buying the $80 call for a credit of $3 1/4. Should XYZ be below $75 at expiration, both options expire worthless. If XYZ is above $80, the spread is worth $5, resulting in a loss of $1 3/4. The put spread had a maximum profit of $3 1/2 for an investment of $1 1/2. Both positions are equivalent. As a credit spread, the risk of the position has to be available and can usually be satisfied with excess margin.

Summary of Spreading

The general rules of spreading are simple:

1. A spread can only be worth as much as the difference of the strike prices of the options that define it.
2. If a spread is purchased, the maximum profit is the maximum value of the spread minus the net amount paid. The maximum loss is the amount paid.
3. If a spread is sold, the maximum profit is the net amount received. The maximum loss is the maximum value of the spread minus that amount.
4. Spreads must be done in a margin account. If a spread is sold, the difference between the credit received and the maximum value of the spread must be available.

LONG STRADDLE

A *long straddle* consists of a long call and a long put with the same strike price and expiration date. By now you know that long calls are profitable if the underlying goes up, and long puts are profitable if the underlying goes down. A long straddle is profitable if the underlying goes up or down substantially.

Motivation

The long straddle is best suited to an environment in which the investor feels a large move is possible, but is unsure as to its direction. Consider a long straddle in a situation where an upcoming earnings report on a stock is expected, or the report of an economic statistic which can move the market is due. A technician can buy a straddle on a stock that has reached a very significant support or resistance level and is expecting the stock to either punch through that level or bounce right off it. In each case, the underlying could respond with a large move in either direction.

At Expiration

XYZ is at $80. The 90-day $80 call is $4 3/4; the 90-day put is $3 1/4. The $80 straddle costs $8 ($800 per straddle). Table 3–13 shows what the profit/loss looks like at expiration. The graph of this table gives the

TABLE 3–13
Peculiar Straddle Shape Evident

Price of XYZ	Long $80 Call	Long $80 Put	Total Value of Straddle	Profit/(Loss) on Straddle
$65	$ 0	$1,500	$1,500	$700
70	0	1,000	1,000	200
75	0	500	500	(300)
80	0	0	0	(800)
85	500	0	500	(300)
90	1,000	0	1,000	200
95	1,500	0	1,500	700

characteristic *V* shape profit/loss profile of the long straddle. It appears to straddle the strike price (see Figure 3–11).

The break-even points of a straddle at expiration are the strike price plus or minus the total premium paid for the call and the put. In this example, the break-even points are $72 ($80 strike price minus $8 cost) and $88 ($80 strike price plus $8 cost).

Risks of the Long Straddle

The risk of this strategy is quite large. Should the underlying not budge, both premiums are lost. However, the maximum loss only occurs at one price at expiration—the strike price of the options. Any move away from that single price immediately begins to lessen the loss because one of the options will have value.

Because of the opportunity to make money from a move in either direction, this strategy can seem too good to be true. In a way, it is. A long call option has a break-even point of the strike price plus the premium; a long put, the strike price minus the premium. The break-even points for the long straddle are the sum of both premiums plus and minus the strike price. A long straddle is the same as buying a call for the price of a call and a put, and buying a put for the price of a put and a call! At expiration, the underlying must have moved enough in either direction to compensate for the total premium paid. In the example, XYZ must be more than 10 percent away from its current price for the position to be profitable. The long straddle buyer must honestly assess the chances of the underlying to make a move of the magnitude required by the break-even prices.

FIGURE 3–11
Long Straddle

Description:	Buy call with strike price I; buy put with strike price I.

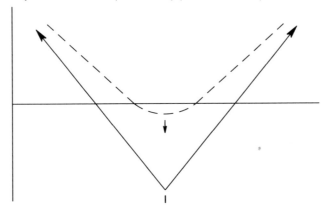

Opinion:	Uncertain—underlying security will move substantially in either direction, but you're unsure which way.
Selection:	Buy call and put with same strike price I when price of underlying security is near I.
Profit:	Increases as underlying security moves in either direction.
Loss:	Limited to sum of premiums paid for call and put.
Break-even:	On upside = Strike price I + Total premiums paid.
	On downside = Strike price I − Total premiums paid.
Time:	Very negative—position has two long options with accelerating decay as expiration nears.
Comments:	Rarely held to expiration due to time effect. Used in anticipation of news that might greatly effect underlying security in either direction.
Equivalencies:	Long 100 shares of underlying, long two puts. Short 100 shares of underlying, long two calls.

Before Expiration

If time is the enemy of long option strategies, it is literally twice as bad for the long straddle.

The long straddle has two clocks running against it, one for the call and one for the put. It should not be a surprise that the long straddle is very sensitive to time decay. Table 3–14 shows the expected value over time of the 90-day, $80 straddle, purchased for $8 as the price of XYZ changes. Because of a long straddle's extreme sensitivity to time, the investor long a straddle can decide to take profits if the underlying makes

TABLE 3–14
Expected Value of $80 Straddle

Price of XYZ	Days to Option Expiration				
	75	60	45	30	15
$95	16 5/8	16 1/4	15 7/8	15 1/2	15 1/4
90	12 1/4	11 3/4	11 1/4	10 3/4	10 1/4
85	9	8 1/4	7 1/2	6 5/8	5 1/2
80	7 1/4	6 1/2	5 1/2	4 1/2	3 1/4
75	7 1/2	7	6 3/8	5 3/4	5 1/4
70	10 5/8	10 1/2	10 1/4	10	10
65	15 1/8	15 1/8	15	15	15

a large move soon after the straddle is purchased. If XYZ runs up to $90 in 15 days, the straddle is worth $12 1/4. If it remains at $90, the position begins to lose time premium. The investor who waits for a continuation of the move finds that he has given back some of that initial profit.

Another reason to consider taking profits is that the position no longer reflects the investor's initial intentions. The straddle now consists of an in-the-money call and an out-of-the-money put. The investor would much rather see XYZ continue to rally. Of course, another 5-point rise in XYZ increases the value of the straddle to twice its purchase price, but the position is also susceptible to a pull-back of part of the move.

Buying a straddle close to expiration does not solve the time decay problem. As expiration approaches, there is less time for the underlying to make a move. If the expected volatility of the XYZ has not changed, the $3 1/4 cost for the 15-day straddle accurately reflects this.

Before rushing to buy this straddle close to expiration ask yourself, "Do I think that XYZ will be above $83 1/4 or below $76 3/4 in 15 days?"

Which Stocks?

One might conclude that the long straddle is best for stocks that show a tendency to make larger moves. However, it may not be wise to base one's choice solely on that basis. As you have seen numerous times, the expected movement in a stock effects option premiums directly via a higher volatility number in the pricing model.

The XYZ $80 straddle in the example had an $8 total premium. If XYZ were a more volatile stock, the premiums of the call and put would be higher. This effect increases the upside break-even point and lowers the downside break-even point by the amount of the additional premium paid. At expiration, XYZ will need to have moved farther for the straddle to be profitable.

LONG STRANGLE

The *long strangle* is very similar to the long straddle. Like the straddle, it is a strategy that reflects one's forecast of a large move in the underlying in either direction. The difference between a strangle and a straddle is that the strike prices of the call and put that make up the strangle are not the same.

At Expiration

If the underlying is between strikes, there are two straddles and two strangles to choose among. Let's say that XYZ is $57 and the 90-day options available are:

Option	Option Price	Option	Option Price
$55 call	$4 5/8	$60 call	$2 1/8
$55 put	$1 1/2	$60 put	$3 7/8

Two strangles can be created from these four options. One consists of the long $60 call and the long $55 put, called the *out-of-the-money strangle*. The other contains the long $55 call and the long $60 put, called the *in-the-money strangle*. The profit/loss diagram of a strangle shows that this strategy's maximum loss occurs over the range of prices between strike prices. In Table 3–15, you can see how the out-of-the money strangle looks at expiration. A strangle has break-even points at expiration of the strike price of the call plus the total premium paid and the strike price of the put option minus the total premium paid. For the strangle in this example, the break-even points are $51 3/8 and $63 5/8. This is a range of plus and minus 10 percent of XYZ's current price of $57 (Figure 3–12).

TABLE 3–15
Strangle

Price of XYZ	Value of $55 Put	Value of $60 Call	Value of Strangle	Profit/Loss of Strangle
$45	$1,000	$ 0	$1,000	$737.50
50	500	0	500	137.50
55	0	0	0	(362.50)
60	0	0	0	(362.50)
65	0	500	500	137.50
70	0	1,000	1,000	737.50

FIGURE 3–12
Long Strangle

Description:	Long put with strike-price I; long call with strike-price II.

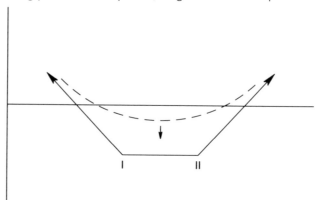

Opinion:	Uncertain—expect underlying security to move substantially, but unsure which way.
Selection:	Buy put I and call II when price of underlying security is between strike prices.
Profit:	Increases as underlying security moves in either direction.
Loss:	Limited to sum of premiums paid for call and put.
Break-even:	On upside = Strike price II + Total premiums paid.
	On downside = Strike price I − Total premiums paid.
Time:	Very negative—position has two long options with accelerating decay as expiration nears.
Comments:	Rarely held to expiration due to time effect. Used in anticipation of news that might greatly effect underlying security in either direction. Costs less than long straddle, but needs bigger move to reach break-even points.
Equivalencies:	Long 100 shares of underlying; buy put I, buy put II. Short 100 shares of underlying; buy call I; buy call II. Buy call I, buy put II.

In-the-Money or Out-of-the-Money?

The out-of-the-money strangle of the $60 call and $55 put costs $3 5/8. By contrast, the in-the-money strangle of the $55 call and $60 put costs $8 1/2. Quite a difference in cost, but the positions are the same! For one, their break-even points are the same. The out-of-the-money strangle has break-even points of $63 5/8 and $51 3/8. The in-the-money strangle has break-even points of $63 1/2 (the $55 call strike plus the $8 1/2 total premium), and $51 1/2 (the $60 put strike minus the $8 1/2 premium). If the positions are the same, they must also have the same risk. The maximum loss of the out-of-the-money strangle is $3 5/8: the maximum loss of its counterpart is $3 1/2.

Why is the risk of the in-the-money strangle only $3 1/2 if it costs $8 1/2? If XYZ is somewhere between $55 and $60, at expiration, the sum of the values of the put and call are $5. For instance, XYZ is $58 at expiration. The $55 call would be $3, and the $60 put is $2. At $56, the call is $1, and the put is $4. Since the sum of the call and put premium will always be $5, the $8 1/2 premium paid for the strangle can only decrease by $3 1/2. This is the risk of the in-the-money strangle.

Strangle or Straddle?

A strangle of an out-of-the-money call and put costs less than the straddle of the at-the-money call and put. As with any long option position, loss is limited to the premium paid for the options. Do not consider buying a strangle in favor of a straddle just because the initial investment is lower. The strangle can cost less, but it is vulnerable to losses over a wider range of prices than the straddle. The straddle only suffers complete loss of the premium paid if the underlying lands at the strike price. Absolute dollar risk should not be the only deciding factor.

Now compare the strangle with the two straddles available. The two straddles are the $55 call and put, and the $60 call and put. The $55 straddle costs $6 1/8 and has break-even points of $61 1/8 and $48 7/8 at expiration. The $60 straddle costs $6 and has break-even points of 66 and 54 at expiration. The strangle costs $3 5/8 and has break-even points of $63 5/8 and $51 3/8.

Which is the best of the three? When a stock is between strike prices, the strangle creates a position which balances the profit potential from a movement of the underlying in either direction. The break-even points of the strangle are 6 5/8 points above and 5 5/8 points below the

FIGURE 3–13
Comparison of Straddles and Strangle

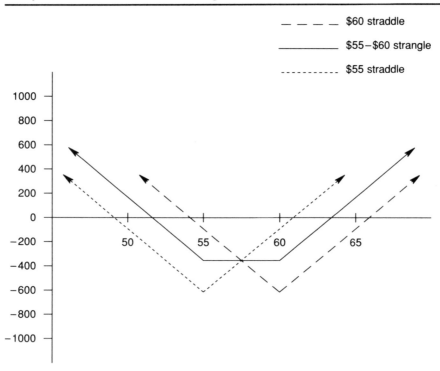

current price. Neither of the straddles does this. The break-even points of the $55 straddle are 4 1/8 points above and 8 1/8 points below XYZ's current price; the $60 straddle, 9 points above and 3 points below. All three positions are presented in Figure 3–13.

What if XYZ were $55? The 90-day options might be priced as follows:

Option	Price	Option	Price	Option	Price
$50 call	$6 3/4	$55 call	$3 3/8	$60 call	$1 3/8
$50 put	$ 5/8	$55 put	$2 1/4	$60 put	$5 1/8

Now the $55 straddle is $5 5/8 with break-even points of $60 5/8 and $49 3/8. The $50 to $60 strangle is $2 with break-evens of $62 and $48.

FIGURE 3–14
Buy One Straddle or Three Strangles?

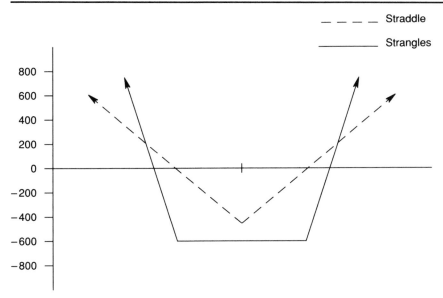

Which is better? Only investors can make that decision. Do they put more emphasis on break-even analysis, absolute dollar risk, or leverage? In terms of leverage, investors can establish three $50 to $60 strangles for almost the same dollar risk as one straddle. The strangles will be a position with six long options (three calls and puts) versus the straddle's two (one call and put). If XYZ makes a big move, the three strangles are much more profitable than the one straddle. However, there is one very important trade-off: The entire premium paid for the strangles is lost if XYZ is between the strike prices of the options. The straddle only suffers total loss of the premium paid at the singular point of the strike price. This is a very aggressive and speculative way to compare strangles to straddles. Figure 3–14 shows why this type of comparison can be so dangerous.

SHORT BUTTERFLY

The *butterfly,* so named because of the "wings" in its profit/loss diagram, is a four-option position. That is, the common short butterfly is created from the purchase of two calls of the same strike price and the sale of one each of the closest in-the-money and out-of-the-money call options.

Assume XYZ is at $55. Use these 90-day option prices from the long strangle discussion.

Option	Price	Option	Price	Option	Price
$50 call	$6 3/4	$55 call	$3 3/8	$60 call	$1 3/8
$50 put	$ 5/8	$55 put	$2 1/4	$60 put	$5 1/8

The short butterfly is:

Short	1	$50 call	$6 3/4	
Long	2	$55 calls	(6 3/4)	(2 × 3 3/8)
Short	1	$60 call	1 3/8	
Net credit			$1 3/8	

At Expiration

The $1 3/8 credit, the maximum profit of this strategy, is achieved if XYZ is above $60 or below $50 at expiration. Below $50, all of the options expire worthless, and the investor keeps the entire net premium received. Above $60, the total value of the two long $55 calls are the same as the total value for the short $50 and $60 calls. For example, at $65, the long $55s are $10 each, for a total of $20. The short $50 is $15 and the short $60 is $5, for a total of $20. The break-even prices for the butterfly are the strike price of the short in-the-money call plus the credit received, and the short out-of-the-money call minus the credit received (Figure 3–15).

The maximum loss occurs at the strike price of the long options, the middle strike. At this price, the investor has a position that is short two options, one worth 5 points and another that is worthless. Unfortunately, the two that were purchased are also worthless. The maximum loss, then, is the credit collected minus the value of the in-the-money short option. In this example it is $3 5/8 ($5 − $1 3/8).

1 Butterfly = 2 Spreads

A short butterfly is a strategy that combines two spreads: a bullish long and a bearish short. This description confirms the limited profit, limited

FIGURE 3–15
Short Butterfly

Description:	Sell 1 of each call with strike price I and III; buy 2 calls with strike price II.

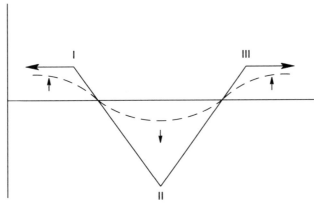

Opinion:	Uncertain—expect underlying security to be below I or above III at expiration.
Selection:	Use when price of underlying security is near strike price II.
Profit:	Net amount of premium received from sales and purchases if underlying below I or above III at expiration.
Loss:	Limited to profit minus value of short spread, strike price I – strike price II, if underlying at strike price II at expiration.
Break-even:	On upside = Net premium received – Strike price III.
	On downside = Net premium received + Strike price I.
Time:	Negative—most dramatic in last month.
Comments:	Cheaper than straddle or strangle because of sold options. Profits truncated at strikes I and III. Done mostly by arbitrageurs to take advantage of pricing relationship among four options. Rarely done by public.
Equivalencies:	Use all puts.

loss of this technique. Spreads were discussed earlier in the chapter. They were described as having both limited profit and limited loss. As a combination of spreads, the butterfly retains these characteristics.

If you break down the example into its spread components, the $1 3/8 credit also results. The $50 to $55 call spread is sold for a $3 3/8 point credit. The $55 to $60 call spread is bought for a $2 point debit. Above $60, each spread is worth its full value, in this example 5 points. Because the strategy is composed of one short spread and one long spread, the 5 point value of the short spread is counteracted by the 5 point asset in the long spread leaving the $1 3/8 credit as profit.

When to Use

There is no good reason for the public investor to use this strategy. The short butterfly is mostly used by professional traders to exploit mispricings among options. It is not done in the public domain.

Here's why. The short butterfly loses money if the underlying stays about where it is—assuming the long options are at-the-money. It loses less as the underlying moves away from the middle strike. The short butterfly looks like the long straddle at prices around the middle strike and, based on this comparison, it appears that the short butterfly should be used when the investor expects the underlying to be somewhere other than the middle strike price at expiration. The $55 straddle costs $5 5/8. The short butterfly has a maximum loss of $3 5/8 at $55. The butterfly looks better at these prices.

On the other hand, the failure of the short butterfly is its inability to provide additional profit should the underlying make a substantial move. The long straddle has the potential for very large profits if the underlying moves well beyond a break-even point. The maximum profit of the butterfly, $1 3/8, is reached very close to the break-even points. The short butterfly hedges away too much of the profit that can be made from a move in the underlying away from the middle strike.

SHORT CONDOR

The *short condor* is a variation of the short butterfly. It also requires four options and is the combination of a short and a long spread. The difference is that the strike prices of the long options are separated. The name condor comes from the larger "wingspan" of the profit/loss diagram, which distinguishes it from the butterfly (Figure 3–16).

An example of a short condor position would be:

Short 1 XYZ $85 call:	$9 7/8
Long 1 XYZ $90 call:	6 1/2
Long 1 XYZ $95 call:	4
Short 1 XYZ $100 call:	2 1/4

These are 90-day option prices when XYZ is $92. The net credit of these four transactions is $1 5/8. As with the short butterfly, it is also the maximum profit if XYZ is above $100 or below $85 at expiration. The

FIGURE 3–16
Short Condor

Description:	Buy calls with strike prices II and III. Sell calls with strike prices I and IV.

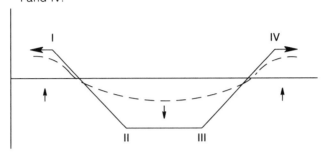

Opinion:	Uncertain—expect underlying security to be below I or above IV at expiration.
Selection:	Use when the price of underlying security is between strike prices II and III.
Profit:	Net premium received from sales and purchases if underlying security is below I or above IV at expiration.
Loss:	Limited to profit minus value of short spread, Strike price I − Strike price II, if underlying between strike prices II and III at expiration.
Break-even:	On upside = Net premium received − Strike price IV.
	On downside = Net premium received + Strike price I.
Time:	Negative—most dramatic in last month.
Comments:	Cheaper than straddle or strangle because of sold options. Profits truncated at strikes I and IV. Done mostly by arbitrageurs to take advantage of pricing relationship among four options. Rarely done by public.
Equivalencies:	Use all puts.

short call spread in this example is $85 to $90; the long spread is $95 to $100. The break-even prices for the condor are the strike price of the short in-the-money call plus the credit received, $86 5/8, and the short out-of-the-money call minus the credit received, $98 3/8.

The short condor suffers its maximum loss over the range of prices between the two long call strike prices. For the short butterfly, it is a single price. Here the risk is $3 3/8—the maximum $1 5/8 profit minus the 5 points the short $85–$90 call spread will be worth between $90 and $95. Above $95 at expiration, the $95 call gains in value. This gain is unchecked by the short $100 call until XYZ goes above $100.

The short condor, with a distance between the long strikes, can be compared to the strangle. The $90 put is $2 7/8, so the $90 put, $95 call strangle costs $6 7/8. Break-even points are $83 1/8 and $101 7/8. The $6 7/8 is lost between $90 and $95. The conclusion reached is that the premium saved by establishing a short condor may not be worth the limited profit potential of the position. Indeed, one could say that the short condor is a strangle that has had its wings clipped!

SHORT STRADDLE

The *short straddle* earns very large profits in a neutral market. No other option strategy is so profitable. Of course, using this technique means very unique and substantial risks if the market does not remain neutral.

A short straddle consists of a short call and a short put of the same strike price. XYZ is at $80. The 90-day $80 call is $4 3/4; the 90-day put is $3 1/4. The $80 straddle can be sold for $8 ($800 per straddle). In Table 3–16, there is a profit/loss picture. The only difference between the short and the long straddles is that the profits have been changed to losses and vice versa.

The graph of the short straddle is the inverted *V* shape profit/loss profile of the short straddle appearing to "straddle" the strike price (Figure 3–17).

Maximum profit is the total premium received; however, there is only one price where this maximum profit is realized—the strike price of the sold options. If the underlying is anywhere other than the strike price, but still within the break-even points, there is a profit, but it is smaller. Outside the break-even points, the potential loss in this strategy is unlimited. The straddle seller has given the potential for unlimited profits *to the buyer*.

TABLE 3–16
Short Straddle

Price of XYZ	Short $80 Call	Short $80 Put	Total Value of Straddle	Profit/(Loss) on Straddle
$65	$ 0	$1,500	$1,500	$(700)
70	0	1,000	1,000	(200)
75	0	500	500	300
80	0	0	0	800
85	500	0	500	300
90	1,000	0	1,000	(200)
95	1,500	0	1,500	(700)

FIGURE 3–17
Short Straddle

Description:	Sell call with strike price I; sell put with strike price I.

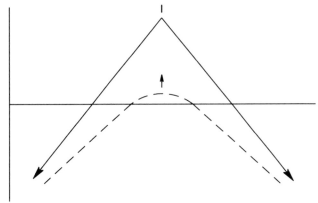

Opinion:	Neutral—underlying security will not move substantially in either direction.
Selection:	Sell call and put with same strike price I when price of underlying security is near strike price I.
Profits:	Limited to sum of premiums received for call and put.
Loss:	Increases as underlying security moves in either direction.
Break-even:	On upside = Strike price I + Premiums received.
	On downside = Strike price I − Premiums received.
Time:	Very positive—position has two short options experiencing accelerating decay as expiration nears.
Comments:	Expecting very ordinary moves in underlying security, within range of break-even points. Great when it works, very large losses when it doesn't.
Equivalencies:	Long 100 shares underlying, short two calls strike price I. Short 100 shares underlying, short two puts strike price I.

The break-even prices at expiration are the total premium received plus and minus the strike price of the options sold.

Motivation

Before options, there was no way for an investor to profit directly from correctly forecasting a narrowly trading market. The only way to improve investment performance was to allocate assets properly. However, asset allocation provides only relative opportunity profit by maximizing investment in sectors that are outperforming and minimizing investment in those underperforming. Without options, there is no way to make money. The short straddle and the three strategies that follow are designed to be profitable when very little happens.

The seller of a straddle expects (needs) the underlying to move in a narrow range around the strike price. In this example, the break-even points are $72 ($80 strike price minus $8 credit) and $88 ($80 strike price plus $8 credit), the same as for the long straddle, some 10 percent away from the current price.

The investor should select this straddle position only if he expects XYZ to trade within plus-or-minus 10 percent of $80 over the next 90 days. Many investors continually forget that selection of the proper option strategy must address the expected price movement of the underlying over time and the consequences of unexpected outcomes. The short straddle is a strategy that could have serious financial results if the underlying moves substantially away from the strike price, e.g., as a result of a takeover bid or a dividend cut.

Time Decay

Say that the straddle sold at $8. If XYZ were to remain at $80, the straddle would drop to $6 1/2 in 30 days. After another 30 days, the straddle decays to $4 5/8. The overall decay is 42 percent. Time is the best friend of all short option strategies!

Risks and Capital Management

The short straddle assumes all the risk of long stock at prices below the downside break-even point at expiration and all the risk of a short position in the stock for prices above the upside break-even point. In effect, the position gets "longer" as prices go down, and "shorter" as prices go up! In more technical terms, as the underlying moves lower, the delta of the put approaches -1; as the underlying moves higher, the call delta approaches $+1$.

The possibility of extensive losses cannot be overemphasized. Short straddles and strangles are very attractive techniques. They beckon the investor with the lure of "free money." After all, these strategies require only a margin deposit which can very often be satisfied with the loan value of securities in the investor's account. This loan value can be used over and over again producing very large returns. This reasoning often results in investors using too much of that loan value in naked option strategies.

Consequences of this type of capital management can be disastrous. It only takes the sale of one ill-timed, short position for the investor to feel the full force of his error. The lack of additional margin to support the increasing requirement can force him to close some or all of the position early. As described earlier, the loss from buying back a short option could eliminate much, if not all, of not only the profits of previous successful positions, but the investor's capital as well.

Capital Required

Since this strategy has naked options, it needs to be supported by an initial margin deposit that is based on the current requirements. This can be higher than the exchange minimums, and your brokerage firm can impose additional criteria. However, since a short straddle can only be unprofitable on one side of the trade (i.e., the underlying is either going up or going down), the requirement will only be the greater of the put or call margin plus the premium of the other side.

SHORT STRANGLE

The goal of the short strangle is to profit from movement in the underlying security over a range of prices. These price limits are defined by the strike prices of the options sold—one call and one put per strangle. Unlike the short straddle, the strike prices of the call and put are different. For example, XYZ is $57 and the 90-options are:

Option	Option Price	Option	Option Price
$55 call	$4 5/8	$60 call	$2 1/8
$55 put	$1 1/2	$60 put	$3 7/8

The out-of-the-money strangle, made up of the $55 put and the $60 call, brings in $3 5/8 in total premium. Break-even points at expiration are $63 5/8 and $51 3/8. These prices are 10 percent above and 9.8 percent below the current price. When the underlying is between strike prices, the strangle more accurately reflects the investor's neutral opinion (Figure 3–18).

FIGURE 3–18
Short Strangle

Description:	Sell put with strike price I; sell short call with strike price II.

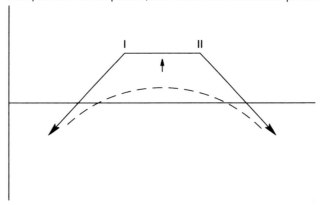

Opinion:	Neutral—underlying security will not move substantially in either direction.
Selection:	Sell put with strike price I and call with strike price II when the price of underlying security is between strike prices.
Profits:	Limited to sum of premiums received for call and put.
Loss:	Increases as underlying security moves in either direction.
Break-even:	On upside = Strike price II + Premiums received.
	On downside = Strike price I − Premiums received.
Time:	Very positive—position has two short options experiencing accelerating decay as expiration nears.
Comments:	Expecting very ordinary moves in underlying security, within range of break-even points. Wonderful when it works; very large losses when it doesn't.
Equivalencies:	Long 100 shares underlying, short one call with strike price I, one with strike price II. Short 100 shares underlying, short one put with strike price I; one with strike price II.

Other comparisons between the short straddle and short strangle are:

1. The short strangle usually brings in less premium because it is most often done with out-of-the-money options.
2. The maximum profit is achieved if the underlying is between the strike prices at expiration. For the straddle, it is at a singular price.
3. As with the short straddle, the short strangle is exposed to unlimited losses if the underlying makes a substantial move to the

upside or the downside. The position gets longer as the underlying goes lower and gets shorter as it goes higher.

A sensible alternative is to start with some protection in place when the position is established. This is examined in the next two sections.

LONG BUTTERFLY

A *long butterfly* is the sale of two at-the-money calls and the purchase of an out- and in-the-money call. Recall that the short butterfly was described as the combination of two spreads that limited the profit and loss of the position. The same is true for the long butterfly. The difference is that the spreads are reversed. Instead of the middle strike being the long calls, they are the short calls.

XYZ is at $85; the 60-day option prices are:

Option	Price	Option	Price	Option	Price
$80 call	$7 1/4	$85 call	$4	$90 call	$2
$80 put	$1 1/8	$85 put	$2 3/4	$90 put	$5 3/4

The long butterfly is:

Long 1 $80 call	$7 1/4	
Short 2 $85 calls	8	(2 × $4)
Long 1 $90 call	2	
Net debit	$1 1/4	

The net debit is the maximum loss of this position if XYZ is below $80 or above $90 at expiration. Below $80, all options expire worthless. Above $90, the long $80 to $85 spread is worth 5 points; so is the short $85 to $90 spread. The values cancel each other out, resulting in the 1 1/4 loss of the initial investment.

Profit, maximized at $85, is 3 3/4. At this price, the $80 call is worth 5 points, and all the other options expire worthless.

Break-even points for the long butterfly are the maximum profit, plus or minus the strike price of the short option. In this example, these prices are $88 3/4 and $81 1/4 respectively (Figure 3–19).

FIGURE 3–19
Long Butterfly

Description:	Buy 1 of each call with strike price I and III. Sell 2 calls with strike-price II

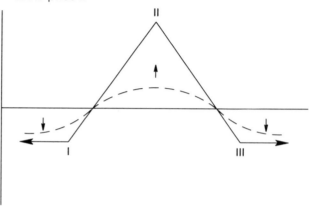

Opinion:	Neutral—underlying security will not be beyond break-even prices at expiration.
Selection:	Use when price of underlying security is near strike price II.
Profit:	Value of long spread minus net premium paid from sales and purchases if underlying security is at strike price II at expiration.
Loss:	Limited to net premium paid if underlying security is beyond strike price I or III at expiration.
Break-even:	On upside = Strike price III − Net premium paid.
	On downside = Strike price I + Net premium paid.
Time:	Positive—most dramatic in last month.
Comments:	Good hedged neutral position. Limits losses if wrong. Because of last month's decay, you should hold to expiration. Less profit potential than short straddle.
Equivalencies:	Use all puts.

Motivation

The long butterfly is used by the investor who wants to profit from a forecast of a narrow trading range for the underlying, but is unwilling to accept the risk of unlimited losses that comes with the sale of either a straddle or strangle.

The long butterfly, then, can be an attractive alternative to the short straddle. First, though, one might ask, "How can a butterfly spread of call options be compared to a straddle composed of a call and a put?"

The answer is something that the investor using options should always remember when analyzing and deciding among strategies: "Place the emphasis on the risk-reward implications of the strategies!" Options can be combined in many different ways to achieve similar results. Put-call parity shows why this is true.

The $85 straddle can be sold for $6 3/4 ($675), the sum of the call and put premiums. This is 3 points more premium than the maximum profit of the butterfly. Instead of selling one straddle for $6 3/4, the investor can buy two butterfly spreads for a total investment of $2 1/2. The $1 1/4 outlay per butterfly is the maximum loss. The maximum profit is $750 ($3 3/4 per butterfly), $75 more than the single straddle.

Break-even points for the straddle are $91 3/4 and $78 1/4. For the butterflies, they are $88 3/4 and $81 1/4. The performance difference is evident in Figure 3–20. One straddle is being compared to two butterflies. Therefore, the profit from the butterflies declines twice as fast. In the diagram, the slopes of the lines from the point of maximum profit demonstrate this effect. The long butterfly can be an effective neutral

FIGURE 3–20
Comparison of Two Long Butterfly Spreads to Short Straddle

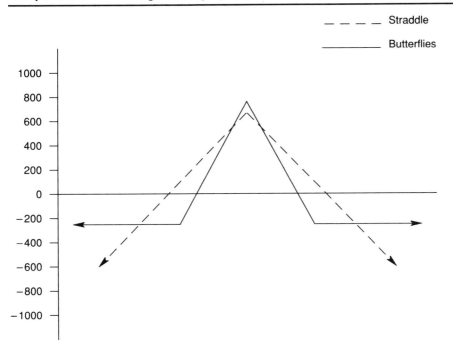

strategy especially for those who would find the excessive losses possible with short straddles hard to accept. The trade-off is the increased speed at which the butterfly achieves its maximum loss.

The Directional Butterfly

The long butterfly has a unique and interesting application for the investor with a directional bias. A long butterfly that can be placed entirely out-of-the-money can be very profitable if the underlying moves ''into'' the profit range of the position. XYZ is $105 and 90-day options are:

$110 call: $3 1/2
$115 call: $1 7/8
$120 call: $1

The butterfly of a long $110, long $120, and short two $115 calls costs $3/4. That is an investment of $75, excluding commissions. If XYZ closes at $115 on expiration Friday, the butterfly is worth its maximum value of 5 points, a 4-to-1 profit. The break-even points are $110 3/4 and 119 1/4.

The caveat is that the investor selecting this type of position cannot be too bullish. Profits will decline between $115 and $119 1/4, and the $3/4 is lost if XYZ is above $120 at expiration. This might be acceptable to the investor with a specific target price and the time frame in mind.

This long butterfly has a very low cost of entry—lower than any of the individual calls or spreads. It is the epitome of the power of options:

> Options allow the investor to maximize his participation in outcomes he considers most likely by creating positions that minimize or eliminate participation or create losses for outcomes he considers less likely.

LONG CONDOR

We need not elaborate on the *long condor*. It has the same risk-reward characteristics as the long butterfly except for the separation of the strike prices of the sold options (Figure 3–21).

Because of the long distance between the two long options, perhaps 15 points or more, the long condor is more effective when used with higher priced securities. For instance, the long condor on a $52 stock could be the long $45 call, short the $50 and $55 calls, and long the $60

FIGURE 3–21
Long Condor

Description:	Sell calls with strike prices II and III; buy calls with strike prices I and IV.

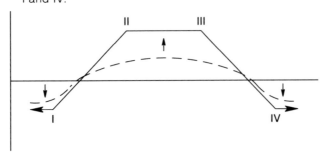

Opinion:	Neutral—underlying security will not be beyond break-even prices at expiration.
Selection:	Use when price of underlying security is between strike prices.
Profit:	Value of long spread minus net premium paid from sales and purchases if underlying security is between strike prices II and III at expiration.
Loss:	Limited to net premium paid if underlying security is above strike price IV or below strike price I at expiration.
Break-even:	On upside = Net premium paid + Strike price I.
	On downside = Net premium paid − Strike price IV.
Time:	Positive—most dramatic in last month.
Comments:	Good hedged neutral position. Limits losses if you're wrong. Because of last month's decay, you should hold to expiration. Less profit potential than short strangle.
Equivalencies:	Use all puts.

call. This 60-day condor would cost $3 1/4 and have only $1 3/4 points potential profit. The 60-day long condor for an $82 stock—long $75 call, short $80 and $85 calls, long $90 call—would cost $2 3/8 and have 2 5/8 points potential profit. Individual 60-day option prices could be:

XYZ at $52		Position	XYZ at $82	
$45 call	$7 3/4	Long	$75 call	$8 3/4
50 call	3 5/8	Short	80 call	5
55 call	1 3/16	Short	85 call	2 1/2
60 call	5/16	Long	90 call	1 1/8
Cost:	$3 1/4		Cost:	$2 3/8

The difference in profitability comes not from the absolute distance between the long options, but from the relative distance. The $45 call is 7 points or 13.5 percent below the stock price. The $75 call is also 7 points below the stock price, but is only 8.5 percent below the current price. Again, the option market has proved that prices accurately reflect options' relation to the price of the underlying. The seemingly better profit/ loss of the long condor on the $82 stock comes at the expense of bringing the points of maximum loss closer to the current price.

NOTES

1. Herbert Filer, *Understanding Put and Call Options* (New York: Crown Publishers, 1959)

PART 2

TRADING STRATEGIES

CHAPTER 4

OPTIONS FOR THE SMALL INVESTOR

An old riddle asks:
What does everybody give and nobody take?
The answer, of course, is advice!

The small investor is bombarded with advice about options. It ranges from dire dissuasions to paeans to the power of leverage. Unfortunately, the advice so proffered is seldom directed to small investors. Perhaps we should define their investment needs. Certainly advice is not needed on hedging portfolios of $500,000. Nor do they need to be told how to buy 50 calls on any one stock. Instead, this book speaks to intelligent people in the marketplace who lack more than the basics in option trading knowledge. For them, we can say: "Yes, you can improve your investing and trading techniques by the sensible utilization of options."

Let's start with someone who has been smart . . .a long position has been taken in a stock at $20 which has subsequently risen to $40. A *double* is nice, but perhaps the stock will move up even farther. For the cautious, a simple option technique such as the following can be very advantageous.

GETTING IN

The Protective Put

This strategy consists of simply buying one put for each hundred shares owned. In this example, you could buy a 40 strike put with an expiration of two to three months. This might cost about 1 1/2 to 2 points per put ($150 to $200). If the stock returned to $20, it could still be sold at $40 by exercising the put. If the stock continued to rise, the put could expire worthless, or be sold for a small amount. There are, of course, some potential negatives here. If the stock stayed in a narrow band—very close to $40—the purchase would seem wasteful, but predicting the future successfully is very difficult and the put acquisition *did* allow you to sleep at night without worrying about the subsequent movement— whether up or down—in the stock.

Opening this chapter with the protective put strategy emphasizes that options have more than one characteristic. While leverage is well known, the protective capacity of options is not. Options can be used to protect, to hedge and even, as in this example, to insure.

The Married Put

This refers to the simultaneous purchase of both stock and an equivalent number of puts on that stock. If these are identified with each other (often by a trailer on the brokerage confirmation), they are said to be *married*. At times, there has been a tax benefit to this technique, but this is not its sole advantage. *Warning:* No one should enter into any tax-related trans- action without advice from a tax professional.

The married put is simply the protective put before the profit has accrued. If the stock, during the life of the put, rises by more than the put's cost, the investor will have a profit. If the stock should fall rather than rise, the loss will be limited to the stock's cost less the put's strike and the put's cost.

Example

Buy 500 shares of XYZ @ 31.
Buy 5 XYZ 3-month 30 puts @ 1.
Maximum loss would be (31 − 30) + 1, per hundred shares.

Phrased another way, you have bought two securities at a cost per hundred of $32 (31 + 1). By exercising the put, you can always recover $30. Therefore the maximum loss is 2 points or 6.25 percent of the initial investment. See Table 4–1.

Couldn't the same goal be accomplished by entering a *stop order* 6 percent below a purchase price? No. Stop orders, while beautiful in

TABLE 4–1
Married Put

	XYZ 31 XYZ 3 mos 30 put 1	Profit/Loss	
Percent Up/Down	Price at Expiration	Stock	Stock and Put
+20%	$37 1/4	+6 1/4	+5 1/4
+10	34 1/8	+3 1/8	+2 1/8
+5	32 1/2	+1 1/2	+ 1/2
–0–	31	–0–	–1
–5	29 1/2	–1 1/2	–2
–10	27 7/8	–3 1/8	–2
–20	24 3/4	–6 1/4	–2

theory, do not always work so well in practice. A random sale of 100 shares can touch off a stop; a stop order can be filled at a price disturbingly below its expected level. When you own a put, *you* control the time and price at which your stock will be sold. The protective put can be especially attractive in four cases: (1) you are afraid of entering the market, (2) you want to buy the particular stock, but are nervous about both its current price and the possibility of its "getting away from you," (3) the stock involved is highly volatile, (4) the stock has a high dividend yield. In this example, if the stock were to go ex-dividend by 50 cents during the life of the put, the risk would be lowered to 1 1/2 points or 4.7 percent.

There are two common criticisms to counter for protective and married puts. When the stock rises, the Monday morning option quarterback says, "You didn't really need the puts and the money was wasted." This is akin, in our view, to the man who calls his insurance broker to complain that, after he bought home insurance, his house didn't burn down!

The second critic is more sophisticated. He says that the 2 to 5 percent cost for three-month protective puts is deceptive; the percentages should be annualized, producing adjusted figures of 8 to 20 percent. This is too expensive and so, he concludes, protective puts cost too much to be practical. Here the basic premise is wrong. You *always* want your house insured, but you need not always insure a stock or an accumulated profit. Protective puts are like every other option strategy: they should be used, not constantly, but when desirable.

Put Purchase versus Short Sale

The obvious way to hedge a short sale is with a long call in a position analogous to the married put. For the following reasons we deem a put purchase as greatly superior to a short sale:

- Your loss is limited—you can lose at most the cost of the put; in the short sale your risk is unlimited.
- You do not need an uptick.
- You do not owe out dividends.
- You never receive a margin call.
- You cannot be panicked into covering.
- You do not have a stop order touched off or filled badly.
- You cannot be involuntarily "bought in" (forced to repurchase the stock).

See Figure 4–1.

FIGURE 4–1
Short XYZ @ 50 versus Long XYZ 50 Put @ 3

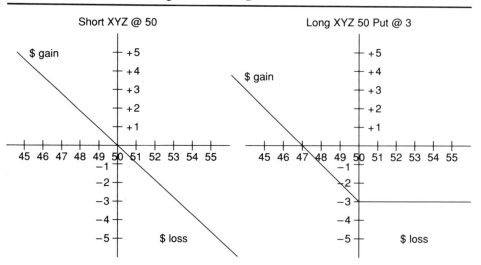

Which graph would you like to depict *your* P&L?

BUYING CALLS

With the reams of literature on call buying, is there really anything new to say on the subject? Yes.

First, make sure that the call that you have selected really fits your expectations for the stock's movement. If you are trying to "scalp" a few points from the stock, you probably shouldn't buy a call at all. If you are looking for a modest rise, you should buy a slightly-in-the-money call. If you anticipate a very large move in the stock, you can buy a slightly-out-of-the-money call. Finally, if you are predicting an absolutely fabulous move in a very brief time (for example, from a takeover), you can contemplate a far-out-of-the-money call. The last strategy should be used sparingly; too often it results in that dreaded actualization of the oft-voiced theoretical warning: loss of 100 percent of investment.

Assume you are considering buying calls on each of three different stocks. They are all trading at the same price—42—but are otherwise quite dissimilar. They are very different in expected *volatility* (how violently or placidly the stock will fluctuate), and you have various expectations for them.

Modest Company	Average volatility	Expected rise—"moderate"
Largemove Inc.	Above average volatility	Expected rise—"healthy"
Fabulous Possibility Co.	Very high volatility	Expected rise—"super"

	2-month calls		
	40	45	50
Modest Company	4	1 3/8	1/8
Largemove Inc.	5	1 3/4	1/4
Fabulous Possibility Co.	6	2 1/4	1/2

Note: Underscore indicates suggested call.

If you are correct in your expectations, you might see moves like this:

Modest Company	+10%	to	46
Largemove Inc.	+15%	to	48 1/4
Fabulous Possibility Co.	+30%	to	55 1/4

		Calls at Expiration			Increase		
		40	45	50	40	45	50
Modest	46	6	1	0	50%	−27%	−100%
Largemove	48 1/4	8 1/4	3 1/4	0	65	86	−100
Fabulous	55 1/4	15 1/4	10 1/4	5 1/4	154	356	950

Note: Underscore indicates suggested call.

Note that, with the expected moves fulfilled, money might be made on many calls (but not usually on far-out-of-the-money). The percentage gain worked out best when the type of call was matched with the expected move.

Of course, you must also note that life sometimes has its little disappointments. If, for example, any of the stocks ended unchanged at 42 you would lose respectively 50, 100, and 100 percent on the three choices.

This is an excellent place to take cognizance of an important point. Buying equal *numerical* amounts of calls is being discussed here. If you had bought equal *dollar* amounts of calls, that would have greatly improved the performance of the farther-out-of-the-money calls. Do not equivocate: that is an extraordinarily **dangerous** way to trade options. When your losses can run to 50 percent or even 100 percent of your investment, you should take care that the loss will be a relatively small dollar amount.

EXPIRATION CYCLES

When *listed options* first began trading, they had quarterly expirations. These were the nearest three months of January, April, July, and October. Later, two other cycles were added: February, May, August, and November, and March, June, September, and December. When *index options* started trading, they expired on a monthly rather than quarterly basis. The popularity of sequential expirations led to the current system. A hybrid type is now used. Equity options all have four expirations (even

TABLE 4–2
Cycles

When Spot Month is	Expiration Months Will Be		
	(newly added month in boldface)		
January	Jan **Feb** Apr Jul	Jan Feb May **Aug**	Jan **Feb** Mar Jun
February	Feb **Mar** Apr Jul	Feb **Mar** May Aug	Feb Mar Jun **Sep**
March	Mar Apr Jul **Oct**	Mar **Apr** May Aug	Mar **Apr** Jun Sep
April	Apr **May** Jul Oct	Apr May Aug **Nov**	Apr **May** Jun Sep
May	May **Jun** Jul Oct	May **Jun** Aug Nov	May Jun Sep **Dec**
June	Jun Jul Oct **Jan**	Jun **Jul** Aug Nov	Jun **Jul** Sep Dec
July	Jul **Aug** Oct Jan	Jul Aug Nov **Feb**	Jul **Aug** Sep Dec
August	Aug **Sep** Oct Jan	Aug **Sep** Nov Feb	Aug Sep Dec **Mar**
September	Sep Oct Jan **Apr**	Sep **Oct** Nov Feb	Sep **Oct** Dec Mar
October	Oct **Nov** Jan Apr	Oct Nov Feb **May**	Oct **Nov** Dec Mar
November	Nov **Dec** Jan Apr	Nov **Dec** Feb May	Nov Dec Mar **Jun**
December	Dec Jan Apr **Jul**	Dec **Jan** Feb May	Dec **Jan** Mar Jun

though the newspapers print only three). These are the nearest two plus two additional taken from one of the original quarterly cycles.

Thus IBM, for instance, would have in January the nearest two months—January and February plus April and July. After the January expiration, the months would be February and March plus April and July. After the February expiration, there would be March and April plus July and October. See Table 4–2.

One result of this system is that you never have to buy the nearest month; there is always a second *spot month*. This is especially important when the near month is halfway or more through its evolution. You do not have to run the risk of the story on the stock materializing, but only after the call has expired. Instead, you can buy the next month out. And it will be only one month away, not three. Thus it won't cost much more, but will significantly increase the probability of making a profit.

Another new thing one can say about buying calls is to take advantage of their low price. No, we do not mean leverage. For example, the fact that a call sells for 10 percent of the price of its underlying stock does not mean you have to buy 10 calls for every 100 shares of stock you were planning to purchase. Instead, you could buy two calls on each of four or five stocks in the same industry. This strategy takes advantage of the lower prices, but for safety through diversification rather than for leverage. It allows you to participate in projected profits, but removes the risk of "right church, wrong pew."

It is worth noting that the *package approach* will often do much better with options than with stocks. This is because with stocks, rises and falls could tend to cancel each other out. With options, the leverage effect operates on the upside while there is a limit to losses on the downside. Now look at the package approach for both computer stocks and their options.

Stock	Price	Call (Market Strike)
Mammoth Mainframes	$150	$7 1/2
Colossal Computers Co.	90	4 1/2
Growing Graphics Group	50	3 1/2
Average Abacus Assoc.	40	3
Inflated Interactions, Inc.	30	2 1/2
Sprouting Systems	20	2

Note: Prices for calls and stocks do not have linear relationships because there are many different determinants involved.

Before continuing, it is necessary to note that the sum of these call premiums is $2,300. Buying four or five calls of each means investing on the order of magnitude of $10,000. The only people who should consider such an investment are those who are very familiar with the risks involved, and who could afford the potential loss. This hypothetical example illustrates the advantage of the package approach. Still, you would have to be bullish on the market overall, very bullish on the computer group, and willing and able to monitor the positions closely. Here is a possible outcome:

	Stock at Expiration	Call Value	Call +/−	Stock +/−
Mammoth Mainframes	$170	$20	+12 1/2	+20
Colossal Computers Co.	80	0	− 4 1/2	−10
Growing Graphics Group	62	12	+ 8 1/2	+12
Average Abacus Assoc.	40	0	− 3	0
Inflated Interactions, Inc.	15	0	− 2 1/2	−15
Sprouting Systems	25	5	+ 3	+ 5
Total			+14	+12

The result: the option package is up more than the stock package. Even more important, the stock gain is 12/380 (3.2%), while the option gain is a whopping 14/23 (60.9 percent)!

COVERED CALL WRITING

Again, so much has been written about this method that remarks here will be restricted. Most important: *never* buy a stock for a covered call, no matter what the projected return, if it is not a stock that you would be comfortable holding. The price level must be acceptable as well. There is absolutely no sense in hearing about an alleged return (to three decimal places) if the stock goes down by more than the premium received. Then you will not have "a return." You will have a *loss*.

At the opposite pole, there have been a lot of takeovers where covered call writers did not participate in very, very large moves. While in theory call writers should not mind that—their stance is to let the buyer try for the long shot—in practice many have become disillusioned and discouraged in these situations. While the number of takeovers has been high, the number of rumored takeovers has been much, much higher. This suggests a strategic solution. Buy as much stock as you are comfortable with; simultaneously write calls on only half the position. With premiums on rumored stocks so high, you still achieve a good return; if the wonderful takeover does come to fruition, half the position achieves the good return, and you are participating fully in the great takeover rise on the other half of the position. Earlier comments about being comfortable with the stock and price apply here with added emphasis. See Figure 4–2.

UNCOVERED PUT WRITING

This strategy fell into disrepute in October 1987 when very large losses hit traders who had written large quantities of uncovered index puts. Nevertheless it is a viable technique and can be used with some restrictions in mind. First, you are dealing here with equity options. That distinction is extremely important. If you have erred in writing an index put, you end up with a debit in your account after it is assigned. This debit does not change if the index subsequently recovers. If you write an equity put which is subsequently assigned, you end up with stock in your account. While its cost could be above its price at the time of writing the

FIGURE 4–2
Covered Write Comparisons

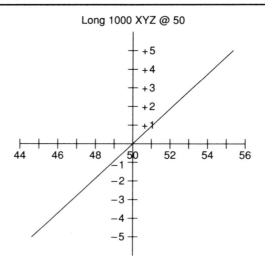

Long 1000 XYZ @ 50

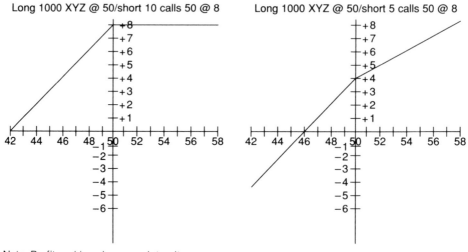

Long 1000 XYZ @ 50/short 10 calls 50 @ 8

Long 1000 XYZ @ 50/short 5 calls 50 @ 8

Note: Profit and loss in one point units.

put, the same would be true of stock purchased at that time and retained. Afterward, you are subject to the familiar risks of stock ownership.

Remarks about being comfortable with the underlying stock apply with equal force to writing uncovered equity puts and writing covered calls.

The great advantage in put writing over covered call writing is the lower initial investment. Policies vary at brokerage firms, but the *minimum* initial margin requirement for an uncovered equity put is 20 percent of the stock price, less any out-of-the-money amount with a minimum of 10 percent of the stock price. The premium must also be left in the account. For a covered call, you are dealing with stock purchase, and so 50 percent must be posted (and reduced by the call premium left in the account). A moment's thought reveals that even with lower put premiums, a higher return can be generated with a similar risk-reward profile. See Table 4–3.

Two other observations are pertinent here. First, the balance of the money that would have been used for stock purchase (cash or margin) can be invested in Treasury bills, thereby enhancing the return without increasing the risk. Second, as with buying calls, the diversification method can be used here. That is, puts might be written on more than one stock to take advantage of the reduced requirements. What should not be done is to write these puts in an amount inappropriate to the possible risk. Contracting to purchase a large quantity of stock because you think that "it can't go down *there*" is not a good approach.

While this has been oversimplified—there is no consideration given to commissions, dividends, or margin interest (although this would apply to the call, not to the put)—the bottom line is that the two strategies have a quite similar risk-reward profile.

If you combine the last two strategies you get covered straddle writing.

TABLE 4–3
Put Write versus Covered Call

	XYZ 50	6 mos call 4	6 mos put 3	
	Covered Call Write		*Uncovered Put Write*	
Successful return (margin)				
Collateral	= 50% $5,000		= 20% $5,000	
	= $2,500		= $1,000	
Minus call premium =	400	Leave put premium		
Out-of-pocket =	$2,100	Out-of-pocket	= $1,000	
Return = 400/2100 =	19%	Return = 300/1000	= 30%	
Annualized return (assumes can be repeated)				
	= 38%		= 60%	
Opportunity loss point =	54		= 53	
Break-even point =	46		= 47	

Note: Commissions not included.

COVERED STRADDLE WRITING

Straddle means many different things to different people. To the IRS, a covered call write is a straddle. To the commodities crowds, a position of long pork bellies and short soybeans is a straddle. So we had better start with a definition. A *straddle* means equal numbers of puts and calls on the same underlying security, with the same expiration and striking price. This means that you can be long or short straddles. Later there is a look at long straddles (or their close cousins—*combinations*), but now it's time to examine short straddles.

But what's a *covered straddle*? Are you covered against the separate risk of a short put and a short call? Yes and no. Being discussed here is the strategic position of long stock/short call/short put. This combines the covered call and the uncovered put (with the same strike). Why would anybody want to do that? Indeed, this could be an appropriate posture if your stock expectations were extremely bullish and/or you wanted to commit less money at this time. Now for a look at "the last word in stocks"—XYZ Corp.

XYZ 50 XYZ 50 call 4 XYZ 50 put 3

By now, you are familiar with posting $2,100 for the covered call write (50 percent of $5,000 less the call premium) and posting $1,000 for the short put (20 percent of $5,000 and leaving the put premium). Thus the initial requirement would be $3,100. The results for this collateral would be: stock up a lot or a little, stock called away and profit from both premiums; stock down, buy a second lot of stock and have its cost reduced by both premiums.

TABLE 4–4
Profit and Loss

	XYZ 50	50 call $4	50 put $3	
Stock Price at Expiration		*Covered Call Write*		*Covered Straddle Write*
$51		+4		+7
50		+4		+7
49		+3		+5
48		+2		+3
47		+1		+1
46 1/2		+1/2	Break-even	0
46	Break-even	0		−1

Another way of looking at the procedure is to contrast it with buying twice as much stock. You would spend more money, post more margin, and pay more in commissions. But your profit percentage might not be higher. See Table 4–4.

SYSTEMATIC WRITING

This term usually refers to the investor whose business, so to speak, is covered call writing. It is contrasted to the trader who occasionally makes use of that strategy to produce incremental income, obtain a downside cushion, or scale out.

Here, *systematic writing* refers to an almost mechanical approach. Start off by writing puts on the stock you have selected. If the stock rises, you are ahead by the premium. If the stock falls, you are assigned on the puts and now own the stock. Then write covered straddles. If the stock rises, you are assigned on the calls and have collected three premiums. If the stock falls, you will be assigned again and have a double position in the stock. Now write as many calls as you are long stock. If the stock rises, you are assigned and have collected four premiums. If the stock falls, you will be long and wrong. But the resulting unrealized loss will have come not from options, but because you chose a stock that went down three times when you had predicted an upward move each time. Even then, you would own the stock at a cost basis that was reduced by four option premiums. See Table 4–5 and Figure 4–3.

SPREADS

Although these examples and illustrations have not referred to commissions, they certainly impact the profitability of any option strategy. This is not an effort to hide transaction costs, but merely to simplify concepts and calculations. However, when it comes to spreads, commissions *do* multiply. A spread of any sort has at least one long option position and at least one short one. This means two commissions going into the trade and perhaps two more to get out. Further, spreads have limited profit potential. The combination of these two factors argues against most spreading tactics for the small investor. An exception may be made for what one could call the far out calendar spread.

TABLE 4–5
Systematic Writing

Jan 3	XYZ 51		No position
Jan 3	XYZ 51	Sell XYZ Mar 50 put 2	
Mar 20	XYZ 48 1/2	Mar 50 put assigned	Long 100 XYZ 48 (50 − 2)
Mar 21	XYZ 48 3/4	Sell XYZ Jun 50 call 3	
		Sell XYZ Jun 50 put 4	Straddle 7
Jun 19	XYZ 47	Jun 50 calls expire	
		Jun 50 puts assigned	Long 200 XYZ
			100 @ 48
			100 @ 43 (50 − 7)
			Avg 200 @ 45 1/2
Jun 20	XYZ 48 1/2	Sell 2 Sep 50 call 3	

Alternate Possibilities

Sep 18 XYZ 52	2 Sep 50 calls assigned	Sep 18 XYZ 48 2 Sep 50 calls expire
	Sell 200 XYZ 53	Cost basis reduced to 42 1/2
	(50 + 3)	(45 1/2 − 3)
	Net profit (53 − 45 1/2) = 7 1/2 × 2	
	= $1,500	
No position		Long 200 XYZ adjusted cost 42 1/2
Ready to sell more options		
Same or another stock		Ready to sell more calls

Note: In either possibility shown, although the stock ended not far from its starting price, you were able to make a good profit.

Far Out Calendar Spread

A calendar spread usually involves the purchase of a farther month option and the simultaneous sale of a nearer month. These will usually be calls if bullish or puts if bearish. It is also usual to opt for a strike just out-of-the-money. Remembering what you learned about expiration cycles, you can buy, for example, the farthest-out call, both in month and strike. Then you can sell the nearest month with a strike below the long leg, but still out-of-the-money. If you have selected wisely and well, the short side expires unassigned (or could be repurchased for a nominal amount), and you still own the long. Then another month can be written, and so on.

It would take some luck as well as sagacity, but it is possible to sell as many as seven different short calls against the same long option.

FIGURE 4–3   Systematic Writing Flow Chart

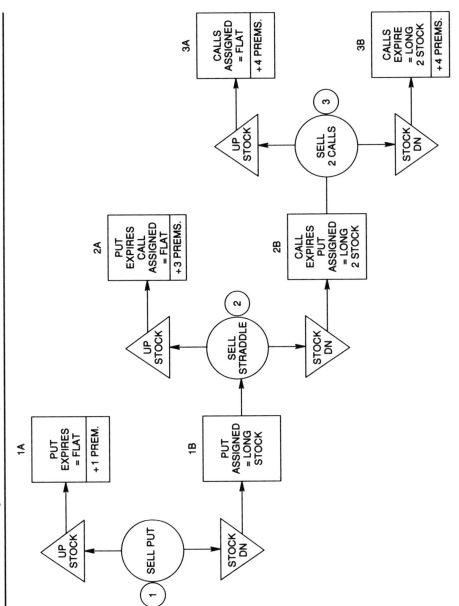

TABLE 4–6
Far Out Calendar Spread (Marvelous Multiple Company)

Fourth Week of	Stock Price	Event	Action
November	$44	July options created	Buy Jul 50 c 5
			Sell Dec 45 c 1
December	44	Dec options have expired	Sell Jan 45 c 1
January	44	Jan options have expired	No action
February	47		Sell Mar 50 c 1
March	49	Mar options have expired	Sell Apr 50 c 2*
April	49	Apr options have expired	No action
May	52	May options have expired	Sell Jun 55 c 4
June	52	June options have expired	No action
July	54	(before July options expired)	Close Jul 50 c 4
Conclusion:	Loss long call	1	
	Gain short calls	9	
	Net profit	8	

* At this point the long cost has been recovered.
Note: This particular scenario has been selected, not as "most likely," but to illustrate the mechanism involved.

Although there would be many commissions, there could be many premiums. These would successfully shrivel the cost of the original long. Not only might this strategy lead to a very low-cost call, incredibly it could lead to a zero—or even negative—cost!

Of course there are, as always, accompanying potential negatives to view. By the time all these trades were finished, the low-cost call might be so far out-of-the-money that it wouldn't be worth very much. Also, the stock could move away quickly, resulting in an assignment on one of the shorts. Obviously, such a technique requires much more monitoring than usual. Still any strategy that holds out the possibility of ending up with a call not far out-of-the-money, with time to run and a zero (or less) cost deserves serious consideration. For the bears, a similar strategy does exist utilizing puts, but be aware of the lower premiums and lower liquidity in put options. See Table 4–6.

GETTING OUT

Most literature on options concentrates on what could be dubbed "getting in." Options can be a very effective tool for getting out of positions as well. One way of achieving this is using the protective put as a means of insuring an accumulated profit. There are two other methods, as follows, for getting out of a position.

Scaling out

Scaling out means making stock sales at successively higher prices. The justification for covered call writing is the return versus the risk, but that is in the context of a zero starting position. If you are long a stock and have reached the stage of ambivalence about its retention, you can write out-of-the-money nearer-term calls against it. This provides a downside cushion and can get you out at a price higher than the current market. If your position is a larger one and your ambivalence has an upward bias, you can write successively higher strikes on portions of the position. This strategy is akin to scaling out (making stock sales at successively higher prices), but could result in higher net returns. See Table 4–7.

Replacement Therapy

This cutely titled technique involves selling out the stock and replacing it with calls. Depending on your outlook, these can be in-, at-, or out-of-the-money calls. In any case, you will have gotten both your profit and

TABLE 4–7
How Covered Call Writing Can Beat Scaling Out

Long	2,000	Supreme Scaling Co. @ 40
		Stock has risen slowly to 48, then spurts to 53
		Sell 5 55 c @ 3

Stock Price at Expiration	Action	Effective Price
56	500 called	58 (55 + 3)
	Sell 5 60 c @ 2	
61	500 called	62 (60 + 2)
64	Sell 5 65 c @ 4	
66	500 called	69 (65 + 4)
	Sell 5 70 c @ 1	
66	70 calls expire	
	Sell 500 @ 66	67 (66 + 1)

Note: Although the stock never rose above 66, this method achieved an average sale price of 64 (not far from the stock's high). Indeed, half of the stock was sold at effective prices above the high for the year!

TABLE 4–8
Replacement Therapy

Long 1,000 Recombinant Replacement cost 40—stock @ 50	
Sell 1,000 @ 50, Buy 10 2 mos. 50 calls @ 3	
$10,000 profit reduced by call purchase to $7,000	
$50,000 investment reduced to $3,000	

Stock Price at Expiration	Additional Profit/Loss
$60	$7,000
58	5,000
56	3,000
54	1,000
52	−1,000
50	−3,000
40	−3,000

Note: The remaining $47,000 is free to be deployed elsewhere. It could be invested in another stock or stocks, in calls or puts, or in Treasury securities.

most of your capital out of the market. Yet you will retain the possibility of participation in farther upside moves in the stock. See Table 4–8.

Enhancement

This is surely a welcome topic! What to do when things are going well is a pleasant problem to encounter. Still, because an option position is going the right way doesn't mean you should just forget about it. Look at a few possibilities. An option (put or call) that you have bought has doubled in value since its purchase. It still has a fair amount of time to run. You could use "OPM".

OPM

OPM can be used in three ways. Here are three examples:

1. Simply sell out half the position. The other half has no upside limit on profits, but you have gotten your *own* capital out of the market.

Example

You are long 10 XYZ calls, original cost 3, now at 6.
Sell 5 calls @ 6 = $3,000 = 10 × $300 = Original cost.
If stock continues up, you still profit, albeit less than maximally. If stock reverses, you can still eke out

more profits. You might make not a penny more, but you don't lose a cent of your original principal. You are still speculating, but with Other People's Money!

2. Sell an equal quantity of a higher/lower (for calls/puts) strike in the same month if that premium is at least equal to your original cost. This creates a spread which limits upside gains, but you can profit by up to the difference between the strikes. And again, this is OPM.

> ### Example
>
> Long 10 XYZ 50 calls cost 3, now at 6.
> Sell 10 XYZ 55 calls @ 3.
> If XYZ ends at 55 or higher, you
> earn an additional profit of 5 points,
> 10 times. If the stock ends between
> 50 and 55, you make some addi-
> tional profit. And, if the stock ends
> below 50, you make no more, but
> your principal is intact.

3. Sell all the options and invest only the *profits* in a different strike and/or month. Once more, you have the potential to pyramid profits with OPM.

> ### Example
>
> Long 10 XYZ Jan 50 calls 3, now at 6.
> Close 10 Jan 50 calls 6 = $6,000.
> Buy 10 Feb 55 calls 3 = $3,000.

You could profit more—you have gained a month's time—if the stock moved still higher. Once again, if the stock fails, your principal is preserved.

Added Profits

Enhancement is not limited to long options. One very common situation is the rapid upward movement of a stock soon after you have done a covered call write. With the earlier comments on expiration cycles in mind, you can do a *diagonal roll*. This consists of buying back the short call and simultaneously writing the next strike one month farther out. Often, this can be accomplished for a nominal cost, equal dollars, or even a small credit. The point here is that, at no extra risk, you have placed yourself in a position to be assigned one strike higher for added profits.

Diagonal Rolling

Example

Jan 2   Buy 500 DDD 38
        Sell 5 Feb 40 calls 2 1/2
Feb 1   DDD at 43
        Buy 5 Feb 40 calls 3 1/2 close
        Sell 5 Mar 45 calls 3 1/4 open

Note that the premium received on the original covered write on Diagonal Data Distributors (DDD) has become irrelevant. So long as you can make the diagonal switch for a low debit or credit, you have little to no additional risk should the stock reverse. You could gain an additional 5 points if the stock continued its uptrend past 45. In fact, you might repeat the maneuver then.

Once you have alerted yourself to enhancement possibilities, many option positions can be thus improved. Like any other market stake, you don't have to do it just because it's there. In all the examples here, the unstated assumption is that the underlying stock will continue to move in the same direction.

REDUCED-RISK TRADING

For the scalpers and market pinpoint-timers, there is a wonderful option strategy available. Start by buying a *combination*—equal quantities of puts and calls on the same underlying stock, with the same expiration month, but with different strikes. These will usually consist of a call strike above the market price of the stock and a put with a strike price below it. This technique is well known: traders use it to profit from a large stock move in *either* direction. The strategy can also be employed in a slightly different fashion.

Assume that after your double purchase, the stock moves down to below the put strike and then hesitates. If you believe it is about to turn up, you could buy stock at that point. If your assumption is correct, you could sell the stock at a point when you thought it would again reverse its trend. If you were wrong, the risk was limited because you could always exercise the put. Similarly, if the stock first rose, you could short it, then buy it back while being protected by the long call. If you are able to get off a couple of good trades, you will probably recover the original cost of the combination. Once that has happened you will be in the stance of having no money invested, and being able to trade back and forth while always being protected. While this trading technique sounds wonderful, it should be attempted by only the most nimble. See Table 4–9.

There is even an enhancement to this tricky technique. When the stock is at your predicted action point, take an offsetting position in options instead of stock! Substitute the sale of an out-of-the-money call for short stock, and the sale of an out-of-the-money put for long stock. In addition to leverage (approximately 20 to 25 percent for the short options instead of 50 percent for the long or short stock), you will also have premium decay working for you. See Table 4–10.

REPAIR

Option Repair

Repair techniques should be a part of every trader's arsenal. They help fix an option and/or stock position that is not going according to plan. Very often, that position might be "repaired"—that is, the profit probability can be increased or the losses can be reduced. While there is an abundance of advice to option traders and investors, that advice usually deals with initiation and occasionally with closure. There has been almost no counseling on what to do when positions go awry. Profits are wonderful, but in real life we have to know what to do about losses.

Let's start with the most frequent position: long calls.

Time—early Jan
XYZ 82 1/2
Mar 100 calls 2 1/4
Mar   95 calls 3 1/8
Mar   90 calls 4 3/8
Mar   85 calls 6 1/4
Mar   80 calls 8 1/4

Assume that you own 12 XYZ Mar 100 calls (purchased in the heat of bullish passion) and have become disturbed about the stock's performance. You still expect a rally, but are dubious about it taking XYZ above 100 (more than 20 percent higher than its current price). Let's (pun intended) look at our options.

TABLE 4–9
Example of Reduced-Risk Trading

Date	XYZ Stock Price	Action
Jan 3	$50	Buy XYZ Feb 55 call @ 1 3/8
4	49 1/2	Buy XYZ Feb 45 put @ 1
5	49 3/4	
6	48 3/4	
9	47 5/8	
10	47	
11	46 1/2	Buy XYZ 46 1/2
12	47	
13	47 1/2	
16	48 1/4	
17	49	Sell XYZ 49 close out, profit 2 1/2
18	49 7/8	
19	50 1/2	
20	51 1/4	
23	51	
24	52 3/8	
25	53 5/8	Sell short XYZ 53 5/8
26	54	
27	54 1/8	
30	53 1/2	
31	53	
Feb 1	52 5/8	
2	52 1/8	
3	51 1/2	
6	51 1/4	Buy XYZ 51 1/4 cover short, profit 2 1/8
7	51	
8	52 1/2	
9	52 7/8	
10	53 3/4	
13	54 7/8	
14	55 5/8	Sell short XYZ 55 5/8
15	56	
16	56 1/2	
17	56 1/8	Exercise Feb 55 call to cover short, profit 5/8. Feb 45 put expires 0.

Conclusion:		
Total *scalp* profit	5 1/4	
Combination spread cost	2 3/8	
Net profit	2 7/8	

Note: The timing here was far from perfect. Nevertheless profits resulted—more than 100 percent of investment (excluding commissions) was gained. It is well to recall the answer of Baron Rothschild when asked how he made all his money: "I always got out too soon."

TABLE 4–10
Reduced-Risk Trading—Using Options!

Date	Action
Jan 11	Sell Feb 40 put 1 1/2
Jan 17	Buy Feb 40 put 1/2 close, profit 1
Jan 25	Sell Feb 60 call 2 7/8
Feb 6	Buy Feb 60 call 3/4 close, profit 2 1/8
Feb 14	Sell Feb 60 call 1 3/4
Feb 17	Feb 60 call expires, profit 1 3/4
	Sell Feb 55 call 1 1/8
	Feb 45 put expires
Conclusion:	Option "scalps" profit 6
	Combination spread cost 2 3/8
	Net profit 3 5/8

Note: Refer to Table 4–9; here, option trades are substituted for stock and similar profit was made while less money was tied up.

1. Hold and Hope

Not so good. Here you frequently find yourself saying:

> *"It will come back, I <u>know</u> it will"* followed by,
>
> *"It will come back, I <u>think</u> it will."* and then,
>
> *"It will come back, I <u>hope</u> it will."* and maybe even,
>
> *"It will come back, I <u>pray</u> it will."*

By the time the hope stage has been reached, it is usually much too late. So you'd better survey some more realistic possibilities.

2. Bite the Bullet

Take (what's left of) the money and run! All too often that's the best way to proceed, although it might be the most underutilized strategy. It's not used so much as it should be because it implies taking a double hit—one to the wallet and one to the ego. The latter is preferable to the former for: "He who fights and runs away/lives to fight another day." And don't forget the improved judgment that results from a difficult experience like this.

If you have elected to eschew both the stubborn hold and the immediate sale, there are other possibilities to evaluate. The most important consideration is to forget about your original cost; it is now irrelevant. Your goal is no longer to produce profits; it is to salvage something from a position that no longer has its previous potential.

3. Trade In
Trade in your "nearly impossibles" for fewer "might-do-it" options or an even smaller number of "more probables."

Replace the 12 100s @ 2 1/4 with   6   90s @ 4 3/8
                   or with   4   85s @ 6 1/4
           or even with   3   80s @ 8 3/4

None of these shifts requires capital infusion. The old 12 generate $2,700 and the new calls cost $2,625, $2,500, and $2,625, respectively. You can't make the great killing you originally lusted after, but keeping half a loaf is better than buying the whole bread and watching it all rot away.

What will happen, if at expiration, XYZ has made a good recovery? A rise of 15 percent would bring XYZ to 94 7/8.

Calls struck at   90   would be worth   4 7/8 ×   6 = $2,925
Calls struck at   85   would be worth   9 7/8 ×   4 = $3,950
Calls struck at   80   would be worth   14 7/8 ×   3 = $4,462.50

Of course, you must also remember:

Calls struck at 100   would be worth   0 × 12 = 0

On the downside, no more money is lost compared to retention of the original 12 calls. Now, a cynic could comment: "If the market does rebound to the upside, you have lost all your profit potential." To demonstrate that this is wrong, calculate break-even points (B/E). Not the usual call purchase B/E point (strike plus premium), but the strategic B/E point. This will allow you to evaluate the comparative efficacy of the strategies. We will ascertain the XYZ price, at option expiration, above which Hold would have outperformed the Trade In tactic.

Trade in to 90   S/B/E 110   Stock needs to rise 33.3%.
Trade in to 85   S/B/E 107 1/2   Stock needs to rise 30.3%.
Trade in to 80   S/B/E 106 5/8   Stock needs to rise 29.2%.

We can verify one of these S/B/Es as an example. An XYZ close at 110 at expiration would produce an intrinsic value of 10 points for each of the 12 calls struck at 100. This total of $12,000 is exactly equal to the worth—20 points each—of the six calls struck at 90.

4. Better Switch
The switch advocated here is not of calls, but of strategies: Change the long call position to a bull spread. This can be done by selling out the

calls to close the position, writing an equal number of the same calls to open a new, short position, and buying an equal number of calls with a lower strike. Here is an example.

Position:	Long	12 XYZ	Mar 100 calls
Action:	Sell	12 XYZ	Mar 100 calls @ 2 1/4 closing
	Sell	12 XYZ	Mar 100 calls @ 2 1/4 opening
	Buy	12 XYZ	Mar 90 calls @ 4 3/8 opening
New position:	Long	12 XYZ	Mar 90 calls
	Short	12 XYZ	Mar 100 calls

Once again, this switch did not require additional capital; a total of 24 calls sold at 2 1/4 produced $5,400 and the 12 calls purchased at 4 3/8 cost only $5,250. We can again calculate the S/B/E. And again it is 110. That is due to XYZ, at expiration, closing above 100, making the 12 spreads worth 10 points apiece. To get more than 10 points each from the original long 12 calls would require a close above 110. In summary: Below 90, each position described does just as poorly; between 90 and 110, this Switch works out better; only above 110 does Hold emerge as the superior strategy.

Note: these repair suggestions might not always be executable at zero cost. They still might be worthwhile doing at small debits.

All spreads must be done in a margin account which has been approved for this type of options trading. In addition to whatever costs were necessary to produce the spread positions, many firms might ask for additional collateral.

Stock Repair

There is another position worth going through the repair review. Although it is seldom talked about from that perspective, it is a strategy that does involve substantial risk: buying naked stock!

The repair strategy examined here is similar to the Better Switch one. Suppose that you are long not 12 XYZ calls, but 1,200 shares of XYZ stock purchased at a price of $100 per share and now selling for 82 1/2. If your outlook is for the stock to recover well, but not all the way, there is an option strategy that can implement that view quite well. Buy 12 XYZ Mar 85 calls @ 6 1/4 and sell 24 Mar 95 calls @ 3 1/8 to produce this position:

> Long 1,200 XYZ
> Long 12 calls Mar 85
> Short 24 calls Mar 95

As before, no additional money is needed (but see the note at the end of the call repair section), and there are no uncovered calls. You now have a combined position of a covered call and a bull spread. There is no additional risk on the downside. On the upside, thanks to your marvelous maneuver, the break-even point for the stock has been lowered. Instead of 100, it has become 92 1/2. To see this, observe the position in a rearranged form:

> Long 1,200 XYZ   Short 12 XYZ Mar 95 calls
> Long 12 XYZ Mar 85 calls   Short 12 XYZ Mar 95 calls

If the stock, at option expiration is 92 1/2 (and you sell it out), you would lose 7 1/2 points per 100 shares. The long calls struck at 85 would each be worth the same 7 1/2 points while the 95 strike calls would expire worthless. The net result would be a breakeven. In other words, using those so-called dangerous and speculative options, you have improved a deteriorated long stock position. Even better, the B/E that was achieved (92 1/2) is very close to 91 1/4. That number is the B/E that would have resulted from a straight averaging down (buy an equal second lot at 82 1/2 and sell both out at 91 1/4). Using options, you obtained a B/E only about a point away from the more traditional technique. We will note impassively that those who do not deign to touch an option would have had the pleasure of spending 1,200 × 82 1/2 = $99,000 to get their B/E! Further, for their almost six-figure expenditure, they would have incurred a doubled downside risk. The final comment here is that the S/B/E is 105. That is, a rise of 22 1/2 points (27.3 percent) would be necessary for Hold to be a superior strategy to Repair.

SUMMARY AND CONCLUSION

Risk Transfer

All too often, option critics erroneously attribute losses to options themselves. These securities are described as speculative, dangerous, and immoral. In fact, options are special securities for the transfer of risk. The risk can be increased as with leverage in long calls; reduced as in married puts or covered calls; or all but eliminated as in protective puts and OPM trading. Option trading is very different from the more familiar stock trading in several ways. These differences are absolutely vital to comprehend and must be constantly kept in mind. We will label the major aspects (although these categories are neither exclusive nor exhaustive) as price, time, KISSes and discipline.

Price and Time

We are all used to thinking that options are cheap (i.e., low priced) compared to stocks, but we may not have fully appreciated the implications. A *point*—$1 per share, $100 per 100 shares, or 1 option—isn't much. Well, it may not be much for stocks, but it's enormous for options. One point on a $50 stock is 2 percent, but the same point on that stock's $4 option is a whopping 25 percent! The moral is that you have to trade options in a much more controlled fashion than you trade stocks.

What is true for price is even more so for time. With stocks you can often afford the luxury of waiting out an adverse move. With options, that waiting period is anathema; it could kill your chances as expiration approaches. In fact, the option buyer will, "always hear/Time's wingèd chariot hurrying near." We observe that time is the friend, not the enemy, of the option *writer*.

As for discipline, it is essential in all aspects of investing, but perhaps nowhere more so than with options. With long options, you run the risk of premium decay up to and including 100 percent loss of investment. With short covered options, you risk loss of opportunity. And with short uncovered options, you face the specter of almost unlimited losses. These negatives are offset by the positive aspects of options: limited risk, good returns, and the lovely lure of leverage.

With these considerations in mind, what should be the approach of the rational investor or trader in options? First, some elementary but effective rules.

A Lot of KISSes

We'll commence with the well-known "KISS" strategy—Keep it Simple, Sweetheart—and extend it to simple, sensible, safe, suitable, and small.

- Keep it simple—don't attempt a diagonal weighted calendar straddle spread if you really just need to buy a call.
- Keep it sensible—don't buy options too far out-of-the-money because they appear "cheap." Even more, don't sell uncovered

options because they're "free money—the stock just can't go that far." The first often produces a 100 percent loss. The second can lead to losses that are fearsome in their magnitude.

- Keep it safe—don't ever risk more than you would be extremely sorry to lose.
- Keep it suitable—just because you read about some alleged mastermind doing something weird and wonderful with options doesn't mean you should try to emulate the operation. Don't try trades or techniques that will take you beyond the *sleeping point*.
- Keep it small—remember the advantages discussed in the buying calls section. It's often better to achieve greater safety through diversification than to try for maximum leverage.

A Little Discipline

Despite all the KISSes, we should note that option losses sometime occur because of the wrong stock, the wrong strategy, and the wrong timing. But beyond these, be aware that decision making for options is radically different from the superficially similar process with stocks. What is needed here is a clarity of viewpoint. Whenever you contemplate an option trade, start out with EYE—Establish Your Expectations. Maybe even write your expectations down on a piece of paper. This can inhibit the rationalizing rituals that so often blind people to the misperformance of their option positions. When a critical point is reached, find that piece of paper and burn it! (Clear your desk first.) This can free you from the now-erroneous expectations.

With these broken, it is time to CYE—Change Your Expectations. How do you know when a critical point is reached? The strange but significant answer to this question is: any way at all! This means that when you EYE, you should not only have at least an approximate idea of when you want to close profitably, you should also have a clear view of an exit point to stem losses. It does not matter whether that exit point is arrived at by fundamental research of the stock involved, by technical readings of the position, by managerial evaluation of the company, by listening to an investment guru, by checking cycles, by gazing at astrological analyses, or by reading chicken entrails! What does matter is that you make the choice that is comfortable for *you* in order to select the exit point. And even more important, when that point is reached, use discipline to stay with your resolve. CYE or lose your money or your opportunity. Phrased succinctly:

If you don't EYE and CYE, you will soon say BYE to your dollars.

Afterword

We have come to the end of this chapter and tried to be instructive without preaching. The chapter started by suggesting that much advice was offered and little accepted. Perhaps our advice will be treated differently. We cannot pretend that options are a panacea. We do believe that there is a plenum, if not a plethora, of option opportunities for both traders and investors. To refrain or refuse to trade with options is sadly to neglect one of the most valuable vehicles in the entire universe of investments. We have tried to explicate some of the myriad possibilities in the large world of options. Naturally, these pages have been able to cover only a small part thereof. For those further interested, there are other chapters in this book and other books to peruse. We hope you will become an option user, even if not an advocate.

CHAPTER 5

INSTITUTIONAL USES
OF OPTIONS

A portfolio manager has many responsibilities beyond those related to specific equity selection. Some involve the broader issues of market timing, portfolio asset allocation, and trade execution. The need to deal with these responsibilities and the ever present pressures to reduce costs were among the driving forces that led to the creation of index options.

Index options have been the fastest growing segment of the industry in recent years, and certain index options markets have become extremely liquid. Because markets are liquid and able to handle sizeable orders, index options are in fact, as well as in theory, a beneficial tool for the knowledgeable portfolio manager.

This chapter explains how a wide variety of options strategies can be used to manage risk and to increase return. In the first section, index option strategies are examined; in the second section, practical advice for using individual equity options is offered.

INTRODUCTION TO PORTFOLIO INSURANCE

Perhaps the most basic use of index options is to insure or to hedge a portfolio against a broad market decline while, at the same time, allowing that portfolio to participate in any market advance. The table below shows the similarities between buying index put options and a standard insurance policy on a car or home.

It is easy to demonstrate how the purchase of index put options can protect the value of a well-diversified portfolio, the make-up of which generally matches the index on which the option is purchased. This concept is illustrated first in a simplified five-stock, $155,375 portfolio that is assumed to track the performance of the S&P 100 Index. The

Insurance Policy	Purchase of Index Put Options
Risk premium	Option time premium
Value of asset	Index level
Face value of policy	Option strike price
Amount of deductible	Index level minus strike price (out-of-the-money amount)
Duration	Time until expiration

potential problem with this assumption for larger portfolios is discussed later.

Consider the five-stock group shown below. Closing prices were taken from *The Wall Street Journal* for June 20, 1988, 92 days from September expiration.

Issue	Number of Shares	Price	Value
Bristol-Myers	500	$40 3/4	$ 20,375
General Motors	600	79 1/2	47,700
K mart	900	34 1/2	31,050
NCR	400	65 1/8	26,050
Ralston Purina	400	75 1/2	30,200
Total value			$155,375

The question here is simply, other than liquidating the portfolio, what can a manager do to protect a portfolio from an expected short-term market decline? Buying puts, of course, is appropriate, but there are two types from which to choose—individual equity and index. So the next step is to analyze potential performance of both types, then compare the results. A portfolio of equity puts that matches the equity holdings in the sample portfolio would look like this (again, closing prices for June 20, 1988):

Issue	Price	Put Option	Price	Quantity	Cost
Bristol-Myers	$40 3/4	Sep 40	$1 3/8	5	$ 687.50
General Motors	79 1/2	Sep 80	3 3/4	6	2,250.00
K mart	34 1/2	Sep 35	2	9	1,800.00
NCR	65 1/8	Sep 65	4 3/8	4	1,750.00
Ralston Purina	75 1/2	Sep 75	2 1/8	4	850.00
Total cost					$7,337.50

How this group of put options would profit with a stock market decline is shown in the next table. Assume that each stock has declined 15 percent (to match the decline in the overall market) at the time of option expiration; thus, there is no time premium left in the option prices.

Issue	Price (Down 15%)	New Option Price	Quantity	Value
Bristol Myers	$34 5/8	$ 5 3/8	5	$ 2,687.50
General Motors	67 1/2	12 1/2	6	7,500.00
K mart	29 3/8	5 3/8	9	5,062.50
NCR	55 3/8	9 5/8	4	3,850.00
Ralston Purina	64 1/8	10 7/8	4	4,350.00
Total put option value after 15% market decline				$23,450.00
Total put option cost				−7,337.00
Total put option profit				$16,113.00

The $16,113 put option profit is the payoff from the insurance policy. This profit directly reduces the total decline of $23,307 in the value of the equities in the portfolio. As a result, the total portfolio declined in value by $7,194 ($23,307 − $16,113). This is only a 4.6 percent decline compared to the overall market and uninsured portfolio decline of 15 percent.

A second insurance strategy is to purchase index put options. On June 20, 1988, the S&P 100 closed at a level of 256.61, and the September 255 put option closed at $9 7/8 (prices taken from *The Wall Street Journal*).

First, it's necessary to calculate the number of options required to insure the equity portfolio. S&P 100 (OEX) options represent a cash settlement value equal to 100 times the index. This means that each option with a strike price of 255 represents a market value of $25,500 (255 × $100). In the example, the equity portfolio has a total beginning value of $155,375. Using the at-the-money Sep 255 put options to insure this portfolio requires purchasing 6 puts ($155,375 divided by $25,500 = 6.09). Obviously, some rounding is always involved in this calculation. At the closing price of 9 7/8, the purchase of 6 put options would cost a total of $5,925 (6 × $987.50).

The next task is to calculate how this insurance strategy benefits the portfolio. First, calculate the index level after a 15 percent decline. Then determine the option price assuming no time premium (a conservative assumption). Finally, calculate the put option profit and resulting benefit to the portfolio.

1. A 15 percent decline in the index from 256.61 results in a level of 216.75 (256.61 × .85).
2. At an index level of 216.75, the 255 put option, at expiration, has a value of $38.25 (255 − 216.75).
3. At $38.25, each index option had a profit of $2,837.50 ($3,825 − $987.50) for a total put option profit of $17,025 ($2,837.50 × 6).

The following table summarizes the effect of these two portfolio strategies.

Equity Options versus Index Options

	S&P 100 Index	Equity Portfolio	Equity Put Options	Six Index Put Options
Beginning value	$256.61	$155,375	$ 7,337	$ 5,925
Ending value	216.75	132,068	23,450	22,950
Change in value	−15%	−23,307	+16,113	+17,025

In this example, the payoff of the two is close enough to be virtually equal. The difference is only $912, which is minor on a $155,375 portfolio. Nevertheless, a closer look at the two alternatives reveals several differences that become important as the portfolio in question gets bigger.

Consider first the issue of manageability. In the simple example given, the purchase of five options is required. All stock issues were chosen with the September option series available 90 days out. In the real world, however, stocks in a diversified portfolio might not have options with 90 days remaining. Due to the way option series are structured and are opened, there are times when only options with 30, 60, and 120 days are available. This means that matching a portfolio of equity puts with an equity portfolio will inevitably result in the purchase of puts with different expirations. When different quantities of puts are added to the variety of expiration months, the management problem becomes obvious.

By contrast, when using equity options, the risk of error is more than losing money. There is also the risk of portfolio disruption. When puts are in-the-money at expiration, there is a great likelihood of automatic exercise. This means that stocks will be automatically sold. For taxable portfolios, the result can be disastrous. Significant extra commission charges from selling stocks and buying them back are other negatives.

There is also the possibility that listed put options are not available on some equities. And even though over-the-counter put options can be available, these options markets are generally not as liquid as the listed options markets. The manager is left to contend with the problems of illiquid markets, such as wide bid/ask spreads and the possible difficulty of entering into or offsetting an options position.

Advantages of Index Options

Fortunately, index options can remedy the disadvantages of equity options. First, consider the issue of manageability. When insuring a portfolio with index options, one quantity of one option series is used. The problem of portfolio disruption is also absent. With the cash settlement feature of index options, there is no risk that individual equities will be sold by automatic exercise.

A lower option commission is another advantage. As previously discussed, at a strike price of 255, one index option covers a market equivalent of $25,500. Compared with a put option on a $50 stock that only covers $5,000 in value (for 100 shares), only one index option is required for every five equity options. This ratio, of course, would be different for every portfolio, depending on the average stock price in the portfolio. The good news is that commission discounts would probably result from buying one larger quantity of index options, compared to buying several smaller quantities of equity puts.

The relative advantages of index options apply to many situations and have fueled the growth of index markets; however, these advantages do not apply in certain situations. For example, in times of market uncertainty, the index options strategy may not be cheaper than an equity one. That index options would be more expensive than equity options seems counterintuitive. Index options represent a diversified portfolio, and diversification generally implies less risk of a broad decline. Consequently, put options with less risk should be cheaper. Yet, in times of market uncertainty, the implied volatility for index options can be higher than for a group of equity options, resulting in a higher price for index options.

In the simple example given, the index put strategy requires a cash outlay of $5,925, and the equity put strategy requires $7,337. Consider also commissions and payoffs. Commissions for six index puts are obviously less than commissions for 28 equity puts on five stocks yet, in the example just outlined, the payoff on the index options was $912 greater.

Overall, the payoff issue is much more uncertain and depends entirely on how well the portfolio in question moves with the index on which the puts are purchased. As long as the two move in tandem, the index put payoff will equal the equity option payoff. However, portfolios weighted in one industry or weighted unlike the index being used have a significant risk of behaving differently. If the manager of a specialized portfolio sees an imminent decline in its equities, there may not be a useful index option available.

STRATEGIC CONSIDERATIONS OF PORTFOLIO INSURANCE

To implement a portfolio insurance strategy, you must evaluate alternatives. Using a general example, this chapter illustrates how each strategy can perform and discusses considerations used in selection.

The Alternatives

Consider the investment alternatives of a portfolio manager with a bearish outlook. One choice is selling the portfolio. While this has many wide ranging implications, it is the ultimate insurance policy. When the portfolio is in cash, it has no risk if a market decline occurs. The second alternative, a variation on this strategy, is selling stock index futures contracts. Although they are not within the realm of this book, this strategy has attracted a considerable following.

Strategy alternatives 3, 4, and 5 are index put option strategies. The third alternative is an index option strategy similar to the example of the five-stock $153,375 portfolio. This method is generally known as Buying a Portfolio Equivalent of At-the-Money Puts. The fourth alternative involves buying the same number of index puts as in the third method, but with a lower strike price. This strategy is called Buying a Portfolio Equivalent of Out-of-the-Money Puts. The final technique is not one that appears obvious to most investors because it involves buying a quantity of puts that is greater than the portfolio equivalent number in strategies 3 and 4. Generally this strategy involves the purchase of a greater number of out-of-the-money puts, so it could be called Buying a Portfolio Multiple of Out-of-the-Money Puts.

How the Strategies Perform

Figure 5–1 illustrates how the portfolio can change in value (vertical axis), given a change in the overall market (horizontal axis) for each of the five alternatives. Lines represent the outcome at expiration. Of course, the strategies would have been implemented at some point prior to expiration.

FIGURE 5–1
Portfolio Insurance Strategies

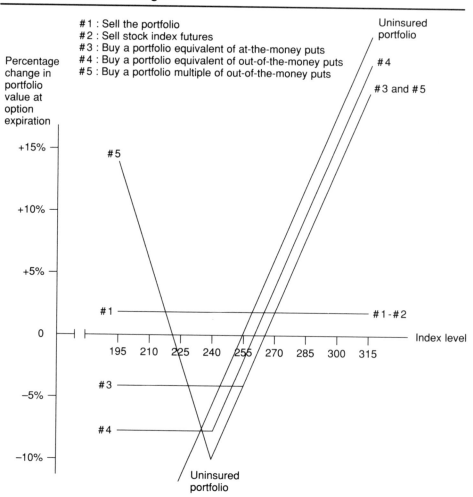

#1 : Sell the portfolio
#2 : Sell stock index futures
#3 : Buy a portfolio equivalent of at-the-money puts
#4 : Buy a portfolio equivalent of out-of-the-money puts
#5 : Buy a portfolio multiple of out-of-the-money puts

Strategy #1: Selling the Portfolio
Converting the portfolio to cash, of course, eliminates risk from market fluctuation. Consequently, the return, regardless of market movement, will be a straight line above zero market movement equal to the interest earned during this time period.

Strategy #2: Selling Stock Index Futures
It is not within the scope of this discussion to cover all the practical difficulties in the execution of this strategy. Suffice it to say that the object of selling stock index futures against an equity portfolio is to eliminate the risk of downside market movement while still owning the portfolio. As a result, at the end of the time period when this strategy is implemented, the return can equal the T-Bill rate of interest. The horizontal line depicting strategy #2 is the same strategy #1 because the dividends on the S+P 100 plus the futures premium equals T-Bill interest.

Strategies #3, #4, and #5: Buying Puts
The best way to explain this method is by using a model portfolio with a total value of $10 million. Assume that the portfolio is broadly diversified and that its performance matches that of the S&P 100 Index. Specifically, assume that the Beta of the portfolio is 1. In this example, the S&P 100 Index stands at a level of 255 when the insurance strategies are implemented. For this example, you can use Table 5–1 on available put option prices.

TABLE 5–1
Index Put Buying Strategies

S&P 100 at 255	
90-Day Put Strike Price	*Option Price*
$255	$11 1/4
250	8 1/4
245	6 3/4
240	4 7/8
235	3 5/8
230	2 5/8

Calculating portfolio equivalent quantity of options:
Number of puts = Portfolio dollar value ÷ (Index level × Multiplier)
For a $10 million portfolio: $10,000,000 ÷ (255 × 100) = 392.

Strategy #3: Buy a Portfolio Equivalent of At-the-Money Puts. As indicated at the bottom of Table 5–1, the purchase of 392 options is required to "fully insure" this portfolio. For strategy #3, using the at-the-money 255 put options and the indicated price of $11 1/4 results in a cash outlay of $441,000 for 90-day "insurance." The results of the total portfolio's performance are summarized both by line #3, Figure 5–1, and by Table 5–2.

Table 5–2 and line #3 in Figure 5–1 demonstrate the two important concepts about portfolio insurance. First, on the downside, the loss in portfolio value is limited to a maximum percentage, even though the market average could fall farther. On the upside, the portfolio remains intact and participates in a market rally; however, on the upside, the portfolio underperforms during the market rally because part of the portfolio is "spent" (and lost) on the put insurance.

A comparison of Figure 5–1 and Table 5–2 reveals an apparent inconsistency. Line #3 in Figure 5–1 is horizontal and represents a constant maximum loss. The Index Percent Change column in Table 5–2, however, indicates that a market decline of increasing proportion actually results in a smaller portfolio loss. How can this inconsistency be explained?

TABLE 5–2
Strategy #3: Buying a Portfolio Equivalent of At-the-Money Puts

To insure a $10 million portfolio, 392 put options, (90-day expiration) with a strike price of 255 are purchased for $441,000 (392 × $1,125).
The balance of $9,559,000 remains invested in a diversified portfolio of equities that matches the performance of the S&P 100.

Index Level at Option Expiration	Index Percent Change	Equity Portfolio Value*	Put Option Value	Total Portfolio Value	Portfolio Percent Change
195	−23.5%	$ 7,312,635	$2,352,000	$ 9,664,635	− 3.4%
210	−17.6	7,876,616	1,764,000	9,640,616	− 3.6
225	−11.8	8,431,038	1,176,000	9,607,038	− 4.1
240	− 5.9	8,995,019	588,000	9,583,019	− 4.2
255	0	9,559,000	0	9,559,000	− 4.4
270	+ 5.9	10,122,981	0	10,122,981	+ 1.2
285	+11.8	10,686,962	0	10,686,962	+ 6.9
300	+17.6	11,241,384	0	11,241,384	+12.4
315	+23.5	11,805,365	0	11,805,365	+18.0

* Dividends are not included.

In theory, as represented by Line #3 in Figure 5–1, the maximum loss in the event of a stable or declining market is the cost of the put options which act like insurance on the portfolio. In the event of a market rise, the portfolio underperforms the market by the cost of the insurance. In practice, however, paying for the put options reduces the amount invested in equities. The result is that 392 puts represent $10 million in market value while only $9,559,000 is invested in equities. On the downside, the puts will rise slightly faster than the decrease in the equities; and on the upside, the equities will rise slightly less than the theoretical $10 million portfolio. It is possible to purchase a number of puts such that a maximum loss will result in the event of a stable or declining market. That number is determined by the use of a linear programming optimizing technique which finds the number of puts equal to the portfolio value being insured. The issue here is that the cost of the put options is part of the total capital whose performance is being measured. Some writers have tried to avoid this issue by assuming that the cost of the put options equals the dividend income or that the puts are purchased with funds outside of the portfolio being insured. A complete discussion of portfolio performance evaluation is beyond the scope of this book, but portfolio managers must face this issue when using option buying strategies.

Strategy #4: Buying a Portfolio Equivalent of Out-of-the-Money Puts. Out-of-the-money puts cost less than at-the-money ones, but if out of-the-money puts are used, the equity portfolio is uninsured against a market decline between the current market level and the strike price of the puts. Consequently, this portfolio insurance strategy is similar to purchasing a policy with a large deductible. In comparison, purchasing at-the-money puts is similar to buying a policy with no deductible.

As Table 5–3 indicates, the purchase of 392 puts with a strike price of 240 (15 points below the current market level) requires a cash outlay of $191,000.

With the out-of-the money puts, the maximum loss in the portfolio is 7.8 percent. This occurs if the market declines to an index level of 240. At this point, the equity portfolio has declined 5.9 percent and the options—at a cost of 1.9 percent—expire worthless. On the upside, the insured portfolio underperforms the market by 1.9 percent—the cost of the put options.

Strategy #5: Buying a Portfolio Multiple of Out-of-the-Money Puts. This put buying strategy has two significant differences from

TABLE 5–3
Strategy #4: Buying a Portfolio Equivalent of Out-of-The-Money Puts

To insure a $10 million portfolio, 392 put options (90-day expiration) with a strike price of 240 are purchased for $191,000 (392 × $487.50).
The balance of $9,809,000 remains invested in a diversified portfolio of equities that matches the performance of the S&P 100.

Index Level at Option Expiration	Index Percent Change	Equity Portfolio Value*	Put Option Value	Total Portfolio Value	Portfolio Percent Change
195	−23.5%	$ 7,503,808	$1,764,000	$ 9,267,808	−7.3%
210	−17.6	8,082,534	1,176,000	9,258,534	−7.4
225	−11.8	8,651,450	588,000	9,239,450	−7.6
240	−5.9	9,230,175	0	9,203,175	−7.7
255	0	9,809,000	0	9,808,900	−1.9
270	+5.9	10,387,625	0	10,387,625	+3.9
285	+11.8	10,966,350	0	10,966,350	+9.7
300	+17.6	11,535,266	0	11,535,266	+15.4
315	+23.5	12,113,991	0	12,113,991	+21.1

* Dividends are not included.

strategies #3 and #4. You can observe the first difference in line #5 in Figure 5–1. With this strategy, the portfolio can actually show an increase in value with a market decline. This occurs because the quantity of puts purchased represents a larger market value than the equity portfolio.

The second significant difference is that there are no strict guidelines as to how many puts to buy. Table 5–4 shows how this strategy performs at different market levels. The reasoning behind the choice of 904 options is as follows: $441,000 was the cost of the at-the-money puts in strategy #3. That dollar amount was chosen as an acceptable amount to risk in terms of underperforming the market in the event of a market rally. Out-of-the-money puts were purchased instead of at-the-money puts due to the desire to take advantage of the leverage feature of options. Obviously, a portfolio manager would have a different market forecast for strategy #5 than for strategy #3.

The cash outlay cost of this strategy is the same as for strategy #3—$441,000. As a result, this portfolio will underperform the market by 4.4 percent if the market remains at the current level of 255 or rallies.

If the market declines slightly, you risk losing a maximum of 10.0 percent. That happens if the market declines to an index level of 240, at

TABLE 5–4
Strategy #5: Buying a Portfolio Multiple of Out-of-The-Money Puts

Use $441,000 to purchase 904 put options (90 day expiration) with a strike price of
240 ($441,000 divided by $487.50).
The balance of $9,559,000 remains invested in a diversified portfolio of equities that
matches the performance of the S&P 100.

Index Level at Option Expiration	Index Percent Change	Equity Portfolio Value*	Put Option Value	Total Portfolio Value	Portfolio Percent Change
195	−23.5%	$ 7,312,635	$4,068,000	$11,380,635	+13.8%
210	−17.6	7,876,616	2,712,000	10,588,616	+5.9
225	−11.8	8,431,038	1,356,000	9,787,038	−2.1
240	−5.9	8,995,019	0	8,995,019	−10.0
255	0	9,559,000	0	9,559,000	−4.4
270	+5.9	10,122,981	0	10,122,981	+1.2
285	+11.8	10,686,962	0	10,686,962	+6.9
300	+17.6	11,241,384	0	11,241,384	+12.4
315	+23.5	11,805,365	0	11,805,365	+18.0

* Dividends are not included.

which point the equity portfolio has declined 5.9 percent and the puts
expiring worthless represent a 4.1 percent loss. Below the index level of
240, however, the leverage effect of the put options comes into play. At
an index level of 225, and a market decline of 11.8 percent, the puts have
increased in value from the cost of $441,000 to $1,358,000; the result is
only a 2.2 percent overall portfolio decline. As the market continues to
decline, the leverage effect of the puts boosts portfolio performance to a
profit position. At an index level of 210, a 17.6 percent market decline,
the portfolio shows a 5.9 percent profit. And at an index level of 195, a
23.5 percent market decline, the portfolio shows a 13.8 percent profit.

All three put option strategies are summarized in Table 5–5.

Choosing a Portfolio Insurance Strategy

In analyzing or choosing an option strategy, there are a number of
important considerations. The first is the cost of the strategy; the second,
the risk. Another important consideration is the portfolio manager's
opinion of the market. Unfortunately, a vague opinion will not suffice.
Because the most popularly traded options typically have a life of less
than six months, market opinion must be specific in terms of direction,

TABLE 5–5
Comparison of Results for Strategies #3, #4, and #5

Index Level at Option Expiration	Percent Change	Percent Change Strategy #3	Percent Change Strategy #4	Percent Change Strategy #5
195	−23.5%	−3.4%	−7.3%	+13.8%
210	−17.6	−3.6	−7.4	+5.9
225	−11.8	−4.1	−7.6	−2.1
240	−5.9	−4.2	−7.7	−10.0
255	0	−4.4	−1.9	−4.4
270	+5.9	+1.2	+3.9	+1.2
285	+11.8	+6.9	+9.7	+6.9
300	+17.6	+12.4	+15.4	+12.4
315	+23.5	+18.0	+21.1	+18.0

Initial portfolio value $10 million
S&P 100 at 255
  Strategy #3: Buying 392 at-the-money puts (a portfolio equivalent quantity).
  Strategy #4: Buying 392 out-of-the-money puts (a portfolio equivalent quantity).
  Strategy #5: Buying 904 out-of-the-money puts (a portfolio multiple quantity).

percentage of movement, and duration. The portfolio manager must also be able to articulate the advantage that options can bring to this particular investment situation.

When the specific market opinion is formulated and the desired benefit is identified, the time frame should then be chosen. As you can see, some strategies are implemented for the life of the option, perhaps as long as six months, and others are implemented for less than one month, at which point the option position is liquidated.

The portfolio manager should also take into account the implied volatility level of options. While it is always better to buy something at the best possible price, the exact level of implied volatility is more important in some situations than in others.

Finally, the expected frequency of use for each strategy deserves discussion.

For a summary of the analytical process in choosing one of these strategies, see the grid in Table 5–6, followed by a detailed explanation of each column.

Column 1: Selling the Portfolio
Selling the portfolio is, in effect, the ultimate insurance policy. Once in cash, there is no risk if the market declines. It is obvious, however, that

TABLE 5–6
Portfolio Insurance Strategy Grid

	Selling the Portfolio	Selling Stock Index Futures	Buying a Portfolio Equivalent of At-the-Money Puts	Buying a Portfolio Equivalent of Out-of-the-Money Puts	Buying a Portfolio Multiple of Out-of-the-Money Puts
Cost	Commissions and impact on market	Discount or premium of futures to real market level	4.4%	1.9%	4.4%
Risk	Miss market rally	Miss market rally	Perform 4.4% worse than market	Maximum loss 7.7%	Maximum loss 10%
Specific market opinion	Long-term bearish	Bearish 4–12 months	Bearish 3 months	Bullish, but worried	Short-term very bearish
Benefit of options	n.a.	n.a.	Market timing portfolio hedge	Disaster insurance	Leverage profit from market decline
Time frame of strategy	1 1/2–3 years	4–12 months	1–3 months	3–6 months	2–4 weeks; will liquidate if market does not begin to move
Implied volatility	n.a.	n.a.	Should buy options at low end of implied volatility range	Relatively unimportant; do not want to buy extremely high implied volatility	Very important; must buy options at low end of implied volatility range
Expected frequency of use	Once in 5–10 years	Once every 2–3 years	Once per year	18–24 months	10 times in 20 years

n.a.: Not applicable.

selling an entire portfolio is not done lightly or frequently. In fact, this would be a major policy decision that would probably occur only at the end of a market cycle. There would undoubtedly be strong fundamental economic considerations, perhaps the forecast of a prolonged recession. Consequently, the portfolio manager would not simply be bearish, he would be predicting a 25 to 40 percent market decline over one to three years. This strategy simply would not be practical for a three-month or even a six-month period.

In the cost/risk area, however, this strategy has many ramifications. For a portfolio of any size, converting all equities to cash is not easy nor inexpensive, and commissions are only part of the cost. The true full cost includes the spread between the current market price and the sale price of the equities. An increase in the supply of a given stock can drive down its price and, for large blocks of stock, this can be a significant discount. For taxable portfolios, this strategy has considerable cost consequences. For individuals with long-term holdings at a very low cost basis, this strategy is virtually impractical.

The ultimate test of cash conversion is the price at which the portfolio is repurchased. The risk, therefore, is being wrong in the market forecast and missing a bull market move. If the repurchase occurs at a market level higher than at the time of sale, this strategy results in an opportunity loss, rather than as a recognizable trading loss.

Column 2: Selling Stock Index Futures

As stated earlier it is not within the purview of this book to discuss all the technicalities of using stock index futures; however, such a contract is equivalent to some dollar value portfolio that matches the underlying index. A portfolio manager seeking protection against a market decline can sell stock index futures contracts against a broadly based equity portfolio with the goal of becoming "neutral the market." Although this is never perfectly achievable, the concept is that the loss experienced by an equity portfolio during a market decline is offset by the profit from the short stock index futures contracts.

This strategy has the advantage of not disrupting the existing equity holdings, which is especially important to taxable portfolios. Other advantages are lower commissions and ease of execution. The ease of execution, however, has been called into question by the October 1987 crash. Nevertheless, the subsequent recovery has shown that this strategy can be implemented satisfactorily for portfolios with values that extend to hundreds of millions of dollars.

Because of the relative ease of entry and exit, the portfolio manager has more flexibility in acting upon bearish market forecasts. If, for example, the institutional investor predicts a 10 percent market correction over three to six months, it would not be practical to sell the portfolio with the goal of buying it all back at a price 10 percent lower. Use of stock index futures contracts, however, could protect a portfolio during this time period.

The risk of this strategy, as with selling all holdings, is missing a market rally. The cost, in addition to commissions, includes any discount or premium to the index at which the futures contracts trades are executed.

Column 3: Buying a Portfolio Equivalent of At-the-Money Index Puts

Although index put options are available with maturities in excess of one year, the most liquid series are in the first six months. Consequently, at the current time, it seems best to limit option insurance strategies to that time frame.

The market opinion required to make a portfolio insurance strategy appropriate must take into account the expected move relative to the price of the option. In the example discussed earlier, the 90-day at-the-money 255 puts were priced at $11 1/4 or 4.4 percent of the index value. This means that the market must decline 4.4 percent for the put position to break even at option expiration. As such, the portfolio manager must have a strong expectation that a market decline in excess of 4.4 percent is likely to occur. To understand why such an expectation is essential, look at the cost/risk of this strategy. The risk is underperforming the market by 4.4 percent—the cost of the put options. If the market remains at the same level or rallies, the put options expire worthless and this insured portfolio underperforms the market by 4.4 percent.

Why would a manager be willing to risk underperforming the market by 4.4 percent during a 90-day period (a 17.6 percent annual rate)? The manager is willing to take this risk because he or she has an extremely bearish view and hopes to beat the market performance by profiting from owning the puts. Clearly, the objective of the option purchase is to have profit and thereby to limit or insure against portfolio losses.

Because the puts in this case are at-the-money, they have the highest price change response to the level of implied volatility. In fact, during the period of 1986 to 1987, at-the-money put options have traded as low as 3 percent of the index (11 percent implied volatility) to 15 percent of the index (45 percent implied volatility). The higher number, of course, occurred in the aftermath of the October 1987 crash. This means that knowledge of implied volatility levels and an opinion of future levels are vital.

Column 4: Buying a Portfolio Equivalent of Out-of-the-Money Puts. What are the implications of buying puts with a strike price below the current market level? At first glance it may seem that there are only two differences between this strategy and buying at-the-money puts: a lower cash outlay (1.9 versus 4.4 percent) and a greater maximum portfolio decline (7.7 versus 4.4 percent). In fact, the other considerations for this strategy—market opinion, time frame, option objective, and implied volatility—are significantly different as well.

Market opinion, as with any equity investment decision, is the place to start. A manager who had a high expectation of a market decline would be willing to pay more for portfolio insurance and would buy at-the-money puts. One who is less certain, but has that "nagging feeling" that a market correction is within the realm of possibility, would be willing to pay a smaller amount.

To make this distinction clearer, consider the following two scenarios. In the first, after a two-and-a-half year bull market, a portfolio manager sees that gradually rising interest rates have not yet been digested by the market. Further, the latest research reports indicate that three major industries are facing labor negotiations and that walkouts in one or two are likely. This institutional investor feels that another major negative development is all it would take to send the market down, and this market experience and knowledge of the political and economic situation make him believe that such an event is likely. In this scenario, the 4.4 percent cost of at-the-money puts is warranted.

In the second scenario, the market has been moving sideways for four months after a 60-day 8 percent rally. The research reports are favorable, and the portfolio manager's fundamental outlook is positive. Experience however, suggests that all may not be as it seems. Bullish sentiment is high, the advance-decline line is sloping downward, and institutional cash holdings are at a low level. The portfolio manager is bullish, but is facing this quandary: Will the overbought condition be resolved by more sideways movement, or by a market correction? The manager is clearly willing to ride out a minor market correction, but he believes in the possibility of a short sharp correction. In this scenario, cheaper insurance is desired. The out-of-the-money puts are the best choice because the portfolio manager is bullish in the longer term and does not want the expensive cost of at-the-money puts to significantly reduce performance, relative to market averages.

What time frame is relevant for purchasing out-of-the-money puts? Because the certainty of the market decline is less than in the first scenario, and because the cash cost is lower per unit of time for longer options, this strategy seems more appropriate for five-, six-, or seven-month options. The overall cost of the strategy is low and, with the timing in doubt, it is best to allow as much time as possible for the insurance to remain in effect.

The level of implied volatility and the objective in using options also need to be addressed. A low level of implied volatility is always favorable when buying options, but is less important when buying out-of-the-money puts than when buying at-the-money puts. Although the change in option price has a nearly linear relationship to the change in volatility, because the overall cost of the out-of-the-money puts is relatively low, a higher level of implied volatility does not significantly change the cost of this strategy as a percentage of the total portfolio. Of course, in extreme conditions such as the aftermath of October 19, 1987, this may not be true, but in normal times, the level of implied volatility does not greatly affect the decision to implement this tactic.

In this portfolio insurance strategy, the objective in purchasing the options is to have them expire—worthless! Strange as it may sound, the portfolio manager actually hopes that these out-of-the-money options expire worthless. After all, a homeowner does not hope that the house burns down so that the insurance policy will provide some compensation. Similarly, a portfolio manager who buys out-of-the-money puts does not hope that the market declines so that the portfolio will lose its value by a lesser percentage than the overall market. This is a hard concept for many investors to digest. But there are times when the experienced money manager recognizes that a sharp market correction, even though not expected, has a probability of occurring that is high enough to justify the expenditure of 1 1/2 to 2 percent of the portfolio on out-of-the-money puts for three to six months of insurance.

Column 5: Buying a Portfolio Multiple of
Out-of-the-Money Puts

Strategy #5 has the possibility of actually profiting from a market decline. The cost of the options is 4.4 percent of the portfolio—the same as strategy #3. However, the risk is the greatest of any of the put buying counterparts. If the overall market drops to an index level of 240 (equivalent to the strike price of the puts), the portfolio loses 10 percent, which would compare unfavorably to an overall market decline of 5.9 percent.

How often is this strategy useful? To quantify the answer, Table 5–4 shows that with an approximate 15 percent market decline, the strategy of buying a portfolio multiple of out-of-the-money puts will actually show a positive return for the entire portfolio. Since 90-day puts are used in the example, it seems reasonable to ask how often the Dow Jones Industrial Average (DJIA) declined by 15 percent or more in 90 days. If this has never happened, the discussion of this method would be no more than an academic exercise. This is a severe yardstick—a 15 percent or greater decline in 90 days. The number of such occurrences is shown in Table 5–7. This has happened only 10 times between 1969 and 1988, about once every other year. With a less strict test, say 12 percent in 100 days, the number of such occurrences is close to once per year. This knowledge should open the eyes of many portfolio managers to the possible benefits of this option strategy.

The objective of this strategy is to take advantage of the leverage aspect of the options and to profit from the anticipated market decline. In order for a portfolio manager to take the risk of performing 10 percent worse than the market, he must be extremely confident of his market opinion. In fact, this strategy has no direct insurance analogy. It is more

TABLE 5–7
10 Times in 20 Years

	Start Date	DJIA	Finish Date	DJIA	Number of Days	Percent Decline
1.	5/14/69	974	7/30/69	788	77	19.0%
2.	11/10/69	871	2/3/70	738	85	15.2
3.	4/9/70	798	5/27/70	631	48	20.9
4.	10/29/73	999	12/5/73	783	37	21.4
5.	6/11/74	865	8/29/74	651	79	24.7
6.	11/6/74	692	12/9/74	570	33	17.6
7.	7/22/77	972	10/19/77	809	89	16.7
8.	2/13/80	918	3/27/80	729	42	20.5
9.	6/30/81	988	9/28/81	807	90	18.3
10.	8/25/87	2,722	10/19/87	1,738	55	36.0

Between 1969 and 1988 the Dow Jones Industrial Average fell more than 15 percent in less than 90 days—10 times.

of a speculation on a market decline. What, then, are the key elements to making this strategy successful? The answer to this question has two parts: the knowledge of implied volatility levels and the choice of the appropriate time frame.

Although the implied volatility level was not significant in strategy #4 (buying a portfolio equivalent of out-of-the-money puts), implied volatility levels are critical in buying a portfolio multiple of out-of-the-money puts. The implied volatility level is important for three reasons. First, because the quantity of options purchased is determined by the dollar amount (or portfolio percentage) allocated, more options can be purchased if the price (implied volatility level) is low. For this example, 4.4 percent of the portfolio was chosen because this is the same amount invested in at-the-money puts in strategy #3. Using this amount clearly demonstrates the effect of leverage when using out-of-the-money options. However, there is no specific rule for the amount allocated when using this strategy.

A second reason the level of implied volatility is important when implementing this strategy is if the puts are purchased at a high implied volatility level, then they will decrease in price rapidly, should implied volatility levels decline. This could happen with or without the market declining as expected. Third, an increase in implied volatility, in addition to appreciation from market movement, greatly adds to the options' increase in price. Consequently, the ideal time to implement this strategy is when implied volatility is low and expected to increase.

The best time frame is similar to the one chosen for any speculation—usually very short. Since success depends on a sharp market move (which, by definition, must be unexpected by the general market), it is likely that in two to four weeks this speculative strategy will prove to work or not. That is the point to sell the options with a profit or no more than a small loss. This is a major difference from the other put buying strategies, in which the plan is to hold them until expiration (although the plan can change at any point before expiration). With this strategy, however, the plan is to sell the options within two to four weeks of their purchase if the anticipated market decline has not begun.

The fact that this method calls for holding the options for no more than a month does not necessarily imply that options with four weeks left until expiration are the best buy. Actually, options that are 15 index points below the current market level and have 90 days or longer until expiration are the preferred choice here. Time decay in option prices is significant in the last 30 days, and option buying strategies using these very short-term options must be planned carefully. If 90-day put options are purchased, they will increase in price either from a sharp down move or an increase in volatility. Perhaps both will happen. When using the 90-day or longer-term options, portfolio managers must have the discipline to liquidate the position at the point when either the strategy has worked successfully, or it has been judged to be unsuccessful.

Where the Insurance Analogy Breaks Down

The term *portfolio insurance* is not used in a strict sense to mean the insurance used by property owners. In fact, many attributes of those policies do not apply to portfolio insurance. First, the home or car owner hopes that he or she never has to make a claim on the policy. Second, mortgage lenders and many state laws require certain types of insurance. Third, home insurance, at least, is generally less than 1 percent annually of the market value of the insured property. Finally, payoffs from home and car insurance (especially the latter) can be several hundred times the premium.

There is certainly no requirement that portfolio managers purchase portfolio insurance. The motivation behind buying put options is a negative market forecast and can entail a desire to profit from the put option purchase. In the previous example of buying at-the-money puts (strategy #3), the total cost of insuring the portfolio for 90 days comes to 4.4 percent of the portfolio; that implies an annual rate of 17.6 percent, which is unquestionably too expensive to be used continuously. Although there are stories of options going up 1,000 percent, most success stories deal with options doubling or tripling rather than multiplying several hundred times.

The conclusion to be drawn from these differences is that portfolio insurance strategies are more properly called *market timing strategies*. They give the portfolio manager several alternatives to use for the purpose of increasing returns and managing market risk. Before the birth of these option products, the range of alternatives available was limited to owning stocks, not owning stocks, or owning a combination of cash and stocks.

Although market timing has its critics, recognize that a manager who changes the portfolio mix between equities and cash is essentially making a market timing decision. Almost by definition, unless a portfolio manager has 100 percent invested in equities all the time, he is a market timer. Consider one who, over the course of time, is "fully invested" at one point, "maintaining cash reserves for buying opportunities" at another point, and "largely in cash waiting for the market to bottom" at a third point in time. Many portfolio managers who make these statements also say, "I am not a market timer," but the motivation behind each of these statements is a market opinion and therefore a market timing opinion. "I am fully invested" means "I am bullish." In this case, the portfolio manager would not be using any of the portfolio insurance strategies discussed above.

"I am maintaining cash reserves for buying opportunities" means "I am long-term bullish but short-term bearish." This situation might dictate being fully invested and employing one of the put buying strategies.

"I am largely in cash" means "I am bearish" and might indicate use of the put buying strategy that profits from a sharp down move. Indeed, looking at portfolio insurance strategies in the light of market timing decisions can give the portfolio manager additional insight into the nature of these tools and their appropriate use.

DYNAMIC HEDGING REDUCES MARKET EXPOSURE

Index put options can be used on a very short-term basis (one to three weeks) to decrease a portfolio's exposure to the equity market during a temporary market decline or during the time it takes to sell individual equities. An example of when this strategy is appropriate is a situation in which a portfolio manager has decided to reduce the equity allocation and is concerned about the effect of a market decline during the two-week period that it will take to select and sell individual equities. To begin with, assume that the S&P 500 Index is at 245. Anticipating a moderate decline in the market, a portfolio manager decides to reduce equity exposure by $7.5 million through the purchase of index puts. A two-month, at-the-money S&P 500 put with a 245 strike is selling at $5 1/8 and has an estimated delta of $-.55$. The manager reduces equity exposure by purchasing 557 index puts [$7.5 million/($100 multiplier × 245 index × .55 delta)]. The cost of this position is $285,000 ($512.50 option premium × 557 options).

Two weeks later, the manager selects the equities to sell. If the index now stands at 241 and the S&P 500 put is $7 7/8, the put position has a value of $443,600, representing a profit of $153,100. Assuming that the equities declined by the same proportion as the index, this profit offsets the $122,400 loss incurred on the sale of the equities.

This strategy is called *dynamic hedging* because the number of index options purchased depends on the delta of the option being used. Because an option's delta changes with market movement, the use of this strategy can involve buying and selling of options during the hedging period.

In the previous example, if the market had moved to an index level of 241 before the individual equities had been chosen, the delta of the 245 put options would have risen to $-.68$. This would have changed the portfolio market value represented by the put options to $9,279,620 (245 × $100 × .68 × 557). Meanwhile, the equity portfolio would be $7,377,600 ($7,500,000 − $122,400). At the index level of 241, only 443 options would be required to hedge the equity portfolio [$7,377,600/ (245 × $100 multiplier × .68 delta)]. Consequently, 114 of the options would be sold, and the portfolio manager would have a new position of "delta equality"—long $7,377,600 of equities and short $7,377,600 represented by index put options. Adjusting the option position could then be repeated until the time when the individual equities were sold, at which point the put options would also be sold.

This dynamic feature could also work if only part of the equities were sold at one time. For example, if the equities were sold in three blocks, each on a different day, the put options would also be sold in three blocks. The goal would be to maintain a short market position in options equal to the long market position in equities until both positions were sold. In this way, the equity market exposure of the portfolio would have been reduced during the period it took to implement the selling program.

Dynamic hedging is perhaps the most frequently misunderstood strategy. It is confused with insurance strategies, and its essentially short-term use is often overlooked. Successful use depends on knowledge of implied volatility levels and the option time decay curve. The portfolio manager must decide on the time period of the dynamic hedge and then carefully examine the possible returns from the options, given a change in market level and implied volatility. If these elements are carefully integrated, a manager can see how effective this tool can be.

INDEX CALL BUYING STRATEGIES

Because index call options replicate a dollar portfolio of the underlying index, it is possible to match a portfolio's total dollar investment by purchasing index call options. The advantages of doing this are similar to the advantages of buying call options on individual equities. For the limited risk of the premium paid, the call buyer can participate in a broad market advance.

There are four general ways to employ index call buying. Three are variations on the same concept of buying calls with the goal of participating in a broad market rally while having limited risk on the downside. These three strategies are: (1) buying a portfolio equivalent quantity of at-the-money index calls, (2) buying a portfolio equivalent quantity of out-of-the-money calls, and (3) buying a portfolio multiple of out-of-the-money calls.

The fourth method of employing index call options is a short-term market timing tool used when increasing a portfolio's equity exposure. Proper use requires knowledge of implied volatility levels and the option's time decay curve, as will be discussed.

In the following examples, assume that the portfolio in question has $10 million in cash and that the S&P 100 Index and related options closed at the prices indicated in Table 5–8.

The 90/10 Strategy

A tactic traditionally known as the *90/10 strategy* enables portfolio managers to achieve two goals simultaneously: capital preservation and potential appreciation from a market rally. This method involves the purchase of index call options with a small portion of a portfolio's capital—say 10 percent—and the purchase of low risk cash equivalents with the remaining 90 percent. Hence the name 90/10. The maximum risk is the premium paid for the calls, and, above the break-even index level implied by the call price, the index call options allow the portfolio to participate dollar for dollar in a market rally.

From Table 5–8, one can calculate that 392 calls are the proper quantity required to replicate a $10 million portfolio. With the S&P 100 Index at 255, each option represents a market value of $25,500

TABLE 5–8
Index Call Buying Strategies

S&P 100 at 255.00 90 days until option expiration

90-Day Call Strike Price	Option Price
$255	$12 1/8
260	9 3/8
265	7 1/4
270	5
275	4 1/4
280	2 7/8

90-day Treasury bills pay 7.0% (annual rate)
Calculating portfolio equivalent quantity of options:
Number of calls = Portfolio dollar value ÷ (Index level × Multiplier)
For a $10 million portfolio: $10,000,000 ÷ (255 × 100) = 392

($100 × Index level of 255) and thus 392 options are required ($10,000,000 divided by $25,500).

The at-the-money calls with a strike price of 255 are purchased at 12 1/8 each for a total cost of $475,202. The remaining balance of $9,524,798 is used to purchase 90-day Treasury bills which pay 7 percent annually, resulting in a maturity value of $9,691,481. Table 5–9 demonstrates how the portfolio of T-bills plus 392 at-the-money calls perform at various index levels.

The percent change column shows that the maximum loss on this portfolio is 3.1 percent (the premium paid for the index calls minus the interest earned on the cash investments). This occurs if the index level declines or remains constant and the calls expire worthless. With any market rally, however, this portfolio of at-the-money calls plus cash will participate in the market advance. If the market rallies to an index level of 285, an 11.8 percent advance, this *cash-plus-calls* portfolio increases in value by 8.7 percent. It is important to note that the maximum loss of the portfolio is also the amount by which the portfolio will underperform the market if the index level rises.

TABLE 5–9
Buying a Portfolio Equivalent of At-the-Money Calls

To replicate a $10 million portfolio, 392 call options (90-day expiration) with a strike
   price of 255 are purchased for $475,202 (392 × $1,212.25).
The balance of $9,524,798 is invested in Treasury bills and earns $166,683
   ($9,524,798 × .07 × .25).

Index Level at Option Expiration	Index Percent Change	Cash Plus Interest Earned	Call Options Value	Total Portfolio Value	Portfolio Percent Change
195	−23.5%	$9,691,481	-0-	$ 9,691,481	− 3.1%
210	−17.6	9,691,481	-0-	9,691,481	− 3.1
225	−11.8	9,691,481	-0-	9,691,481	− 3.1
240	− 5.9	9,691,481	-0-	9,961,481	− 3.1
255	-0-	9,691,481	-0-	9,691,481	− 3.1
270	+ 5.9	9,691,481	$ 588,000	10,279,481	+ 2.8
285	+11.8	9,691,481	1,176,000	10,867,481	+ 8.7
300	+17.6	9,691,481	1,764,000	11,455,481	+14.5
315	+23.5	9,691,481	2,352,000	12,043,481	+20.4

Low Cost Participation with Out-of-the-Money Calls

Participation in a market rally can be achieved by buying out-of-the-
money options. This method requires less cash outlay than buying at-the-
money index call options, although participation in the rally begins at a
later point in the market rise. One can determine by trial and error that
purchasing 392 options with a strike price of 270 at a total cost of
$196,000 ($500 each × 392) almost equals the interest earned of $171,570
on the remaining cash balance of $9,804,000. Table 5–10 illustrates how
this cash plus index call buying strategy performs at different index
levels.

   This strategy has a maximum potential loss of 0.2 percent (the
difference between the cost of the calls and the interest earned). With a
broad market advance, however, this tactic does not work until the index
reaches a level of 270—the strike price of the options. If, for example,
the market rallies to an index level of 300, a 17.6 percent advance, this
cash-plus-calls portfolio will achieve an 11.5 percent increase. This
portfolio has underperformed the index by 6.1 percent. You can calculate this by adding the cost of the calls minus the interest earned to the

TABLE 5–10
Buying a Portfolio Equivalent of Out-of-the-Money Calls

To replicate a $10 million portfolio, 392 call options (90-day expiration) with a strike
price of 270 are purchased for $196,000 (392 × $500).
The balance of $9,804,000 is invested in Treasury bills and earns $171,570
($9,804,000 × .07 × .25).

Index Level at Option Expiration	Index Percent Change	Cash Plus Interest Earned	Call Options Value	Total Portfolio Value	Portfolio Percent Change
195	−23.5%	$9,975,570	0	$ 9,975,570	− 0.2%
210	−17.6	9,975,570	0	9,975,570	− 0.2
225	−11.8	9,975,570	0	9,975,570	− 0.2
240	− 5.9	9,975,570	0	9,975,570	− 0.2
255	0	9,975,570	0	9,975,570	− 0.2
270	+ 5.9	9,975,570	0	9,975,570	− 0.2
285	+11.8	9,975,570	$ 588,000	10,563,570	+ 5.6
300	+17.6	9,975,570	1,176,000	11,151,570	+11.5
315	+23.5	9,975,570	1,764,000	11,739,570	+17.4

difference between the strike price of the calls and the index level at the time of the call purchase. In this example, the cost of the calls minus the interest is $24,430, or 0.2 percent of the $10 million portfolio. The difference between the strike price of the calls (270) and the index level at the time of the call purchase (255) is 15 points, or 5.9 percent of the index level. Adding these figures together gives you 6.1 percent, the amount by which the portfolio using this call buying strategy will underperform the market in a broad market rally.

Leverage with Out-of-the Money Calls

In this strategy, a quantity of out-of-the-money calls greater than the portfolio-equivalent number is purchased so that the portfolio's performance will be increased by the leverage aspect of options. Determining the quantity to be purchased is a subjective decision. One commonly employed practice is to calculate the dollar amount required to purchase at-the-money calls as in strategy 1 and then use that dollar amount to purchase as many out-of-the-money calls as possible from strategy 2. In this case, $475,202, the amount used to purchase index call options in strategy 1, will purchase 950 out-of-the-money 270 calls ($475,202 divided by $500 each). The upside leverage payoff of this strategy is demonstrated in Table 5–11.

If the market rallies to an index level of 300, a 17.6 percent advance, this cash-plus-calls portfolio increases by 25.4 percent, outperforming the market by 7.8 percent. At an index level of 315, this portfolio outperforms the market by 16.5 percent.

This portfolio will continue to outperform the index at an increasing rate because 950 calls with a strike price of 270 represent the portfolio equivalent of $25,650,000 ($27,000 × 950). By comparison, a $10 million portfolio at an index level of 255 would have grown only to $10,588,235 at an index level of 270.

Upside leverage does not come without a cost, however. For any decline in the index level, the maximum potential loss is 3.1 percent (the same as in the 90/10 strategy), the premium paid for the calls less the interest earned on the cash investments. This, however, is not the worst case for the portfolio manager who is evaluated on his performance in comparison to the performance of the market and his peers. The worst case for the manager occurs when the market rallies only slightly to an index level of 270. At this point, the index has risen 5.9 percent and with the 270 calls expiring worthless, this cash-plus-calls portfolio loses 3.1

TABLE 5–11
Buying a Portfolio Multiple of Out-of-the Money Calls

Use $475,202 to purchase 950 call options (90-day expiration) with a strike price of 270 ($475,202 divided by $500).
The balance of $9,524,798 is invested in Treasury bills and earns $166,683 ($9,524,798 × .07 × .25).

Index Level at Option Expiration	Index Percent Change	Cash Plus Interest Earned	Call Option Value	Total Portfolio Value	Portfolio Percent Change
195	−23.5%	$9,691,481	0	$ 9,691,481	− 3.1%
210	−17.6	9,691,481	0	9,691,481	− 3.1
225	−11.8	9,691,481	0	9,691,481	− 3.1
240	− 5.9	9,691,481	0	9,691,481	− 3.1
255	0	9,691,481	0	9,691,481	− 3.1
270	+ 5.9	9,691,481	0	9,691,481	− 3.1
285	+11.8	9,691,481	$1,425,000	11,116,481	+11.2
300	+17.6	9,691,481	2,850,000	12,541,481	+25.4
315	+23.5	9,691,481	4,275,000	13,966,481	+40.0

percent. This means that the portfolio has underperformed the market by 9 percent.

Choosing the Appropriate Call Buying Strategy

Table 5–12 summarizes and compares the percentage changes in the portfolio for call buying strategies 1, 2, and 3 at various index levels.

Different payoff opportunities for each imply that various market environments and outlooks lead to the selection of each method.

Again, there are important considerations in selecting the appropriate strategy. The first is the cost of the strategy; the second is the risk. Risk is defined in terms of comparing the performance of the cash-plus-calls portfolio and the overall market performance. Market opinion, in all the required specificity described earlier, must be taken into account and the benefit to be derived from buying calls must be clearly identified. Other considerations are the time frame for implementation and the implied volatility level. Finally, no strategy can be used continuously, so the next section reviews how often a particular one might reasonably be implemented.

TABLE 5–12
Comparison of Results in Index Call Buying Strategies 1, 2, 3

Index Level at Option Expiration	Index Percent Change	Percent Change Strategy 1	Percent Change Strategy 2	Portfolio Percent Change Strategy 3
195	−23.5%	− 3.1%	− 0.2%	− 3.1%
210	−17.6	− 3.1	− 0.2	− 3.1
225	−11.8	− 3.1	− 0.2	− 3.1
240	− 5.9	− 3.1	− 0.2	− 3.1
255	0	− 3.1	− 0.2	− 3.1
270	+ 5.9	+ 2.8	− 0.2	− 3.1
285	+11.5	+ 8.7	+ 5.6	+11.2
300	+17.6	+14.5	+11.5	+25.4
315	+23.5	+20.4	+17.4	+40.0

Initial portfolio value $10 million
S&P 100 at 255.
   Strategy 1: Buying 392 at-the-money calls (a portfolio equivalent quantity).
   Strategy 2: Buying 392 out-of-the-money calls (a portfolio equivalent quantity).
   Strategy 3: Buying 950 out-of-the-money calls (a portfolio multiple quantity).

Analysis for Choosing Index Call Buying Strategy 3
Gaining Leverage

The payoff table for this strategy shows the model $10 million portfolio significantly outperforming the general market in a major rally. Consequently, market opinion must be extremely bullish for the very near term. Specifically, the portfolio manager must be looking for an increase in the index level from 255 to at least 285, an 11.5 percent market advance. Above that level, the cash-plus-calls portfolio increasingly outperforms the market. This move must be expected to begin in the very near future, probably within two to four weeks.

Although it may come as a surprise to many investors, this kind of rally occurs, on average, nearly once per year. Such a rally occurred in August 1982 when the Dow Jones Industrial Average rallied from 790 to 950 (a 20 percent advance) in two weeks. Table 5–13 lists similar moves since 1970.

This strategy would be employed to take advantage of the leverage aspect of options. A portfolio manager who employs this strategy must

TABLE 5–13
19 Times in 20 Years

	Start Date	DJIA	Finish Date	DJIA	Number of Days	Percent Rise
1.	5/26/70	628	6/19/70	728	24	15.9%
2.	7/7/70	669	9/8/70	773	63	15.5
3.	11/19/70	775	2/16/71	890	89	17.9
4.	11/23/71	790	1/18/72	917	56	16.0
5.	10/16/72	921	1/11/73	1,067	87	15.8
6.	8/22/73	851	10/29/73	985	67	15.7
7.	9/30/74	598	11/6/74	692	37	15.7
8.	12/9/74	579	2/21/79	749	74	29.3
9.	4/7/75	742	6/30/75	878	84	18.3
10.	12/8/75	821	2/25/75	994	79	21.0
11.	3/1/78	743	5/17/78	858	77	15.4
12.	3/27/80	730	6/17/80	887	82	21.5
13.	8/9/82	770	10/22/82	1,051	74	36.4
14.	2/2/83	1,046	4/29/83	1,226	86	17.2
15.	10/7/85	1,324	12/30/85	1,550	84	17.0
16.	1/22/86	1,502	4/21/86	1,856	88	23.5
17.	1/5/87	1,971	4/3/87	2,390	87	21.2
18.	5/29/87	2,291	8/25/87	2,722	88	18.8
19.	12/4/87	1,766	2/29/88	2,071	86	17.2

Between 1969 and 1988 the DJIA rose more than 15 percent 19 times in less than 90 days.

be sufficiently confident of a short-term bullish market opinion that allows for a possible reward, despite the risk of underperforming the market by 9.0 percent.

The time frame for this strategy is necessarily short. The portfolio manager's unusually bullish forecast must be prompted by something—a news event, a technical condition in the market, or some other pending development. Generally speaking, in such a situation the manager will know within two weeks to a month if his or her forecast is being realized. Consequently, the time to liquidate the option position is when the strategy is successful or when it becomes apparent that it is not working.

Deciding which options to buy is another matter. Expecting a major rally to begin in the next two to four weeks does not mean that the front-month options are necessarily the right choice. This strategy is a short-term bullish volatility play, and two events can make it profitable: a market rally or an increase in implied volatility. With the front-month options so close to expiration, it is unlikely that they will benefit much from an increase in implied volatility. Also, if the market rally starts later than expected, these options can expire just before the market rallies through the strike price. Farther out options have a higher absolute cost, but have the advantages of benefiting from an increase in implied volatility and a longer life to enable a bullish market forecast to materialize. A portfolio manager must weigh these trade-offs when choosing which option expiration to buy.

Implied volatility is an important consideration when buying the farther out options. If the strategy is to buy 90-day options and sell them in two to four weeks if the rally has not started, the buy decision is best implemented with a thorough knowledge of implied volatility levels. Implied volatility changes can have a greater impact on the price of a 90-day option than time decay. If, instead, the strategy is to buy front-month options with three to four weeks until expiration and let them expire if the rally does not occur, implied volatility is not important. In this situation, the approach is to take a low-cost, short-term option risk; the total price, not implied volatility, can be the most important factor.

The considerations for index call buying strategies are summarized in Table 5–14.

Analysis for Choosing Index Call Buying Strategy 2
Strategy 2 (buying a portfolio equivalent of out-of-the-money calls) is employed for completely different reasons and has completely different criteria than does strategy 3, yet both use out-of-the-money calls.

TABLE 5–14
Index Call Buying Strategy Selection Grid

	Strategy 1 Buying a Portfolio Equivalent of At-the-Money Calls	Strategy 2 Buying a Portfolio Equivalent of Out-of-the- Money Calls	Strategy 3 Buying a Portfolio Multiple of Out-of-the- Money Calls
Cost	4.75%	2.00%	4.75%
Risk	Underperform general market by 3.1%	Underperform general market by 6.1%	Underperform general market by 10%
Specific market opinion	Bullish on pending developments, worried about sharp down move	Short-term bearish but worried about missing big market advance	Very bullish short term
Benefit of options	Expensive insurance (no deductible)	Low-cost insurance	Leverage
Time frame of implementation	1 month maximum	Buy 3–6 month options; willing to let them expire	2–6 weeks, then close out if not successful
Implied volatility	Should be on low end of range	Not an important consideration	Important consideration: Need low implied volatility
Expected frequency of use	As needed, depending on cash position of portfolio	As needed, depending on cash position of portfolio	Once every year, on average

Examining payoff Table 5–10, one can ask: Why would a portfolio manager be willing to risk underperforming the market by 6 percent? The answer is that he or she has a bearish outlook and purchases calls for insurance. This strategy could be employed near the end of a bear market when a portfolio manager is in cash and still bearish, but is looking for an acceptable price level at which to buy stocks. This manager is looking for the market to bottom in the next two to four months and is planning to be fully invested at that point. In the meantime, upside protection is needed in case the market rallies sharply and unexpectedly, as it so often does at the end of bear markets. By owning call options, the portfolio manager insures participation in an upside rally.

Had this strategy been employed during the 20 percent market rise in August 1982, a cash-plus-calls portfolio could have increased by 14 percent. It underperformed the market by 6 percent, but the portfolio manager was bearish and out of stocks. The cost of options was approximately equal to interest income, and the options were an insurance policy against missing a big market rally.

The optimal time frame for any conventional insurance policy is for as long as possible. With this strategy, the manager must determine over what time period the portfolio will become fully invested, and plan the option purchase for that period. Generally, with this strategy, options would be purchased with a view to carrying them until expiration. If the market did not rally while this portfolio was becoming fully invested, the options would expire worthless—similar to any insurance policy expiring when no claim is made. The benefit to the portfolio in this case is the ability to buy individual equities at a lower market level.

Implied volatility is not a major consideration here. A few out-of-the-money options are being purchased, and changes in implied volatility is not a meaningful percentage of the total portfolio. This strategy is designed as insurance against a major market move, so it is not likely that these options would be sold in the event of a quick market run-up or an increase in implied volatility. Doing so would eliminate the insurance before the portfolio was invested in equities.

This strategy can be employed whenever one has cash to invest, and when one is short-to-medium-term bearish and waiting to buy individual equities. That might be as infrequently as at the end of each bear market cycle, or as frequently as when new funds are received for investing in equities.

Analysis for Choosing Index Call Buying Strategy 1
Strategy 1 (buying a portfolio equivalent of at-the-money calls) is similar to strategy 2 in that the portfolio participates in a market rally but underperforms the market—in this case by 3.1 percent. Also, at-the-money calls are more than twice as expensive as out-of-the-money calls.

What then must the market forecast be, and why purchase these expensive calls? The market forecast must be bullish, but the reason, again, is insurance.

There are two classic situations when this strategy is appropriate. The first is a major news event such as a presidential election. The portfolio manager predicts that the market will rally sharply after the election, but he or she realizes that the election results may cause the market to decline. In this situation, underperforming the market by 3.1 percent on the upside is a favorable trade-off relative to outperforming the market on the downside—a maximum loss of 3.1 percent versus a potentially significant market decline.

The second situation is one in which the money manager cannot afford to lose due to contractual obligations and, without the limited risk nature of call options, would otherwise be forced to buy only fixed income investments. For example, assume a corporate treasurer must make a fixed pension contribution at some point in the future. If the money is available now and the treasurer is bullish, equities would not be appropriate due to the risk of a market decline. Any available funds, however, in excess of the fixed obligation (interest or excess accumulated funds) could be used to purchase call options, thereby insuring participation in a market rally.

In this strategy, the market forecast is more important than the implied volatility level of the options. Obviously, buying options when implied volatility levels are low is always advantageous. But with this strategy, matching the market forecast to the break-even index level of the call option strategy is the determining consideration. For example, in a bull market, when new investment funds are coming to a portfolio manager, index calls may be the quickest and easiest way to commit the funds to the market.

DYNAMIC HEDGING INCREASES
MARKET EXPOSURE

Using call options to provide additional market exposure is a strategy with different implications than the insurance and leverage strategies just discussed. The goal here is to replicate market performance during the time it takes to shift a portfolio from cash investments into individual equity issues.

For example, assume that the S&P 500 Index is currently at 248. Anticipating a rapid advance in the market, the professional manager decides to commit an added $5 million to equities. Market exposure is initially increased by purchasing S&P 500 index calls. The plan is that stocks will be purchased as specific issues are selected and the amounts to be invested in each are determined. This professional investor decides to use one-month S&P 500 calls with a 245 strike. These sell for $5 3/4 and have an estimated delta of .70. To create an immediate $5 million exposure to the market on a point-for-point basis, 288 calls are bought [$5 million exposure/($100 multiplier × 248 index value × .70 delta)]. This represents an initial outlay of $165,600 ($575 premium × 288 calls).

One week later, the manager purchases a group of stocks to make up a $5 million equity investment. Assuming that the S&P 500 advances to 252 and the calls are trading at $8 3/8, then the call position is valued at $241,200 ($837.50 × 288 calls). The calls can then be sold for a net profit of $75,600 ($241,200 − $165,600) as the stocks are purchased. Assuming that the selected stocks increased in proportion to the index, the outlay for the stocks will be $5,080,600. The $80,600 increase in stock price is mostly offset by the $75,600 profit in the option position, which provided immediate participation in the market advance.

A logical question is, what would have happened if the market declined? Quite simply, the loss on the index calls would have been largely offset by the decrease in the purchase price of the stocks. Remember that the calls were purchased so that market exposure was increased immediately, with results very nearly the same as purchasing a portfolio of equities.

This strategy is sometimes called *dynamic hedging,* because the delta of an option changes as the index level changes. Consequently, maintaining approximate equality between the initially desired portfolio and the index options requires buying and selling options as the market fluctuates. This process is known as *adjusting* and explains why the strategy is dynamic.

In the example just given, assume that on the day the 288 calls are purchased the market rallies to an index level of 250, the options increase to 7 1/8, and the delta of each one rises to .75. At this point, a $5,000,000 equity portfolio would have risen to $5,040,000 [$5,000,000 × (250/248)]; 288 calls with a delta of .75, however, replicate a $5,400,000 portfolio (288 × 25 index level × $100 multiplier × .75 delta). The proper number of calls for a $5,040,000 portfolio is 269 [$5,040,000/(250 index level × $100 multiplier × .75 delta)]. Consequently, at the end of day one, with the index up 2 points, 19 calls would be sold so that the call option position remained in balance with the desired equity portfolio.

To make this successful, the time period must be chosen carefully and the portfolio manager must have considerable knowledge of implied volatility levels. This is a very short-term strategy. Time decay is a significant element here. If options are held too long, it is possible that time decay can take away all, or at least most of, the profit from owning them during a market rally. Depending on which options are purchased, this strategy is most effective in the two-to-four-week time frame.

Changes in implied volatility can also impact this strategy. The call option purchaser must have a basis for believing that implied volatility is not going to decline significantly during the period that dynamic hedging is implemented. Forecasting implied volatility requires knowledge and experience, but is not an impossibly difficult task.

REDUCING VOLATILITY BY WRITING COVERED CALLS

Covered call writing is a popular strategy among institutional investors. Selling call options against individual stocks reduces the variability of returns associated with stock ownership and enhances returns in stable or declining markets. Writing S&P 500 Index calls against a well-diversified portfolio can provide the same benefits on a portfolio-wide basis.

For example, assume that the S&P 500 Index is at 250 and that a diversified $10 million portfolio approximately matches the index and yields 3.4 percent. Expecting the market to remain within a 10 percent range over the next three months, the manager decides to sell 90-day, at-the-money index calls with a premium of 12 1/2. Dividing the value of the portfolio by the contract size times the index level, you can determine that 400 index calls can be sold against this portfolio [$10,000,000/ (250 index level × $100 multiplier)].

Figure 5–2 illustrates the return profile for this position at expiration under different market conditions.

In Table 5–15, column 4 lists changes in the call position under different market scenarios. Assuming that the stocks increase in proportion to the index, if the market advances 10 percent by expiration, the value of the portfolio will increase by $1 million. The value of the call option at expiration is 25, which is the in-the-money amount (275 − 250). Loss on the short call position is $12 1/2, which is the in-the-money amount minus the premium received ($25 − 12 1/2). Therefore, the total call position shows a $500,000 loss ($1,250 per contract × 400 contracts). If the call option expires at- or out-of-the money, it will expire worthless and the seller will keep the total $500,000 premium.

FIGURE 5–2

Writing Index Calls against an Equity Portfolio (reduces volatility while increasing cash flow)

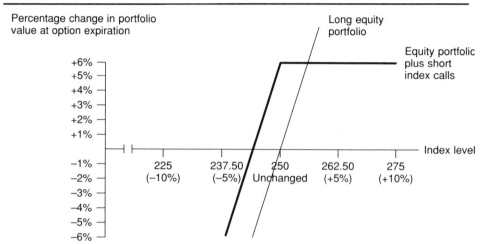

Column 6 in Table 5–15 shows a three-month portfolio dividend of $85,000 (3.4 percent annual yield for three months on $10 million). The dividend is constant and is not dependent on market movements. The net change in the combined option/stock position is indicated in column 7, which is the sum of the values in columns 3, 4, and 6. The maximum profit from the combined position is $585,000. No matter how far the index advances, there is no potential for appreciation beyond the premium. Should the market decline, the combined position will outperform a position consisting of only stocks. If the market declines by 5 percent, the value of a stock portfolio will decline by $500,000 less dividends of $85,000, while the value of the portfolio covered with call options will actually increase by the amount of the dividend.

The premiums earned by writing covered calls provide a cushion against loss in a declining market, and extra income in a flat market. This is an effective strategy for institutional investors who: (1) want to supplement the dividend income of a portfolio, (2) want to reduce the downside risk of a portfolio, (3) are willing to exchange upside potential for downside protection, or (4) believe that call premiums are overvalued.

The risk-reward characteristics of a covered writing strategy changes, depending on whether in-the-money or out-of-the-money op-

TABLE 5–15
Writing Index Calls on a Diversified Portfolio

1 Range of Market Outcome	2 S&P 100 Expiration Level	3 Change in Equity Position	4 Change in Options' Position	5 Value of Options' Position	6 Dividends	7 Profit/ Loss Combined Portfolio	8 Value of Combined Portfolio	9 Percent Change (unannualized)	10 Profit/ Loss Portfolio	11 Value of Unprotected Portfolio
10%	275	$1,000,000	$-500,000	$1,000,000	$85,000	$585,000	$10,585,000	5.85%	$1,085,000	$11,085,000
5	262.50	500,000	-0-	500,000	85,000	585,000	10,585,000	5.85	585,000	10,585,000
0	250	-0-	500,000	-0-	85,000	585,000	10,585,000	5.85	85,000	10,085,000
-5	237.50	-500,000	500,000	-0-	85,000	85,000	10,085,000	0.85	-415,000	9,585,000
-10	225	-1,000,000	500,000	-0-	85,000	(415,000)	9,585,000	-4.15	-915,000	9,085,000

FIGURE 5–3

Writing Index Calls against an Equity Portfolio (a comparison of strike price selection)

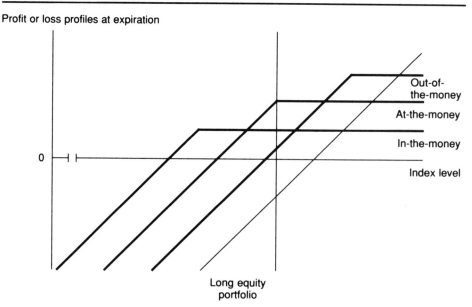

Profit or loss profiles at expiration

Out-of-the-money

At-the-money

In-the-money

Index level

0

Long equity portfolio

tions are used. Some differences are graphically presented in Figure 5–3. A portfolio manager who writes in-the-money options exchanges upside potential for premium income that provides downside protection. The more a call is in-the-money, the more protection it provides. A manager who writes at- or out-of-the-money options participates more fully in a market advance, but limits downside protection on the portfolio. Whether the option is in- or out-of-the-money, however, covered call writing does not totally insulate a portfolio from a severe market decline.

The Fence Strategy

To build a *fence* around possible returns, combine two strategies previously discussed: buying an index put option for insurance and, at the same time, selling an index call to reduce volatility and enhance portfolio income. This is demonstrated graphically in Figure 5–4 and numerically in Table 5–16. With an overall market decline, the long index puts limit the possible loss, while the returns from a market advance are limited by the sale of the index calls.

FIGURE 5–4
Fence Strategy

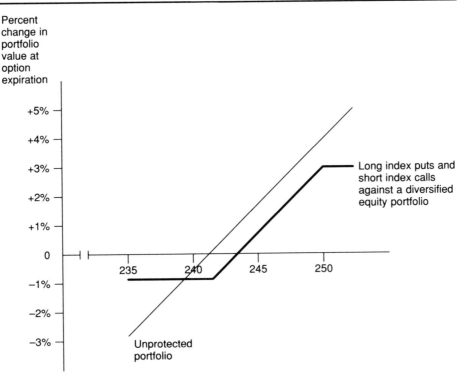

Percent change in portfolio value at option expiration

Long index puts and short index calls against a diversified equity portfolio

Unprotected portfolio

There is no real insurance analogy for the combination of these two strategies. This strategy is based on the portfolio manager's desire to lower the net cost of insurance (the put purchase) by giving up some upside profit potential (the covered call sale). A portfolio manager who expects the market to decline sharply, but feels that implied volatility levels are too high, might consider simultaneously selling a call option and buying a put option.

For example, with the S&P 100 Index at 241.00, a $10 million portfolio can be insured for 60 days by buying 414 240 puts [$10,000,000/ (241.00 × $100)]. At a price of 8 3/8 each, the total cost is $346,725 (414 × 837.50). The index level at which the put option purchase breaks even is 231.50 (240 − 8 1/2). This represents a market decline of 4 percent ((241.00 − 231.50)/241.00). The cost of the puts could be re-duced by selling the index calls with a 250 strike price for $5 each. The total premium received from the sale of 414 calls would be $207,000 ($500 × 414). This would lower the net cost of the strategy to $144,900.

TABLE 5–16
The Fence Strategy with a Diversified Portfolio

1 Range of Market Outcome	2 S&P 100 Expiration Level	3 Change in Equity Position	4 Change in Options' Position	5 Value of Options' Position	6 Dividends	7 Profit/(Loss) Combined Portfolio	8 Value of Combined Portfolio	9 Percent Change (unannualized)	10 Profit/(Loss) Unprotected Portfolio	11 Value of Unprotected Portfolio
10%	265	$1,000,000	$(765,900)	$−621,000	$85,000	$319,100	$10,319,100	3.2%	$1,085,000	$11,085,000
3.7	250	370,000	(144,900)	-0-	85,000	310,100	10,310,100	3.1	455,000	10,455,000
2.3	246.50	230,000	(144,900)	-0-	85,000	170,100	10,170,100	1.7	315,000	10,315,000
-0-	241	-0-	(144,900)	-0-	85,000	(59,900)	9,940,100	−0.6	85,000	10,085,000
−1.9	236.50	(190,000)	-0-	144,900	85,000	(105,000)	9,895,000	−1.0	(105,000)	9,895,000
−10	217	(1,000,000)	807,300	952,200	85,000	(107,700)	9,892,300	−1.1	(915,000)	9,085,000

Sale of the calls would also raise the downside break-even index level to 236.50 (240.00 − 3.50) which represents a market decline of 1.9 percent. While this level of downside protection is attractive compared to the break-even level of the put purchase alone, this benefit is not achieved without a cost. That cost is limiting the upside potential of the portfolio to an index level of 250. Above that level, the short calls will lose as the market (and the portfolio) rises.

The risk/reward profile for the combined strategy of buying a put and selling a call is presented in Table 5–16. This table describes the returns the investment manager could expect from a $10 million portfolio protected by the fence strategy (purchase of puts strike 240 and sale of calls strike 250). Figure 5–4 presents a picture of the return profile at option expiration.

In the fence strategy, the long put limits the downside risk, and the short call limits the upside potential. The fence is often seen as a "low cost method" of buying insurance, and it is frequently thought to be excellent if the insurance can be bought for "nothing." In some cases, calls which are closer to the money can be sold for a premium equal to or greater than the cost of puts, which are slightly farther from the money. Note, however, that focusing exclusively on the cost of the strategy ignores other important factors central to portfolio management. General issues of managing risk and reward are, by their very nature, subjective. Any investment decision is a decision that the prevailing market price is "wrong" in some sense. The decision to buy a stock presumes that the market is valuing a stock too low. Option trading decisions are no different in this basic sense. Portfolio managers buy puts as insurance because they believe the put premiums relative to current market levels and their market forecast represent a fair risk-reward ratio relative to owning a portfolio without insurance.

At a given decision point, a portfolio manager should consider the fence strategy as a viable alternative, but not because of its "low cost" alone. The first consideration should be the market forecast. The second should be the portfolio's objective, and third should be the knowledge of current implied volatility levels.

The Portfolio Repair Strategy

A variation of the repair strategy for individual equity issues discussed in Chapter 4 can also benefit broadly based portfolios that have experienced a 10 to 15 percent decline. Assume that $10 million was invested in a diversified group of equities, the performance of which closely follows the S&P 500 Index when it was at 345. If the index had subsequently declined 12 percent to 303.60, the portfolio could have a value of $8.8 million. By using options on the S&P 500 Index, the break-even point on this portfolio can be lowered to an index level of 325, instead of 345. Here's how it works.

The strategy is to buy one at-the-money call option and sell two out-of-the-money call options at a total net cost that is very low. With the S&P 500 Index at 303.60, the 305 calls are at-the-money calls. A $10 million portfolio equivalent of these calls comes to 328 [$10,000,000 ÷ (305 × $100)]. At a price of $14 each, the cost of 328 calls is $459,200. The second part of the strategy is to sell twice as many index calls with a strike price of 325. At a price of $6 1/2 each, 656 of the calls can be sold for $426,400. This reduces the total cost of the strategy to $32,800.

What has this accomplished? The long at-the-money index calls essentially double the market exposure of the equity portfolio. This means that the portfolio can recoup its losses in half the market rise required by the equity portfolio alone. Portfolio appreciation, however, is limited to the level of the short index call options—in this case an S&P 500 Index level of 325. Above that point, the short calls begin to appreciate in value and therefore offset additional gains in the long calls and the equity portfolio. How this strategy works is demonstrated in tabular form in Table 5–17 and graphically in Figure 5–5.

In the example just given, note the use of S&P 500 Index options, instead of the more popular S&P 100 Index options. The reason this was done relates to the early exercise feature of American options. Because index options are *cash settled,* there is an additional risk in applying the repair strategy to a portfolio, a risk that does not exist when using equity options to repair a loss on an individual stock.

In the case of the equity options repair strategy, early exercise does not create additional risk, because the exercised short call can be met by delivering stock or by assuming a short stock position which can then be met by the exercise of the lower strike price call option. For instance, assume the owner of a $44 stock decided to repair his unrealized loss by purchasing one $45 call and selling two $50 calls with the same expiration date. And assume the stock then rose to $55 and one week prior to expiration, both short $50 calls were exercised. Against one of these $50 calls he delivered his long 100 shares of stock; against the other $50 call he exercised his $45 call, which enabled him to deliver stock against the

TABLE 5–17
Portfolio Values at Option Expiration

Equity Portfolio	Index Level	Percent Gain	Long 328 305 Calls	Short 656 325 Calls	Total Portfolio Value*
$ 8,800,000	303.60	0	0	0	$ 8,800,000
8,840,480	305.00	.46%	0	0	8,840,480
8,985,680	310.00	2.11	$ 164,000	0	9,149,680
9,130,000	315.00	3.75	328,000	0	9,458,000
9,275,000	320.00	5.40	492,000	0	9,767,200
9,420,400	325.00	7.05	656,000	0	10,076,400
9,565,600	330.00	8.70	820,000	$ (328,000)	10,057,600
9,709,920	335.00	10.34	984,000	(656,000)	10,037,920
9,855,120	340.00	11.99	1,148,000	(984,000)	10,019,120
10,000,320	345.00	13.64	1,312.000	(1,312,000)	10,000,320

* This table assumes the option strategy was executed at net $0 cost. The $32,800 cost in the example must be subtracted from these figures in this column to arrive at the true portfolio value. However, it must be realized that under different market conditions, the net cost can be higher or lower than $32,800.

FIGURE 5–5
Portfolio Repair Strategy

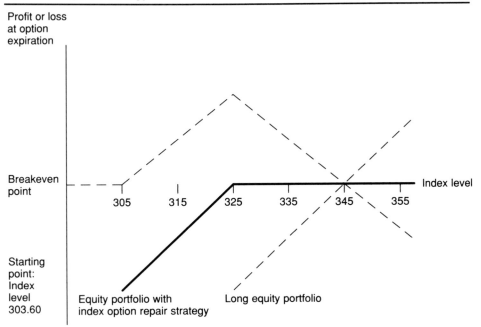

second short call as well. Between the time that notice was received of the exercise and the time he was able to exercise his $45 call, there was no market exposure because the short $50 call (when exercised) turned into short stock. As the short stock fluctuated, the long $45 call also fluctuated because it was deep-in-the-money.

Yet in the case of index options, the portfolio manager must deliver cash against a call which is exercised—an obligation that never changes. He is still left with the long portfolio and the long call options which have the lower strike. Consequently, he is long twice what is desired until he can sell the long call options. If the market opens substantially lower, the long calls would be sold at an index level below the level where he had to settle the short calls exercised against him.

The way to avoid this "overnight risk" or "early exercise risk" is to use European style options, such as the S&P 500 Index options, on which early exercise is not permitted. No early exercise privilege means these options are generally cheaper. Sometimes this will affect the pricing relationship of at-the-money and out-of-the-money options. As a result, it can be necessary to use different strike prices than optimally desired or to use an expiration farther out than with American style options.

Selling Equity Puts: A Portfolio Management View

Selling equity puts is, without question, the most controversial of all option strategies. It is viewed as highly risky and very speculative. Some critics have gone so far as to blame the October 19, 1987, crash in part on a large number of *naked* put sellers. But is all this true?

Chapter 3 demonstrated that selling puts has exactly the same payoff diagram as covered writing does. In Chapter 2, the discussion of put-call parity also demonstrated that the two strategies are identical.

Nevertheless, selling puts continues to be vilified while covered writing is accepted as a safe, conservative strategy. During an Options Institute class in July 1988, an opinion poll was taken of 32 participants. Twenty-two said that selling puts was "risky," and 28 said that selling puts was "inappropriate for institutions." Twenty-five said that selling puts was "inappropriate for individuals." In contrast, 29 people said that covered writing is "conservative." Only five thought that covered writing was "inappropriate for institutions," and none thought it "inappropriate for individuals."

Why the difference? There *"seem"* to be three reasons. First, do not overlook that options are complicated. People may believe that the two strategies are different because they have not been introduced to the concept of put-call parity. They may have also heard or read about the risk of *naked put selling*.

Second, for some inexplicable reason, there is a tendency to analyze a covered write from the point of view of, "how much can I make?" Whereas the tendency is to analyze selling puts from the point of view of, "how much can I lose?"

Third, the use of margin changes the profit or loss potential as a percentage of capital. And, typically, the put seller uses margin while the covered writer does not. Consequently, stories about losses from selling puts on margin—so-called *naked puts*—tend to be more dramatic than stories from covered writers who can brag that, "the $2 call I sold expired worthless," even though the stock declined $10.

This discussion is a good introduction for considering equity put selling from a portfolio management perspective because a comparison of the institutional and the individual speculator is most instructive. Their goals are different; the capital they manage is different; and the way they can benefit from options is often different.

It is important to make a clear distinction between a portfolio manager and a speculator. A speculator, for the purposes of this discussion, has limited capital, uses margin, and concentrates on one or two stock or option positions at a time.

The portfolio manager, by comparison, does not use margin and is constantly preoccupied with a portfolio of securities, probably at least 25 individual issues. Absolute quantity of capital is not the distinguishing feature because there are many very large speculators; however, a portfolio manager has diversified his investments so that he does not consider himself to have limited capital.

With these clear distinctions in mind, the first obvious difference is in the willingness to buy the stock on which the puts are sold. The speculator has no intention of buying and owning the stocks. If the stocks are put to the speculator, this means that he was wrong. The stocks would be sold immediately. The portfolio manager, however, has sold puts on stocks that he is willing to own and that he would like to buy at a price below the current market price. In fact, when a money manager sells puts on a group of stocks, he fully expects to get some delivered to him. Thus, delivery of stock is not viewed as being wrong; it is viewed as buying a good stock at a good price.

There is a sharp difference in goals between the speculator and the portfolio manager. The speculator simply wants to collect the premium from the sale of the put option. The institutional investor, however, is content with either of these two outcomes: collecting the premium or taking delivery of the stock. The result over time is income enhancement to the portfolio by collecting option premiums.

The very different risk profiles of the two investors is not so obvious. The speculator, as a result of selling puts on margin, stands the risk of losing a high percentage of capital. This is especially true if a speculator is *fully margined*. A portfolio manager views the risk profile quite differently. First, selling puts for the portfolio manager is actually less risky than owning stocks! Because selling a put is similar to buying stock at a lower price, the cash-collateralized put seller loses less than the owner of a stock when the market declines. Second, because the portfolio manager sells puts on stocks considered desirable for the portfolio, he or she would be very disappointed if the market rallies and these stocks were not in the portfolio. Consequently, the risk for this professional manager is missing the big market rally—quite a difference from the speculator who does not care what happens to a stock when it is above the strike price of the sold put.

This difference in perceived risk implies a significantly different market opinion when initiating the put selling strategy. The speculator is neutral to bullish and does not want the stock to decline. Anything else is O.K. The speculator is not wildly bullish, or he would buy calls. The portfolio manager, however, has the goal of buying stocks cheaper. If a manager thought prices would rally, he would buy stocks now. To sell puts, therefore, the manager must be forecasting a neutral to bearish market. In the absence of options, a manager would be placing bids for stock under the market, expecting prices to dip so that the bids can be filled. Selling puts can accomplish the same result without a stock dipping to the desired price as long as the stock stays below the strike price of the put.

For example, assume that a stock is trading at $50 and the appropriate $50 put option can be sold for $2. A portfolio manager, who is short-term bearish but willing to buy this stock, could place an order to buy the stock at $48. If the stock drops to $48 1/2 and rallies back to $50, the manager still owns no stock. If the stock dropped to $45, the stock would have been purchased at $48 and would have experienced a $3 loss. If the stock rose to $55, the portfolio manager would have been wrong and made nothing.

Selling the $50 put option, however, makes two of these situations better and has the same outcome as the third. If the put is exercised, the portfolio manager has effectively bought the stock at $48. If the stock price declines to $45, there is a $3 loss exactly as just described. At $50, the portfolio manager is a buyer of stock at $48, gaining a $2 profit. In the case of the rally to $55, he or she still collects the $2 option premium. This is a nice consolation prize when the short-term market forecast was wrong!

Viewed in its proper context, then, cash-collateralized put selling is a valuable income enhancement strategy for portfolio managers.

COVERED WRITING VERSUS PUT SELLING: FINDING A DIFFERENCE WHERE THERE IS NONE

Starting from a cash investment and going to either a covered write or a short put results in exactly the same payoff diagram. But if these strategies are used over time to enhance portfolio performance, there is a difference in timing as to when each should be implemented.

A portfolio manager who is fully invested, but is willing to sell some of the equities at higher prices, finds the strategy of selling covered calls attractive. This means that the manager is neutral to bullish and looking for a place to raise cash.

The portfolio manager most likely to sell puts, however, has cash and is looking for lower prices at which he hopes to buy stocks. Selling puts is the appropriate strategy with this neutral to short-term bearish market opinion.

When considering the market cycle over the course of several months, the distinction is very obvious. A portfolio manager should be a covered call seller when willing to sell stocks and a cash-collateralized put seller when willing to buy stocks.

CHAPTER 6

THE BUSINESS OF
MARKET MAKING

For any option order that enters the pit, market makers must bid to buy or offer to sell. They are required to make a two-sided market on demand. In fulfilling these responsibilities, the market maker's goal is to accept only the amount of risk he is able to bear and to control his overall risk by trading away the particular risks he is unwilling or unable to retain for himself.

THE ROLE OF OPTIONS MARKET MAKERS

Beyond that, the market-making function is a critical component in the investment and capital formation process for four reasons. First, market makers add liquidity to the financial markets. Whether backed by large or small amounts of capital, each one has a willingness to assume risk and therefore contributes to the overall market's ability to facilitate the purchase and sale of securities with reduced price fluctuations.

Second, price efficiency is increased by the market-making function. As will be discussed later, many market makers conduct their trading through *hedging*—a process by which one security is bought and another with equal or similar risk characteristics is sold. By acting in this way, market makers keep the prices of similar securities in line with each other, no matter where the security is traded. This condition is called *price efficiency* and the presence of options market makers increases price efficiency.

Third, because hedging keeps prices efficient, options market makers also increase the ability of financial markets to transfer risk. Financial markets are comprised of many participants who are willing to accept particular risks in the expectation of adequate compensation because they are better situated to accept those risks, or perhaps more expert in controlling them. The hedging process conducted by options market makers transfers risk between different market participants who would not, for a number of reasons, trade among themselves.

Fourth, by bidding, offering, and trading, options market makers provide valuable price information that is transmitted across all markets and is used in the decision-making process of other participants.

The Business of Market Making

Market making in the option pits is a business—one with its own special set of risks and rewards. Actually, the job is notorious for both big rewards and high risks; however, this reputation is only partly deserved. In some crucial respects, the "high rollers" label that often comes to mind when you think of floor traders can be misleading. In fact, the real job centers in controlling and minimizing risks. Despite the job's reputation, it's not the high-rolling gamblers who are successful over the long run.

The skill of market making is looking at trades, not in isolation, but in combinations to be bundled together as packages. A market maker attempts to trade those combinations that allow him to realize a profit and, at the same time, allow him to hedge away unwanted exposure by means of offsetting trades. The market maker's ideal trade is an *arbitrage*—a trade where there is a profit to be taken without retaining any accompanying risk.

Arbitrage trades are typically found in shades and colorations, not in pure, perfect form. A pure arbitrage—a truly rare find—is one where exactly the same fungible product can be bought and sold simultaneously at two different prices, bringing a genuinely riskless profit. Any variation from this incurs risk. Once, perhaps, there were such trades, when stock traders bought a stock in New York and jumped on their horses to ride hell-bent for Philadelphia to sell it at a price a point higher. But even then there was risk. Either the horse or the stock could take a tumble during the ride!

What options market makers typically look for, however, is not the perfect arbitrage, but a *synthetic arbitrage*. They try to synthesize one instrument out of a combination of others, and then to buy and sell the same package of risks for a profit. Their goal is to establish this low-risk combination of offsetting trades for a net profit on the whole package.

Measuring and evaluating risks can be a highly mathematical task, so that eliminating them is a highly quantitative enterprise. Ultimately, a synthetic arbitrage is a *mathematical arbitrage,* one where the mathematical characteristics of one set of instruments are combined to offset the mathematical characteristics of another. It should be clear that the market maker's job demands the fast thinking and discipline for which it is renowned, as well as complex analysis and careful judgment. A large part of being successful lies in the ability to spot synthetic arbitrage trades.

Large and Small Operations

Most market makers are "independents," trading for their own accounts. They trade as individuals relying on their experience and on the information they can gather standing in the pits. They can rely on PCs to help tally their trades and look over their positions after the close of the markets, and they may well have computer printouts or "sheets " of theoretical option prices over a range of underlying prices and volatilities. Independent market makers, however, usually trade without computer backup during the day.

As financial markets in stocks, currencies, and interest rate and other instruments have evolved and become increasingly sophisticated and interdependent, so have the options markets matured. Over the years, a range of firms have developed; they vary in their theoretical sophistication, in the complexity of their organizations, and in the power and complexity of their computer systems. Some are well capitalized, with perhaps $100 to $200 million or more behind them. They have developed sophisticated proprietary computer systems which employ their own quantitative approach to help evaluate and control their positions. They are not brokers; they do not serve customers. Instead, they are organizations trading for their own accounts.

These large firms can have dozens of traders both upstairs (off the trading floor) and down (actually in the pits on various trading floors). These firms maintain a presence on the floors of the exchanges that trade underlying instruments as well as on the floors of various options exchanges. They are organized to gather and make use of a wide range of information, both from the floors and from outside the pits. For example, their upstairs operations monitor news from many sources and relay it internally. They relay not only the news, but its anticipated impact, in the form of output from their computer models.

In between the independent market maker and the very large organization are firms with various structures, sizes, and styles. Some are simply organized teams of individual traders. Others try to differentiate roles so that some members concentrate on gathering information and providing analysis from outside the pits, while others function on the floors.

Styles of Options Trading

Besides differences in size and organization, there are differences in style among traders and trading organizations. The techniques market makers use to limit risk are multifaceted. While this section describes various styles, it is necessary to recognize that market makers can use any or all of these techniques during a day, depending on the ebb and flow of orders into the pits and the types of trades possible.

Day traders tend to hold small positions for very short times to reduce their risk and they often do not make any real attempt to hedge risks during the day. *Theoretical traders* buy what their quantitative models say, in theory, is cheap and sell what is overpriced. *Spread traders* make markets primarily in spread positions, which they then incorporate into their own overall positions. *Premium sellers* tend to sell more options than they buy because this strategy pays off as long as nothing out of the ordinary happens, but they must hurry to hedge their risks when an unusually large move does occur. And then there are those risk takers who "get a hunch, and bet a bunch."

These differences in style reflect not only how market makers take on risk and try to control it, but also how their attitudes differ. Some, such as the small independent day traders, or *scalpers*, are willing to accept the risks of briefly holding a long or short position. Others (often, but not exclusively, the larger organizations) make every attempt to hedge away as much of their risk as they can. This makes it possible for them to trade more theoretically and to hold their positions for longer periods—perhaps weeks—while they wait for prices to behave in a way that makes the theoretical edge pay off.

Together, these various styles for managing risk determine the role of the options market within the broader financial markets. The different styles of market making (arbitrageurs, day traders, theoretical traders, spreaders, and scalpers) determine how risk is distributed throughout the options markets and how much risk is transferred from the pits to outside markets.

HOW MARKET MAKERS PRICE OPTIONS

In a sense, the key to successful market making is very simple. The prescription for success is: Buy options that are cheap, sell those that are expensive, and yet eliminate the risks.

Market makers use a variety of approaches to the business, but few, if any, simply buy calls or sell puts when they are bullish and buy puts or sell calls when they're bearish. While most will *scalp* trades or *leg* into spreads on a short-term basis, they will generally not try to employ the long-term strategy of taking advantage of moves in underlying prices. The risk of simply taking direction bets, or taking on any one kind of exposure for that matter, is just too great. Those who do so don't survive over the long run.

All market makers attempt to control the risks of their positions, most of them by spreading options against other options or the underlying stocks or index futures. Easy as the prescription for synthetic arbitrage sounds, there is great skill in knowing how to follow it. First, the market maker must know what is mispriced. Second, he needs to know how to hedge away the unwanted risks. The two problems can be treated as different sides of the same coin. If the market maker can enter two or more offsetting trades that cancel out the risk, and if he can do this for a net profit, he has solved both problems.

Relative Pricing and Arbitrage Spreads

Market makers in the pit often don't need to worry about whether an option is actually overpriced or underpriced in some absolute sense. What matters is whether an option is mispriced *relative* to the underlying stock or to other options at any given point in time so that the market maker can create a spread and reduce the risk of buying or selling the option.

There are a few such basic arbitrage spreads that will be examined in detail later. These spreads determine the price relationships that the underlying stocks and their various options should have to each other. When the basic price relationships don't hold, there is an opportunity for profit. The first thing that market makers learn to do when they enter the pit is to watch for the basic arbitrages. If the arbitrages are there to be done at current prices, traders spread options against options, or options against the underlying stock, until their own buying and selling pressure forces the prices back into line and the possibility of further arbitrage disappears.

Synthetic Equivalents

To expand on this point, a market maker quickly learns to think in terms of synthetic equivalents. He compares prices of different combinations of puts, calls, and stock that have the very same risk exposure. Then, by buying the underpriced and selling the overpriced, he takes advantage of any mispricings and, at the same time, cancels out his net exposure by establishing an arbitrage spread. In fact, this basic technique is a fundamental part of the way that a market maker thinks when he considers what he can do at current prices.

Looking at option positions in terms of synthetic equivalents reveals alternatives. Pricing synthetic equivalents is part of the apparent "magic" in market making. It is key to understanding the professional's ability to begin making bids and offers within seconds after walking into a pit.

Let's first consider some forms of risk and examine some simple ways that the risk of one position can offset the risk in another. Owning a stock (being long the stock) is the most obvious way to take on exposure to the direction the stock price moves. Assume you are simply bullish. If the stock rises, you make money; if it falls, you lose. In either direction, the value of your position varies dollar for dollar with any change in stock price. So if you are long a stock, you clearly have direction risk.

There is an equivalent way of being long or bullish about direction— an equivalent way to acquire the same exposure with the same risk. By holding a combination of a long call and a short put (with the same strike and expiration), your exposure to movements in the stock price is identical to owning the stock itself. So a position combining a long call with a short put is called *synthetic long stock*. Why is this so? Suppose XYZ stock is trading at $100.

1. If you own the stock, you gain a dollar for every point it rises above $100 and lose a dollar for each point it falls. Now consider two at-the-money options.
2. If you own a $100 call, at expiration your position is worth a dollar for each point the stock has risen over $100. On the other hand, your call is worth nothing if the stock falls below $100.
3. If you are short a put, your position has lost a dollar for each point the stock has fallen below $100 by expiration. The short put has no value at expiration if the stock is above $100.

So the combination of (2) and (3), a long call and a short put, is synthetically equivalent to (1), holding long stock. If the stock price rises, the call is worth a dollar for each point the stock is above $100 and the short put is worthless. But should the stock fall, the long call has no value and the short put loses a dollar for each point below $100. Think for a minute about how you might take advantage of synthetically equivalent positions. At expiration, synthetic long stock and real long stock show the same net gain or loss with any change in stock price. The two equivalent positions have the same potential for gain and the same risk of loss when the stock price moves. Thus, by buying one and selling the other, you can eliminate the most significant form of position risk, namely, exposure to the direction of price movement. Buying stock and selling synthetic stock, or the reverse, results in no net direction exposure. The positions cancel because what you make on one, you lose on the other.

Not only is there a synthetic equivalent for long stock, there is a synthetic equivalent for any option or stock position. (See Table 6–1). Market makers quickly learn to price options in terms of the basic stock and option positions, together with their synthetic equivalents. If prices of any options (or stocks for that matter) get out of line with other prices, market makers quickly spot the discrepancy and consider how to use the mispricing to position themselves in the option and its synthetic counterpart.

Conversions and Reversals

You've had a brief look at the basic idea of buying one instrument and selling its synthetic equivalent. Ready for more?

The two most basic forms of option arbitrage are the *conversion* and reverse conversion or *reversal*. If a market maker can buy long stock and sell synthetic long stock (or the reverse) for a net price difference that

TABLE 6–1
Synthetic Equivalents for Stocks and Options

Position	Synthetic Equivalent
Long stock	Long call, short put
Long call	Long stock, long put
Long put	Short stock, long call
Short stock	Short call, long put
Short call	Short stock, short put
Short put	Long stock, short call

more than covers his costs, the combination of trades ought to net a profit with no direction risk. What matters is not the price of the call, put, or stock itself in isolation, but the relative price of the offsetting pieces.

For example, suppose a market maker finds 100 calls, expiring in 30 days, trading at $4 1/4 and the puts at $3 1/4 with the underlying stock trading at $100. He simply puts together the three pieces: selling the call, buying the put, and buying the stock. He takes in $1 and, at the same time, hedges away his exposure to any changes in the price of the stock prior to expiration.

Assume that carrying the stock until expiration (tying up his funds at $100 per share) costs him $100 × 10% interest rate × 1/12 of a year = 83 cents. His net profit, assuming no other costs and risks, is about 17 cents which he can earn with no stock price exposure. All calculations should be multiplied by 100 because options cover 100 shares of stock. Furthermore, of course, appropriate interest rates need to be used in the calculation to reflect actual costs.

There is no reason to think of a conversion exclusively in terms of long stock and short synthetic stock. From Table 6–1, it is clear that a conversion can be viewed in terms of the other pieces. A conversion can be either a long call and a short synthetic call, or a short put and a long synthetic put, as well as long stock and short synthetic stock.

Of course, the opposite strategy, a *reverse conversion* or reversal, can be established if the call and put prices are out of line in the opposite direction. If, for example, the $100 call were offered at $4 and the put were $3 1/2 bid, a market maker could buy the underpriced call, sell the expensive put, and sell the stock short for a net debit to his account of 50 cents. He could then earn interest on the $100 he received from the sale of the stock to generate a net positive return with no direction exposure.

Exclusive Deal on Interest
Readers may not be familiar with the concept of earning interest when stock is sold short because brokerage firms generally do not pay interest to individual customers. Market makers, however, who short large quantities of stock are allowed to keep the cash received when borrowed stock is sold. The cash is then invested in T-bills, and the interest income is a significant part of the profit from a reverse conversion position.

It should be apparent that the current level of interest rates determines whether a conversion or reversal is profitable. For that reason, these spreads are known as *interest rate plays*. Using his own appropriate current interest rate, a market maker calculates his "cost of carry'' for the position, including the receipt of a dividend (long stock) or the payment of one (short stock). He then knows the size of the credit or debit that would make a conversion or reversal profitable, and he can examine current option prices with those values in mind.

Market makers who enter conversions and reversals have largely eliminated their stock price risk, but they are still subject to the risk that interest rates will move against them prior to expiration. (For that reason, market makers may try to balance the number of conversions they put on against the number of reversals in order to hedge their interest rate exposure.)

There is no need to restrict this strategy to at-the-money options. As long as the put and call have the same strike price, a combination of a long call and a short put has the same direction exposure as holding the stock. However, parity, the intrinsic value of the in-the-money option, must be considered in computing the cost of carrying the spread until expiration.

For example, consider using a put and a call with a strike price of $90 and the stock trading at $100. The $90 call will be $10 in-the-money and will be trading at a price somewhere in excess of $10. Perhaps the call is trading at $12 3/4, and the put at $2. This means that the conversion, which requires buying the stock and selling the call, requires about $10 less investment for the holding period until expiration.

The strategy here is to put on the conversion whenever the difference between the option prices, after netting out parity, allows you to take in more than 75 cents, and to do the reversal if it costs less than 75 cents to put on the spread. This is because the cost of carry for the conversion is approximately ($100 for the stock − $10 parity received for the call) × 10% interest rate × 1/12 of a year = 75 cents.

An additional technicality to consider is that one cannot invest the full $100 price of the stock at the current rate of interest. A fee must be paid for borrowing the stock to sell short, and there are transaction costs to entering and exiting the spread. So the conversion might be profitable if the option prices differed by more than 85 cents, and the reversal might be profitable if the price difference were 55 cents or less.

To take some specific option prices, suppose a market maker finds the $90 call offered at $12 1/2 while there is $2 bid for the $90 put. He buys the call and sells the put for a total debit of $10 1/2. At the same time, he sells the stock for $100 and invests the money (minus approximately $10 he had to pay for the option spread) for a month to earn about 75 cents. After it's all over, he can buy back the stock and take off the spread. He will have taken in 75 cents in interest income and paid out 50 cents for the options, after netting out $10 parity.

Whether the options are at-the-money (or not) alters, but does not invalidate, the pricing relationship between puts and calls with the same strike. Because of these basic arbitrage spreads, at-the-money calls should be more expensive than the puts by the cost of carrying the stock until expiration. Out-of-the-money options should be priced so that the difference between the call and the put, after parity has been netted out, reflects carry costs (or interest) for the total amount invested.

If prices of any options get out of line with other prices, market makers quickly spot the mispricing, then buy whatever is cheap and sell whatever is relatively expensive—its synthetic equivalent—until their own buying and selling pressure forces prices back into line. In doing so, they are performing an important role in the stock and option markets. By forcing options and the underlying stocks to be priced appropriately relative to each other, market makers enforce pricing efficiency among the options and across the option and stock markets.

Dividends

Dividends also alter price relationships, but they do not abrogate basic pricing principles. In general, the value of a stock must be discounted by the amount of the dividend on the *ex-dividend date* (that date is the day before which an invester must have purchased the stock in order to receive the dividend). Absent of other relevant happenings, the price of a $100 stock paying a $1 dividend should be expected to fall by $1 on the ex-dividend date, and holders of record on that date should receive $1. Since the stock is worth less, an approaching ex-dividend date means that calls should be less valuable and puts more valuable. To be precise, the value of a long call and a short put together ought to be worth less by approximately the amount of the dividend than they would be without it.

The implications for conversions and reversals are fairly straightforward. If you put on the conversion—buy the stock, buy the put, and sell the call—then (since you own the stock), you can expect to receive the dividend in the mail. That means your cost of carrying the conversion is reduced by the amount of the dividend. The difference between the price you receive for selling the call and the price you must pay to buy the put—after you net out parity—needs only to exceed the new cost of carry to be profitable. That is, the call price, minus the put price after netting out parity, must be at least enough to compensate for the interest expense of holding the stock (minus the dividend that you receive). Algebraically this is expressed as:

Call price − Put price (− Call parity or + Put parity) >
Interest expense − Dividend received.

For the reversal to be profitable, the amount you must pay for the call, minus the price you receive for the put, must be less than you can expect to receive for investing the price of the stock until expiration, minus the value of the dividend which you have to pay out because you are short the stock. Algebraically this is:

Call price − Put price (− Call parity or + Put parity) <
Interest income − Dividend payout.

The basic arbitrage price relations remain intact, after some arithmetic adjustments, among all the options and their underlying stock, and market makers can establish conversions or reversals without extreme risk at all strike prices, whether or not dividends are anticipated.

Hidden Risks

From the calculations just covered, it should be apparent that arbitrage trades typically net a market maker only very small profits. The key to using these trades is to minimize any and all risks. One substantial loss can eat up all the profits from many such transactions.

This is a point well worth noting in trying to understand what a market maker does for a living. One who fails to spot a risk can lose all the profits he's made over a week, a month, or even a whole year. Two particular risks market makers must be aware of when they consider putting on reversals are especially instructive because they typify the kinds of hidden risks that many market makers learn to guard against only after harsh, expensive experience.

First, the possibility that the stock might close precisely at $100 on the day of January expiration, so that neither option is worth exercising, poses a danger to anyone carrying a synthetic long or short stock position as part of a spread. If the stock price is "pinned" precisely at the strike price at expiration so that no exercise occurs, the position can be left with direction exposure at expiration. This is sometimes referred to as *pin risk*.

Second, a reversal generates a profit because the funds received for selling the stock short can be invested until the spread is taken off—

presumably until the options expire. Any reversal that involves in-the-money puts—especially if they are deep-in-the-money—involves the danger that the (short) puts will be exercised early. Early exercise would force the spread to be closed out prior to expiration. The market maker would be forced to buy back the stock when it is put to him or her. As a consequence, the interest income generated from the spread would be less, perhaps significantly less, than he or she anticipated based on the calculation for the full holding period.

Many a rookie market maker who bought out-of-the-money calls that looked cheap—intending to sell the puts and sell the stock short, then earn interest on the funds until expiration—has found himself getting "bagged" on the reversal. He thought he was hedged against any move in the price of the stock. But then he saw the price of the stock fall and found that his short puts had been exercised well in advance of expiration. Early exercise of the puts cut off the interest income he expected over the life of the options.

To see just how dangerous it can be to trade in these supposedly "riskless" arbitrage spreads, consider this extreme, but not unheard of, case. Suppose a $32 stock goes ex-dividend tomorrow and is paying a special $5 dividend. Assume further that the options expire after the ex-dividend date, but before this week is out. Entering a conversion or reversal in this stock could be a disaster for the unwary market maker. Let's see how this might work.

Ordinarily, you might expect the 30 puts, which are $2 out-of-the-money with a few days of life remaining, to be almost worthless; and you would expect the 30 calls to be worth only their inherent value of $2 because you would expect to exercise them today, prior to the ex-dividend date tomorrow. So you might consider buying the call and selling the put (and hedging with short stock) if you could pay anything less than $2.

In fact, if you pay $2 for the reversal, you will lose money. The put is worth $3, even though it is out-of-the-money! Tomorrow when the stock goes ex-dividend, the stock price can be expected to drop by $5. Thus, assuming nothing else extraordinary happens, the stock drops to $27 so that the put is $3 in-the-money. That means that later this week the put is exercised for its $3 inherent value before it expires, so the reversal should be a credit spread. That is, you should demand to be paid at least $1 to put on the reversal (because you will want to exercise your long call immediately for $2, and the short put will be worth $3 after the ex-date). Settling for anything less than a $1 credit in "buying" the synthetic stock would prove very expensive. It is the not-so-apparent risks that can prove costly to novice market makers who aren't careful in examining "riskless" trades.

Box Spreads

So far this chapter has explained why puts and calls with the same strike price must bear certain price relationships and how market makers can establish an arbitrage position if a put-call pair gets out of line. There are also other price relations that hold among options with different strike prices, and there are still other relations that hold among options with different expiration dates. Each of these relationships deserves a look.

Suppose a market maker finds two put-call pairs with different strikes that have their prices out of line in opposite respects—in one case the calls are cheap compared to the puts and in the other, the calls are expensive. For example, the $90 strike call is cheap relative to the $90 put, while the $100 strike call is expensive relative to the put.

The market maker's strategy here is to do a conversion using the $100 strike options and a reversal using the $90 strike options. Specifically, he should sell synthetic stock with the $100 strike options (sell the call and buy the put), and he should buy synthetic stock using the $90 strike. Against his short and long synthetic stock positions, he should buy and sell stock. Of course, the last step is superfluous. The two stock transactions simply net out. He can sell synthetic stock at one strike price and buy synthetic stock at another, and the option positions alone offset each other.

This strategy—long synthetic stock at one strike and short synthetic stock at another (long call, short put and short call, long put, all with the same expiration)—is a basic arbitrage spread called a *box spread*. Box pricing relationships hold among options of all strike prices with the same expiration. For example, there is a 90–100 box, a 100–110 box, a 90–110 box, a 100–120 box, and so forth. If any option gets out of line, it can be bought or sold and hedged using any appropriate combination of three other options to create long and short synthetic stock at two different strikes.

As with conversion or reversal, there are various ways of thinking about a box. They are listed in Table 6–2. It is important for market makers to recognize boxes under any and all of these descriptions because it allows them to compare prices for various spreads, seen as components of other spreads, as well as for individual options and their

TABLE 6-2
Ways of Thinking of a 90–100 Box Spread

1. Long 90 call, short 90 put, short 100 call, long 100 put
2. Long synthetic stock using 90 strike and short synthetic stock using 100 strike
3. Long 90–100 call, bull spread and long 90–100 put, bear spread
4. Short 90–100 call, bear spread and short 90–100 put, bull spread
5. Long 90–100 mambo-combo (in-the-money call and in-the-money put, also called *guts*) and short 90–100 strangle for surf and turf (out-of-the-money call and out-of-the-money put, also called *wings*)

synthetic counterparts. A mispriced call bull spread or *mambo-combo* (an in-the-money call and an in-the-money put) can be turned into a box just as readily as a mispriced put-call pair can be turned into a conversion or a box.

Box Pricing

Like conversions and reversals, box spreads should generally be regarded as interest rate plays. They are arbitrage trades in the sense that they can be expected to produce a profit whenever (1) you pay a net debit for the options that will be more than offset by the interest income returned while you hold the position, or (2) you receive a net credit that exceeds your cost of carrying the position.

To put it differently, if you buy a box, (i.e., buy synthetic stock—buy call, sell put—at the lower strike price and buy the put and sell the call at the higher), you must buy an in-the-money call and/or an in-the-money put. You are selling less expensive, out-of-the-money options. You should then expect to pay approximately the total inherent value of the in-the-money options. Normally, the four options net out to make the cost of buying a box approximately equal to the difference between the strikes. A box with strikes 5 points apart costs about $5 because of parity in the in-the-money options, and a 10-point box costs about $10 in inherent values.

More precisely (assuming no early exercise), a 10-point box should trade for the present value of $10 at expiration ($10 minus the cost of carrying the $10 investment for the life of the options). This means that boxes, like conversions and reversals, are interest rate sensitive. The price of a box spread reflects both the cost of carry for the spread for the period until the options expire and the market maker's risk from interest rate fluctuations for that period (as well as any additional costs from entering or exiting the spread).

There are some important additional factors for a market maker to keep in mind. For instance, a box comprised of American options often involves buying or selling deep-in-the-money puts, and these puts are likely to be exercised prior to expiration. If this happens, it changes the cost of carry calculations for holding the spread.

Suppose you sell a 110–120 box with the stock trading at $100 and 30 days left until expiration. That is, you sell the $110 call and the $120 put and buy the $120 call and the $110 put. You receive something in the neighborhood of $10, which is the parity value in the box (the difference between $20 for the $120 puts that you sell and $10 for the $110 puts you buy).

The Bottom Line

The question in pricing the box is: How much less than $10 should you be willing to take, given that you earn interest on the proceeds? To answer, calculate that you can invest $10 for one month at 10 percent interest to earn about 8 cents. This implies that you might be willing to sell the box for anything in excess of $9.92—8 cents less than the $10 parity value.

But there is another risk here. The deep-in-the-money $120 put will almost certainly be exercised very soon, perhaps immediately. The box does not generate 8 cents in income, since you soon have the stock put to you and, instead of the 110–120 box, you are forced to carry the $110 conversion. (You have long stock, short the $110 synthetic stock, unless you decide to exercise your own $110 put.) Clearly, you need to demand more than $10, not less, if you want to sell the box.

As a general rule, if you are short a put and the corresponding call falls below the cost of carrying the conversion, you can expect to have the stock put to you. If you have established a short box position with this in mind (so that you have covered the expense of carrying the conversion in the event of early exercise), then, when the put is exercised, selling out the "left-over" long call can produce a bonus.

Extra Premium

As can be seen, if you are selling puts that are deep-in-the-money, you need to demand extra premium. Similarly, in-the-money puts on expensive stocks command extra premium because the carry cost for holding the stock is higher. If you sell an in-the-money put on a high-priced stock—as part of a reversal, for instance—this means that you must demand more because the put may well be exercised early, ending the income from the reversal. A market maker who is not alert to these extra complications quickly learns the painful consequences.

Advantages
Trading in conversions, reversals, and boxes gives a market maker advantages in addition to the small arbitrage profits available from the spreads themselves. Holding positions with no net exposure, but involving many options, provides a market maker with a great deal of flexibility. He has a ready inventory of long and short options, making it much easier to trade in and out of positions as the market moves. It becomes easier for him to accept some small amount of direction exposure for a short time to take advantage of movement that he sees in the market.

Consider the following example of using a box spread in a bear market. A market maker is long a box spread. He bought synthetic stock at the lower strike and sold an out-of-the-money call and bought an in-the-money put at the higher strike. Meanwhile, the stock price has dropped to a point where the short out-of-the-money call is priced below the short stock interest rebate for the stock.

The market maker can now position himself to take advantage of *bounces* in the falling market (bounces are when the market begins to go back up). He can buy in his short call with the expectation of exercising his deep-in-the-money put very soon to establish a reversal. Now, if the market bounces after he has *covered* his short call, the market maker has two alternatives available. First, he can choose to go ahead with his initial strategy by early exercising his put to establish a reversal. On the other hand, he can decide to sell out the call once again. This re-establishes the short synthetic stock position for his original box. As such, this tactic allows him to re-establish his original box to capture a *scalp profit* from the amount the call price rose during the bounce.

Jelly Rolls and More

It is November. Suppose that a market maker finds two mispriced put-call pairs. This time they have the same strike price, but differ in expiration cycle. That is, he finds an expensive call and a relatively cheap put (with a January expiration) and a cheap call and expensive put (with an April expiration), all with a $100 strike price. He then does a conversion with one pair and a reversal with the other, just as he would to establish a box. In this case, he should sell synthetic stock using the January options and buy synthetic stock using the April options. To hedge, he could buy stock to offset his January options and sell stock to offset his April position. The stock positions net out, at least until January expiration, leaving him with short January synthetic stock and long April synthetic stock.

This position is called a *jelly roll,* commonly shortened to *roll.* It is the basic arbitrage that interrelates options across various expirations, and, together with conversions and box spreads, it serves as the basis for valuing all options in relation to other options.

Jelly rolls may sound like complicated spreads—long a call with one expiration, short a call with a second expiration, and the reverse with the corresponding puts. But they are fairly easy to spot because they can be seen as two *time spreads.* And time spreads trade frequently in the pits. (See the discussion of trading time spreads later.)

Pricing jelly rolls is fairly straightforward, once you understand conversions and reversals. A long jelly roll like the one just described (long the April 100 call, short the put and short the January 100 call, long the put) simply turns into a reversal at January expiration. To see this, consider what happens at January expiration. Either the stock price is above $100, in which case the short January call is exercised, leaving the market maker short stock and long April synthetic stock; or the stock price is below $100, in which case the long put should be exercised to produce the same position. In either case, the market maker has a reversal with three months' life left in the options. Long or short jelly rolls are priced as if they were reversals or conversions with three-month carry periods.

Of course, there are more of these basic arbitrage spreads. A spread involving put-call pairs with different strikes as well as different expirations is called a *time box.* Such a combination is a box that lasts until near-term expiration and then turns into a conversion or reversal for the time remaining until the farther-term options expire.

In each case, there are risks and complications to consider. Arbitrage spreads can seem risk free at first glance, but experienced market makers know the hidden risks involved in each kind and can quickly price the spreads to compensate. They have learned from experience which spreads require a premium and which spreads shouldn't be entered at all.

THEORETICAL VALUES AND VOLATILITY

Options have a host of uses for end users in controlling and modifying various forms of risk. Indeed, options are capable of repackaging risks in infinitely many ways and can be used to eliminate, accept, or transfer combinations of exposure and risk. A glance at Table 6–3 should make it clear that different spreads carry different degrees of exposure. Option position risks can be classified into four fundamental types:

1. Exposure to the direction of the underlying security's price moves.
2. Exposure to the size of an underlying price move because a

TABLE 6–3
Risks (and Rewards) of Arbitrage Spreads

	Direction Risk/Reward	Volatility Risk	Time Decay Risk	Interest Rate Risk
Long/short stock*	High	—	—	Low
Long naked options*	Moderate to high	—	High	Moderate
Short naked options*	Moderate to high	High	—	Moderate
Bull/bear spreads*	Moderate	Moderate	Moderate	Low
Conversion/reversal*	Low to none	Low to none	Low to none	High
Long box*	Low to none	Low to none	Low to none	High
Short box*	Moderate	Low to none	Low to none	High
Jelly roll*	Low to none	Low to none	Low to none	High
Long time spread*	Low to moderate	Low	Low	Low
Short time spread*	Moderate	Moderate	Moderate	Moderate
Backspread (long options delta neutral)	—	—	High	Low
Vertical spread (short options delta neutral)	—	High	—	Low
Long butterflys*	Low	Low	Low to moderate	Low
Short butterflys*	Low to moderate	Low to moderate	Moderate to high	Low

* Denotes spreads that are one-to-one in nature and are regularly quoted as spreads in most option pits.

substantial move in one direction can undo a hedge constructed to remove direction exposure.

3. Exposure to the volatility of stock prices—the amount of price movement without regard to its direction.
4. Exposure to changes in the cost of carry (changes that derive primarily from variations in short-term interest rates or changes that can result from inaccurately forecasted dividends).

In buying or selling options, market makers take on exposure to each of these forms of risk. They can then choose either to accept them or to hedge them away, totally or partially. The arbitrage spreads discussed earlier are examples of strategies for eliminating direction exposure and, in most cases, size and volatility exposure.

Market makers would be fulfilling their role in its simplest form if they simply bought whatever options were undervalued, sold options that were overvalued, and then proceeded to eliminate all the risks entirely. Of course, this is much too simple to be practicable. In fact, market makers accept uncertainty when they buy or sell options; and, in practice, they must leave some risks unhedged. Competition often forces them to accept some risks just to be included in trades. Sometimes there are no immediate and efficient means available to eliminate all the risks. If, for example, all options are underpriced for a period, there are no expensive options to sell that will enable the market maker both to establish a hedge and to lock in his edge.

More often, market makers accept and retain particular risks with studied intent. When they find options significantly underpriced, they may well be willing to accept certain risks in buying the options as long as they can eliminate the most dramatic and potentially devastating ones.

Most simply will not accept direction risk for more than a very short time. There are many, usually individuals, whose style is to *scalp* or *day trade,* trying to take advantage of intra-day price trends by buying calls and selling puts when stock prices are on the way up, or reversing the tactic when prices fall. Even these traders trade out of their positions as quickly as possible as a means of minimizing danger, and none retain any heavy exposure to the direction of stock prices overnight. It's just too easy to sustain a devastating loss when taking on this kind of exposure.

On the other hand, most market makers are willing to accept some volatility exposure that comes with being net long or net short options. For the same reasons they are unwilling to accept direction exposure— largely because a sudden big price move in the wrong direction could put them out of business—they are willing to take on volatility exposure. In other words, if they can hedge away their immediate exposure to the direction of prices, a sudden move in underlying price is unlikely to result in a major loss. Although the volatility component in option premiums can increase or decrease dramatically, even a fairly large change in volatility would be unlikely to be devastating.

Now let's look at how market makers decide when to take on volatility exposure, taking a chance in expectation of a profit. To put it another way, we'll look at how traders decide when options are over- or underpriced, when the mispricing doesn't reflect some interest rate versus cost-of-carry considerations.

A Tool for Accepting Volatility Exposure

Earlier, you saw how interest rate and dividend considerations affect price relationships among different options, and between options and their underlying stocks. You saw how market makers determine theoretically correct option values, given current prices for other options, and how they act upon relative mispricings when they discover them to create spreads sensitive only to interest rate fluctuations (and perhaps changes in dividends).

Consider for a moment the factors that affect the price of an option—the variables in the option pricing models. These include:

- The current underlying stock price.
- The strike price.
- The time remaining in the option.
- The current interest rates.
- The expected dividend.
- The projected volatility of the underlying instrument.

One can make fairly reliable projections about short-term interest rates or dividends over the next few months, and it is simple to determine a value for the current stock price, strike price, and time remaining until expiration. The one determinant of option values difficult to ascertain—and even more difficult to project—is the volatility of the underlying instrument.

If you could correctly assess how volatility will contribute to the total value of options, you would have a handle on all the components of option value. You've already seen how market makers assess the value of the interest rate and dividend contributions. Knowing the volatility component would allow them to determine a single theoretically correct price for each option.

Indeed, this is just what many try to do. They purchase volatility research or, in the case of large firms, do their own research to project the volatility of the underlying instruments over the life of the options. Then they plug those volatility numbers into one of the option pricing formulas to generate a computer printout of theoretical values, or *sheets,* for the options they are trading. Armed with such a table, a professional can price options individually. He or she can decide that an option is mispriced, even though it is in line with the current prices of its counterparts.

This greatly increases flexibility. In addition to trading in the basic arbitrage spreads that take advantage of interest rate and other carrying costs, these market makers can compare market prices and theoretical values. Then they can buy and sell options one by one, intending to repackage them into appropriate bundles to eliminate risks. With a sound idea of a theoretically correct price, a market maker can buy underpriced options or sell overpriced ones. He or she can then decide independently to hedge away those unwanted risks and retain those he or she is willing to carry.

One way for market makers to think of a table of theoretical values is as a tool for deciding when to accept volatility exposure. If the volatility component in the option value is currently mispriced, market makers can position themselves to take advantage of this by buying or selling options and hedging away other forms of risk, especially direction exposure.

Volatility Premium

Assessing the value of options is fairly straightforward, except for the portion of the premium accounted for by volatility. It is easy to calculate the advantage of holding a deep-in-the-money $90 strike call option that costs a bit more than $10 in place of the $100 stock itself, and it is easy to compute the effect on the value of an in-the-money call when the stock pays a dividend.

It is much more difficult, both in theory and in practice, to determine the value of a call option that offers the opportunity to buy a stock currently trading at $100, if and only if the stock price is above $100 on a certain date in the future. This kind of calculation involves some fairly complex statistics and analysis of probabilities.

Briefly, the value of an option is a function of how likely it is to finish in-the-money and how far in-the-money. Historical research shows that, over time, stock prices approximate what statistics calls a "log-normal distribution" or "bell curve." This tells a great deal about how likely a stock's price is to be at any given level two, three, or six months from now.

First, researchers know that the chance of a stock going up by $10 in a given time period is about the same as its dropping $10. We know then that a call that is $10 out-of-the-money ought to have about the same volatility premium as a put $10 out-of-the-money. Researchers also know the put-call parity thesis: Put price minus call price should equal parity, or, a put and a call with the same strike price should have the same volatility premium.

Furthermore, knowing that stock prices are statistically normal over time, it is possible to compute about how likely a stock is to be up or down by 5, 10, or 20 percent during the life of an option. The volatility (technically the standard deviation of the distribution) of an underlying stock of, for example, 25 percent simply means that the stock has a certain likelihood (about a one third chance) of being up or down by 25 percent in any one-year period. From this it is easy to determine the probability of any size price move for any time period—in this case, the time left in the life of an option.

A volatility number indicates how active the underlying stock is expected to be. This in turn indicates the likelihood that an option has value prior to expiration, either because it is now out-of-the-money (but may finish in-the-money), or because it is now in-the-money and offers some protection. If, over a very long period, you bought options priced exactly at their (correct) theoretical values, i.e., with the correct volatility estimate, you could expect that on the average the rate of return on a typical option would be at least as great as the rate of return for the stock. This explains the justification for the option market: Expected returns from options should equal or exceed expected returns from stocks.

An Edge and a Hedge

Another way of looking at this is that, over the long run, you would do well if you bought underpriced options and sold overpriced ones. In fact, we can say just how well you should do. Over the long run, just enough options should finish in-the-money enough of the time that you should come out ahead by the total difference between actual market prices and theoretical values. Thus, buying options that are priced below theoretical value, or selling options that are priced above value, gives an investor a theoretical edge. The difficulty is to survive for the long run, so that trading options in relation to their theoretical values has the chance to pay off.

In the short run, any trade can go against you. Buying an under-priced call, for instance, may or may not pay off, depending primarily on whether the underlying price rises by expiration. The likelihood that it pays off enough to provide a return that corresponds exactly to its theoretical value is minuscule. Trading on the basis of theoretical values pays off only as a long-term strategy.

The market maker, who accepts volatility exposure and trades on the basis of a sheet of theoretical values, must find a way to reduce the risk that buying or selling options will produce disastrous short-term results. For this purpose, market makers use a trading strategy called *delta neutral spreading*. As the name implies, it is a technique to take the worst risks out of option trading by minimizing *delta* (short for direction exposure).

Delta

Many people acquainted with options know that the price of an option generally changes slower than the price of the underlying stock. If the stock rises $2, an at-the-money call option can rise by only $1 and an out-of-the-money call can increase by only a few cents. An in-the-money put might lose $1.50 and an out-of-the-money put might lose 25 or 50 cents.

The delta of an option is the measure of how its price changes in relation to a move in the price of the underlying stock. Technically, delta is the rate at which the option value increases or decreases as a percent of any change in the underlying stock price. Delta tells you how much the option price should change, given a $1 move in the stock.

Thus, a 50 delta call can be expected to change in value by 50 percent of any change in the price of the stock; and a −25 delta put should rise by 25 percent of the amount of any fall in the stock price. This also means, of course, that two 50 delta options change price at the same rate (by 100 percent) as 100 shares of stock.

Many traders are familiar with delta in terms of the *hedge ratio*—the number of options it takes, given the current price of the stock and time left in the option, to hedge 100 shares of stock. It should be clear why delta provides the hedge ratio. It takes four −25 delta puts, each moving at −25 percent the rate of changes in the stock price, to protect 100 shares of stock; it takes 80 shares of short stock to offset an 80 delta call.

Similarly, two short 50 delta calls hedge 100 shares of long stock, and three long 33 delta calls offset the effect of a price move on 100 shares of short stock.

In other words, delta is the number of stock shares necessary to produce a change in dollar value equivalent to any dollar change in the option. You can be *long delta*—equivalent to holding a long stock position—or *short delta*, in which case your net delta is negative and is equivalent to a short stock position. Furthermore, it is often convenient to think of the underlying stock itself in terms of deltas. One hundred shares of stock will change value at the same rate as a 100 delta option. Stock can be thought of as having 100 deltas—its value changes at 100 percent the rate of its own price, and option deltas can be thought of in terms of equivalent shares of stock.

Knowing this, it is a simple matter to neutralize the price exposure of any stock or option position, however complex. You simply calculate the *net delta* by adding and subtracting the deltas of all the component options and the underlying stock.

For example, a position consisting of four long 75 delta calls, two long -50 delta puts, and 100 shares of long stock has a net delta of $+300$ deltas ($4 \times 75 - 2 \times 50 + 100$), so the position gains or loses value at a rate three times any change in the stock price.

To take a second example, a position including three short 50 delta calls, two short -25 delta puts, and 100 shares of short stock has a net delta of -200, that is, ($-3 \times 50 - [2 \times -25] - 100$). The overall position loses 2 points for every 1 point gain in stock price, and it gains $1 for every 50 cents the stock declines.

Curve

Things aren't quite as simple as this, however. Hedging a position against price exposure can't be done once and for all. It is important to note that delta gives the correct hedge ratio (and relative rate of price change) *only for the current price of the underlying stock,* and only for the current volatility and time until expiration. Because option prices respond to changes in underlying price in a way that is non-linear, or curved, there is a further risk that a hedged or delta neutral position will acquire direction risk by becoming unhedged.

The term *curve* refers to this characteristic of option positions to change their direction exposure with any large move in stock price. Any sizable move in stock price produces an accompanying change in the hedge ratio. A stock price move can cause a fully hedged or "riskless" position to take on direction exposure and to become unhedged at a different underlying price. The amount of curve, or change in price exposure, is indicated by the so-called *gamma* of an option or option position.

A market maker who finds some expensive 50 delta, at-the-money calls can't just sell 20 calls and buy 1,000 shares of stock and be done with it. This will do as a start. But he must constantly adjust the hedge as the stock price changes, or as time decay or other factors change, for they produce concomitant changes in delta.

If the stock price suddenly runs up and the calls move into the money, their deltas rise. For example, if call deltas rise to 60, the trader would be long 1,000 shares of stock or 1,000 deltas, but would now be short 20 60-delta calls or $-1,200$ deltas (-20 calls $\times$ 60 deltas each). His position would have acquired a net delta of -200. He would be short the equivalent of 200 shares of stock while the stock price is rising.

The solution, of course, is to rehedge the position by buying 200 more shares of stock or by buying back about three short calls. Either of these adjustments probably means that he has lost money on the spread. Either he must buy more stock at a higher price to stay hedged, or he must buy back calls that have gone up in value.

A market maker can be *long curve* or *short curve*. If a market maker's position is net long options or long curve, his position responds to an upward move in the stock price by increasing its delta (and responds to a price decline by decreasing the delta). A position that is long curve multiplies the bet in the direction of any price move. Conversely, a position that is short curve responds to a major price move by increasing the bet against a continuation of the trend. Either way, the position requires constant adjustment in the face of trending prices to remain hedged and avoid taking on price exposure.

Volatility Plays

The kind of "dynamic" option trading that requires constantly adjusting a long or short option position to retain minimal price exposure—to maintain a zero net delta—allows market makers to buy and sell options to act upon their projections about volatility, yet still avoid betting on the direction prices will move. Market makers typically use a *delta neutral* strategy to implement their views when they think the volatility premium in options is mispriced. That is, when current prices do not accurately reflect the volatility they expect over the life of the options.

Market makers are often willing to take a position based on volatility projections. Sometimes this is done tacitly by relying on theoretical values that incorporate a volatility estimate. Often they establish positions quite consciously because they believe implied volatility is too high or too low and that actual volatility will differ from implied.

In fact, those market makers who concentrate on using theoretical values in making markets come to think of option prices explicitly in terms of volatility. They think and speak of options in terms of their *implied volatilities* and compare the "implied" to their own projections for volatility over the near term. Implied volatility is simply another way of thinking about current prices; it is the volatility that the current option price "implies" that the underlying stock must have over the life of the option for the price to be correct. More technically, implied volatility is the number you get if you plug the current option price into a mathematical option pricing model and run the formula backward to solve for the volatility, instead of the option price.

High option prices reflect high implied volatility. An expensive option reflects the fact that the marketplace has built a high volatility estimate into the current price of the option. It shows that the market is expecting a lot of movement in the underlying stock before expiration to justify the increase.

What market makers are doing when they buy cheap options and decide to hedge them with the underlying stock—often called *back-spreading*—is anticipating that over time the options will pay off by finishing enough in-the-money (or by offering enough protection to a stock position) to more than compensate for their current price. Conversely, by selling expensive options against a stock position, they are anticipating against high volatility, prior to expiration.

Positioning to Accept Other Types of Exposure

By buying what they think are underpriced options, traders are positioned to profit if volatility rises. They often refer to such positions by saying they are *long volatility*, and they describe positions where they have sold overpriced options to take advantage of a decline in volatility premiums as being *short volatility*. Among other risks, then, a position that is long volatility is exposed if volatility declines. What's more, a trade in favor of volatility is a trade against time passing with no action. So a trader who is long volatility is exposed to time decay, even when implied volatility remains constant.

There are other ways to make volatility plays. Just as delta measures the rate at which option price changes with a change in stock price, another measure, usually called *vega* (or sometimes *kappa* or *tau*) indicates an option's sensitivity to changes in volatility itself.

Vega tells you the rate you can expect an option's price to change with a 1 percent change in underlying volatility. The higher the vega, the faster an option responds if volatility kicks up, and the quicker the option loses premium if volatility dies.

It follows that at-the-money contracts can be expected to have higher vegas than out-of-the-money or deep-in-the-money options. The volatility component of their premiums is much larger and is thus more sensitive to any change in volatility. It also follows that a farther-term option has a higher vega than a near-term option. The greater time remaining for volatility to act makes their premiums more responsive to changes in volatility.

This offers market makers a variety of ways to spread options against options, and vegas against vegas, to take advantage of the different rates at which options can be expected to respond to changes in volatility.

For example, time spreads can be used to make volatility plays. By buying a time spread, a market maker can act on an expectation that volatility premium will rise. In general, by spreading options with different expirations and, at the same time, keeping the overall position delta neutral, traders can construct low-risk positions that profit when the volatility premium in one option expands or contracts faster than another.

A market maker can also trade *vega neutral* and thus hedge away his exposure to volatility changes. When he finds a disparity between two implied volatilities, by spreading one option against the other in a ratio that produces a zero net vega, he can wait for the high and low implied volatilities to come back into line, without exposing himself to the risk that volatility will change drastically in either direction.

Akin to the delta and vega thermometers, there are measures of other kinds of sensitivity and risk. They can be used to indicate risks to be avoided or eliminated, or they can be used to search out ways to take on just the exposure a market maker wants to accept.

As pointed out earlier, the mathematical measure of the curve or direction instability of an option position is the *gamma*. This measure tells you the rate at which you can expect delta to change with stock price. It indicates how fast an option position can be expected to become unhedged, if there is a move in the underlying.

Gamma can be used to recognize unstable hedges and to anticipate the size of price moves that require quick readjustment of the hedge. By buying and selling options with offsetting gammas (to reduce curve), a market maker can greatly increase the stability of his hedge across a range of underlying prices.

Just as delta is dependent on the current price of the underlying stock, it is also dependent on the time left in the life of an option and on the volatility premium built into the current price of the option. Any delta neutral spread must be adjusted to maintain its neutrality as time decay occurs. Moreover, it must be rehedged as market conditions change to produce different implied volatilities.

Similarly, a market maker can hedge away his exposure to volatility or to time decay by trying to neutralize vega and *theta,* the measure of time decay, just as he can hedge away gamma. Of course, when he does, he no longer has a position that benefits from an increase in volatility. Once all the risks are hedged away, the position becomes a pure arbitrage. All this can, in turn, demand further adjustment by buying or selling stock to compensate for the effect on the net delta of the position in neutralizing the other forms of exposure. Table 6–4 summarizes the types of risks inherent in basic spread positions.

Removing the Risks of Index Options

You've seen how market makers can use various combinations of equity options, together with underlying stocks, to selectively remove any or all

TABLE 6–4
Types of Exposure for Basic Spreads

	No Delta	Long Delta	Short Delta
No curve	Basic arbitrage spreads (conversion, box, jelly roll)	Long or synthetic stock	Short or synthetic stock
Long curve	Long option delta-neutral spreads; long options versus stock; long straddle or strangle; option-to-option ratio spreads; net long options	Long call	Long put
Short curve	Opposite to entry directly above	Short put	Short call

TABLE 6–4 (concluded)

	No Delta	Long Delta	Short Delta
No volatility	Basic arbs	Long or synthetic stock	Short or synthetic stock
Long volatility	Long at-the-money time spread; delta-neutral spreads, net long options; long straddle or strangle; (not option-option ratio spreads)	Long call; long time spread with stock below strike	Long put; long time spread with stock above strike
Short volatility	Opposite to entry directly above	Short put; short time spread with stock above strike	Short call; short time spread with stock below strike

	No Curve	Long Curve	Short Curve
No volatility	Basic arbs	—	No such spreads
Long volatility	Long ratio time spread (e.g., +1 May, −2 Jan. options)	Net long options	Long a-t-m time spread
Short volatility	Opposite to entry directly above	Short a-t-m time spread	Net short options

Accompanying Risks

No delta	No current price risk	No curve	No risk from price instability
Long delta	Downside price risk	Long curve	Risk after large price move; risk from time decay
Short delta	Upside price risk	Short curve	Risk from any large price move
No volatility	No exposure to changes in expectations		
Long volatility	Risk from decrease in volatility expectations; risk from time decay		
Short volatility	Risk from any sudden change in expectations		

of the risks inherent in buying and selling mispriced options. By eliminating risks selectively, they can construct positions that contain precisely the amount of exposure desired. Most frequently, they trade against the market's assessment of the volatility of a single underlying stock by buying or selling options. Then they use the stock itself to remove exposure to the direction of price movement.

In the index pits, market makers use the same approach to take positions on the volatility of the market as a whole—at least as measured by a particular index such as the S&P 100. They position themselves as net buyers or sellers of index options and then neutralize the index delta. This leaves them with no net exposure to market direction, but with a position that profits from an increase or decrease in volatility premium that reflects their own view of index volatility.

A dilemma arises when making markets in index options that traders don't encounter when they trade options against a single underlying stock. When market makers trade equity options, they have a good, "clean" underlying in the stock itself. They can be secure in the knowledge that their stock and option positions function as a bona fide hedge to offset each other because the options settle into the stock itself. Ultimately, options even turn into a stock position, either because they expire worthless or because they are exercised directly into the stock.

On the other hand, for the S&P 100 (OEX) and other cash settled index options, there is no such underlying instrument available to provide a reliable hedge. The OEX underlying is a capitalization weighted index, containing different numbers of shares of 100 different stocks. OEX options do not settle into shares of the stocks themselves. Instead, a cash settlement at expiration compensates for the difference in value between the expiration-day index value and the strike price of the options. There is no perfect way to adopt a position in the underlying index itself, short of holding the appropriate number of shares of 100 different stocks—an alternative that is simply too cumbersome and too costly to be feasible.

Surrogates

As a result, market makers typically choose some surrogate for the underlying index. Most turn to the S&P 500 Index and use the S&P 500 Index Futures (an index traded at the Chicago Mercantile Exchange). Others use "baskets" of 10, 20, or more stocks as a representative sample of the 100, which they expect to move in tandem with the actual S&P 100 Index. Still others opt for some combination of stocks and futures to serve as an accurate representation to track the underlying index.

All these alternatives share the same drawback, to a greater or lesser extent. Every surrogate shows some tracking error in any given period and, consequently, all involve some *basis risk*. That is, the *basis* (or duplication in the price movement between the surrogate being used to replicate the 100 and the index itself) varies from period to period. For any given period, the surrogate can gain or lose value, relative to the S&P 100 Index itself. Therefore a market maker's hedge can gain or lose value, relative to the option position it is being used to offset. A market maker must take the risk that his hedge is ineffective to this extent every time he uses a substitute.

In addition to basis risk, market makers face problems maintaining their hedge when exercise occurs. When OEX options are exercised, it's a *cash settlement*. This means that the market makers' option positions are eliminated in favor of cash, yet the position adopted in the surrogate for the underlying S&P 100, whether a position in index futures or a basket of stocks, is unaffected by the exercise. The market maker, left with an unhedged position in his surrogate for the underlying index, must accept considerable exposure.

This represents a problem not only at expiration, but at any time the market maker (short options) finds options getting deep in-the-money. If the market maker is short deep-in-the-money, American options like the OEX, against a position in the actual stocks, the options can be exercised on any given day. This leaves the rest of the position in the stocks and equity options entirely unhedged because the index options settle for cash while the stock position remains unaffected by the early exercise. The misfortunate market maker starts the next day with a huge *leg*, totally exposed to any sudden move in the market.

Trading a Portfolio Delta-Neutral

You have seen that the basic strategy market makers use, whether they are trading equity or index options, is to buy or sell mispriced options and then to repackage options in bundles that eliminate unwanted risks. Such bundles can be small or large, combining an option or two with a position in the underlying instrument, or packaging together a number of options with different strike prices and expirations.

Furthermore, just as you can control the exposure of any position combining a single underlying stock or index and its options, you can also control various forms of exposure for a whole portfolio of stocks and options by treating the whole portfolio as one huge bundle of options and underlying instruments.

The same alternatives available for managing the exposure of a portfolio of stocks can be used to manage a portfolio of options. Fortunately, all the different types of exposure are simply additive. If volatility exposure on one contract is X and volatility exposure on another is Y, the total exposure to changes in volatility is just $X + Y$. This is also true for direction exposure and all other forms of risk. This means the overall delta or total exposure to market direction can be controlled with index products. Similarly, you can control the exposure of your portfolio as a whole to changes in market volatility and time decay with index options.

How to Do It
Starting with the most basic kind of position, suppose you owned a portfolio of 50 or 60 stocks with no option position. Obviously such a portfolio's price exposure could be neutralized with S&P 100 (OEX) options. After all, controlling portfolio price exposure is precisely one of the purposes for which the OEX was designed.

To eliminate price exposure, first compute the *beta* of your stock portfolio relative to the S&P 100 Index, and calculate the number of options required to match the dollar value of your stock holdings. Then, by selling index calls to neutralize the upside exposure and buying puts to protect the downside, you can design a hedge that neutralizes the portfolio against any price move.

The same general approach also works for a portfolio that includes equity options, along with the underlying stocks. However, the portfolio cannot be neutralized with this simple technique across a sizable range of market values. Remember that options change their own exposure with moves in the underlying stocks, as well as with changes in time and volatility.

At any given time and market level, the net delta for each stock, taken together with its options, indicates current exposure to price movement in that stock. Simply think of *option deltas* as shares of stock currently held. By totaling the current option deltas and the shares of actual stock held, you end up with a *net delta* which tells you your position in equivalent shares held. (Note again that this number changes over time and changes in stock price.)

If you know your current net delta stock by stock, you have a measure of your current exposure in each stock. This, in turn, enables you to neutralize your current market price exposure with index options, just as if you held a portfolio of the stocks alone. By selling index calls and buying puts, assuming your overall position is long (your portfolio net delta is positive), you can maintain a zero net delta for the whole portfolio.

Of course, you are not restricted to using index options to control price exposure. Clearly, you can always buy and sell the stocks themselves. Furthermore, with some additional minor adjustments for beta, you can also use S&P 500 Index Futures to control your market direction exposure in much the same way you could adjust the net delta of a position in a single stock's options by buying and selling the underlying stock. You can use any index options that fit the makeup of your holdings, not only as one more tool for controlling direction exposure, but also for helping control other forms of exposure.

A good way to close this topic is with one final, provocative point. Market makers can control more risks than just their exposure to market direction at a portfolio level. A portfolio of stocks and options has a net gamma, a net vega, and a net exposure to time decay, just as it has a net delta. All these forms of risk can be addressed at both the micro-level of individual securities and at the macro-level with index products in the portfolio.

This is certainly not to say that the intricacies of how to go about controlling these risks at a portfolio level are easy, either in theory or in practice. It is to suggest, however, that market making in its purest form, where the market maker buys and sells options and eliminates all the risks it is possible to hedge, can be done in a wide variety of ways with a host of instruments.

Obviously, a market maker or market-making organization must have a fairly large position to even consider controlling exposure at a portfolio level, instead of stock by stock. Nearly all floor traders approach the task of managing their risk in discrete chunks, largely because they are standing in the pit where it's easier to control exposure a bit at a time. By bundling together combinations of options and stocks into groups (each of which is relatively free of those risks), a market maker can move on to other trades without undue concern over how each new purchase or sale will affect the exposure already inherent in the overall position.

TIME SPREADS, BUTTERFLIES, AND OTHER TRADING TOOLS

In theory at least, the basic arbitrage spreads have no exposure to underlying price movement—not to direction, size, or volatility. Often it's not easy to establish an arbitrage to lock in the edge from mispriced options. There are two other spreads that are not truly arbitrages, but that do deserve special discussion because they are staple items in a market maker's toolbox. They play a basic role in his or her strategies for bundling options into low-risk spreads to take advantage of mispricings and for trading in and out of other spread positions.

Butterflies and *time spreads* are themselves low-risk combinations of options. What's more, they can be recombined in various ways to produce arbitrage positions with even lower risks. For this reason, market makers learn to price and trade butterflies along with the basic arbitrage spreads even before they begin trading. Veteran traders keep their eyes on time spreads to give them a feel for price relations across different expirations.

While these two types of spreads retain some risks besides interest rate exposure, they are low-risk positions because all forms of exposure are at least partially hedged. However, establishing a time spread or a butterfly is to accept some risk. It is to take a position on both the price at expiration and the upcoming volatility of the underlying stock.

From Figure 6–1, it may be apparent that both kinds of spreads result in a profit or loss depending on whether the stock price lies within a particular range when expiration arrives. It might also be clear that there is indeed a volatility component to the pricing of these spreads, though it is dampened by the fact that the spreads include both long and short options.

Time Spreads

A one-to-one time spread (also called a *calendar* or a *horizontal spread*) simply involves buying a call (or a put) with one expiration and selling the same strike call (put) with a different expiration. For example, buying a call time spread in November, which would result in a debit to the market maker's account, might involve buying a more expensive April call and selling a near-term January call with the same strike.

The value of a time spread at any given point during the life of the

FIGURE 6–1

Profit and Loss Profiles for Butterflies and Time Spreads

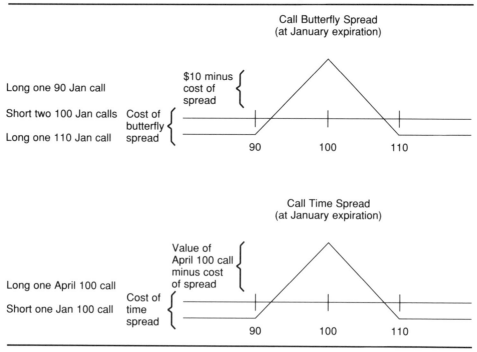

two options (including the moment of expiration for the near-term option) is just the difference between the values of the long and the short
options. The spread value of a one-to-one call or put spread is the value
of the more expensive farther-term option, minus the value of the nearer-
term option. At near-term expiration, the expiring option is worth its
inherent value. (If an in-the-money, it is worth parity; if an out-of-the-
money, it is worth nothing.) At expiration, the spread is worth the value
of the far-term option with parity netted out.

Assuming three months between the option expirations, the value of
a time spread is three months' worth of time value or volatility premium.
Note that this may not be the same as the time value of an option that
expires three months from today. The particular three-month period
covered is important. Whether dividends are expected or there is potential for important news during the period beginning with the near-term
expiration and ending with the farther-out expiration, can make a major
difference in spread value.

You may recall time spreads from the discussion of jelly rolls because a jelly roll arbitrage across two expirations can be seen as composed of two time spreads—a long (short) call time spread and a short (long) put time spread. Market makers often use jelly rolls as expiration approaches to *roll* other positions into the next expiration—hence the name *roll*. Doing so is simply a matter of trading in expiring options for others with more distant expirations—a matter of trading time spreads.

The important points to note for now are:

1. The availability of low-risk time spreads gives market makers a host of alternatives as expiration approaches besides closing out all their expiring option positions, or letting all their in-the-money options be exercised into stock positions.
2. Time spreads (and jelly rolls) allow market makers to extend pricing relationships across different expirations so that risks can be controlled, or even totally neutralized.
3. Time spreads allow market makers to manage their positions over different time periods. They can adjust their exposure in light of not only *what* they expect to happen, but also *when* they expect it to happen.
4. Time spreads, either one-to-one or in other ratios, can be used to manage other risks inherent in options besides just direction exposure. Hedging option positions with other options having different expirations provides a technique that is crucial for controlling exposure to volatility and time decay.

Primarily because they are so critical for controlling position risks, time spreads are frequently traded on the floor and priced as spreads. They are not nearly as important for their role as speculative vehicles as they are for their role as risk management tools.

Trading Time Spreads: A Conflict in Intuition

Time spreads are unusual among the strategies traders have at their disposal. They are rarely put on as freestanding spreads; more often they are used as a hedge in conjunction with other spreads. This stems from an odd combination of characteristics that make time spreads too inactive in price to make much money, but still capable of serving as an effective hedge.

It's curious that a spread that does not move enough to justify putting it on for its own sake is used to hedge something else. Although a time spread does not show the dramatic range in value that characterizes its counterparts, it responds predictably to changes in the market and can be relied on to offset the effects on another spread.

Nonetheless, time spreads are worth using as trading vehicles in their own right, and it is important to understand how they behave. These spreads have a peculiar kind of exposure to each of the various determinants of option price—underlying price, interest rates, dividends, volatility, and time. What's more, the nature of this exposure changes as time passes or as the spread moves farther in- or out-of-the-money.

Assume you're long a time spread with two months until near-term expiration (you're long a 120-day option and short a 60-day option with the same strike). Now take a look at the risks and the profit potential.

The spread, with 60 days left in the short options, does very little for a while unless something dramatic happens. An at-the-money time spread remains passive, earning little money as time decay slowly erodes the short options, until rapid time decay begins to affect the near-term options about five or six weeks prior to expiration. (In-the-money or out-of-the-money time spreads gain very little from time decay, since there is little time value to erode in the short options.) In this sense, the time spread is like a *vertical*—selling options against the underlying or against deeper in-the-money options; it profits from inactivity as time goes by.

If a time spread is established at-the-money and the underlying price moves away from strike, however, it can be expected to lose value since the spread is long time premium and the time premium in options that are away-from-the-money is much less than the time premium of those at-the-money. In this way, too, time spreads are like verticals: a move away from strike in the underlying price produces a loss.

There are some important respects, however, in which time spreads are unlike verticals. In many ways, time spreads behave more like *backspreads*—the mirror images of verticals. This makes the behavior of time spreads seem counter-intuitive to traders used to trading volatility by dealing in backspreads and verticals.

You expect a vertical, like a time spread, to gain from time decay and lose from a large price move, but in a vertical spread you are net short volatility premium. A time spread is long volatility premium. The value of the spread, after all, is just the difference in volatility premium between a long option with a lot of time (or volatility premium), and a short option with relatively little volatility premium. Consequently, a time spread is like a backspread and unlike a vertical in the way it responds to implied volatility: An increase in implied volatility benefits the spread and a decrease produces a loss.

Yet, unlike a backspread (like a vertical), an at-the-money time spread is hurt by a large price move usually associated with high volatility. If prices move away from strike, there is little of the volatility component left in the price of either option, so there is little difference between the two option prices and little value left in the spread. Not only do you lose more volatility premium in the far-term option, but there is less time value left in the near-term option left to decay. So room for profit from time decay has dried up.

For similar reasons, anything that might alter the effective expiration date—a large dividend, a takeover, a major restructuring—dramatically reduces the value of the time spread because the far-term options are worth no more than the near-terms. If this happens, the holder of the spread loses whatever he paid for it.

All this should help make clear why time spreads can seem so counterintuitive and even unpredictable. If you are long an at-the-money time spread, you want stability and you profit from time decay, despite the fact that you are long time premium. You are long volatility premium, but you don't want volatility—or at least not a big price move. You want higher implied volatility, but you don't want underlying prices to exhibit volatility by moving away from the strike price.

What makes a time spread attractive as a trading vehicle is that it allows you to bet in favor of stability and time decay, but with limited risk. You can lose only what you paid for the spread.

Furthermore, time spreads are quite predictable in various ways. Dividends and interest rate changes affect them in very predictable ways. For example, suppose you suspect interest rates are going up. Remember that a far-term call has a greater interest rate component than a near-term. An increase in interest rates benefits your far-term options more than the near-terms. You can play it the opposite way with puts where the effect of interest rates is negative.

The strategy can be inverted for dividend plays to anticipate a higher or lower dividend than generally expected. The value of calls, for example, involves subtracting the expected dividend. A dividend increase, assuming it affects two dividends prior to far-term expiration versus one before near-term expiration, reduces the price of the far-term option more than the near.

However, the most common scenario is one where nothing much

changes very dramatically—not dividends, not interest rates, not implied volatility, and not any dramatic movement in underlying price. This is the kind of scenario where an at-the-money time spread can be established to produce a profit without much risk. The risk is simply that the spread value collapses if something dramatic does happen. When a time spread moves away from-the-money, it becomes very cheap.

This risk has a flip side: Time spreads that are already away from the money are very cheap, and they have the potential to expand dramatically under certain conditions. They can function as valuable hedges in combination with other spreads. They can provide cheap disaster insurance. If, for instance, your overall position has exposure at a particular price level above or below current prices, buying out-of-the-money time spreads at that level can be an effective hedge for that exposure. Out-of-the-money time spreads are a cheap hedge if the underlying price moves toward strike.

Although they are a complex and sometimes counter-intuitive trading tool, time spreads can also be extremely valuable to experienced traders who take the trouble to learn their intricacies.

Butterflies

A *butterfly spread* is a combination of four options (all calls or all puts) involving three strike prices, though just one expiration. A long butterfly—one that involves buying the "wings"—is composed of a long option, two short options at the next higher strike, and a long option at the strike above that. For example, a 50–55–60 call butterfly consists of a long $50 call, two short $55 calls, and a long $60 call. The corresponding put butterfly simply substitutes puts for calls, so it includes a long $50 put, two short $55 puts, and a long $60 put.

An alternative way to think of a butterfly is to pair the options as bull and bear spreads, also called *vertical spreads*. A long 50–55–60 butterfly is a $50–$55 call (put) bull spread combined with a $55–$60 call (put) bear spread.

Profit/Loss Profiles
Butterflies are limited risk, limited profit spreads. Taken by itself and carried to expiration, a butterfly spread succeeds or fails to make a profit depending on whether the underlying stock price closes at expiration within a particular range. The optimal result for a long butterfly is for the stock to close exactly at the middle strike price. In the example just

given, having the stock close precisely at $55 would leave the two short $55 options and the long out-of-the-money option worthless with the in-the-money option worth a full $5. The spread would be worth $5 at expiration.

Any move away from the middle strike price makes the spread less valuable. The call butterfly, for instance, loses value from $55 down because the long in-the-money $50 call loses; it loses value from $55 up because the two short $55 calls produce twice as much loss as any gain from the single long $50 call.

Butterflies have limited stock price exposure, however. They cannot produce a loss greater than the premium initially paid for the spread. To return to the call butterfly at expiration, below $50 all the options, long or short, are worthless, so the spread cannot lose more than you have invested in it. At $60 the values of the long $50 call and the two short $55 calls cancel (while the $60 call is worthless). As price escalates above $60, the two long options gain value at the same rate the two short options lose. In no case, then, should the spread result in a loss greater than the initial investment. Thus, a long butterfly is exposed to losses on either side of the middle strike price across the "body" of the butterfly, but the exposure is limited by the butterfly's "wings." Partly because of their limited loss features, butterflies are especially valuable as *inventory*—tools for trading in and out of other positions.

The way butterflies respond to price swings is unique. With options that have a great deal of time left, a butterfly does not react dramatically to moderate price moves. Only large moves produce a significant response in the spread price. So sensitivity to price movement is reduced to a minimum if expiration exceeds 60 days.

Volatility affects butterflies, but, again, their sensitivity is minimal as long as there is a lot of time remaining. Time decay does affect a butterfly, primarily because the out-of-the-money options become completely worthless, but most decay comes in the last few weeks before expiration.

All this means that for the farther-out options, a butterfly is a very effective tool for packaging trades into low-risk bundles to be thrown into *the spread hopper* and set aside until needed. Price movement won't hurt butterflies day by day, and they can always be taken back out of the hopper when there is an opportunity to use the inventory.

Typically, the same profit/loss profile as a butterfly can be achieved by selling the mid-strike straddle and buying the surrounding strangle—a spread nicknamed the *iron butterfly*. For example, the profit profile from a 50–55–60 call or put butterfly could be duplicated by selling the $55 straddle and buying the $50 put and $60 call or the 50–60 strangle.

You've seen how jelly rolls can be seen as combinations of time spreads, which in turn can be separated and recombined into other spreads. Similarly, butterflies can be seen as combinations of bull and bear spreads, which in turn can be recombined to form *boxes*. By buying a call butterfly, for instance, and hedging the risks by simultaneously selling a put butterfly, you can establish a *double box* or *double butterfly* spread (for example, a long 50–55 box and a short 55–60 box) that is free of direction and volatility exposure. (See Table 6–5 for a look at some of the various combinations.)

A look back at Figure 6–1 should make it clear that butterflies and time spreads have very similar value (or profit/loss) profiles. For times well prior to near-term expiration, the way time spread values change with underlying price is virtually identical to the way butterflies respond to price changes.

This suggests that the two spreads might be used to offset each other's risks. Not only can call butterflies be hedged against put butterflies (to form double boxes or double butterflies), and call time spreads hedged with put time spreads (to form jelly rolls), but market makers can also trade time spreads and butterflies against each other to form an indefinite number of reduced-risk positions.

What's more, each of the spreads can be extended in various ways to produce an array of spreads with an array of risk profiles. Butterflies,

TABLE 6–5
Some Ways to Think about Butterflies and Boxes

Long 50–55–60 call butterfly	Long 50 call	Short two 55 calls Long 60 call
	or	
	50–55 call bull spread	55–60 call bear spread
Long 50–55–60 put butterfly	Long 50 put	Short two 55 puts Long 60 put
	or	
	50–55 put bull spread	55–60 put bear spread
Long 50–55—60 iron butterfly	Long 50 put and 60 call	Short 55 call and short 55 put
	or	
	Long 50–60 strangle	Short 55 straddle
Double box or double butterfly	Long 50–55 box and short 55–60 box	Long 50–55–60 call butterfly and short 50–55–60 put butterfly

for instance, need not be restricted to consecutive strikes. You might, for example, want to construct a 50–55–65–70 butterfly by getting long the 50–55 call spread and short the 65–70 call spread.

The combinations for constructing different versions of the basic butterfly are limited only by the number of strikes available. A common name for any of these elongated butterflies is the *condor*. Other nicknames for this sort of spread are the *top hat, flat-top,* or *pan-head butterfly*. Condors have elongated profit patterns, hence the name. (The body is longer than a mere butterfly.) Unlike the basic, consecutive-strike butterfly, there is no single point at which the profit is maximum. Instead there is a fairly large range (determined by the strikes selected and their prices) over which the spread earns its maximum profit. The profit profile at expiration is illustrated in Figure 6–2. Typically, condors are much more expensive than basic, three-strike butterflies because they have an extended profit zone. This squares with intuition: Anyone willing to take a view about the stock that requires the price to fall within a narrow range should have to pay less than someone who wants to profit across a broader range.

Trading Butterflies
Butterflies offer the trader a multitude of alternatives and almost unlimited flexibility. To see this, take another look at the equivalence between a basic call and an iron butterfly.

If you start with a call butterfly (e.g., long the 50 call, short two 55s and long a 60), then sell a 50–55 box (a totally neutral addition), notice that you end up with an iron butterfly. You end up short the $55 straddle and long the $50 put and the $60 call. It follows from this that selling the straddle and buying the strangle should put a credit in your account because, in effect, you are short a box for a large credit and long a butterfly for a small debit.

FIGURE 6–2
Profit Profile for a Top Hat, Flat-Top, or Pan-Head Butterfly

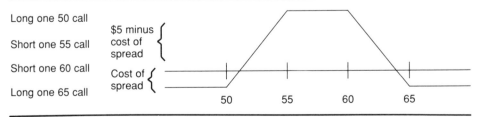

The beauty of the butterfly is that it gives the market maker the ability to make a mistake—yet various ways to correct it. He has three other sides of a trade to make up for the errant initial trade. If, for example, he buys one option, and that trade seems to be going against him, he can sell two options and wait for the third side to come his way. On the other hand, if he sells a call option and it starts to go against him, he can buy a deeper call and wait to sell the higher bear spread at a better price.

The only way a trader really gets hurt moving in and out of butterflies is in very *whippy markets*. Then he can either buy the strangle and sell the straddle when it gets to his price; or he can sell the strangle when the market is whipping back and forth within a narrow range, then buy the strangle when it comes to his price.

Characteristics of butterflies change dramatically as time till expiration becomes short. What was a low-risk spread takes on several types of exposure that just weren't there before. But as a trading vehicle while there are several weeks left in the option contracts, butterflies are a nearly perfect trader's tool.

WHAT IT TAKES TO BECOME A MARKET MAKER

Becoming a market maker may seem a simple matter of joining an exchange and starting to trade, but there is a great deal more to it. Becoming a market maker amounts to starting a business—one that could range in size from one person trading on his or her own small account independently, to a large and complex operation. Setting up such an operation requires both a heavy capital investment and a heavy investment in time, energy, and hard work.

More importantly, market-making demands some very special expertise. Developing that expertise requires native ability and a lot of homework, practice, and experience. The next part takes a careful look at the knowledge and skills market makers have to acquire. First, though, here's a brief look at some of the requirements for setting up a market-making business.

Costs and Commitments of Market Making

First, of course, are capital considerations. Trying to run any undercapitalized business is very risky. Market-making is no exception; a market maker needs adequate trading capital to survive, even for the short term.

Currently, "adequate" means an amount in excess of $100,000, even if the market maker plans to trade independently only in his own "small" account.

The second major capital consideration is arranging for a seat. Memberships on the major futures and options exchanges are now priced in the neighborhood of $300,000 to $500,000. In addition to full memberships, some exchanges offer less costly partial memberships or trading permits with trading rights for a limited number of products. Alternatively, seats can be leased for about $3,000 to $6,000 a month to leave capital free for trading.

Additional costs include initial fees in the neighborhood of $1,250, plus the on-going costs of doing business, such as securing office space, hiring a clerk, and obtaining computer facilities. Other daily costs to anticipate are paying the basic contract rate, arranging a volume discount, forking over fees for stock executions or index futures trades, and so on.

But it's more than a thousand dollars here, a thousand there. Ever think about where you train for trading pits? Well, nearly every business or profession has a structured and often institutionalized way to learn the ropes and get started. Doctors and lawyers go through professional schools and internships; engineers train on the job after mastering the technical material in undergraduate and graduate programs; and other businesses have lengthy formal training programs. Our industry, however, lacks a formal or standardized structure for initiating new traders into the business.

To make things worse, this is probably one of the most expensive businesses in which to get started because it involves such high financial risk. Part of the cost of entry into this business is the cost of inexperience. Not every market maker loses money in his first month, but a great many do; not every market maker blows out in his first month, but some do that too. Any tally of the cost of entry for the business of market making as a whole needs to reflect the enormous total cost of the collective experiences of all new traders.

When asked to add the total start-up costs involved for all neophytes— both the survivors and the bankrupt—to arrive at an average, the consensus among veterans is in the $50,000 to $100,000 range. That, most agree, is the *average cost* before a market maker turns the corner.

There are some ways to cut the cost of inexperience. The Options Institute at the CBOE conducts simulated trading for new market makers on its floor. Other learning tools include books, games, videotapes, seminars, classes, and paper trading. Computer-based trading simulators employ state-of-the-art technology to replicate the environment in which trading occurs. While these tools are no substitute for time on the trading floor, they offer knowledge and preparation that can contribute to the bottom-line of a market maker's actual trading.

Clearly, the financial investment required for market making is substantial, and there are additional forms of investment required. Before you can trade, you need to be approved for exchange membership, a process that can take several weeks, and you need a letter of guarantee from a clearing firm. Selecting an exchange and a clearing firm are important and difficult decisions, decisions which require diligent homework.

Choosing an Exchange

The exchange the trader chooses determines the environment in which he or she will work. Every floor, indeed every pit, has a culture of its own. Although it may be hard to judge how a particular floor will feel as a place to spend long days standing in a crowd of traders, there are some key factors that determine the culture of a floor.

The first is whether an exchange is regulated by the Securities and Exchange Commission (SEC) or by the Commodity Futures Trading Commission (CFTC). This is important, not only because some of the rules are different, but also because the history and evolution of trading practices in the securities markets differ significantly from those in the futures markets. The New York Stock Exchange, as you know, is the dominant stock trading institution in the securities markets. Its long-established decorum and trading style, and its system which separates specialists providing liquidity from brokers filling customers' orders, have had an important impact on the development of SEC regulated option markets, such as the CBOE. For example, a market maker on the CBOE, the dominant options trading institution, cannot act as both a broker (filling a customer order) and a market maker in options on the same underlying stock during the same day. This proscription has not been part of the tradition on futures exchanges, although regulation separating the principal and agency function has been under consideration in recent years. Capital requirements also differ between SEC and CFTC regulated exchanges.

Futures pits have a tradition where *locals* (individuals who trade for their own accounts) provide liquidity in an open outcry system that gives all those making markets equal access to trades and equal responsibility for providing liquidity and accepting risk. *Scalping*—accepting risk by simply holding unhedged long or short positions for brief periods during the day—has been the style in the futures markets for over a century. Traders can enter spread positions to reduce their risk, but often they don't.

For that reason, trading options fits into a different environment on a futures' floor. That is not to say that there is anything about the theory of trading options on futures that makes it inherently more risky, or even very different from trading equity or cash settled options. Options on futures do differ in some theoretical respects from equity options and from options on cash, but these are differences that a market maker can adjust to fairly quickly. Over the long term, it is the floor environment and culture that are more important considerations in choosing an exchange.

Other considerations include the volume and the volatility in the options you intend to trade. Not only does greater volume mean getting a chance at more trades, it also means that it is easier to transfer risk. Liquidity is crucial to reducing risk. On the other side of the coin is the fact that bid-ask spreads are typically wider when option volumes are lower (to compensate for the greater risk).

The volatility of the underlying instrument is important because it determines the premium and the fluctuations in premium for the options. Higher volatility produces higher premiums and more opportunities; low, steady, and unchanging volatility means that the value of options and the number of opportunities for profit are reduced. For example, CBOE's OEX is the most active option product in the world. Its volatility ranges typically between 15 and 25 percent, making it a relatively volatile product. Thus, OEX options offer both opportunities for profit and liquidity for controlling risk.

Choosing a Clearing Firm

A market maker's clearing firm plays a major role in his business. New market makers usually operate out of the clearing firm's office space, so the clearing firm influences all of his work time outside the pit. The cost structure that the market maker negotiates with the clearing firm has an impact on his cost of doing business, and on his potential for success.

Many clearing firms offer a wide array of services. The basic services every one offers include clearing trades, accounting services (partial), and guaranteeing the market maker's trades. In addition, the firm might provide office space, secretarial services, educational facilities, and formal education programs. Different clearing firms offer different services and cost structures. And, of course, the costs rise with the amount of service. New traders ordinarily opt for an arrangement that offers the lowest clearing costs. Seasoned traders often demand more services, but generally they are also in a better position to negotiate rates.

An important consideration for new market makers is what a clearing firm offers to help them learn the business. Some have well developed education programs, including videotaped lectures, written materials, and perhaps even formal classes. One firm even offers a computerized instructional package to help the novice learn option pricing, spreading techniques, and methods to respond to changes in the market. In addition, clearing firms differ in their atmosphere. At some, experienced market makers are very willing to help newcomers and spend time with them; at others, mentoring is absent.

Partnerships and Backing

Adequate capital is crucial to success as a market maker. The arrangements between individual market makers and their backers vary greatly. In the past, backers typically negotiated a 50:50 split with a cut-off after a $50,000 loss. But in the past, a higher percentage of newcomers turned a profit. Today, typically only one out of five will be successful. A typical contract calls for a 30 percent cut for the market maker and a 70 percent cut for the backer to compensate the backer for his greater risk.

Frequently, sponsorship arrangements evolve out of an initial role as a clerk. A newcomer who learns the business by working for an experienced trader as a clerk often develops the relationship so that he takes more and more responsibility until he eventually becomes a market maker himself, backed by his mentor. Such arrangements vary from the new trader receiving a guaranteed salary and some minimal percent of profits to receiving a percentage of the profits based on a sliding scale. A typical scale might offer no participation for the first $50,000 in profits, 5 percent participation in the next $50,000, 10 percent for profits from $100,000 to $150,000, 15 percent from $150,000 to $250,000, and 20 percent above $250,000.

There are also partnerships among traders and arrangements where the backers play no role whatever in trading. An experienced team of market makers and clerks might arrange for backing up to several million dollars by negotiating participation in profits ranging anywhere from 30 percent to 70 percent.

Success

Successful traders are often asked, "What's it take to be a market maker?" Composure and the ability to respond intelligently to the unexpected, for starters. There's just no such thing as a "typical day" in the marketplace. There's rarely a day when everything goes as expected so that the market maker is prepared for everything that happens. Perhaps one of the key ingredients for being a market maker is enjoying that kind of daily variety. It's potentially very frustrating, but market makers are often people who enjoy the uncertainty, instability, and lack of structure.

What does it take to succeed instead of survive in the pits? It takes a combination of discipline and expertise, and discipline that outweighs expertise more than in most jobs. What marks the superior trader is the discipline to execute properly and the discipline to maintain the strategies he or she intended to employ. Success requires the ability to respond in a structured way in an unstructured environment.

Expertise is crucial too, especially today. Expertise among traders has risen dramatically, so competition has become very stiff, yet profit margins are small. A market maker who is going to stand out over the long run has to develop expertise out of experience. In particular, the experience the market maker gains from facing that first "crisis" is unsurpassed. How he handles it isn't as important for the long run as what he learns from it. That first crisis, and others that follow, mold a trader, and his talent for acquiring skill from experience is a major ingredient of success.

REFLECTIONS ON WHAT THE FUTURE HOLDS

The listed options business has evolved since its start in April 1973. Market makers who relied on "market feel" and "guts" have largely been replaced by arbitrage traders and mathematicians who trade for slight price discrepancies, rather than for "the big kill." This trend toward sophistication will continue, not only because of new technology, but also as a result of the increased awareness of price risk, which is inherent in any aspect of the securities business. Because the market maker's function is to transfer risk between longer-term investors, there will always be room for new and improved methods of managing this risk transfer role.

The October 1987 and 1989 crashes are dramatic examples of price risk that is ever present in the securities business. In recent years, every major market has experienced similar volatility. From crude oil to Treasury bonds, and from agricultural commodities to currencies, every market in the world has attracted headlines at one time or another when price movements panic. The lesson for any participant is that risk management is crucial, and all investors and traders must be flexible enough to change with the evolving environment.

In addition to improved risk management, some challenges markets will face are the development of new trading techniques, applications of technology, trading structures, and extended trading hours.

New trading techniques can arise from new theoretical insights or from the listing of new products. Past milestones in the options business were the development of the Black-Scholes options pricing model, the introduction of put options, and the creation of cash settled index options. Each created a new ballgame at the time of its introduction. New products, such as cash settled interest rate options and deliverable "baskets" of equities to settle options, might change the rules again.

Modern applications of technology will continue to further the efficiency of analyzing and acting upon market information. Although computers may never replace the human decision-making process, there undoubtedly will be continuing discoveries of new ways to use the computer's ability to track prices and to identify price discrepancies. Undoubtedly, new developments will translate this information into trade execution.

Indeed, new trading structures will arise. Although the specialist system has historically dominated equity trading, and the open-outcry auction market system has been prominent in option trading, no one can say with certainty that these market structures will persist indefinitely. The CBOE has experimented with the Designated Primary Market Maker (DPM) system which has some similarities to the specialist system, and the New York Stock Exchange has applied a market-making structure to its stock basket product. What's more, off-floor computer-based trading will challenge floor-based trading. So trading procedures and rules for access that are suitable to computer usage will need to be invented.

Extended trading hours via longer hours of floor trading, or via computer-based trading, are the result of international financial markets. Trading around the world has grown in importance, and U.S. exchanges must face up to the challenge to maintain market share. Of course, extended hours are only part of meeting the global challenge. U.S. exchanges must continue to have markets with the most liquidity and with the highest integrity—or the business will go elsewhere.

PART 3

REAL TIME APPLICATIONS

CHAPTER 7

USING OPTION MARKET INFORMATION TO MAKE STOCK MARKET DECISIONS

Listed options are stock market derivatives. As such, it would seem that looking at option price data to make stock market decisions is "putting the cart before the horse." Actually there are several logical reasons for analyzing option price data. One relates to a basic objective of the option markets, which is to determine a "fair" value for the derivative security. The fair value is a price for an option that favors neither the buyer nor the seller. Indeed, the listed option market is unusual in its quest for price efficiency. While the efficient market theory says that all information that is publicly known about a company is included in its price, this market is the only one that uses a mathematical model to arrive at an efficient or "fair" value.

As you have seen in previous chapters, the variables used in pricing models contain very useful information. First of all, option premiums contain an opinion about the future volatility of the stock price, i.e., the range of prices in which the market expects the stock to trade. Second, option premiums must also take into account an expectation for short-term interest rates, since market makers finance their positions based on the spread between puts and calls. Third, option prices take into account an expectation for a stock's future dividends. For example, when a company is expected to make a change in its dividend policy, options premiums can reflect the anticipated change.

Another reason for studying this market is the nature of the use of options.

Listed options are ideal vehicles for speculation. This means they offer the potential to analyze the psychology of speculators. Options are also excellent tools for managing risk. Therefore, contained within an option price is an opinion regarding the risk of the underlying security, which is very valuable information for those who have invested, or are contemplating an investment, in a particular security.

Finally, listed options incorporate a time assumption. The timeframe is short by traditional investment analysis standards. Most options have expirations of 90 days or fewer. Few fundamental approaches to analysis cover a time period this short. Normal technical analysis does not state a time period. Indeed, with quarterly performance analysis increasing in importance, information that is directly aimed at the short term is increasingly in demand.

This chapter examines three methods of analyzing the option market. The first method seeks to determine the investment sentiment of option-oriented investors; the second examines premiums. Then the third explores the inner workings of an option pricing model in an attempt to determine the market movement expectations contained within the option price.

THE PUT-CALL RATIO

Sentiment indicators have long been a favorite technical analysis tool. Contrary indicators are those that mean the exact opposite of what they say. If such an indicator is registering a large percentage of bullish investors, the reading is considered bearish, given the assumption that most speculators are wrong most of the time. Prior to the introduction of listed options, *odd-lot volume* was a favorite contrary indicator. An odd lot is fewer than 100 shares of stock. Odd-lot buyers or sellers were generally considered to be at the bottom of the investment sophistication barrel, and thus were assumed likely to be making the wrong decision at key times in the market. The epitome of the odd-lot indicators was the number of odd-lot short sales. The arrival of listed options, along with an inflation rate that turned many odd lots into round lots, diminished the value of this indicator.

In recent years, the percentage of bullish investment advisors has become a popular sentiment indicator. Just as with individual investors, a relatively large number of bullish advisors is deemed to be bearish on Wall Street. Each week, investment advisors are polled in an effort to measure their bullishness, and the analyses are published frequently in various financial publications.

Buyers of options are generally considered speculators. Speculators are thought to be on the wrong side of the market most of the time, especially at market extremes. Logic would then suggest that an examination of the number of puts traded versus the number of calls might provide an ideal *contrary sentiment indicator*.

The CBOE publishes two put-call ratios. The S&P 100 Put-Call Ratio is calculated by dividing the number of puts traded on the popular OEX options during the analysis period by the number of calls traded. The CBOE Equity Put-Call Ratio makes the same calculation for puts and calls on individual stocks traded on the exchange. Some brokerage firms maintain their own put-call ratio calculations. The CBOE ratios can be found each week in the "Market Laboratory" section of *Barron's*.

A put-call ratio of 70 : 100 for the S&P 100 (70 puts for every 100 calls), considered as a contrarian sentiment indicator, could be viewed as a bullish reading. It takes only a 65 : 100 ratio to reach a similar conclusion for the CBOE Equity Put-Call Ratio.

The difference reflects an opinion that index traders are somehow less vulnerable to "contrary indicator disease" than individual equity players. To reach contrarian bearish readings, the ratios must record a reading of 40 : 100 (40 puts for every 100 calls).

Figure 7–1 shows the S&P 100 (OEX) Index graphed; it can be compared with both CBOE put-call ratios also in the figure. Some users prefer to plot a moving average to more clearly define the trend, thus helping filter out short-term "noise" that can be present in the numbers.

When using put-call ratios, it is important to remember that not all option activity reflects the trading of speculators. In fact, more than half the volume of trades comes from investment professionals and market makers. The percentage of public trades is a changing number, reflecting the overall condition of the market. It would seem logical that the value of examining put-call ratios would be greater during periods of high market interest by the public.

Remember also when viewing a put-call ratio that there is a direct, definable relative value between puts and calls. Traders on the floor of an exchange can "create" a put option by buying a call and selling the underlying stock short. They can create a call by buying a put and buying the stock. This process is known as *conversion*. They would choose to do this trade, or the reverse, if the prices for either option get out of line. This means that high call volume can generate high put volume and vice versa.

FIGURE 7–1

S & P 100 Index (OEX)—1988

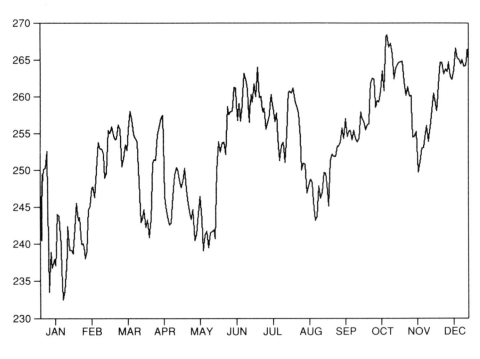

CBOE Equity Put/Call Ratio—1988

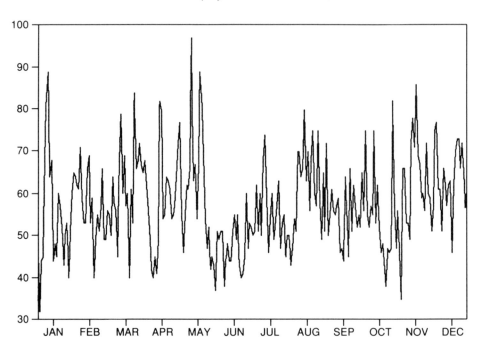

FIGURE 7–1 (*concluded*)

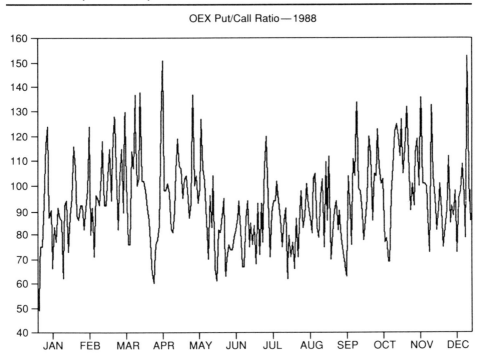

OEX Put/Call Ratio—1988

While on the subject of volume, note that option volume is a moving target. A volume of 1,000 contracts does not necessarily mean there is a buyer or seller of that many options, although there might be. When an order reaches the floor of an exchange, the market maker can simply purchase the contracts for his or her own account. If the option is not desired, the trader can offset the new position by making a trade in the underlying security or another option. Offsetting a position with other option contracts pyramids the volume of such trading.

With all these caveats in mind, the put-call ratio can provide valuable market insight. As with most technical indicators, though, successful use of the number is probably more of an art than a science.

OPTION PREMIUMS

The amount by which an option price exceeds its intrinsic value is called the *premium*. An option's *intrinsic value* is the difference between the current value of the stock and the strike price of the option. Premiums are the "product" of the options market. All of the fundamental, psychological, and mathematical factors in the market are incorporated in their value. Monitoring the level of premiums and their relationship is one of the simplest—and probably one of the most important—ways option market information can be used to make stock decisions.

If the strike price of the option is at or above the price of the stock (in the case of a call), or at or below the price of the stock (in the case of a put), the entire price of the option is premium. The level of premiums is an important consideration for option traders—and for stock traders.

Traders in general want to be the sellers when premiums are high, buyers when they are low. The problem is that what is relatively high or low is known for certain only *after* the fact. In other words, by looking at a chart of historical option premiums, the viewer can say what would have been the best approach for a trader to have taken. For example, if premiums had been declining, the trader should have been a seller, since the level obviously had been too high in the past.

Option Premium Indexes

The CBOE calculates a dual index of option premiums. The index estimates the value of a theoretical call and put option on a stock of average market volatility selling at $100. The options have a strike price of $100 and expire in 180 days. Figure 7–2 shows the put and call premium levels, according to the CBOE Put and Call Option Premium Indexes, since the inception of listed option trading. As the chart shows, both put and call premium levels rise and fall together. This is due to the direct relationship between the two, and it reflects the fact that the most important factor in option pricing is the volatility assumption, which is the same for both contracts.

Of the two indexes, put premium levels might be the most revealing and the easiest for investors to understand. A purchased *put option* represents the right, but not the obligation, to sell a stock at the strike price for a stated period of time. Puts are often used as insurance to protect a profit in the underlying stock. The seller of a put can be viewed as taking a position on risk equivalent to that of an insurance company. Just as in the more traditional forms of insurance, premium level is a key consideration. If insurance premiums turn out to have been too high, the insurance company will make a higher than expected profit. Higher profits attract other companies to the business and eventually lead to lower premiums. The same thing happens in the case of put options. Figure 7–3 shows the level of option premiums in 1988. The fact that put

FIGURE 7–2
CBOE Put and Call Option Premium Indexes

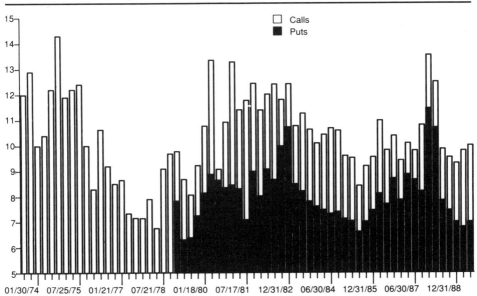

and call premium levels steadily declined during the year means that option writers earned a higher than expected return.

As is the case with the put-call ratio, a chart on the level of option premiums provides valuable perspective. Traditionally, one can be found each week in "The Striking Price" column of *Barron's*. This chart shows the trend of premium levels over the last six months.

The long-term picture of premium levels suggests a cycle. In the insurance business, the premium cycle is an important consideration. The same might be true for the listed option business, although the history of the business is still too short to make such a statement with certainty. If so, the volatility cycle can provide additional insight into the underlying market.

In addition, the long-term chart shows that the difference between put and call premium levels is not constant. The reason for this variance is the conversion process discussed previously. A put option can be converted into a call by simply buying the stock while holding the put. Actually, the process of conversion is one of the keys to efficient option pricing. The conversion process means that the long put, long stock position is equal in risk and return to a long call, long T-bill position. In order for this relationship to be true, the call option usually has a higher

FIGURE 7–3
The CBOE Put and Call Option Premium Indexes

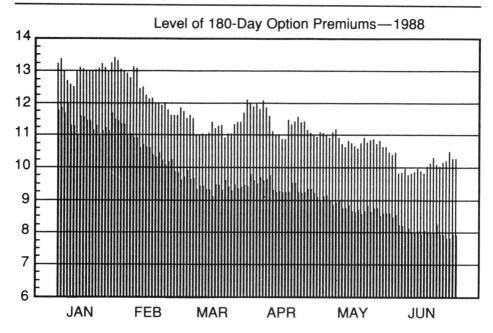

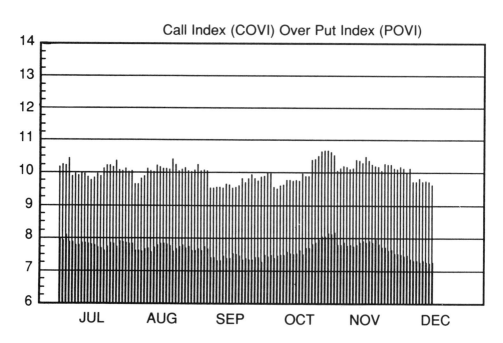

value than the put. This is true because under most conditions the dividend yield on the stock is less than the T-bill yield. As short-term interest rates rise and fall, the spread between the value of the call and the put premium index changes. When the short-term yield on T-bills rises, the value of the equity should decline, all other factors being the same. This tends to hold the put-call relationship steady.

Confidence Index
In actual practice, it has often been observed that at times both short-term yields and stock prices increase. This leads to an increase in the spread between bond and stock yields. *Barron's* publishes a number of yield spread indicators, the best known being the Confidence Index. The Confidence Index is calculated by dividing a high-grade bond index by an intermediate-grade index. Changes in the relationship are used to measure the confidence of investors. At some point it is assumed that investors will become overconfident. The CBOE Put and Call Option Premium Indexes provide a simple way of calculating a yield spread. Since the results are based on a 180-day assumption, simply multiplying the spread by two gives an annualized spread. Figure 7–4 shows how the relationship has changed in the past.

FIGURE 7–4
Option Premium Derived Yield Spread

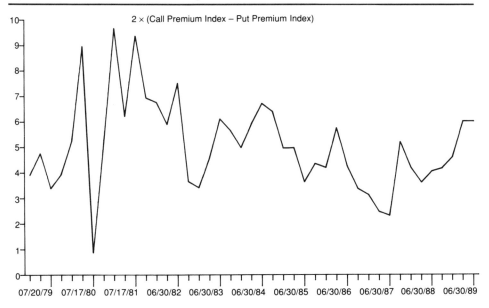

IMPLIED VOLATILITY

An option pricing model requires the following input variables: stock price, exercise price, time, interest rate, stock dividend, and expected volatility. Of these, volatility is the only unknown variable, yet it is the most important. *Volatility* is defined for pricing model purposes as the standard deviation of the daily percentage price change for the stock, annualized. To estimate the volatility of a stock, the stock price changes for a recent time period can be analyzed. The volatility for the stock determined in this manner is called the *historic volatility*.

Calculating the value of an option using historic price volatility often results in a theoretical price that is different from that in the actual market. This means either that the option is out of line with its value, or that the volatility being used by others in the market varies from the historic. Because the option market has become relatively efficient since its birth in 1973, it is more often the latter reason—that expected volatility is different from historical volatility. To determine what this assumed volatility factor is, the pricing model can be employed. If the price of the option is used as an input, and the model is solved for the volatility assumption, the resulting factor is called *implied volatility*.

Implied volatility can help an investor analyze the market in several ways. A chart of implied volatility provides the same perspective as the chart of option premiums discussed in the previous section. If a stock's implied volatility has been declining, it can be assumed that option writers have been earning at a higher rate than expected. If implied volatility is in an uptrend, option buyers have probably been net winners. A sudden change in the trend of implied volatility might indicate a substantial fundamental event in the company or the market.

The average investor has to search a little to find volatility numbers. Many online computer services compute an implied volatility for each underlying stock every day. The *Daily Graphs Option Guide* includes the historic volatility each week in its statistical section. Sooner or later the media will discover that implied volatility is an important statistic, and it will be included along with stock dividend and price earnings multiples in the daily stock quotations page.

When looking at an implied volatility for a stock, remember that the number can vary from option to option within a family of options. It can also change for in-the-money or out-of-the-money types. For this reason, most services use a filtering process, or weight more heavily the more liquid at-the-money contracts. The most important consideration is that the service remain consistent in applying its rules. Remember also that as a stock's options become less liquid, the implied volatility becomes a volatile number. This would suggest that decisions based on implied volatility would be better for liquid issues than those less often traded.

The implied volatility of the stock is a vital consideration for a trader. The higher the implied volatility, the greater the percentage move in the underlying stock needed to double the value of the option. Table 7–1 shows the dollar price movement for the underlying stock needed to double the value of an at-the-money option. It states that a stock selling at $60, whose options assume a volatility of 30 percent, has to increase in price by 4 1/2 points for the $60 option to double in value, all other factors remaining the same. This table only considers an option with 45 days until expiration. Contracts with more days to expiration would need greater price movement. Another use for implied volatility could be to estimate the expected price range for a stock for a particular time period. This is based on the idea that an upper and lower price for the stock can be determined, above or below which the volatility would be wrong. Table 7–2 presents the implied price range for stocks of varying implied volatilities and price over the next 45 days. This table states that a stock selling at $60 with an implied volatility of 30 percent has an implied price range of 18 points.

Price range is determined using an option pricing model. To find the upper limit, the price of the stock is increased until the dollar price movement in the option equals that of the stock. This is referred to as a *delta* of 1. The same process is used to determine the lower limit. The

TABLE 7–1
Ten-Day Price Movement of Stock Necessary to Double the Value of an At-the-Money Option with 45 Days Until Expiration

Implied Volatility	Beginning Stock Price				
	$20	$40	$60	$80	$100
15%	3/4	1 5/8	2 3/8	3 3/8	4 1/8
20	1 1/8	2	3 1/8	4 1/8	5 3/8
25	1 3/8	2 1/2	3 3/4	5	6 3/8
30	1 5/8	2 7/8	4 1/2	6	7 3/4
35	1 3/4	3 3/8	5 1/4	7	8 3/4
40	1 7/8	3 7/8	6	8	10
45	2 1/8	4 3/8	6 3/4	9	11
50	2 3/8	4 7/8	7 3/8	10	12 1/4

TABLE 7–2
Implied 45-Day Price Range

Implied Volatility	Beginning Stock Price				
	$20	$40	$60	$80	$100
15%	3	6 1/2	9 1/2	13 1/2	16 1/2
20	4 1/2	8	12 1/2	16 1/2	21 1/2
25	5 1/2	10	15	20	25 1/2
30	6 1/2	11 1/2	18	24	31
35	7	13 1/2	21	28	35
40	7 1/2	15 1/2	24	32	40
45	8 1/2	17 1/2	27	36	44
50	9 1/2	19 1/2	29 1/2	40	49

difference between the upper and lower limit is the expected price range. Again, the greater the time frame, the larger the expected price range.

For those who like rules of thumb (recognizing the dubious origin of the term) the approximate expected price range for a stock for the time period under consideration can be determined by multiplying the at-the-money call option price by 8.

At this point it is important to remember that the options market considers stocks to be efficiently priced and price movement to be random. In other words, a stock is always considered to be at the center of its expected volatility price range. Applying the implied price ranges to the table of the stock might lead to a different conclusion.

A research service in Vienna, Virginia, publishes an options market newsletter that is almost entirely devoted to an analysis of implied volatility. The firm's owner holds a belief that a stock has a longer-term price trend that is directly related to the investment fundamentals of the company. In the short term, the price of the stock bounces randomly around this trend as buy and sell orders are received, and as the overall market oscillates. The more volatile the stock, the wider the range of possible price fluctuations. The research service estimates the location of each optionable entity within its expected price distribution. The information is then used to determine the most appropriate risk management strategy and stock to employ in the strategy.

The firm's approach contains three steps. Step one calls for determining the location of the overall market in its expected price range. This step determines the most appropriate risk management strategy and is considered to be 50 percent of the decision process. If the market is in the upper part of its expected price range, a defensive or bearish position is assumed. The listed options market offers a number of strategies for such a situation. In the defensive list are *overwriting* (the sale of call options against exiting stock positions) and the purchase of *protective puts* (puts purchased as insurance against a stock price deline). Possible bearish positions include the speculative purchase of puts or *bear spreads* (the purchase of a put combined with the sale of a lower priced put, for example).

If the market is judged to be in the lower part of its implied range, bullish positions are considered. Possible bullish strategies include *buy-write* (the purchase of stock and sale of a call option); *underwrite* (the sale of cash-secured put options); and buy call and *bull spreads*. All of these positions offer the possibility of profit if the underlying stock increases in value.

The midrange for the market is possibly the most important consideration in the strategy decision process. This is because it is expected that the market will be in this area most of the time. This assumption is based on the normal distribution assumption for market values in the expected price range. Option pricing models assume that two thirds of stock price observations will be in an area that represents one third of the price range. If the market is in the mid-range, a strategy that would result in a profit if the price of the underlying stock is little changed would be preferred. These option positions are called *neutral strategies*. Possible neutral strategies include bull and bear spreads, *straddles* (the sale of a put and a call with the same strike price and expiration date), and buy-write or underwrite (discussed as bullish positions, but also applicable in the neutral area because they can produce a profit if the underlying stock price remains unchanged).

The strategy selection process just discussed can be visualized using The Option Strategy Spectrum (see Figure 7–5).

The Option Strategy Spectrum

Bullish	Neutral	Bearish
Market in lower part of expected price range	Market in middle part of expected price range	Market in upper part of expected price range

Once a market strategy has been established, the process of stock selection is started. This selection process has two parts, stock risk analysis and industry group analysis. Each stock is assigned to one of 20

FIGURE 7–5
The Option Strategy Spectrum

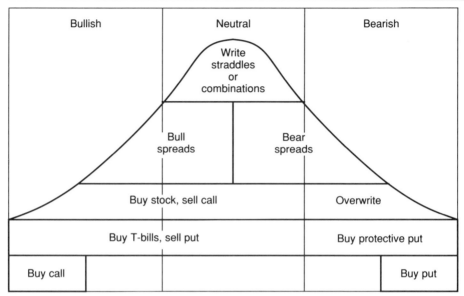

Source: The Option Strategy Spectrum was developed by Jim Yates, President of DYR Associates, Vienna, Virginia.

industry groups. The average position of all stocks in the group is determined so that an analysis can be made about an individual issue. If the individual issue differs dramatically from that of its industry group, it can indicate that an abnormal fundamental condition exists. This is important because the implied volatility analysis assumes a "normal" market.

The analysis of the market and industry group can be viewed as market risk analysis; this evaluation constitutes 75 percent of the decision process. The final step is to identify the location of the individual stock. This step is called nonmarket risk analysis.

Table 7–3 can be used to estimate the location of a stock within its normal expected price distribution in a 90-day time frame. The needed ingredients are the stock's price, its 50-day average price, and its implied volatility. The first step in using the table is to determine the stock's percentage variation from the 50-day average. Then using the implied volatility, you can determine if this variation is sufficient to place the stock one, two, or three standard deviations above or below this trend.

TABLE 7–3
Percentage Deviation from Trend Necessary to Attain Options Strategy Spectrum Zones for Various Levels of Implied Volatility

Implied Volatility	Zones					
	1	2	3	4	5	6
5	−3	−2	−1	0	1	2	3
10	−6	−4	−2	0	2	4	6
15	−9	−6	−3	0	3	6	9
20	−12	−8	−4	0	4	8	12
25	−15	−10	−5	0	5	10	15
30	−18	−12	−6	0	6	12	18
35	−21	−14	−7	0	7	14	21
40	−24	−16	−8	0	8	16	24
45	−27	−18	−9	0	9	18	27
50	−30	−20	−10	0	10	20	30
55	−33	−22	−11	0	11	22	33
60	−36	−24	−12	0	12	24	36
65	−39	−26	−13	0	13	26	39
70	−42	−28	−14	0	14	28	42
75	−45	−30	−15	0	15	30	45
80	−48	−32	−16	0	16	32	48

The importance of volatility in the listed options market cannot be overstated. The entire market rests on the efficient market concept of randomness and lognormal price distribution. As the single most important factor in determining the value of a option, implied volatility is a critical factor in market risk analysis.

SUMMARY

The listed options market can be the most efficient equity market. As such, data derived from the market can provide valuable perspective regarding expectations. The perspective gained from an an analysis of the listed options market, when combined with longer-term fundamental or technical analysis, should allow the investor to make significant use of a valuable risk management tool.

CHAPTER 8

INSTITUTIONAL CASE STUDIES

During the 1980s the U.S. stock market provided opportunities for exceptional profits as well as for dramatic losses. The market advanced from 800 on the Dow Average in August 1982 to 2700 by August 1987, and then plummeted more than 500 points on October 19, 1987. Volatility in stock prices became the concern of institutional investors, and strategies to manage volatility were actively marketed to institutional clients.

This chapter presents two case studies about portfolio risk management, which were written at the Darden Graduate School of Business at the University of Virginia.* These cases were developed from interviews with fund managers after reviewing the investment environment between 1986 and 1988. They represent examples of the use of options contracts in a period surrounding the exceptional market volatility from 1986 to 1988, a particularly appropriate time to study equity and index options in the context of portfolio risk management. Investors had become conditioned to success in this market; indeed, many youthful traders, brokers, analysts, and portfolio managers, entering the business after 1981, had never experienced a bear market before the October 1987 debacle.

During the summer of 1987 as the stock market continued to climb, individual and institutional investors became increasingly apprehensive about the market's ability to sustain its current level. More and more money managers began to seek protection for paper gains by using the options and futures markets, trading long puts, short calls, and short stock index futures positions. The fledgling industry of providing portfolio insurance to institutional money managers received increased atten-

---

* Case studies are published here with the permission of Michael A. Berry.

tion because it promised cheap "insurance." At the height of the 1987 bull market, it is estimated that more than $100 billion of pension fund money was "insured" using the techniques analyzed in these cases.

Case One, T. David Brown, is set prior to the market decline of 1987. In this scenario, a mutual fund money manager is advising a client seeking insurance protection during the fall of 1986. Analysis of this case requires an understanding of portfolio insurance concepts and the means by which it can be implemented. The case discussion should distinguish among various strategies for insuring portfolios and consider when these strategies are appropriate to implement. Discussion can also focus either on quantitative dimensions involving the comparative costs and benefits of insurance strategies, or the qualitative aspects of the advantages and disadvantages of portfolio insurance, compared to traditional hedging strategies.

The market environment following the October 1987 crash is equally rich for studying the options markets. Prognosticators suggested that a recession was imminent and forecasted further declines in the equity market. The widespread failure of the stock index futures market to provide portfolio insurance as promised, and their apparent dramatic effect on stock price volatility, caused widespread concern among portfolio managers who utilized these protection techniques.

Case Two, Rocky Mountain High, describes a situation following the market decline in which use of the futures market had been limited by public concern about the impact of index futures contracts on market volatility. As such, the analyst devised insurance strategies using listed options, instead of dynamic insurance techniques.

These case situations portray the importance of understanding the trade-offs between the derivative and equity markets for individual and institutional investors attempting to modify the risk-return profile of their portfolios. You are encouraged to analyze each one and attempt a solution to the problem. After doing this, you can compare your analyses to the solutions provided following each case. It should be noted that these solutions represent only one possible answer. Many different feasible solutions exist, depending on the risk preferences and investment objectives that you believe are appropriate.

T. David Brown

Bob Whitney, the new options strategist for the investment management firm of T. David Brown, gazed out his office window, overlooking the harbor in Seattle, and contemplated the job he had been asked to accomplish. T. David Brown managed a family of mutual funds and accounts for corporate pension plans. Bob had been asked by senior management to design and implement several option-related investment strategies that would appeal to pension plan sponsors in the particularly turbulent equity markets. Bob knew he would not be able to sacrifice much return potential in his product development plans.

Whitney noted that employee benefit plan sponsors typically traded well-diversified portfolios of stocks that tracked the major indexes quite well. Brown's clients often diversified across mutual funds, and pension fund clients in particular tended to invest in multi-managed portfolios that closely tracked the market. In fact, plan sponsors had popularized the idea of "indexing" early in the 1970s when some sponsors believed that it was difficult to outperform the market and they did not want to increase their risk exposure in excess of the market through active management. Whitney's objective, taking the current market into account, was to design strategies to add value and reduce the risk of the portfolios.

The past months had seen increasing short-term volatility in the stock market, which suggested a lack of confidence among investors. A decline seemed likely. In Bob's opinion, the Dow had peaked at 1850, and he was surprised to see it approach 2000 in early September 1986. He noted that there had been major corrections of 3 to 5 percent in June, July, and September; he did not expect to see the stock market return to these dizzying heights for some time.

PORTFOLIO INSURANCE

Beginning in 1984, the major "sell-side" institutions on Wall Street had popularized a number of strategies using the options and futures markets to protect the value of an equity or bond portfolio. These strategies, collectively known as *portfolio insurance,* had been implemented in various ways. A plan sponsor might buy an index put against a portfolio; buy puts on individual stocks; buy index calls and money market securities; buy individual calls and money market securities; sell stock index futures to create a synthetic put; or sell the individual stocks, and "go to cash."

H. Nicholas Hanson, at Salomon Brothers, had written a paper on portfolio insurance in which he explained the use of puts as insurance as follows:

> Consider an investor who buys one share of a stock at a price of $100. Profit or loss from the stock position is shown by the dashed line in Figure 8–1 which is a 45 degree line through the purchase price of $100. Assume that the investor also purchases a put option on that stock with a strike price of $100. The profit and loss line for the put only is shown in Figure 8–1. If the stock is above $100 at option expiration, the put buyer will lose the put premium; but if the price falls below $100, the put buyer will profit after the stock price falls by the cost of the put. Now consider the profit and loss line for the portfolio composed of the stock plus the put shown as the

FIGURE 8–1
Long Stock–Long Put Return Pattern

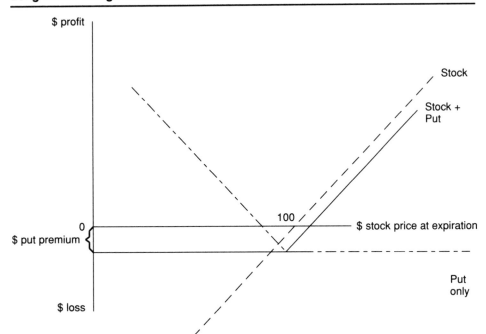

solid line in Figure 8–1. If the stock increases in value, the buyer will not exercise the put but will be entitled to the entire capital gain of the stock, less the price paid for the put. Should the stock decrease below $100, the buyer will exercise the option and receive $100 per share for the stock. The maximum possible loss is the cost of the put.

For every stock price above $100 the stock-put position will underperform the stock by the put premium. For stock prices below $100, the investor's loss will be limited to the cost of the put. The investor has thus insured the stock position against a price decline in the same way that a homeowner insures a house against loss due to fire.[1]

Whitney felt that evidence provided in the 1984 Salomon Brothers report suggested that portfolio insurance was worthwhile. Hanson ran a simulation of a portfolio insurance program using an S&P 500 Index fund protected by three-month at-the-money European index puts from mid-1970 until 1983. The puts were purchased at the beginning of each quarter and held through the quarter. At the end of each period, they were exercised if their value was positive. The put prices were derived using a dividend-adjusted Black-Scholes model. The simulation reinvested quarterly dividends. The results of the simulation are shown in Exhibit 1. Here is what Hanson found:

> The insured index funds outperformed the uninsured index fund by nearly 200 basis points per year on a compound annual basis, resulting in approximately 25 percent more wealth at the end of the 13.5-year period. We believe that this was particularly significant since the overall market was in a larger-than-average uptrend over this time span. Evidently, the ability to avoid the small number of disastrous quarters that did occur during this period made it possible for the insured index fund to outperform the uninsured index fund, even though its downside risk was obviously less, and an average quarterly premium of 2.2 percent was paid for the puts. In [Exhibit 1], a comparison between the insured and uninsured index funds over various calendar-year periods is given.

Hanson's simulation used European puts, which could only be exercised at the end of the period, instead of American puts, which could be exercised at any time throughout the period, but which would be more expensive.[2] Exhibit 1 also shows the results of the simulation if the put

---

[1] Salomon Brothers report, by H. Nicholas Hanson, Ph.D., Vice President, Futures and Options Research, Stock Research Department, 1984. More excerpts are given in the following paragraphs.

[2] An option contract that allows its holder to exercise before expiration is termed an *American option*. In contrast, a *European option* may not be exercised before expiration. Therefore, an American option is always worth at least as much as a European option.

EXHIBIT 1
S&P 500 Index Fund Insured with Put Options

	S&P 500				Insured Index Fund I*			Insured Index Fund II†		
	Quarter-End Price	Qtr Div	Quarter Return	Annual Return	Put Price	Quarter Return	Annual Return	Put Price	Quarter Return	Annual Return
1970										
2Q	72.72	—	—		1.83	—		2.83	—	
3Q	84.21	0.78	16.9%		1.46	14.0%		2.12	12.5%	
4Q	92.15	0.79	10.4	29.0%‡	1.11	8.5	23.7%‡	1.65	7.7	21.1%‡
1971										
1Q	100.31	0.75	9.7		1.53	8.4		1.33	7.7	
2Q	99.70	0.78	0.2		2.13	-0.7		1.35	-0.5	
3Q	98.34	0.77	-0.6		2.17	-1.3		2.17	0.6	
4Q	102.09	0.77	4.6	14.2	1.33	2.3	8.6	2.34	2.3	9.0
1972										
1Q	107.20	0.75	5.7		1.59	4.4		1.37	3.4	
2Q	107.14	0.78	0.7		1.78	-0.7		1.57	-0.5	
3Q	110.55	0.78	3.9		1.77	2.2		1.77	2.4	
4Q	118.05	0.84	7.5	19.0	2.22	5.8	12.1	1.76	5.8	11.4
1973										
1Q	111.52	0.77	-4.9		3.08	-1.2		1.99	-0.8	
2Q	104.26	0.83	-5.8		1.96	-2.0		2.77	-1.0	
3Q	108.43	0.83	4.8		4.04	2.9		2.13	2.1	
4Q	97.55	0.95	-9.2	-14.7	2.81	-2.7	-3.1	3.58	-1.1	-0.9
1974										
1Q	93.98	0.83	-2.8		2.47	-2.0		2.66	-2.7	
2Q	86.00	0.89	-7.5		3.90	-1.6		2.39	-1.8	
3Q	63.54	0.92	-25.0		3.24	-3.3		3.12	-1.7	
4Q	68.56	0.96	9.4	-26.3	2.28	4.1	-2.9	3.36	4.3	-2.1

EXHIBIT 1 (continued)

	S&P 500				Insured Index Fund I*			Insured Index Fund II†		
	Quarter-End Price	Qtr Div	Quarter Return	Annual Return	Put Price	Quarter Return	Annual Return	Put Price	Quarter Return	Annual Return
1975										
1Q	83.36	0.90	22.9		2.20	18.9		2.85	17.2	
2Q	95.19	0.93	15.3		2.60	12.3		2.41	11.5	
3Q	83.87	0.92	-10.9		1.94	-1.7		2.27	-1.5	
4Q	90.19	0.93	8.6	37.1	2.19	6.2	39.5	2.19	5.8	36.1
1976										
1Q	102.77	0.91	15.0		2.10	12.2		2.50	12.2	
2Q	104.28	1.00	2.4		1.67	0.4		2.08	0.0	
3Q	105.24	1.01	1.9		2.19	0.3		1.78	-0.1	
4Q	107.46	1.13	3.2	23.8	1.64	1.1	14.2	2.28	1.5	13.8
1977										
1Q	98.42	1.05	-7.4		1.77	-0.5		1.58	-1.1	
2Q	100.48	1.17	3.3		1.53	1.5		1.73	1.7	
3Q	96.53	1.15	-2.8		1.84	-0.4		1.46	-0.6	
4Q	95.10	1.30	-0.1	-7.2	1.55	-0.5	0.0	1.74	-0.2	-0.2
1978										
1Q	89.21	1.18	-5.0		2.03	-0.4		1.50	-0.6	
2Q	95.53	1.28	8.5		1.68	6.1		2.06	6.7	
3Q	102.54	1.26	8.7		3.11	6.8		1.71	6.4	
4Q	96.11	1.35	-5.0	6.5	1.47	-1.7	11.0	2.78	-0.3	12.5
1979										
1Q	101.59	1.31	7.1		1.36	5.5		1.56	4.1	
2Q	102.91	1.42	2.7		1.63	1.3		1.43	1.1	
3Q	109.32	1.43	7.6		2.45	5.9		1.61	6.1	
4Q	107.94	1.54	0.1	18.5	3.00	-0.8	12.3	2.18	-0.1	11.6

1980									
1Q	102.09	1.46	-4.1		2.10	-1.4		2.68	-0.7
2Q	114.24	1.56	13.4		3.03	11.1		3.03	10.5
3Q	125.46	1.56	11.2		3.28	8.3		2.80	8.3
4Q	135.76	1.58	9.5	32.4	2.60	6.7	26.6	3.11	7.1	27.4
1981									
1Q	136.00	1.58	1.3		1.61	-0.6		2.88	-0.9
2Q	131.25	1.67	-2.3		2.81	0.0		1.37	-0.9
3Q	116.18	1.69	-10.2		1.91	-0.8		2.56	0.2
4Q	122.55	1.69	6.9	-4.9	3.06	5.2	3.8	2.36	4.6	3.0
1982									
1Q	111.91	1.67	-7.3		1.79	-1.1		2.64	-0.6
2Q	109.61	1.76	-0.5		3.28	-0.0		1.81	-0.8
3Q	120.42	1.73	11.4		5.16	8.2		4.22	9.6
4Q	140.64	1.71	18.2	21.5	3.92	13.4	21.3	5.85	14.2	23.6
1983									
1Q	152.96	1.71	10.0		2.91	7.0		4.10	5.6
2Q	168.11	1.79	11.1		3.76	9.0		3.11	8.2
3Q	166.07	1.79	-0.1		2.45	-1.1		3.74	-0.8
4Q	164.93	1.80	0.4	22.5	—	-0.4	14.8	—	-1.1	12.0
Cumulative return			311.0%			414.3%			403.3%
Compound annual return			11.0			12.9			12.7

* Using actual standard deviation for quarter.
† Using previous quarter's standard deviation.
‡ Six-month return.

EXHIBIT 1 (concluded)   Cumulative Returns for Insured and Uninsured Index Funds (in percent)

Insured S&P 500 Index Fund

Until Year-End	From Year-End												
	1970	1971	1972	1973	1974	1975	1976	1977	1978	1979	1980	1981	1982
1971	8.6												
1972	21.7	12.1											
1973	18.0	8.6	-3.1										
1974	14.5	5.5	-5.9	-2.9									
1975	59.8	47.1	31.3	35.5	39.5								
1976	82.5	68.0	49.9	54.7	59.3	14.2							
1977	82.5	68.0	49.9	54.7	59.3	14.2	0.0						
1978	102.6	86.5	66.4	71.7	76.8	26.8	11.0	11.0					
1979	127.5	109.5	86.8	92.8	98.6	42.4	24.7	24.7	12.3				
1980	188.0	165.2	136.5	144.1	151.4	80.2	57.8	57.8	42.2	26.6			
1981	198.9	175.2	145.5	153.4	161.0	87.1	63.8	63.8	47.6	31.4	3.8		
1982	262.6	233.9	197.8	207.4	216.5	126.9	98.7	98.7	79.0	59.4	25.9	21.3	
1983	316.3	283.3	241.9	252.9	263.4	160.5	128.1	128.1	105.5	83.0	44.5	39.3	14.8

Uninsured S&P 500 Index Fund

Until Year-End	From Year-End												
	1970	1971	1972	1973	1974	1975	1976	1977	1978	1979	1980	1981	1982
1971	14.2												
1972	35.9	19.0											
1973	15.9	1.5	-14.7										
1974	-14.6	-25.2	-37.1	-26.3									
1975	17.1	2.6	-13.8	1.0	37.1								
1976	45.0	27.0	6.7	25.1	69.7	23.8							
1977	34.6	17.8	-1.0	16.1	57.5	14.9	-7.2						
1978	43.3	25.5	5.5	23.6	67.7	22.4	-1.2	6.5					
1979	69.8	48.7	25.0	46.5	98.8	45.0	17.1	26.2	18.5				
1980	124.8	96.9	65.5	94.0	163.2	92.0	55.1	67.1	56.9	32.4			
1981	113.8	87.2	57.3	84.5	150.3	82.6	47.5	58.9	49.2	25.9	-4.9		
1982	159.8	127.5	91.2	124.1	204.1	121.8	79.2	93.1	81.3	53.0	15.5	21.5	
1983	218.3	178.7	134.2	174.6	272.5	171.7	119.5	136.5	122.1	87.4	41.5	48.8	22.5

prices were increased by 5 percent. Even so, Hanson's report still favored the insurance strategy:

> Thus, prices nearly 20 percent higher than those shown in [Exhibit 1] could have been paid for the puts, and the cumulative return of the insured index fund would still have nearly matched that of the uninsured index fund.

In the past, an equity portfolio manager sensing a market decline in the making could reduce risk only by selling stocks or shift from more aggressive to more defensive securities. A plan sponsor could draw capital from equity managers and shift the funds to money market or similar funds, or move funds from more aggressive to more defensive managers. For sponsors, meeting infrequently, timing changes was more difficult. The new synthetic instruments offered both managers and sponsors the opportunity to move more capital, often more expeditiously and usually with lower transaction costs.

In Whitney's view, all these new strategies seemed to have different advantages and disadvantages. For instance, portfolio insurance, like any other insurance policy, was not free. If the plan trustees were not uncomfortable with the level of volatility in the market, they might consider the cost of the insurance too great for the decrease in expected return from the premium. Regarding the cost of portfolio insurance, Hanson compared:

> dynamic portfolio insurance programs with static insurance programs. By static we mean purchasing listed (or over-the-counter) index put options to protect the portfolio. An example of a dynamic insurance "tree" to protect a stock (or portfolio) initially priced at $100 for 13 weeks is shown in [Exhibit 2]. The numbers at each "node" of the tree—in the boxes—represent the amount of stock and cash held in the replicating portfolio, and are determined as follows. Using the Black-Scholes formula, the fair value of a European put struck at $100 is determined for the stock price and time until expiration represented by that particular box. The fair value of the put is then added to the stock price to determine the static portfolio value. The hedge ratio gives the number of shares required in the dynamic portfolio. Since both the dynamic and static portfolios must have the same value, the amount of cash to be held is found by subtracting the amount invested in stock (hedge ratio times stock price) from the static portfolio value. For example, assume that the stock is initially at $100 and will pay no dividend over the next 13 weeks. The fair value of a European put struck at $100 using a risk-free rate of zero and an annual standard deviation of 14.42 percent (2 percent per week) and having 13 weeks until

expiration is $2.88. The cost of establishing the static portfolio (long one share of stock plus long one put) is $102.88. The hedge ratio is 0.5144, so that the dynamic portfolio will contain 0.5144 share of stock worth $51.44. Since the value of the dynamic portfolio must also be $102.88, the amount of cash held is simply $102.88 minus $51.44, or $51.44. This procedure is repeated at each box.

One difference between dynamic and static insurance is that dynamic insurance is path dependent. For example, in the extreme case in Exhibit 2, if the stock price remains constant at $100 over the next 13 weeks, some stock would be sold and the proceeds held in cash. By the end of the period, the portfolio would still be worth $102.88—$50 in stock, $50 in cash, and $2.88 which was removed from the portfolio during the 13 weeks, returning the original cost of the put. The Hanson report concluded:

> In effect, the insurance would have cost nothing since the stock exhibited zero volatility. The actual cost of the insurance in a dynamic strategy will depend on the experienced volatility, whereas that of the static strategy is fixed by the initial cost of the put, which is a function of the anticipated volatility. In cases where the experienced volatility is greater than the anticipated volatility, the dynamic strategy will cost more. And this neglects the transaction costs associated with rebalancing, which can be formidable and rise with increasing volatility.

*****

Certainly, some general statements regarding the relative merits of using a dynamic strategy instead of a static strategy can be made. If the volatility implied by the put price is believed to be too high (that is, the listed put is overpriced), the dynamic strategy might be preferable, since its cost for insurance will depend on the actual experienced (and presumably lower) volatility.

*****

. . . with a dynamic strategy the investor can tailor insurance to his specifications. [For example, one can dynamically replicate a three-year European put, an instrument that currently is not traded on any exchange.]

PLAN SPONSORS

Throughout the 1980s, pension plan sponsors had discovered and utilized equity options to an extent not before contemplated. From its modest beginnings with options listed on 16 stocks in 1973, the CBOE

EXHIBIT 2 Dynamic Insurance Tree

Stock Price

Weeks until Expiration		88	90	92	94	96	98	100	102	104	106	108	110	112
13	S	3.63	6.93	12.08	19.32	28.61	39.55	51.44	63.44	74.78	84.88	93.43	100.40	105.96
	C	96.48	93.29	88.35	81.44	72.65	62.41	51.44	40.57	30.58	22.00	15.12	9.92	6.23
12	S	3.09	6.17	11.15	18.36	27.80	39.06	51.38	63.82	75.51	85.80	94.40	101.29	106.69
	C	96.99	94.01	89.22	82.33	73.37	62.79	51.38	40.08	29.75	21.00	14.09	8.99	5.46
11	S	2.56	5.39	10.16	17.31	26.90	38.52	51.32	64.26	76.32	86.82	95.44	102.22	107.43
	C	97.50	94.76	90.15	83.30	74.17	63.22	51.32	39.53	28.84	19.89	12.98	8.02	4.69
10	S	2.05	4.60	9.11	16.15	25.88	37.90	51.26	64.76	77.25	87.95	96.56	103.19	108.18
	C	98.00	95.52	91.15	84.38	75.09	63.72	51.26	38.91	27.81	18.68	11.79	7.00	3.92
9	S	1.57	3.79	8.00	14.88	24.74	37.19	51.20	65.34	78.31	89.22	97.78	104.20	108.92
	C	96.46	96.30	92.22	85.57	76.13	64.31	51.20	38.21	26.64	17.33	10.51	5.95	3.15
8	S	1.13	3.00	6.82	13.47	23.42	36.37	51.13	66.04	79.54	90.64	99.10	105.23	109.64
	C	98.89	97.07	93.35	86.91	77.34	65.01	51.13	37.38	25.30	15.82	9.14	4.88	2.41
7	S	0.74	2.22	5.58	11.89	21.90	35.39	51.06	66.88	80.98	92.25	100.52	106.28	110.31
	C	99.27	97.82	94.55	88.41	78.76	65.85	51.06	36.40	23.73	14.12	7.66	3.79	1.72
6	S	0.43	1.51	4.30	10.13	20.09	34.20	50.98	67.93	82.72	94.09	102.03	107.32	110.91
	C	99.58	98.52	95.79	90.11	80.45	66.89	50.98	35.21	21.88	12.20	6.10	2.73	1.10
5	S	0.20	0.88	3.01	8.15	17.91	32.71	50.89	69.27	84.84	96.19	103.61	108.28	111.41
	C	99.80	99.13	97.04	92.02	82.52	68.23	50.89	33.71	19.63	10.01	4.47	1.75	0.60
4	S	0.07	0.40	1.79	5.96	15.21	30.75	50.80	71.07	87.52	98.60	105.20	109.11	111.76
	C	99.94	99.60	98.23	94.15	85.10	70.03	50.80	31.73	16.84	7.54	2.84	0.91	0.24
3	S	0.01	0.11	0.77	3.61	11.79	28.00	50.69	73.65	90.99	101.27	106.64	109.69	111.94
	C	99.99	99.89	99.23	96.44	88.41	72.59	50.69	28.96	13.24	4.80	1.37	0.31	0.06
2	S	0.00	0.01	0.15	1.40	7.34	23.71	50.56	77.78	95.62	103.98	107.66	109.96	112.00
	C	100.00	99.99	99.85	98.62	92.75	76.69	50.56	24.63	8.49	2.04	0.34	0.04	0.00
1	S	0.00	0.00	0.00	0.10	2.03	15.54	50.40	85.82	101.47	105.82	107.99	110.00	112.00
	C	100.00	100.00	100.00	99.90	97.99	84.62	50.40	16.35	2.55	0.18	0.01	0.00	0.00
0	S	0.00	0.00	0.00	0.00	0.00	0.00	50.00	102.00	104.00	106.00	108.00	110.00	112.00
	C	100.00	100.00	100.00	100.00	100.00	100.00	50.00	0.00	0.00	0.00	0.00	0.00	0.00

S = Dollars invested in stock.   C = Dollars held in cash.   Risk-free rate = 0%.   Weekly standard deviation = 2%.

had innovated a number of products, including calls and puts on individual equities and indexes. In particular, the option on the S&P 100 Index (OEX) had been extremely successful, and plan sponsors were becoming more aware of its potential. Historically, more than 40 percent of large (over $1 billion) employee benefit plans used equity options both to control risk and create "extra" return. This meant that options were not strangers to these plan sponsors. Index options, however, were a more recent innovation, and Whitney wondered how to proceed with his product development ideas.

Whitney was scheduled to present a strategy to the plan sponsors for the Kreiger Employee Benefit Fund in mid-October. This client had been invested in several of the Brown mutual funds, and performance had been hurt in the market declines in June, July, and September. Kreiger wanted to explore some approaches to the choppy markets that had hurt its investment results.

Employee Benefit Plans' Risk Exposure

Many pension plans had grown to enormous size, with the median in the $500 million range. Moreover, a large number of plans had grown to several billion dollars in assets by the mid-1980s. This necessarily meant the insurance programs would have to cope with a need for liquidity in the implementation of their plans. On the other hand, most funds were quite well diversified with holdings in stocks, fixed-income instruments, real estate, and the money market. With this much size and diversification, active management was difficult, and plan sponsors were often faced with the task of diversifying across money managers and styles, rather than across the individual financial instruments themselves. In short, many plans found themselves approaching *closet indexing* (i.e., closely tracking the market in composite).

In the 1980s, some sponsors began to experiment with overwrite (selling calls against stocks owned) and buy-write programs. These programs promised to reduce downside risk exposure for part of the portfolio at modest sacrifice of upside potential. Since sponsors tend to be risk conscious in exercising their fiduciary responsibilities, limiting downside risk was attractive to them during periods of adverse equity market movements. Exhibit 3 provides an example of the performance of some of these funds.

EXHIBIT 3

Performance of Option Funds (risk and diversification 3/83–3/86; percent return 3/83–3/86)

Name of Fund	Manage Co	IO	Assets (mil$)	Load Fee	Alpha	Beta	R2	Std Dev	Annual Rate of Return
Colonial Option Inc TR	COLONL	GI	1,383	Yes	−1.9	0.73	82	2.9	15.3%
Analytic Optioned Equity	ANALYT	GI	86	No	−1.8	0.55	89	2.1	13.3
Putnam Option Income I	PUTNAM	GI	1,191	Yes	−5.0	0.78	79	3.1	12.3
First Invest. Option	FSTINV	GI	195	Yes	−4.2	0.64	52	3.2	11.6
Kemper Option Income FD	KEMPER	GI	783	Yes	−3.4	0.52	81	2.1	11.0
Gateway Option Income	GATEWY	GI	28	No	−2.9	0.47	79	1.8	11.0
Unweighted Averages			611		−3.2	0.62	77	2.5	12.4
Weighted Averages						0.69	79	2.8	
STANDARD & POOR 500					0.0	1.00	100	3.6	21.1
SALOMON BROS CORP BONDS					4.5	0.52	35	3.1	20.0

Note: Alpha expressed per annum; standard deviation expressed per month. Six entries reported.

These overwrite programs had been sold to the sponsors as "free lunches." The option-related programs promised to increase average returns over a typical market cycle, while reducing downside risk. Unfortunately, the equity markets of the mid-1980s were very strong, and the strategies did not work as well as had been hoped. Reaction to the tests was therefore mixed and only a small part of equity portfolios were protected through the option strategies.

In the 1980s, both the fixed-income and equity markets were strong. By the mid-1980s, most pension funds had become significantly overfunded relative to actuarial requirements and pension funding costs, relative to payrolls, were declining sharply. After a trying decade of rising pension costs and inadequate funding during the 1970s, pension sponsors were increasingly conscious of protecting the sound funding levels now achieved.

As the equity market continued to rise sharply in early 1986, sponsors increasingly questioned whether a significant market correction might be forthcoming. From June to September, daily and weekly market volatility increased, and there were several sharp, although short-lived, market breaks that added to this concern. In the previous decade, fixed-income securities—particularly those with long maturities—had become substantially more volatile and the covariance between long-term fixed-income and equity returns had increased. Fixed-income alternatives no longer appeared to be an attractive way of reducing exposure to an adverse equity market. The growing and active promotion of portfolio insurance as an alternative way of reducing potential market exposure found an increasingly receptive audience among the more nervous plan sponsors. Whitney estimated that the market for portfolio insurance in one form or another was $75 billion and was growing rapidly.

Finally, the overriding impetus for a new view on portfolio insurance had come from tremendous volatility in the markets over the past year. From September 1985 to the present, the Dow had increased by more than 500 points—about 33 percent. During that period there had been eight major declines followed by recoveries. Clearly, short-term volatility in the equity markets had increased dramatically and index options, priced on volatility, might be the best vehicles to offset these impacts for Brown's client base. Whitney wanted to devise both an active and a passive investment strategy in this regard.

INDEX OPTIONS

The market for index options had increased in volume by more than 500 percent in 1984 alone. The growing liquidity of the index option market, particularly in the near-term contracts, had encouraged more plan sponsors to consider these instruments for use in their insurance plans. In addition to the innovation of broad market options, numerous other industry and sector option products had been introduced in 1984 and 1985. In September of 1986, it was clear that institutional investors were intrigued by these products.

Several characteristics distinguished stock index options from their equity counterparts. First, index options were settled in cash. Active investors liked this feature because it reduced the turnover of traditional portfolios when the stock was called away. Some believed that it would increase dividend income. The cash settlement was equal to the difference between the option's strike price and the closing price of the index. Second, Whitney believed that the index option was priced somewhat differently than the individual equity option. He was familiar with the Black-Scholes option pricing model (OPM), which derived prices based on estimates of volatility and interest rates. Whitney believed that market expectations were a pricing determinant in the case of index options. In fact, he resolved to determine if a relationship existed between index futures and index options. He wondered if perhaps the index options were somehow priced "off" the index futures.

Stock index futures and stock index options appeared to offer distinct advantages. By buying index puts, a sponsor knew in advance the cost of the insurance and the benefits that could develop. By selling stock index futures (creating a *synthetic put)*, the seller could not determine the actual cost in advance and had to accept the pricing risk of the futures contract. This fact alone seemed to weigh heavily in favor of index options in these markets. Whitney did realize, however, that the futures contract allowed creation of both a strike price and an expiration date, if one is willing to accept its pricing risk. Index options had to be rolled forward in this regard.

Index options seemed to have several other significant advantages, but Whitney was not sure how to quantify them. Instant diversification was one advantage that was difficult to achieve with a buy-write strategy. Index options seemed to offer higher premiums than their equity counterparts, written on the same portfolio. Finally, index options seemed to offer improved performance—especially in volatile markets. Whitney did not believe that this had been appreciated by corporate sponsors currently involved in buy-write programs.

BOB WHITNEY

Whitney returned to his computer terminal. He noticed that the market had become more volatile in the past few weeks. This had been variously attributed to interest-rate concerns and to the impact of institutional buy-and-sell programs on the equity markets. He noted that a record of over 2 million options had traded in the past week, with the popular OEX accounting for almost 1.5 million contracts. Puts had soared in price, reflecting expectations of the future course of the stock market. The OEX September 235 had risen to 15 1/2 from 2 3/4. The put-call ratio at 1.04 seemed to indicate minimal downside risk in the short term. But Whitney didn't feel comfortable with an optimistic forecast of the market, given these facts. He was certain that increased market volatility had turned the psychology of the market sour.

Given the performance of the market in the past quarter and the accompanying returns on the Kreiger portfolio, Whitney began to sort out his thoughts on a strategy to manage risk and return more effectively, using dynamic portfolio insurance or listed options. Exhibit 4 shows recent weekly closing prices for the S&P 100 and 500 Indexes and the calculation of their 1986 volatility from January 10 to September 5. Exhibit 5 provides information on S&P 100 put premiums over the past year.

Whitney's objective is to develop a systematic investment program that might meet Kreiger's concerns about undue volatility in its equity account.

Questions for Discussion

1. Define portfolio insurance and describe various strategies using options that represent portfolio insurance. Explain why strategies such as (1) covered call writing, (2) general market timing, and (3) asset allocations between stocks, bonds, and cash differ from portfolio insurance strategies.
2. Why insure a portfolio? What are the advantages of following a portfolio insurance strategy? What are the disadvantages? Com-

EXHIBIT 4
Indices and Volatility (calculation of standard deviation of daily percentage)

1986 Date	OEX S&P 100	Price Relative (S_t / S_{t-1})	Natural Logarithm Log R_t	Deviation from Average (Log R_t − Avg. Log R_t)	Squared Deviation (Log R_t − Avg. Log Price Relative)
Jan 10	200.61				
17	202.35	1.009	0.00864	0.004	0.00001
24	199.93	0.988	−0.01203	−0.017	0.00028
31	204.00	1.020	0.02015	0.015	0.00023
Feb 07	207.49	1.017	0.01696	0.012	0.00015
14	212.38	1.024	0.02329	0.018	0.00034
21	217.57	1.024	0.02414	0.019	0.00037
28	217.57	1.000	0.00000	−0.005	0.00002
Mar 07	215.05	0.988	−0.01165	−0.016	0.00027
14	225.44	1.048	0.04718	0.042	0.00179
21	222.22	0.986	−0.01439	−0.019	0.00037
28	227.60	1.024	0.02392	0.019	0.00036
Apr 04	218.41	0.960	−0.04122	−0.046	0.00212
11	224.58	1.028	0.02786	0.023	0.00053
18	230.40	1.026	0.02558	0.021	0.00043
25	233.01	1.011	0.01126	0.006	0.00004

EXHIBIT 4 (continued)

1986 Date	OEX S&P 100	Price Relative (S_t/S_{t-1})	Natural Logarithm $Log\ R_t$	Deviation from Average $(Log\ R_t - Avg.\ Log\ R_t)$	Squared Deviation $(Log\ R_t - Avg.\ Log\ Price\ Relative)$
May 02	225.84	0.969	-0.03125	-0.036	0.00130
09	228.02	1.010	0.00961	0.005	0.00002
16	222.14	0.974	-0.02613	-0.031	0.00096
23	230.26	1.037	0.03590	0.031	0.00097
30	236.05	1.025	0.02483	0.020	0.00040
Jun 06	235.69	0.998	-0.00153	-0.006	0.00004
13	235.17	0.998	-0.00221	-0.007	0.00005
20	235.88	1.003	0.00301	-0.002	0.00000
27	236.57	1.003	0.00292	-0.002	0.00000
Jul 03	238.20	1.007	0.00687	0.002	0.00000
11	229.21	0.962	-0.03847	-0.043	0.00188
18	224.16	0.978	-0.02228	-0.027	0.00073
25	226.14	1.009	0.00879	0.004	0.00002
Aug 01	220.46	0.975	-0.02544	-0.030	0.00092
08	222.67	1.010	0.00997	0.005	0.00003
15	231.57	1.040	0.03919	0.034	0.00118
22	234.42	1.012	0.01223	0.007	0.00005
29	237.32	1.012	0.01230	0.007	0.00006
Sep 05	236.41	0.996	-0.00384	-0.009	0.00008
		Average =	0.0048295		0.00047
				Variance =	
				(Avg. squared deviation)	

Variance of average log of price relative $\times$ (34/33) = 0.00048
To convert to annual variance: $\times$ 365 or 0.17675
SIGMA — Annual volatility = Square root or 0.42041

EXHIBIT 4 (continued)
Indices and Volatility (calculation of standard deviation of daily percentage)

1986 Date	SPX S&P 500	Price Relative (S_t/S_{t-1})	Natural Logarithm Log R_t	Deviation from Average (Log R_t − Avg. Log R_t)	Squared Deviation (Log R_t − Avg. Log Price Relative)
Jan 10	205.96				
17	208.43	1.012	0.01192	0.006	0.00004
24	206.43	0.990	-0.00964	-0.015	0.00024
31	211.78	1.026	0.02559	0.020	0.00039
Feb 07	214.56	1.013	0.01304	0.007	0.00005
14	219.76	1.024	0.02395	0.018	0.00033
21	224.62	1.022	0.02187	0.016	0.00026
28	226.92	1.010	0.01019	0.004	0.00002
Mar 07	225.57	0.994	-0.00597	-0.012	0.00014
14	236.55	1.049	0.04753	0.042	0.00175
21	233.34	0.986	-0.01366	-0.019	0.00038
28	238.97	1.024	0.02384	0.018	0.00033
Apr 04	228.69	0.957	-0.04397	-0.050	0.00247
11	235.97	1.032	0.03134	0.026	0.00065
18	242.38	1.027	0.02680	0.021	0.00044
25	242.29	1.000	-0.00037	-0.006	0.00004
May 02	234.79	0.969	-0.03144	-0.037	0.00138
09	237.85	1.013	0.01295	0.007	0.00005
16	232.76	0.979	-0.02163	-0.027	0.00075
23	241.35	1.037	0.03624	0.030	0.00093
30	247.35	1.025	0.02456	0.019	0.00035

EXHIBIT 4 (concluded)

1986 Date	SPX S&P 500	Price Relative (S_t/S_{t-1})	Natural Logarithm $Log\ R_t$	Deviation from Average $(Log\ R_t - Avg.\ Log\ R_t)$	Squared Deviation $(Log\ R_t - Avg.\ Log\ Price\ Relative)$
Jun 06	245.67	0.993	-0.00682	-0.013	0.00016
13	245.73	1.000	0.00024	-0.006	0.00003
20	247.58	1.008	0.00750	0.002	0.00000
27	249.60	1.008	0.00813	0.002	0.00001
Jul 03	251.79	1.009	0.00874	0.003	0.00001
11	242.22	0.962	-0.03875	-0.045	0.00198
18	236.36	0.976	-0.02449	-0.030	0.00091
25	240.22	1.016	0.01620	0.010	0.00011
Aug 01	234.91	0.978	-0.02235	-0.028	0.00079
08	236.88	1.008	0.00835	0.003	0.00001
15	247.15	1.043	0.04244	0.037	0.00135
22	250.19	1.012	0.01223	0.006	0.00004
29	252.93	1.011	0.01089	0.005	0.00003
Sep 05	250.47	0.990	-0.00977	-0.016	0.00024
		Average =	0.0057546	Variance = (Avg. squared deviation)	0.00049

Variance of average log of price relative × (34/33) = 0.00050
To convert to annual variance: × 365 or 0.18427
SIGMA – Annual volatility = Square root or 0.42927

EXHIBIT 5
Standard & Poor's 100 Options (OEX)

October 1, 1985

Strike Price	Calls Last			Puts Last		
	Oct.	Nov.	Dec.	Oct.	Nov.	Dec.
165	11.000	12.250		0.063	0.188	0.438
170	7.000	7.500	7.875	0.188	0.750	1.125
175	2.750	4.000	4.750	3.125	1.750	2.375
180	0.375	1.500	2.375	4.000	4.750	5.250
185	0.063	0.438	1.000	8.375	9.250	9.625
190	0.063	0.125	0.188	14.000	13.875	14.500
195	0.063	0.063				
200	0.063	0.063				

November 1, 1985

Strike Price	Calls Last			Puts Last		
	Nov.	Dec.	Jan.	Nov.	Dec.	Jan.
165	12.750	13.000	13.250	0.063	0.063	0.125
170	8.250	8.250	8.750	0.125	0.188	0.438
175	3.375	4.250	5.125	0.813	0.750	1.125
180	0.688	1.750	2.500	3.375	1.938	2.438
185	0.063	1.500	1.063	8.250	4.500	4.875
190				13.750	8.375	9.500
195						

EXHIBIT 5 (continued)

December 3, 1985

Strike Price	Calls Last			Puts Last		
	Dec.	Jan.	Feb.	Dec.	Jan.	Feb.
165	23.750	24.000			0.063	
170	19.125	19.500			0.063	
175	14.000	14.500	14.750	0.063	0.063	0.063
180	9.125	9.875	10.000	0.063	0.125	0.188
185	4.500	5.750	6.375	0.063	0.563	0.438
190	1.875	2.875	3.750	0.688	1.625	1.000
195	0.313	1.188	1.938	2.688	3.875	2.250
200	0.063	0.500	0.938	6.625	7.250	4.750
205				11.375	11.500	7.625

January 2, 1986

Strike Price	Calls Last			Puts Last		
	Jan.	Feb.	March	Jan.	Feb.	March
170	37.500					
175	32.500	31.500				
180	26.000	26.750	28.000		0.063	0.188
185	22.000	22.500	22.000	0.063	0.188	0.375
190	16.000	17.000	16.750	0.063	0.500	0.938
195	11.500	12.500	14.250	0.188	1.063	1.750
200	6.750	6.750	11.125	0.875	2.313	2.750
205	3.500	5.375	6.500	2.375	4.250	4.750
210	1.188	3.125	4.125	5.500	7.125	7.000
215	0.375	1.563	2.875	9.750	9.250	11.000

February 3, 1986

Strike Price	Calls Last			Puts Last		
	Feb.	March	April	Feb.	March	April
180	22.250	24.000	21.000		0.125	
185	20.000	20.000	16.500	0.063	0.313	0.750
190	14.754	15.625	12.750	0.125	0.813	1.438
195	9.875	11.625	9.500	0.625	1.688	2.625
200	6.000	7.875	6.500	1.750	3.250	4.000
205	3.000	5.000	4.375	3.875	5.375	6.375
210	1.125	3.000	2.688	7.000	8.500	11.000
215	0.375	1.625	1.563	11.500	12.500	13.000
220	0.063	0.750			17.750	16.750

March 3, 1986

Strike Price	Calls Last			Puts Last		
	March	April	May	March	April	May
180	39.250			0.063		
185	33.000			0.063	0.063	0.188
190	27.500	29.500		0.063	0.188	0.375
195	23.000	24.250	25.500	0.063	0.375	0.750
200	17.750	19.250	21.375	0.125	0.750	1.313
205	13.000	14.500	15.750	0.375	1.438	2.250
210	8.750	11.000	12.125	1.188	2.563	3.625
215	5.250	7.750	9.125	2.875	4.500	5.625
220	2.750	5.125	6.875	5.750	7.000	8.250
225	1.188	3.125	4.750	9.000	9.875	10.500
230	0.438	1.875	3.250	12.000	13.000	14.000

EXHIBIT 5 (continued)

April 1, 1986

Strike Price	Calls Last			Puts Last		
	April	May	June	April	May	June
185	40.000	40.000		0.063	0.063	
190	34.000	35.000		0.063	0.063	
195	29.500	31.000	30.500	0.063	0.063	5.800
200	23.750	24.250	25.000	0.063	0.250	1.063
205	19.000	20.500	23.000	0.063	0.438	1.875
210	13.875	15.625	18.000	0.125	0.938	1.875
215	9.625	12.750	14.875	0.375	0.938	4.500
220	6.000	9.000	11.750	1.125	3.000	6.325
225	3.125	6.500	9.000	2.688	5.000	8.000
230	0.625	2.875	5.000	5.250	7.500	13.500
240				12.000	14.125	

May 1, 1986

Strike Price	Calls Last			Puts Last		
	May	June	July	May	June	July
195	33.375					
200	26.625	29.000		0.063	0.250	
205	23.750	21.500		0.063	0.625	
210	16.625	19.625	20.000	0.125	1.063	2.000
215	11.500	14.250	16.500	0.438	2.125	3.000
220	7.250	11.250	12.000	1.375	3.500	4.625
225	4.000	7.125	9.250	3.250	5.625	6.750
230	2.125	4.750	7.750	6.500	8.500	9.500
235	1.000	3.125	5.000	10.250	11.875	12.500
240	0.375	1.875	3.500	14.500	15.500	13.250
245	0.125	1.000	2.375	19.250	19.250	19.250

June 2, 1986

	Calls Last			Puts Last		
Strike Price	June	July	August	June	July	August
200	38.750					
205	31.375			0.063	0.063	0.250
210	28.500	27.750	22.500	0.063	0.125	0.375
215	22.000	22.250	19.750	0.063	0.313	0.688
220	16.500	17.375	14.500	0.125	0.750	1.250
225	11.750	12.875	10.500	0.125	1.375	2.188
230	7.375	9.125	7.375	1.375	2.688	3.625
235	4.125	6.250		3.250	5.000	6.000
240	1.938	4.000		6.125	7.875	
245	0.750	2.313		10.000	10.750	
250	0.250	1.188		12.750	13.000	

July 1, 1986

	Calls Last		Puts Last
Strike Price	July	August	July
220			0.063
225			0.250
230			0.813
235	5.125	0.188	2.250
240	2.438		4.750
245	0.875		
250	0.188		

EXHIBIT 5 (concluded)

August 1, 1986

Strike Price	Calls Last			Puts Last		
	Oct.	Nov.	Dec.	Oct.	Nov.	Dec.
205	18.500	18.625		0.063	0.563	2.125
210	13.000	15.000	16.500	0.188	1.250	2.063
215	8.125	10.250	12.875	0.750	2.500	3.625
220	4.000	7.125	9.250	2.250	4.125	5.625
225	1.688	4.500	6.500	5.125	7.250	8.375
230	0.625	2.750	4.375	9.000	10.500	10.750
235	0.188	1.625	2.938	13.500	14.000	14.500
240	0.063	0.875	1.875	18.000	18.000	
245	0.063	0.438	1.250	23.000	22.500	
250	0.063	0.250	0.750		26.625	
255		0.125	0.500			

September 2, 1986

Strike Price	Calls Last			Puts Last		
	Sept.	Oct.	Nov.	Sept.	Oct.	Nov.
205	28.000	29.000		0.063	0.063	
210	23.000	22.000		0.063	0.125	0.313
215	17.625	19.000	19.000	0.063	0.375	0.563
220	12.750	13.750	15.125	0.125	0.688	0.875
225	8.500	10.000	12.250	0.125	1.125	1.563
230	4.750	7.000	8.500	1.125	2.750	2.625
235	3.313	4.500	5.625	2.813	4.500	4.125
240	0.625	2.438	3.500	5.750	7.125	6.125
245	0.313	1.125	2.125	8.375	10.000	8.375
250	0.063	0.563		12.750	13.500	13.250
255						

Source: The Wall Street Journal

pare an insurance strategy based on index options to one developed using individual equity options. Does it matter if the options are European or American?
3. How is a dynamic insurance strategy implemented? Why are the option pricing model and the option hedge ratio critical to the dynamic insurance strategy? Compare a dynamic insurance strategy to a static insurance strategy which uses index or individual options.
4. Evaluate the data in Exhibit 1, and explain their implications regarding static portfolio insurance. What criticisms would you make regarding the simulation results? Why are such simulations termed "sample period dependent"?

COMMENTS ON CASE ONE, T. DAVID BROWN

Objectives of the Case

Analysis should help you develop a more complete understanding of how options can be used to define and control risk in equity portfolios. Thorough understanding of the material in Chapter 5, Institutional Uses of Options, will facilitate discussion of the more subtle issues involved in this case. The analysis should begin by developing a concise definition of the term *portfolio insurance* and the strategies that can be used to insure equity portfolios. Next, the advantages and disadvantages of portfolio insurance can be listed, followed by a comparison of dynamic insurance strategies to those which use individual and index puts and calls.

Data in each exhibit can be examined and related to the topic of risk modification using options. Analysis of the case should conclude with a recommended investment strategy for Bob Whitney and his clients. This case has been used effectively in The Options Institute Program for Institutional Investors, and the suggested analysis here incorporates numerous comments and suggestions made by seminar participants during discussions.

The Problem

Bob Whitney is the options and futures strategist for T. David Brown, a mutual fund company in Seattle. The case is set in the fall of 1986, a period following a major market increase from below 900 on the DJIA in August 1982 to nearly 2000 in August 1986. Institutional investors are becoming apprehensive as the market continues to rise, and Whitney is trying to devise a plan which will protect the gains in the equity portfolios of his institutional clients.

Whitney must decide whether or not T. David Brown should provide portfolio insurance strategies to his clients, and if so, the most cost efficient manner to achieve this protection. He is aware that each dollar of client capital used for insurance premiums cannot be allocated to the purchase of T. David Brown's mutual funds.

Topics for Discussion

Prior to the market crash of October 1987, portfolio insurance was a rapidly growing equity strategy. This case focuses on the concept of portfolio insurance, the reasons it appeals to institutional investors, and the way it can be implemented. It is estimated that the amount of insured funds grew from a few billion dollars in 1983 to $100 billion by 1987. Many pension sponsors had significant gains in both stocks and bonds over this period, to the extent they became overfunded. The cost of new funding was declining rapidly in relation to payroll. As equities continued to increase in 1987 and stocks appeared more and more overvalued by historic standards, managers sought protection against a major market reversal, yet they were reluctant to give up participation in future market advances. Portfolio insurance strategies emerged as a low-cost procedure to achieve these objectives.

A Definition of Portfolio Insurance and Representative Portfolio Insurance Strategies

In the analysis, it is important to first establish a definition for portfolio insurance and to differentiate the expected returns of an insured portfolio to those from other types of hedging strategies. *Portfolio insurance* is defined as an investment strategy in which (1) the probability of loss is expressed as some percentage of the portfolio's value, including zero percent, and (2) the return is a predictable percentage of the increase in a reference portfolio (e.g., the S&P 500). Strategies that meet the definition of portfolio insurance are described in Chapter 5, and they include the purchase of protective puts, buying calls and Treasury bills, as well as dynamic asset allocation using stock index futures or the actual stocks. These are reviewed briefly here.

Portfolio Insurance Strategies. The most intuitive example of a portfolio insurance strategy is the purchase of equity or index puts on stocks currently held in a portfolio. The cost of the insurance is the put premium and the maximum loss, in insurance terms, the *deductible,* is the amount by which the puts are out-of-the-money. For example, on a stock with a price of $100, if the six-month $95 put is purchased for $2, the maximum loss is $5 (excluding the cost of the put), regardless of the stock's price in six months. Thus, the policy has a $5 deductible. If the stock appreciates above $100, the total gain less the cost of the put accrues to the stockholder. The stockholder shares by a predictable relationship in the price appreciation of the stock.

Another portfolio insurance strategy is the purchase of equity or index call options with a small percentage of the portfolio's total funds, say 10 percent, and investment of the remainder in Treasury bills. The downside loss is limited to the cost of the calls less the Treasury bill interest if the stocks decline. If the market appreciates, the calls increase in value and the profit earned is the total price appreciation of the stock above the option's striking price, less the cost of the calls, plus interest on the Treasury bills.

To see how the put and call strategies are associated, recall the put-call parity relationship presented in Chapter 2. Put-call parity describes how the price of the put, call, stock, and the interest rate must be related for fair value to exist for the options. Figure 2–19 in Chapter 2 shows that a riskless relationship which should earn the return of a riskless bond, $B,$ is created by a position which is long stock, $S,$ long an at-the-money put, $P,$ and short an at-the-money call, $C,$ with both options having the same exercise price and maturity. This can be expressed as: $B = S + P - C.$

Since this is an equality for European options, the relationship can be rearranged by transferring the call premium, $C,$ to the left of the equal sign, to show that $B + C = S + P.$ That is, purchase of a bond plus a long at-the-money call will give the same payoff as an investment in the stock plus purchase of an at-the-money put, and both represent strategies of portfolio insurance. The put-call parity idea will be used later to equate strategies involving the sale of puts and calls.

Another way to insure a portfolio is to use dynamic insurance, also described in Chapter 5. This method is based on the creation of a synthetic put by frequent rebalancing of funds (e.g., weekly or daily) between the stock (or stock index futures) and Treasury bills. The objective is to replicate the payoff of put plus a long stock position. Mechanics of this strategy are in the section describing dynamic insurance.

Distribution of Portfolio Returns

Insight into the way options modify a portfolio's risk is gained by comparing the possible distribution of returns for insured portfolios containing options to portfolios composed only of stocks and bonds. Typically, the distribution of returns from an all equity or debt-equity portfolio is approximately normal, generally conforming to the familiar bell-shaped curve shown in Exhibit 6A. If the portfolio manager lowers the investment in this stock portfolio by increasing investment in cash or bonds, it reduces variability, represented by the spread in the distribution, pulling in the tails and making it more peaked. However, the distribution still retains its symmetric shape.

Returns for the S&P 500 Index.   Relating this concept to the case, the distribution of quarterly returns for the S&P 500 Index given in Exhibit 1 is plotted in Exhibit 6B. The value above each bar is the midpoint of the percentage range for the bar and the height of the bar indicates the proportion of the 54 quarterly returns which had a return in that 5 percentage interval. For example, about 25 percent of all quarterly returns were between 0 and +5 percent indicated by the bar labeled "2.50%." The mean return for this distribution is 3.02 percent, and the variability, as measured by the standard deviation of returns, is 8.6 percent.

EXHIBIT 6A
Representative Normally Distributed Security Returns

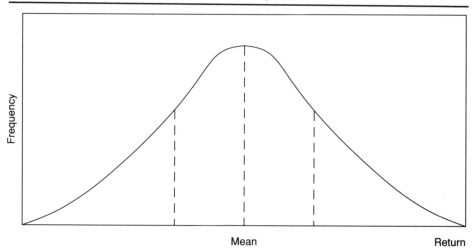

EXHIBIT 6B
Distribution of Quarterly Returns for the S&P 500 from 1970 to 1983

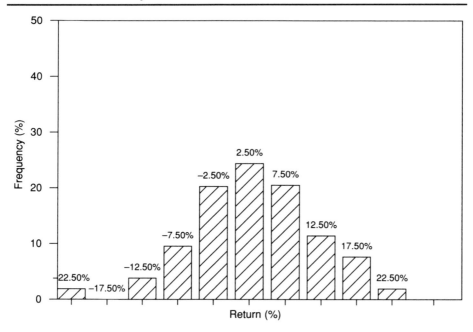

Returns for Insured Portfolios. Consider now the return distribution for an insured portfolio. Because losses for an insured portfolio are defined and gains accrue at a known relationship to the reference portfolio, the distribution of returns for insured portfolios possess the characteristic of positive skewness. A stylized graph of a protective put portfolio is shown in Exhibit 7A which is overlaid on the normal distribution of the underlying stock portfolio. The protective put distribution is truncated on the downside at the defined loss value, and has a long tail toward the positive returns, thus the term *positive skewness*. A graph of the returns from buying calls (10 percent) and investing in Treasury bills (90 percent) would look virtually the same as this protective put graph.

Consider the distribution of the quarterly returns for the protective put portfolio, called the Insured Index Fund I as shown in Exhibit 7B. These quarterly returns are given in Exhibit 1 of the case. Exhibit 7B shows that about 41 percent of the quarterly returns from the protective put strategy are between −5 and 0 percent. The mean return of 3.05 percent for this distribution is slightly greater than the mean of 3.02 percent for the S&P 500 portfolio, and the standard deviation of 5.2 percent is significantly lower than 8.6 percent for the S&P 500. The

EXHIBIT 7A
Stylized Return Distribution for a Protective Put Portfolio

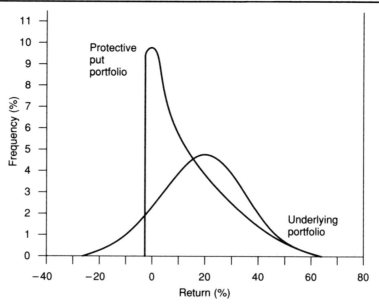

EXHIBIT 7B
Distribution of Quarterly Returns for the Insured Index Fund I from 1970 to 1983

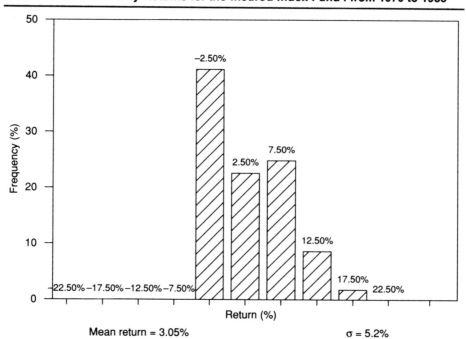

reduced variability is achieved by eliminating the returns below the mean, an action highly valued by investors.

It should not be inferred that the use of portfolio insurance produces returns about the same as or greater than an equity portfolio, since any empirical test is data dependent on the period from which the sample is taken. However, maintaining an insured position on an equity portfolio always reduces the portfolio's risk. Thus, it should be expected that the reduced risk of the protected put strategy leads to lower returns over a long period of time for an insured portfolio, compared to an all-equity one.

Comparison of Quarterly Returns

These concepts can be developed further by examining the data presented in Exhibit 1. First, note that when the quarterly returns on the index are positive, the insured index funds have positive (but smaller), returns, caused by the cost of the put. However, when the S&P 500 has a loss, the loss for the insured fund is much less, reflecting the insurance dimension of the put. The largest loss for the S&P 500 in quarter 3 of 1974, −25 percent, is paired with the insured portfolio's largest loss of only −3.3 percent. The greatest gain for the S&P 500, +22.9 percent in quarter 1 of 1975 is paired with a gain of 18.9 percent for the Insured Fund I.

Next, note how the results between the uninsured S&P 500 and the insured index fund vary relative to the time period in which the simulation is begun. Cumulative returns for each strategy are given at the end of Exhibit 1. If the entire data period from June 1970 until December 1983 is used, the cumulative return for the insured fund is 414.3 percent and for the S&P 500, it is 311.0 percent. Large losses, incurred by the index in 1973 and 1974, depressed its performance over the entire period. By avoiding the large losses in those two years, the insured fund earned a superior return, compared to the S&P 500 Index. However, if the simulation is begun in January 1975, the uninsured S&P 500 portfolio outperformed the insured fund, 272.5 versus 263.4 percent. The same is true if the data begin in January 1978, 1979, 1980, 1982, or 1983.

Finally, a word of caution should be noted about the simulation results presented on Exhibit 1. As with any simulation, the results are dependent on how well the simulation reflects reality. These results are driven by the option pricing model, its inputs which are used to calculate option premiums, and the assumption that transactions would have occurred at model prices. For example, if volatility estimates used to price the options in the simulation were systematically lower than those which would have been used in actual trading, severe option underpricing would exist. The insured portfolio strategy would appear better than it really would have been.

Strategies Which Do Not Represent Portfolio Insurance

When discussing the concept of portfolio insurance, seminar participants sometimes suggest strategies that do not conform to the definition of portfolio insurance. Frequently mentioned are covered call writing, market timing, and portfolio rebalancing (e.g., allocation between stocks, bonds, and cash).

Covered Call Writing

Covered call writing can be termed *hedging,* but it does not conform to either part of the definition of portfolio insurance. Instead, the covered writing portfolio participates in losses of the reference portfolio while it limits the portfolio's gains to the call's striking price, plus the option premium received. For example, assume that a six month at-the-money call is sold on a $100 stock for $6. The most that can be earned from this position is $6 plus any dividends paid by the stock. On the downside, if the stock falls below $94, the stockholder shares dollar for dollar in the loss in the stock.

Exhibit 3 contains performance statistics for six mutual funds which follow the strategy of covered call writing. Over the period of March 1983 through March 1986 these funds earned an average annual return of 12.4 percent, compared to 21.1 percent for the S&P 500. Their risk, as measured by beta or standard deviation, was lower than the market, but not proportional to their significantly lower returns.

The Distribution of Covered Call Returns

A stylized return distribution for a covered call portfolio is shown in Exhibit 8. For this strategy, the return distribution is truncated on the right side, reflecting the limited gains which can be earned, while the left tail extends toward the negative returns which occur when the underlying portfolio of stocks falls in price. Variability in this distribution is less than the stock portfolio as shown by the more compact range of returns, however the lowered variability comes about by eliminating the returns above the mean—an undesirable effect.

EXHIBIT 8
Stylized Distribution of Returns for the Strategy of Covered Call Writing

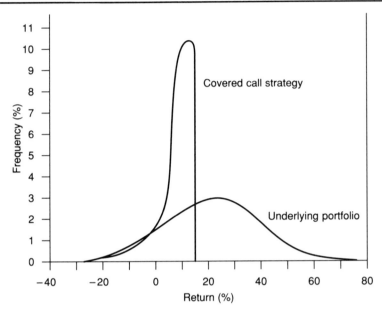

The put strategy equivalent to covered writing, expressed as $S - C$, is the sale of a put combined with an investment in Treasury bills equal to the put's exercise price, $B - P$. This can be derived by rearranging the put-call parity relationship from $B = S + P - C$, to $B - P = S - C$. The distribution of expected returns for a sell put, buy Treasury bills portfolio theoretically will be identical to the covered writing strategy, and thus would look like Exhibit 8.

Market Timing

The strategy of market timing is sometimes compared to the insurance technique called *dynamic insurance,* however, they are quite different in concept and execution. The objective of dynamic insurance is to replicate the performance of a portfolio composed of the stock, plus puts purchased on the portfolio (the protective put strategy). Allocations between cash and equities is not based on the predicted direction in the market, but instead is derived from a mathematical algorithm which specifies the required allocation between stocks and the riskless asset needed to replicate a protective put portfolio.

Conversely, under market timing the allocation between stocks, bonds, and cash is made according to factors which the timer believes is going to cause the market to rise or fall. It is the timer's objective to profit by anticipating market movements. However, if the timer is wrong and the market falls when a rise was predicted, there is no floor protection level to reduce losses. On the other hand, assume that the market timer moves to cash and bonds from equities in anticipation of a market decline, but the market rises instead. The portfolio does not share in the market increase. Neither part of the definition for portfolio insurance is met by a market timing strategy, even though dynamic insurance (like market timing) does involve movement of funds between equities and cash.

Portfolio Rebalancing

Similar to market timing, the strategy of portfolio rebalancing based on expected market movements does not represent portfolio insurance. As discussed earlier, changing the allocation among stocks and less risky assets, such as bonds or cash, alters the expected return distribution by pulling in the extreme returns in the tails of the distribution and making it more peaked as shown in Exhibit 9. However, there is no floor return on

EXHIBIT 9
Stylized Distributions of an All Equity Portfolio and a Portfolio of 60 Percent Equity, 40 Percent Bonds

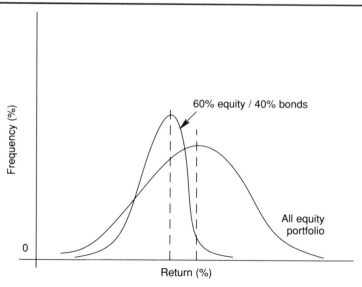

the downside to protect the portfolio from losses during market declines. The rebalanced portfolio with reduced equity exposure just does not fall as much as an all equity portfolio on the downside, nor does it appreciate as much when the market rises.

Empirical Evidence about Insured Portfolio Performance

Several studies have compared the performance of portfolios containing options to equity portfolios over lengthy market periods. While results of this research cannot be generalized to specific future markets, the findings can enhance appreciation of how options can be used to mold return distributions to meet particular investment objectives. If the traditional relationship holds between return and risk, over a long period of time it should be expected that an all equity, uninsured portfolio earns a higher return than one which is continually insured, because the uninsured one has greater risk. Results of one study which compares the performance of four option strategies to an equity portfolio over a 20½ year period are shown in Exhibit 10.

The Sample
The 129 stocks used as the sample represent all stocks on which listed options were available in May 1980. Stock prices, dividends, and interest rate information were used to calculate premiums for at-the-money put and call options using a modified Black-Scholes option pricing model. In

EXHIBIT 10
Return Distribution Statistics for Stock and Option Strategies, July 1963–December 1983 (quarterly returns)

Strategy	Mean Return	Volatility (σ)	Skewness	Maximum Loss
Equity portfolio of 129 stocks	3.69%	9.91%	− .2259	−24.4%
Buy calls (10%)/buy T-bills (90%)	3.84	8.22	+ .5021	− 7.0
Covered call writing	2.42	5.23	−1.6163	−20.9
Buy puts/buy stock	3.14	5.06	+ .8260	− 4.5
Sell puts/buy T-bills	1.77	4.40	− .9769	−15.3

Source: Gary L. Trennepohl, James Booth, and Hassan Tehranian, "An Empirical Analysis of Insured Portfolio Strategies Using Listed Options," *Journal of Financial Research* 11, no. 1 (Spring 1988).

each option strategy, the option position was established at the beginning of each three-month period and closed at the end of the period. For example, under the covered call writing strategy, an at-the-money three-month call was sold against each share of stock in the 129 stock portfolio at the beginning of each quarter. It was assumed that any call in-the-money at the end of the quarter was bought back; all others were allowed to expire worthless. For any strategy involving stocks, it was assumed that all dividends received were reinvested in the portfolio at the end of each quarter.

Portfolio Performance
Statistics about the return distributions of different strategies are presented in Exhibit 10. The buy calls (10%)/buy T-bills (90%) strategy had the largest three-month return with slightly less risk than the 129 stock portfolio. By contrast, the protective put portfolio (buy puts/buy stock), had a slightly lower return than the stock portfolio, but about half the risk (return variability). The insured portfolios, buy calls (10%)/buy T-bills (90%) and buy puts/buy stock, were positively skewed with a small maximum loss, while the covered write strategy and its equivalent sell puts/buy T-bills, exhibited lower returns and volatility, and negative skewness. These two strategies suffered smaller maximum losses than the stock portfolio due to option premiums received in the quarter the market incurred its largest decline (quarter 3 of 1974).

How insured strategies perform relative to a stock portfolio depends on the particular market period and thus cannot be generalized to the future. What is true is that the insured strategy will have a smaller maximum loss near the promised floor return, and positive skewness in its returns representing participation in the gains of the reference portfolio.

Why Insure a Portfolio?

Understanding how options modify a portfolio's return distribution is essential when evaluating benefits and costs of an insured portfolio strategy. Investors should compare their investment objectives and their attitudes toward risk to evaluate the advantages and disadvantages regarding portfolio insurance strategies. Theoretical arguments suggest that portfolio insurance should be considered by investors having one of the following characteristics:

1. Their tolerance to risk increases as their wealth increases, more than the average investor's. Pension fund managers, for example, may be willing to accept more risk once they have achieved the minimum required return on their portfolio. Portfolio insurance provides participation in further gains if they occur while protecting the current value of the portfolio.
2. Their expectations are more optimistic than the average investor's, such as fund managers who believe they will outperform the market by superior stock selection. The costs of portfolio insurance can be paid from the excess returns they expect to generate, while the insurance protects them from unforeseen market downturns.

Advantages of Portfolio Insurance
The advantages of using portfolio insurance, which frequently are suggested during case discussion, include the following:

1. "Catastrophe insurance"—it protects a portfolio from severe, unexpected market declines.
2. Capital preservation—it protects gains in your portfolio.
3. Flexible risk control—it enables the portfolio manager to control risk in the portfolio without disturbing major equity positions.
4. It allows for participation in market advances while limiting losses during market declines.
5. It can be implemented independent of the active equity managers.
6. It eliminates the need for market timing and portfolio rebalancing decisions, which often are imprecise and detract from portfolio performance.
7. "Job insurance"—An insured portfolio does not incur large losses in a severe market downturn, thus portfolio managers do not have to explain why they did not foresee the downturn and take action to reduce the portfolio's risk. In short, they save their jobs.

Disadvantages of Portfolio Insurance
1. It is complex and can be difficult to explain to clients and board members.
2. It has a cost. Maintaining an insured portfolio through time can detract from performance. Board members and clients might ask why these costs are being incurred when the market is rising.

3. Dynamic insurance using futures or the sale of stocks might not work in times of severe market downturns, such as occurred in October 1987.

Portfolio Insurance Using Index Puts Compared to Individual Equity Options

Greater understanding of the differences between index and individual options is gained by exploring how portfolio insurance strategies differ using these instruments. Information presented in Chapter 5 can be used to develop this comparison.

Difference in Payoffs

Recall that the payoffs can differ between index and individual options depending on how the prices of individual securities change in the portfolio. It is not possible to predict which produces the greatest payoff over a particular future period. The comparison in Chapter 5 between portfolios insured by index and individual puts shows little difference in profit between the two strategies; however, other examples could be constructed in which the results differ dramatically.

Differences in Premiums Caused by Differences in Risk

The costs of index puts or calls generally is lower than buying a portfolio of individual options. To understand why, it is necessary to divide the total risk (price volatility) present in any security into its two components. One source of price volatility is general market factors, which affect the prices of all stocks; this is called *systematic risk*. The other component is volatility caused by factors unique to each firm, called *unsystematic risk*. Between 40 and 60 percent of the price changes in the typical security is systematic, related to changes in the market; the remainder can be attributed to unsystematic risk. The combination of systematic and unsystematic risk represents total risk of the security. As securities are combined into portfolios, the unsystematic risk of each security tends to offset the unsystematic volatility in other stocks, and total risk in the portfolio declines as portfolio size increases. This is just a complex way to explain the common rule that investors should diversify their holdings.

Diversification and Risk. The act of diversification quickly reduces the unsystematic risk in an equity portfolio toward the limiting value of risk in the market portfolio. Since the market portfolio is fully diversified, it contains only systematic risk. Exhibit 11 shows how price volatility, or risk, in a portfolio changes as the portfolio size is increased. Risk is plotted on the vertical axis and the number of securities in the portfolio are plotted on the horizontal axis. The curve, representing total portfolio risk, falls toward the line indicating the risk of the S&P 500. Points on the curve are determined by calculating the average volatility of all portfolios containing one stock, two stocks, three stocks, etc. An average 20-stock portfolio has about 95 percent less unsystematic risk than is present in the average individual security. The systematic portion of risk forms a floor on the level of risk-reduction possible by diversification since the totally diversified market portfolio, as represented by the S&P 500, contains only systematic risk.

Pricing Index and Individual Options.   Considering the systematic and unsystematic components of risk, the differential in pricing between individual and index options now can be resolved. Recall from Chapter 2 that the price of an option is directly affected by the volatility of its underlying security. The higher the volatility, the higher the option's price. The volatility estimate used to price options on individual securities reflects the security's total risk, including the systematic and unsys-

EXHIBIT 11
The Relationship between Portfolio Size and Portfolio Risk

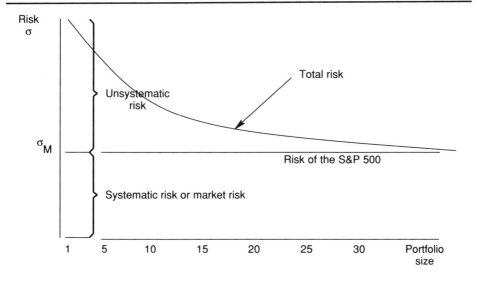

tematic components. The volatility estimate used to price options on an index, say the S&P 500, represents the total risk of the index, but it contains only systematic risk because the unsystematic risk component in the market portfolio has been removed by diversification. The lower volatility estimate means that it costs less, relatively speaking, to purchase one S&P 500 Index put than individual puts on 500 securities. If the objective is to insure the portfolio, not each security, the purchase of index puts is the most cost effective technique. Buying individual equity options "overinsures" the portfolio because the total risk of each stock is protected.

Portfolio Tracking

Fund managers must consider how their holdings track the portfolio underlying the index option. If the relationship between the two is high, using index options can be cost effective insurance. If the relationship is not high, it might be necessary to use individual options or to engage in dynamic insurance.

Settlement Procedures

The settlement procedure differs between individual and index options and can influence which options are selected. Index options are settled in cash while individual options are exercised by delivery of the underlying stock. Obviously either index or individual options can be traded before expiration on the floor of the options exchange. Also, portfolio insurance strategies, involving the purchase of puts or calls, are not subject to unexpected exercise since the purchaser determines when the option is exercised. However, strategies involving the sale of individual options, such as covered writing, expose the writer to potentially unexpected exercise of the call and sale of the underlying security with accompanying costs and tax consequences.

American versus European Options

Finally, the question of using European or American options also should be explored relative to index and individual options. Currently, all exchange traded individual options are American, meaning that they can be exercised at any time. However, some index options, the S&P 500 series for example, are European, meaning that they can be exercised only at expiration. When insuring a portfolio, which option to use primarily depends on the fund manager's objectives. A European option can be cheaper than an American option on the same underlying security with identical attributes (e.g., time to expiration and strike). This happens because there is a cost associated with the privilege of early exercise afforded by the American option. If the objective is to insure a portfolio over some defined time horizon, say one year, and the ability to exercise the option has no value to the fund manager, it is more cost effective to purchase European index options. However, if the alternative of actually trading the underlying security has value to the fund manager, using individual equity options should be considered. It is not possible to obtain or deliver securities by exercising an index option.

What Is Dynamic Insurance and How Is It Accomplished?

Dynamic insurance is derived from the theory underlying the Black-Scholes option pricing model. It is an attempt to create an arbitrage portfolio composed of the underlying security and the riskless asset, say Treasury bills, which will have payoff identical to an option over a short time period. This insight regarding the arbitrage portfolio enabled Black and Scholes to develop their option pricing model. The amount to allocate to each security at each point in time is determined by the option's delta, or hedge ratio.

The Black-Scholes Call Option Pricing Model
The Black-Scholes call option pricing model is given as,

$$C = N(X_1)S - N(X_2)Ee^{-rT}$$

where C is the price of a European call, $N(X_1)$ and $N(X_2)$ are probabilities, S is the price of the stock, E is the exercise price of the option, and e^{-rT} is the present value operator using the interest rate, r, over time period, T. $N(X_1)$ also is called the delta, or hedge ratio of the call, a value between 0 and 1. For our discussion we assume that the stock pays no dividends.[3] It is helpful to express the call pricing equation as:

Call price = (Call hedge ratio)(Stock price) − Borrowing

That is, the call on one share of stock is replicated by a long position in a fractional share of stock which is financed primarily by borrowing.

---

[3] Option pricing models are available that can price American options on dividend paying stocks. However, the basics of option replication are the same as used in the standard Black-Scholes option pricing model shown here.

Replicating a Call
For example, consider an at-the-money three-month call on a $100 stock, with a volatility of .1442 (annualized), and an interest rate of 8%. Solving the Black-Scholes equation shows that the call should have a price of $3.90, and a delta of .62. This means that the replicating portfolio will be constructed by buying .62 shares of stock financed by borrowing $58.10,

$$\$3.90 = .62(\$100) - \$58.10.$$

The $3.90 added to the portfolio, represents the call buyer's investment in the position.

A change in any of the five factors influencing the value of a call will cause a change in the hedge ratio and thus change the allocation between the stock and the amount borrowed. For example, assume that immediately after establishing the replicating portfolio, the price of the stock increases to $102. In this case the call value will change to $5.24 and the delta will increase to .72. The replicating portfolio must be adjusted by buying .10 shares of stock, which is totally financed by borrowing. A decrease in the stock price would cause a decline in hedge ratio, requiring stock to be sold. In theory, the replicating portfolio will be totally self-financing through time, additional shares are purchased by increased borrowing, and the sale of stock which occurs when the stock price falls is used to repay borrowed funds.

Pricing a Put
The option pricing model also can be used to price a put, by changing the signs on the stock, riskless asset positions, and the $N(X)$ values in the equation.

$$P = -N(-X_1)S + N(-X_2)Ee^{-rT}$$

Thus, a put can be replicated by shorting the stock and lending the proceeds at the riskless rate.

$$\text{Put} = (\text{Put hedge ratio})(\text{Stock}) + \text{Lending}$$

The hedge ratio for a put will lie between 0 and -01.0; as the stock price falls the hedge ratio moves toward -1.0, while an increase in the stock price causes the hedge ratio to move toward 0. Also, it is useful to know that the hedge ratio for the put equals the call hedge ratio minus one.

Replicating a Put
Consider replicating a three-month, at-the-money put on the same $100 dollar stock described above. The value of the put is $2.01 and the hedge

ratio is $-.38$, meaning that the replicating portfolio will contain a short position in .38 shares of stock. The proceeds from the short sale plus $2.01 will be invested at the riskless rate of interest. If the stock price rises immediately to $102, the put hedge ratio will change to $-.28$ and the put price will fall to $1.35. The replicating portfolio will be rebalanced by purchasing .10 shares of stock (ie. $.38 - .28$), which is financed by reducing the lending position.

While the replicating portfolio is self-financing in theory, that will rarely be the case in practice. Because the replicating portfolio is re-balanced at discrete intervals rather than continuously, there will be some slippage in the value of the replicating portfolio compared to the option. The degree of slippage primarily will be a function of the re-balancing interval used (e.g. one day versus one week) and the volatility of the security experienced over the period covered by the replicating portfolio.

Replicating a Protective Put Portfolio
The replicating portfolios described above create the position of a long call or long put. However, for the purpose of this case it is important to understand how the replicating portfolio is constructed when the inves-tor is combining the replicated long put with a long position in the underlying security, producing the protective put portfolio. First, note that the delta of the stock is 1.0, since the delta indicates the percentage change in the security's price relative to a change in the price of the underlying stock. To determine the delta of the long stock and long put position, the deltas of the securities are added together. Using the $100 stock from the example above, the protective put portfolio of the stock plus the put would have a delta of .72, $[(+ 1.0) + (- .38)]$. (Recall that this also is the delta of the at-the-money three-month call on the same security.) Thus, the synthetically insured portfolio would consist of .72 shares of the underlying stock and investment in the riskless asset as determined earlier.

The Dynamic Insurance Tree
The data in Exhibit 2 of the case, Dynamic Insurance Tree, illustrate how the replicated protective put portfolio would behave through time. In this example, the stock is at $100 and has a volatility of 14.42%, annualized (2% weekly). The replicated at-the-money European put has 13 weeks to expiration, and it is assumed that the interest rate is 0%. The put pre-mium determined by the model is $2.88, and the put option delta is $-.4856$. Combining the put and stock position produces a delta for the

portfolio of .5144 which equals the call delta, or hedge ratio, given in the case. Thus the dynamic asset allocation portfolio would consist of a long position in .5144 shares of the underlying stock costing $51.44, and lending equal to $51.44. The total replicating portfolio value, $102.88, is equal to the value of one long share of stock, $100, and a put, $2.88.

Reallocations in the replicating portfolio caused by changes in the stock price or time to expiration can be determined by the stock/cash amounts shown in the exhibit. To see that this strategy represents an insured portfolio, note that the last row, "zero time to maturity", shows that the portfolio will have a value of $100 if the stock is below $100 in price, and some amount above $100 if the stock is above that value.

An interesting point of reference as suggested in the case, is to examine the composition of the replicating portfolio down the $100 stock price column, thus assuming that the stock does not change in price during the entire 13-week period. Each week, the reduction in time to expiration moves the delta towards zero, thus reducing the investment in the underlying security and the lending portfolio. This is accomplished by selling a small amount of stock each week and liquidating a portion of the riskless asset investment, enabling some cash to be removed from the portfolio each week. In this unrealistic example of no price volatility, the excess cash withdrawn over 13 weeks amounts to $2.88 (the original cost of the put), indicating that the put was costless. (This result may be intuitive. The value of an option on a stock whose future price is known with certainty is the present value of the difference between the known future price and the exercise price of the option.)

The Cost of Dynamic Insurance
This example may suggest that there is no cost attached to a protective put insurance strategy based on dynamic insurance; however, that conclusion is incorrect. Note that when the strategy was implemented in week 13, a total of $102.88 was invested in portfolio, $51.44 was allocated to the stock, and $51.44 was invested in the riskless asset. There was no payment of the option premium up front, but its cost is imbedded in the funds loaned at the riskless rate. Whether or not funds will be recovered, or additional funds added to the dynamic insurance portfolio, will be determined by the volatility of the stock over the period of the insurance. Recall that the option price of $2.88 was calculated using an estimated stock volatility of 14.42 percent. If the volatility experienced over the life of the insured portfolio is less than this amount, the cost for the insurance protection will be less than $2.88. If the volatility is greater than 14.42

percent, cash will have to be added to the replicating portfolio causing the protection to cost more. These relationships can be demonstrated by following different stock price paths from the top to the bottom of Exhibit 2.

A Comparison of Dynamic Insurance to Static Insurance Using Listed Options

Dynamic insurance is an alternative to listed options for creating an insured portfolio. Most fund managers who attempt to insure their portfolios using dynamic insurance use the stock index futures markets to hedge the underlying equity portfolio, rather than trading in stocks. When futures are used, the portfolio insurer shorts sufficient futures contracts (each short futures contract has a delta of -1.0) to create a delta on the equity portion of the portfolio equal to that specified by the option model. Whether stock index futures or stocks are used, the trading mechanics are essentially the same.

Why Consider a Dynamic Insurance Strategy?
To make the comparison between static and dynamic insurance, it first is necessary to establish why a manager would consider implementing portfolio insurance with the dynamic strategy, which can appear unnecessarily complicated and transaction intensive. The following reasons are frequently mentioned as advantages of dynamic insurance:

1. Listed options may not be available on indexes which track a particular fund's portfolio.
2. Listed options may not have the exercise price, maturity, or be of the desired type (American or European.) For example, insurers often use a one-year time horizon for the insurance, and until the S&P 500 contract was introduced, no listed contract was available with this maturity. Also, most insurers prefer a European contract because the early exercise option is of no value to them. Options can be created with dynamic insurance having the exact characteristics desired by the fund manager.
3. The fund is so large that the listed option market does not have sufficient liquidity.

Given that reasons exist for the consideration of dynamic insurance, the following comparisons between listed options and dynamic insurance should be developed.

1. The dynamic insurance strategy requires continual rebalancing of the positions; the use of listed options does not. Consequently dynamic insurance positions can get whipsawed in a volatile, nondirectional market.
2. Large jumps in stock prices can be disastrous for the dynamic insurer, as was evident in the market crash of October 1987. Static insurance strategies using listed options, which require no trading in a volatile market, performed well during the crash and are unaffected by large jumps in the market.
3. Transactions costs can be significant with the dynamic insurance strategy.
4. The cost of the protection under the dynamic insurance strategy is unknown when the insurance is implemented. If market volatility is less than that used to price listed options when the positions are first established, its realized cost will be below the listed options; if volatility is greater, the cost will be higher.

Two main points should emerge from the comparison. First, a cost for the insurance exists for the dynamic strategy, even though it is not as obvious as the put premium in the static strategy. The main difference is that the cost for the static strategy is known when the position is established, while the cost for the dynamic counterpart is unknown until the insurance position is terminated. Second, because the static insurer does not have to trade in volatile markets, the protection afforded by listed puts is much greater than that of the dynamic insurance program. Because of the difficult market conditions during the market correction on October 19 and 20 in 1987, many dynamic insurers terminated trading, leaving their portfolios uninsured during that period.

Analyzing Data from Case Exhibits 4 and 5

At this point in the analysis, the major qualitative issues in the case have been developed. Further quantitative analysis can be performed using the data presented in Exhibits 4 and 5. Suggested activities include:

1. Exhibit 4 illustrates how the volatility of the S&P 100 Index can be calculated. It can be helpful to work through the calculations to become familiar with the mathematical procedure. In addition, the implied volatility in the OEX options presented in Exhibit 5

can be compared to the past volatility calculated in Exhibit 4. Implied volatility for OEX options in today's market also can be contrasted with implied volatility from Exhibit 5 and actual volatility calculated in Exhibit 4.

2. Premiums for the OEX puts and calls presented in Exhibit 5 can be used to simulate various static insurance programs. Performance of the insured portfolios can be compared to performance of the uninsured index to determine which strategy would have achieved the best results over this period.

Bob Whitney's Recommendation

A careful analysis of all these topics presented should enable Bob Whitney to make an informed decision about the use of portfolio insurance for his client's portfolios. The principal concepts developed in the case discussion include:

1. Portfolio insurance reduces portfolio risk by limiting losses, while allowing participation in market advances. It differs from market hedging strategies, such as market timing or asset mix decisions.
2. Portfolio insurance has a cost, whether the insurance is obtained by the purchase of listed individual or index puts, or by dynamic rebalancing.
3. Empirical evidence suggests that portfolio insurance strategies would have performed well over extended market periods, reducing volatility while earning returns similar to a portfolio of equity securities.
4. The costs of insurance differ between index and individual puts because of the type of risk used to price the options. The cost of dynamic rebalancing is unknown at the beginning of the insurance period and is determined by the volatility over the insurance period.
5. Insurance with listed options is effective in volatile markets, while dynamic insurance can break down in severe market declines.

The recommendation that Whitney makes to his clients should depend on his assessment of the market's future direction and his attitude toward risk. If there is a sufficient concern that the market is overvalued and that gains should be protected, a portfolio insurance strategy should be recommended. Based on information presented in the case, portfolio insurance is an appropriate strategy for Whitney's clients.

Assuming that Whitney's portfolios track closely with the S&P 100 or S&P 500 Indexes, the purchase of index puts with a known cost appears to be the most secure move. While the use of listed puts can appear more costly than dynamic insurance because of the "up front" premium, dynamic insurance has a cost as well. It is just not as easily identified.

In retrospect, insurance with index puts would have been a wise decision. The equity portfolios would have participated in the market advance until August 1987, and the insurance would have become quite valuable when the crash occurred.

What decision did Whitney actually make? In the fall of 1986 he opted for the dynamic insurance strategy. It worked quite well over the next year as the DJIA increased from 1900 to 2772. Unfortunately, the volatility of the market increased in September 1987; by October, the futures market was unable to absorb mounting selling pressures as dynamic insurers attempted to rebalance their portfolios in a declining market.

During trading on October 19, 1987, future prices became delinked from the underlying stocks because of the inability to obtain timely stock price quotes. Most dynamic insurers suspended futures trading, causing their portfolios to become uninsured. Dynamic insurance turned out to be ineffective during severe market volatility—a time when insurance is needed the most. It has been suggested that investors who implemented dynamic insurance strategies using the futures market realized a 60 per cent level of insurance, compared to hedging with listed puts. Moreover, the dynamic strategy has been blamed for accentuating the market crash of October 19.

Case Two, Rocky Mountain High, involves an investment situation in which the static hedging techniques using the S&P 500 put options contract (SPX) was used prior to the October 1987 crash with positive results. This case, however, forces the reader to make risk modification decisions in a radically different market environment than the first case.

Rocky Mountain High

On January 18, 1988, Jay Tracey, vice president of Berger Associates, was working on an appropriate investment strategy for the One Hundred Fund, a $10.5 million no-load mutual fund. The current investment environment was not as friendly as it had been during the past few years. A sudden drop in the Dow Jones Industrial Average during October of last year had sent tremendous shock waves through the financial markets. Worse, the period following the crash was marked by further uncertainty, high volatility, and continued declines. And the fourth quarter of 1987 had been particularly tough on growth stocks.

The One Hundred Fund, classified as a growth fund, primarily purchased equities of both growth and emerging growth companies. This afternoon, Tracey is meeting with Bill Berger, president of Berger Associates, and Will Nicholson, vice president, to discuss an appropriate portfolio strategy for the fund. Given the current market conditions and the pool of available securities, these portfolio managers would have to make some difficult decisions. Since all three worked on this account, Tracey wanted to outline several distinct alternatives for all of them to examine in order to establish the investment strategy for the fund over the next few months.

Company Background

In 1973, Bill Berger founded Berger Associates, an investment management firm located in Denver, Colorado. Berger Associates managed debt and equity portfolios and had over 100 accounts, composed of individual portfolios, company pension and profit-sharing programs, and two mutual funds. Four portfolio managers (Bill Berger, Lloyd Joshel, Jay Tracey, and Will Nicholson) shared management responsibility for each account and made all investment decisions together.

The firm's central investment philosophy was that profitable, successful companies result in profitable, successful investments, whereas mediocre ones produce mediocre investment returns. Berger Associates primarily used earnings growth, dividend growth, and return on equity as performance measurements to identify those companies whose returns have been the highest and most consistent. This strategy motivated them to have a long-term orientation. Berger Associates did not speculate on short-term price movements to produce results. Berger Associates' goal was to double the value of its accounts every five years.

The Summer of 87

The One Hundred Fund gained 26.6 percent from January through July, and Tracey and Berger were pleased with this performance. Although the market continued to advance, both managers realized that new highs also represent potential danger. Current price-earnings multiples, price-to-book values, and dividend yields indicated that the market was valued at an historically rich level. If the market retreated from its current valuation, the One Hundred Fund might decrease dramatically.

During a company meeting, Berger said, "Jay, I'm concerned about a precipitous market decline, which could be as high as 20 percent. I do not believe that the likelihood of such a decline is very large, but if it should happen, our shareholders would probably ask, 'Didn't you guys know that the market was overvalued?' Our only response would be, 'Yes, but we didn't think that the market would correct itself this time.' We had better look into some downside protection." The only questions that remained were what type of protection to obtain and how much should they be prepared to pay.

At the following week's discussion, Tracey presented several options that addressed those concerns. He said, "There are essentially three ways to go: convert to cash, short the futures market, or buy index puts. Increasing cash means liquidating some of our current positions, which would have tax implications from capital gains. We would also limit the fund's participation in any market advances. Since we're not forecasting a bear market, I suggest that we do not increase cash. The second alternative is to short the futures market. The major benefit of this option is that we do not have up-front costs, and the hedge is effective at this level, like buying puts at-the-money. The major drawback, however, is that we cannot quantify the total cost of this strategy. If the market continues to advance, we may ultimately have to convert equities to cash to cover a short future position. In any case, we cut off our upside exactly to the extent of our hedge. As I see it, we want to limit our downside while still participating in market advances. We can use index puts to accomplish this objective. We know our up-front costs and can decide the total amount that we pay for protection. In addition, our current investments remain intact to take advantage of market advances.''

Berger agreed with this strategy and directed Tracey and Nicholson to determine how many puts to buy for the fund. The prospectus of the One Hundred Fund limited the purchase of index options to 1 percent of the fund's net asset value at any one time. Berger, however, wished to keep the cost of protection to less than 1 percent annually. During the past two years, the firm had used index puts to hedge many of its other portfolios, and these positions had never produced a profit. Considering these previous experiences, the managers decided to limit the cost of buying index puts. Given this cost constraint, Tracey developed a table of various market declines, reproduced in Exhibit 1, that outlined the required number of contracts and their maximum purchase price. Index puts were bought in July and August for the One Hundred Fund, and the original purchase and ultimate results are reproduced in Exhibit 2.

The October Crash

After a week of sliding prices, the Dow Jones Industrial Average dropped 508 points on Monday, October 19, 1987. Wall Street had not experienced such an enormous decline in one trading day since 1914. Stock prices across the market plummeted. The firm's stocks were not spared from this disaster, but declines in the portfolio's long positions were offset by gains in the index puts. The November 285 puts in the One Hundred Fund were purchased for $27,206, and at the end of the day's trading, these contracts were valued at $2.275 million! Although Tracey believed this valuation may not have been realizable that day because of the option market's illiquidity, the success of this strategy was undeniable.

While most portfolios experienced tremendous declines, the One Hundred Fund's value actually increased by 52 cents per share. The One Hundred Fund's market positions on October 16 and 19 are illustrated in Exhibits 3 and 4. On October 21, Nicholson sold the puts for $1.6 million. This sale was done for two reasons. First, on October 19, Tracey and Berger managers believed that the puts were trading at an unsustainably high premium of 15 points over the intrinsic value. Second, the resulting cash from the sale would act as a partial buffer against any further decline, so the fund would not sacrifice its gain from the options. Now was the time to stay in cash and weather the storm, Tracey commented.

EXHIBIT 1
S&P Index Option Table—August 28, 1987 (S&P 100 Index equals 322.40)

Market Decline: Percent and Index Value

Quantity–Price per Contract*

Strike Price	-5% 306.28	-10% 290.16	-15% 274.04	-20% 257.92	-25% 241.80	-30% 225.68	-100% 0.00
$322.4	3.10–.81	3.10–.81	3.10–.81	3.10–.81	3.10–.81	3.10–.81	3.10–.81
320	3.64–.69	3.35–.75	3.26–.77	3.22–.78	3.20–.78	3.18–.79	3.13–.80
315	5.73–.44	4.03–.62	3.66–.68	3.50–.71	3.42–.73	3.36–.74	3.17–.79
310		5.04–.50	4.17–.60	3.84–.65	3.67–.68	3.56–.70	3.23–.77
305		6.74–.37	4.84–.52	4.25–.59	3.96–.63	3.78–.66	3.28–.76
300		10.16–.25	5.78–.43	4.75–.53	4.30–.58	4.04–.62	3.33–.75
295		20.66–.12	7.16–.35	5.39–.46	4.70–.53	4.33–.58	3.39–.74
290			9.40–.27	6.23–.40	5.19–.48	4.66–.54	3.45–.72
285			13.69–.18	7.39–.34	5.79–.43	5.06–.49	3.51–.71
280			25.17–.10	9.06–.28	6.54–.38	5.52–.45	3.57–.70

* Here's what the numbers mean. Taking the first pair, for an option with a strike price of $322.40 and a forecasted decline of 5 percent, you would buy a total of 3.10 contracts at a price of 81 cents per contract. In the second pair, you would buy 3.64 contracts for 69 cents each.

Note: For every $100,000 in the One Hundred Fund, only $1,000 can be spent annually for options. Since these options have a maximum life of 3 months, $250 can be spent for each contract per $100,000 asset value.

EXHIBIT 2
Options—Purchases and Sales (The One Hundred Fund)

Date	Option Purchased	Cost	Result
7/22/87	S&P 100 puts SEP 270	$41,825	Expired 9/19/87
7/22/87	S&P 100 puts SEP 265	26,200	Expired 9/19/87
8/31/87	S&P 100 puts NOV 285	27,206	Sold on 10/21/87 for $1,623,695

EXHIBIT 3
Market Value—10/16/87 (The One Hundred Fund)

Securities	Shares	Price	Market Value
Abbott Labs	9,000	$ 52.00	$ 468,000
Acuson Corp.	15,000	17.25	258,750
Citicorp	7,500	53.13	398,475
Computer Associates	18,000	28.25	508,500
Cypress Semiconductor	15,000	12.50	187,500
EG&G, Inc.	12,000	38.88	466,560
Franklin Resources	11,250	21.75	244,688
Hanson Trust	20,000	13.38	267,600
Home Depot	20,000	20.00	400,000
I.M.S. International	9,000	30.38	273,420
Intel Corp.	10,000	52.00	520,000
Lin Broadcasting	6,000	46.00	276,000
Mayfair Industries	12,000	8.00	96,000
Medco Containment	4,064	33.13	134,640
Philip Morris	3,000	102.63	307,890
Reuters Holdings	7,000	74.63	522,410
Saatchi & Saatchi	13,333	25.88	345,058
Safety-Kleen Corp.	10,000	35.63	356,300
Student Loan Marketing	7,000	79.75	558,250
T. Rowe Price	16,200	33.75	546,750
Telerate, Inc.	20,000	18.13	362,600
20th Century Industries	15,000	25.50	382,500
V F Corp.	12,000	34.00	408,000
Wal-Mart Stores	13,000	30.00	390,000
Waste Management	7,000	40.00	280,000
Wheelabrator Tech	15,000	20.88	313,200
S&P 100 put Nov 285	325	14.00	455,000
U.S. Treasury bills		98.49	984,875
Total market value			$10,712,966
Net asset value per share			$23.11

EXHIBIT 4
Market Value—10/19/87 (The One Hundred Fund)

Securities	Shares	Price	Market Value
Abbott Labs	9,000	$45.50	$ 409,500
Acuson Corp.	15,000	13.75	206,250
Citicorp	7,500	37.00	277,500
Computer Associates	18,000	21.25	382,500
Cypress Semiconductor	15,000	9.50	142,500
EG&G, Inc.	12,000	33.63	403,560
Franklin Resources	11,250	17.00	191,250
Hanson Trust	20,000	9.88	197,600
Home Depot	20,000	15.50	310,000
I.M.S. International	9,000	28.00	252,000
Intel Corp.	10,000	42.00	420,000
Lin Broadcasting	6,000	43.38	260,280
Mayfair Industries	12,000	7.00	84,000
Medco Containment	4,064	30.75	124,968
Philip Morris	3,000	97.00	291,000
Reuters Holdings	7,000	58.75	411,250
Saatchi & Saatchi	13,333	22.38	298,393
Safety-Kleen Corp.	10,000	32.63	326,300
Student Loan Marketing	7,000	70.00	490,000
T. Rowe Price	16,200	31.00	502,200
Telerate, Inc.	20,000	10.50	210,000
20th Century Industries	15,000	23.38	350,700
V F Corp.	12,000	25.50	306,000
Wal-Mart Stores	13,000	27.25	354,250
Waste Management	7,000	31.00	217,000
Wheelabrator Tech	15,000	18.50	277,500
S&P 100 put Nov 285	325	70.00	2,275,000
U.S. Treasury bills		98.49	984,875
Total market value			$10,956,376
Net asset value per share			$23.63

(Exhibit 5 illustrates the weekly closings of the Dow Jones Industrial Averages from October 2, 1987, to January 15, 1988.)

At the end of the year, the One Hundred Fund had gained 15.7 percent, even though its fourth quarter performance was a negative 7.5 percent. These figures compared very favorably to market indexes. The reinvested Dow gained 5.6 percent for the entire year and lost 24.6 percent in the fourth quarter. S&P 500 experienced similar results, gaining 5.3 percent for the year and losing 22.5 percent in the fourth quarter. The One Hundred Fund's put options prevented its earlier gains from being wiped out in one trading day.

EXHIBIT 5
The Stock Market in Late 1987

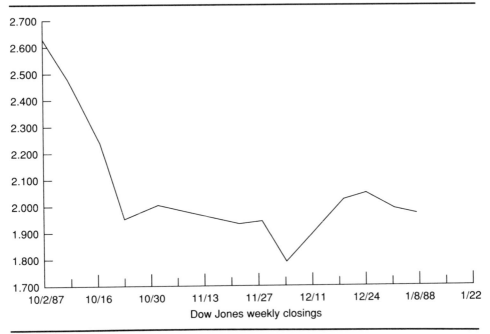

Dow Jones weekly closings

January 1988—A New Dawn

The Dow opened the new year at 1939; the market of 1988 was clearly not the same market as the summer of 1987. A five-year bullish uptrend had been broken, and for the first time, serious doubt had haunted previously confident investors. Since market valuations had returned to the middle of their historic ranges, Tracey thought that the overall risks inherent in the market at 2700 were not necessarily present at current price levels. The new risks, however, were significant. Investor confidence was low, some analysts forecasted a recession, and trade and budget deficits continued.

Tracey and Berger believed the market had seen its lows. They thought the market had declined enough to be classified as a complete bear market, and the economic outlook was still positive. Although they could not yet call the beginning of a definite uptrend, they thought the seeds for market advancement were in place. Tracey knew, however, that he could not ignore the possibility of a downturn. If one did occur, he envisioned the possible downside at about 10 to 12 percent.

Another element of the current market was the available prices for growth stocks. Relative to the price-earnings ratio of the S&P 500, current price-earnings multiples for emerging growth companies were at an all-time low. Over the past two-and-a-half years, these stocks had traded between 1.1 and 2.2 times the market multiple. They were currently trading at market multiples for the first time since 1977 and only the third time in 27 years.

Tracey believed investors, responding to declines in blue chip stocks, had driven the prices of growth stocks below their intrinsic values. He figured that buying growth stocks at such attractive values would be, in some sense, a defensive way to proceed. This strategy, however, was dangerous. Although Tracey perceived value differences between small stocks and blue chips, he believed a further market decline would probably drive the prices of growth stocks down as well. Just the other day, however, Berger was saying, ''Human nature being what it is, we will see people buying these stocks again. Highly successful, profitable companies are still the best defense in the battle of long-term investment survival.''

STRATEGY ALTERNATIVES ALONG
THE NEW FRONTIER

Tracey's market forecast was mixed. He currently weighed undervaluation in growth stocks and the potential for a new bull market advance against the possibility of a continued market retreat.

Searching for a strategy that could be flexible and defensive, he identified several distinct alternatives: move into cash, short the futures market, buy index puts, or sell call options. Each alternative was advantageous, depending on which aspect of his market forecast that he weighted the most. The risks that Jay was willing to accept, combined with his forecast, should have identified the optimum alternative for the One Hundred Fund.

Cash Conversion

Increasing the fund's cash was a possibility, and Berger had already done this during the past few months. This strategy was more appropriate than puts during a continuing market decline because it preserved the portfolio's value. Tracey thought that the probability of this kind of market was low. Thus, he did not perceive the potential benefits of increasing cash outweighing the costs. One of the costs of conversion was capital gains tax from liquidating some of the older positions in the fund. Another important cost was that the fund would not be in place to participate in a market advance. Tracey believed values currently in the market, along with a possible advancement, made this strategy less attractive.

Futures

The next alternative was to short the futures market. Exhibit 6 reproduces the prices in the futures market as of January 15. Tracey realized that this alternative was attractive if the market continued to retreat. The One Hundred Fund could take a short position without any up-front costs, and this position would increase in value if the market declined. Tracey referred to this as a "synthetic cash" position that actually reduced exposure to both declines and advances in the market; therefore, it had the disadvantage of limiting the upside to the extent of the hedge. Its principal advantage, however, was the relative convenience in adjusting the degree of exposure, which was an asset allocation issue. The effectiveness of this strategy depended on smooth and continuous prices at which to enter and exit the futures market. Jay did not believe that this caveat held true during October 19. In short, the objective of protection might be achieved, but the possibility of advancement could be limited.

Index Puts

The third alternative was to return to the option markets and buy index puts. This strategy had worked beautifully in October when these instruments protected the funds from catastrophic declines. This alternative was attractive because it provided downside protection at a known cost in addition to allowing participation in a market upswing. Before he could ultimately decide, Tracey wanted to rework his option table using the current value of the S&P 100 Index and the available strike prices. His basic impression was that put option premiums in today's market (reproduced in Exhibit 7) were higher than he was willing to spend. If this was true, he could rework his analysis.

    Given more expensive premiums, Tracey could recommend an increase in the amount that the fund should be willing to pay annually. He considered increasing the dollar cost of put options up to 2 to 3 percent of

EXHIBIT 6
Future Prices on January 15, 1988 (S&P 500 Index)

	Open	High	Low	Settle	Change	High	Low	Open Interest
March	246.50	248.10	244.00	247.45	+1.20	344.90	181.00	114,595
June	247.70	249.40	245.60	249.05	+1.30	347.90	190.00	1,383

Index: High, 247.00; low, 243.97; close, 245.91, +0.09

Source: *The Wall Street Journal*, January 18, 1988.

EXHIBIT 7
Options—Prices on 1/15/88 (S&P 100 Index)

Strike Price	Calls			Puts		
	Jan.	Feb.	March	Jan.	Feb.	March
$185					1.063	
190				0.063	1.375	
195				0.063	1.875	
200				0.063	2.313	
205				0.125	2.875	
210	27.500	31.500		0.188	3.500	6.000
215	23.125			0.313	4.750	7.125
220	18.250	22.250		0.438	5.750	8.750
225	13.500	19.000		0.938	6.875	9.500
230	9.500	15.000	17.750	1.625	8.250	13.000
235	5.500	11.750	15.000	2.750	10.250	12.750
240	2.688	9.250	12.000	4.750	12.500	16.250
245	1.125	6.750	10.250	8.500	14.500	19.000
250	0.500	4.875	8.000	12.500	18.500	22.500
255	0.125	3.375	6.500	18.750	22.000	23.000

the fund's net asset value. Alternatively, the fund could consider purchasing put options with strike prices farther out-of-the money. Although this would lower costs, market volatility would have to be higher than Tracey currently foresaw for these instruments to be protective.

Cost was a critical factor in this analysis, but Tracey also believed that fiduciary duty was important. The investment philosophy at Berger Associates continually stressed long-term investments, rather than speculation in financial securities. Was there a price for options that separated a justifiable hedge versus a speculative position? Tracey estimated the probability of a second catastrophic decline as so low that he had to balance his basic inclination to hedge the downside versus participate on the upside. Jay was not positive, however, where this demarcation line existed for the One Hundred Fund.

Indeed, Tracey believed that selling call options against the One Hundred Fund might be another alternative worth considering. He was also intrigued with the possibility of using a dynamic hedging strategy in the options market. Tracey reasoned that he might reduce the costs of buying put options to protect the portfolio by using the hedge ratio from the Black-Scholes formula to help establish a delta neutral portfolio. This might provide a low-cost partial insurance plan for the One Hundred Fund.

Questions for Discussion

1. Describe Tracey's opinions about current market conditions. In light of this environment, compare the strategies of buying index puts, shorting stock index futures, covered call writing, and converting to cash.
2. Should Tracey consider a strategy of buying what he perceives to be undervalued growth stocks? How can he hedge this position using options?
3. Evaluate the strategy of buying deep out-of-the-money puts. How does it change the expected returns from the portfolio? In what market environment is it most effective?
4. Should Tracey consider writing calls against stock held in the portfolio? Compare the expected returns from covered call writing to buying protective puts. In what market environment can covered call writing enhance portfolio value?
5. Given the market environment in January 1988, what strategy would you recommend that Tracey pursue? Why?

COMMENTS ON CASE TWO, ROCKY MOUNTAIN HIGH

Objectives of the Case

Rocky Mountain High focuses on alternative techniques for hedging against stock market declines. Four strategies are suggested in the case for consideration: converting to cash, shorting the futures market, buying index puts, and writing calls. Tracey needs to make a recommendation regarding which of these alternatives is most suitable under the market conditions in January 1988.

He is a vice president of Berger Associates, a Denver firm that manages the One Hundred Fund, a growth fund that invests primarily in equity of growth companies. Tracey had anticipated the stock market crash of October 19, 1987, and had hedged the fund's position by purchasing Standard & Poor's 100 Index puts. As a result, the value of the fund actually increased 52 cents per share that day and grew 15.7 percent over the year of 1987.

It is recommended that Case One, T. David Brown, be discussed prior to analyzing Rocky Mountain High. Discussion in the second case then can focus on an evaluation of option strategies for portfolio risk management over two different market periods. As such a valuable exercise is to evaluate how portfolio risk management decisions are affected by the different market conditions in 1987 and 1988.

The Problem

In January 1988, the time period for the case, Tracey believes that the market will rise, but he also feels that a decline of 10 to 15 percent is possible. Therefore, he wants to hedge the fund against losses, but not at the expense of participating in possible market growth. To meet these objectives, several alternatives were suggested in the case. Tracey could (1) buy index puts again, but the premiums now appear too high, (2) move into cash, (3) short the futures market, or (4) write calls. The problem is to determine which strategy should be recommended and why.

Topics for Discussion

Tracey had successfully hedged the One Hundred Fund's position against the October 19, 1987, stock market crash by purchasing S&P 100 Index puts. Now, with the S&P 500 and the Dow averages down 22.5 and 24.6 percent, respectively, the five-year bull market appeared to have come to a close. Tracey, however, believed that the market had bottomed and would experience some growth, but he was not willing to rule out a downturn of 10 to 12 percent. He wanted to protect the fund against a market decline, while allowing it to participate in the anticipated advance.

Market Conditions and Strategies to Hedge the Portfolio's Value

The strategies under consideration which would protect the fund against loss while allowing it to appreciate with market advances were the purchase of index puts and the sale of stock index futures. Both conform to the definition of portfolio insurance as developed in the analysis of the previous case, T. David Brown. Call writing and cash conversion provide some hedge against portfolio losses, but do not produce appreciation when the market advances. Tracey had used the strategy of purchasing index puts in 1987 with great success.

The Market Environment in 1988. Evaluating Tracey's perception of the market in January 1988 is a useful starting point. Information already presented suggests that:

1. Tracey believed that the market was overvalued in 1987 when the Dow was at 2700, but he did not believe it was overvalued in 1988, at a level of 1939.
2. Investor confidence was low and investors were skittish about the stock market in 1988. The reverse was true in 1987.
3. The near-term economic outlook was in question as some analysts projected a recession. The budget and trade deficits remained large. Tracey, however, was more optimistic about the economic prospects.
4. The market was volatile, having not yet settled into a pattern of growth or retreat (see Exhibit 5.)

Alternative Strategies for Portfolio Protection

A complete analysis of various portfolio insurance strategies was presented in the case solution to T. David Brown. Some of the important points about each one relative to the 1988 market environment are summarized here.

Buying Index Puts. What are the advantages and disadvantages of buying index puts? On the positive side, their cost is known at the beginning of the period and if the market advances, they expire without having to be exercised. If the market declines, index puts increase in value. This relationship between put and stock positions produces the desirable positive skewness in protective put portfolio returns.

Disadvantages of index puts include:

1. They represent a sunk cost incurred at the beginning of the hedging period. If the market holds steady or continues to advance, the puts expire worthless. To maintain portfolio insurance, it is necessary to roll the puts over, thus increasing costs of the strategy.
2. Because of recent market volatility, index puts carry a high relative premium. It is doubtful that much protection could be purchased if the One Hundred Fund maintains its limit of 1 percent of portfolio value for the purchase of options. Put options are inappropriate if a more cost-effective alternative exists.

Using Stock Index Futures. The strategy of dynamic insurance using stock index futures, as analyzed in T. David Brown, fell into disrepute after the market debacle of October 19, 1987. Whether true or not, many investors and regulators believed that dynamic insurance strategies using stock index futures helped cause the severe market decline in October 1987. Since this insurance strategy was ineffective when most needed, money managers turned to other techniques for hedging portfolio value.

While dynamic insurance using futures may not be a viable alternative, Tracey considered selling stock index futures to create a short hedge for the equity portfolio. The advantage of this strategy is that no up-front cost is paid. The short position is lifted at some future date by repurchasing the contracts at the market price. Gain or loss on the futures contracts can be offset by loss or gain in the underlying portfolio. Shorting futures creates essentially the same result as selling a portion of the equity portfolio at the market's current level, without incurring transaction costs or tax consequences. The disadvantage of this strategy, compared to using listed puts, is that it limits gains in the portfolio if the market advances since the futures would be covered at a loss.

Compare using futures to the purchase of index puts. If short positions are taken in stock index futures, they must be covered at a loss if the market rises, which would offset dollar for dollar the gains in the portfolio. Alternatively, index puts would be allowed to expire worthless. The distribution of expected portfolio returns from shorting futures against the equity portfolio remains normal, it just exhibits less volatility. The distribution when using protective puts is positively skewed, an outcome desired by most investors.

Call Writing. Using data from Exhibit 7, an analysis of index call writing can be conducted. If index options are overvalued as Tracey believes, the strategy of call writing is appropriate. However, as described in the case solution to T. David Brown, a call writing portfolio has limited upside potential determined by the striking price of the options.

Given Tracey's somewhat optimistic outlook, call writing using out-of-the-money calls may be a viable method. Compared to put buying, call writing works best in a flat market with lower than expected volatility. The sale of calls would provide current income, which could cushion declines in the portfolio value if the market falls. Also, recall that index options are settled in cash; consequently, Tracey would have to plan for the liquidity needed if the options are in-the-money at maturity.

When evaluating the call writing portfolio, it should be noted that if the market advances beyond the option's striking price, no further gain in the portfolio will occur. Alternatively, the portfolio will share dollar for dollar if the market declines. This relationship produces the negative skewness in call writing returns as shown previously in Exhibit 8 to the T. David Brown case.

Converting to Cash. The cash strategy protects the portfolio against declines, but allows no participation in market advances. Tracey should consider this alternative only if convinced a market decline is imminent.

Alternatives to Buying At-The-Money Puts

Tracey is hesitant about purchasing at-the-money index puts because of their cost and the limited funds which he can commit to the strategy. As an alternative, Tracey can consider purchase of out-of-the-money index puts, selling index calls, or selling individual calls on selected stocks.

Buying Out-of-the-Money Index Puts. The strategy of buying out-of-the-money index puts lowers the floor level of protection for the portfolio. It is akin to raising the deductible of an insurance policy. The advantage of raising the deductible is that protection is less costly; the disadvantage is that the market must decline by a larger amount before the protection has any value. Data in Exhibit 7 can be used to determine the costs of out-of-the-money put strategies for various striking prices.

Similar to the concept of raising the deductible on an insurance policy to protect only against a catastrophic loss, the farther puts are out-of-the-money, the greater the market can decline before the portfolio is protected. If Tracey believes that a decline of 10 to 12 percent is the maximum, it is unlikely that out-of-the-money puts can provide much protection.

To demonstrate this, consider again the expected return distributions for a protective put portfolio and an equity portfolio, shown in Exhibit 7 in the T. David Brown case. As the striking price of the puts is lowered, the positive skewness declines and the floor moves to the left. The protective put distribution approaches the shape of the normally distributed equity portfolio as striking prices for puts are lowered.

Buying Individual Puts. Another strategy with lower cost is the purchase of growth stocks and individual puts on each position. Tracey believes that certain growth stocks are attractively priced, but he suspects the market will decline. The purchase of individual puts on selected securities provides protection for a specific part of the portfolio, while enabling profits to be made if the market appreciates.

JAY TRACEY'S RECOMMENDATION

A comparison of market conditions between September 1986 and January 1988 set the groundwork for determining an appropriate strategy for Tracey in the 1988 market environment. Factors important to his decision are:

1. Stocks appear more properly valued, compared to 1986. He believes that a decline of 10 to 12 percent is possible, but not likely.
2. Certain growth stocks are attractively priced.
3. The market had been volatile and option premiums were high, reflecting that volatility.
4. Only 1 percent of the fund's value could be used to purchase options.
5. Dynamic hedging strategies based on stock index futures were not considered a viable alternative.
6. Tracey wanted some protection against a market decline, but he hoped to participate in any market advance.

Given these considerations, it appears that Tracey can most effectively meet his objectives by selling out-of-the-money calls, or buying out-of-the-money puts against stocks held in the portfolio. Selling calls with a strike above current market levels allows for some participation in a market advance, and the premiums would help offset losses in a market decline. In addition, call premiums appear high as a result of recent market volatility. However, if the market moves dramatically in either direction, the call writing strategy underperforms a put buying or futures hedging portfolio.

Buying out-of-the-money puts also should be considered because of its low cost. If the market declines, some protection probably can be realized from the puts. If the market appreciates, the equity portfolio can participate in the gains. However, it should be emphasized that the potential returns from call writing differ greatly from that of put buying. Tracey's convictions about the future direction of the market should ultimately determine which strategy is selected.

APPENDIX

COMPUTER SOFTWARE FOR THE OPTIONS INVESTOR: A GUIDE TO SOFTWARE AND DATA VENDORS

The massive amount of information generated by the options markets makes the computer an indispensable tool for sifting through trading possibilities. Evaluating prices, volatilities, and trading strategies demands the computer's help to make timely decisions.

As the following Contents indicates, the section on software is divided into seven sections. *Custom Programming* is an individualized consulting service in which new software is created for specific customer needs.

Options Analytics calculate theoretical values. Systems differ in the mathematical models they use but, in most cases, do not differ significantly in the results they generate. These systems might include capabilities for generating such variables as implied volatility, and the theoretical values for delta, gamma, theta, and vega. The capabilities of these types of systems vary greatly.

Portfolio Management software takes the theoretical calculations to another level. In addition to doing calculations for one option or for a set of options, these software packages can perform theoretical calculations for an entire position of options and underlying securities. In addition, these packages can do many of the accounting functions that are usually done by time-sharing or service bureaus.

Risk Management software, which frequently comes as part of a portfolio management software package, performs strategy or position simulations for analyses over a range of underlying prices, volatilities, and time. Typically, net value, profit or loss, and margin requirements or sensitivities can be calculated so that a trader can estimate the risk-reward profile of a position, given certain changes in market conditions.

Software Vendors is a list of companies that sell a variety of software packages—some they have written themselves and some they market for others. There is some necessary overlapping with the preceding categories.

Technical Analysis software provides charting and analyses of stock prices and/or commodity prices. Frequently, these services offer the capability of calculating such technical market indicators as moving averages, trend lines, stochastics, and relative strength indexes. A user must concern himself or herself with the database each of these systems requires. Some use online databases, while others use historical databases which require periodic updating. Cost and database requirements vary greatly.

Trading Systems are software packages that make trade recommendations based on certain assumptions about market behavior. Some systems fully disclose their trading techniques and provide calculations and trading signals. Other systems do not make full disclosure and only provide trading recommendations.

The section on Data Vendors is divided into three categories: those providing only databases, those providing only quotes, and those providing both.

Databases of historical price information are provided in a wide range of subject matter. Updating methods vary. Some database vendors specialize in stock options and stock prices, others specialize in futures options and futures prices. There are also those specializing in options on physicals and the price information on the related underlying. Certain systems have real-time, online data, using databases that are updated continuously. Some have daily data and are updated via a telephone modem; others use keyboard or disk input.

Quote Vendors supply price data on options and underlying instruments. Data typically include open, high, low, close, volume and open interest. Data can be transmitted real-time, delayed, or as requested. Receiving real-time data is significantly more expensive than delayed data because distribution of real-time data incurs exchange fees, payable to the particular options exchange.

SELECTING AN OPTION TRADING SYSTEM

With the many different capabilities and costs of the options systems available, trying to decide which one is right for you is certainly not easy. Here is a brief guide to help you make a decision.

First, decide on which markets you want to concentrate. Few option trading systems work on all types. Most systems analyze stock and stock index options; fewer include cash markets or options on futures.

Second, decide what type of data you need. Receiving real-time data incurs exchange fees, payable to the particular options exchange. This monthly fee can substantially increase the cost of your systems. If you can get by with delayed data or no data feed at all, you can save a great deal of money.

Third, decide what database capabilities you need. Not all systems are able to save price data and charts. If you are able to create your own database for prices, you could purchase a less expensive analysis product. Decide if you want charts and if you need your system to help you with your trade accounting.

Fourth, decide what analytical capabilities you need. Some systems offer technical analyses of the underlying markets. Many offer a feature—trade alerts—which signals the user when a real-time price is reached. Charting capabilities vary widely. Option pricing calculations also range from very simple to quite complicated. When picking out your first system, do not be afraid to select one that performs some functions that you do not fully understand: This can be a good way to learn more about options.

Finally, select your software before buying any hardware. This is probably the most important guideline. Trying to fit a system into an existing computer is often disappointing. After choosing your software, look for hardware that is cost-effective in running that software. Paying a little more for a higher quality computer is generally a good idea. Your system costs you the most money when it does not work, causing you to lose trading opportunities.

CONTENTS[1]

Software

Custom Programming
Options Analytics
Portfolio Management

---

[1] © Chicago Board Options Exchange, September 1989. All rights reserved. Printed in U.S.A.

Risk Management
Software Vendors, Peripherals Vendors
Technical Analysis
Trading Systems

Data Vendors

Database
Quote Vendors
Databases and Quote Vendors

By providing the following information, the CBOE does not endorse any product, service, or company. Although every effort has been made to collect correct information, CBOE cannot guarantee its accuracy.

Custom Programming

Fortunet Inc.
2995 Woodside Rd.
Suite 400
Woodside, CA 94062
415–368–7655
Tom Johnson, president
• Develops custom software for commercial hedgers, corporate treasury departments and financial institutions. Price subject to contract terms.

Mortimer & Associates Inc.
7900-27 Baymeadows Circle East
Jacksonville, FL 32256
904–739–2424
Rick Mortimer, president
• Custom software development for complex option positions. Price negotiable.

National Computer Network Corp.
223 W. Jackson Blvd.
Suite 1202
Chicago, IL 60606
312–427–5125
Tom McDonald, director of marketing
• Writes custom software programs. Call for price. (Also see listings under Software Vendors and Databases.)

OPA Software
P. O. Box 90658
Los Angeles, CA 90009
800–321–4100; 213–545–3716
Loren Bellocchio, marketing director
• Writes custom programs. Price negotiated. (also see listing in Options Analytics.)

Options Analytics

Automated Trading Systems Inc.
40 Exchange Place
New York, NY 10005
212–968–0800
Kenneth Troy, vice president
financial systems group
* ULTRA
  Analytical options software for
  PCs and minicomputers. Begins at
  $1,200. (Also see listing in
  Portfolio Management.)

BARRA
1995 University Ave.
Suite 400
Berkeley, CA 94704
415–548–5442
Barbara Hodges, manager of
marketing communications
Kamal Duggirala, director of
broker/dealer services
* Options and futures analytical
  software and trading
  workstations. Includes options
  valuation models, strategy
  evaluation, and position/risk
  analysis for markets in six
  countries. Call for price.

Bond-Tech Inc.
P.O. Box 192
Englewood, OH 45322
513–836–3991
Roger A. Cox, President
* FISTS-Fixed-Income Security
  Trading System
  Cash, financial futures, and
  options pricing and analysis.
  Options modules within program

offer valuation choice of Black-
Scholes or Cox-Ross-Rubinstein
pricing models. $1,250.

Chronometrics, Inc.
1901 Raymond Dr.
Suite 7
Northbrook, IL 60062-6714
312–272–0949
H. Phillip Becker, president
* COMPACT
  Commodity Put and Call Trading
  System includes OEX valuation
  and calculates contract
  relationship to S&P 500 futures.
  Hourly and monthly rates
  available.

Coast Investment Software
8851 Albatross Dr.
Huntington Beach, CA 92646
714–968–1978
Joe DiNapoli, president
* Fibnodes
  Fibonacci retracement and
  objective calculator for intra-day
  or position trading designed for
  fast user interaction. Not copy-
  protected. $795.

* The CIS Trading Package
  Graphics package with unique
  technical studies for stocks and
  futures. $495.

Coherent Software Systems
771 Anthony Rd.
Portsmouth, RI 02871
401–683–5886

Meg Jackson, marketing director

- Rory Tycoon™ Options Trader
  Retrieves quotes and analyzes
  more than 50 possible trades.
  $49.95. (Also see listing in
  Portfolio Management.)

The Comhedge Partnership

210 Sylvan Ave.
Englewood Cliffs, NJ 07632
201–569–3522

Lillian Zito, manager

- The Option Calculator
  Evaluates and analyzes option
  premiums according to Black-
  Scholes pricing model. $500.
  (Also see listings in Portfolio
  Management and Trading
  Systems.)

Commodity Communications Corp.

250 S. Wacker Dr.
Suite 1150
Chicago, IL 60606
800–621–2628; 312–977–9067

Paul Huske, sales manager

- Option Source
  Online quotations and real-time
  trading evaluation and simulations
  for OEX and options on futures.
  Call for price.

Com-Tech Software

141 W. Jackson Blvd.
Suite 1531–A
Chicago, IL 60604
414–248–6489; 312–341–7547

Nancy Geldermann Williams,
partner

- Option Master
  Theoretical values and position
  analysis for all options—equities
  and futures. $500.

Emerging Market Technologies, Inc.

Presidential Commons
Suite 10
3781 Presidential Parkway
Atlanta, GA 30341
404–350–9043

Jeffrey S. Multz, president

- Invest Now!®
  Equity and option calculator for
  determining profitability and
  return on investment. Personal:
  $79. Professional: $129.

- Telescan™
  Charting, technical analysis, and
  fundamental indicators package
  for equities, options, futures,
  bonds, and mutual funds. Works
  in conjunction with Telescan
  Database. $79. (Also see listing
  under Software Vendors.)

FBS Systems Inc.

P.O. Drawer 248
Aledo, IL 61231
309–582–5628

Norman Brown, president

- Put-N-Call
  Options calculator based on
  Black-Scholes pricing model.
  Calculates theoretical values and
  sensitivity analysis. $99.

FinCalc, Inc.

2241 N. Dayton St.
Chicago, IL 60614
312–327–4257

Robert McDonald, president

- The Option Analyst
  A set of Lotus 1–2–3®
  spreadsheets based on Black-
  Scholes formula. Analyzes
  options, spreads, and positions

including an underlying stock. What-if capability enables the user to change all inputs. $110.

H & H Scientific Inc.
13507 Pendleton St.
Fort Washington, MD 20744
301–292–2958
Herschel Pilloff, president
* The Stock Option Analysis Program (SOAP)
  Analytical program based on Black-Scholes pricing model includes spreads and what-if capabilities. $150.
* The Stock Option Scanner (SOS)
  Ranks top 50 and bottom 50 positions on data entered for up to 3,000 positions. $150.

Integrated Analytics Corp.
13315 Washington Blvd.
Los Angeles, CA 90066
321–578–5052
Dale Prouty, president
* MarketMind
  Real-time intelligent market monitor for options, stocks, and futures based on trader's own strategies. Call for price.

Intelligent Trading Systems, Inc.
327 S. LaSalle St.
Suite 545
Chicago, IL 60604
312–341–9599
Robert J. Santos
* Wall Street Trading
  Pricing and valuation system with Lotus Signal™ tracks real-time prices, theoretical values, and

portfolio values. Also creates charts. Call for price.

International Advanced Models Inc.
P.O. Box 1019
Oak Brook, IL 60522
312–369–8461
Michael Tentner, president
* IAM Option Strategist
  Examines behavior of up to 10 user-defined strategies based on modified Black-Scholes formula. Plots strategy returns. $124.50.
* IAM Option Investor
  Calculates daily return of strategy based on user-specified price behavior of underlying instrument. $144.50.

Knight-Ridder Financial Information
55 Broadway
New York, NY 10006
212–269–1110
Sales representative
* TradeCenter
  PC-based real-time graphics and analytical trading service covering all major cash and exchange markets. Call for price. (Also see listing in Quote Vendors.)

Market Software Inc.
440 S. LaSalle St.
Suite 2424
Chicago, IL 60605
312–906–3370
Robert Beckmann, president
* Professional Options Advisor
  Analytic software for equity, index, and futures options. Evaluates trades and portfolio; generates delta sheets. $795.

MarketView Software Inc.
2020 Dean St.
Suite D–1
St. Charles, IL 60174
Chris Moore, regional sales manager
312–663–7330
Jeff Thomas, regional sales manager
212–608–6305
• MarketView
Analytic software for OEX and options on futures. OptionView module includes historical volatility, real-time theoretical values, and what-if scenarios. Begins at $400 per month.

Maxus Systems International
20 Waterside Plaza
Suite 13G
New York, NY 10010
212–481–3688
Sean Mansfield, president
• Capri
Real-time analytic and portfolio management system for options on equities indexes, bonds, futures, and currencies. Interfaces with online data feeds and Microsoft® Excel. Starts at $995.

Montgomery Investment Group
332 Pine St.
Suite 514
San Francisco, CA 94104
415–986–6991
George Montgomery, principal
• Options 1–2–3
• Options XL
Option spreadsheet analysis for use with Lotus 1–2–3® or

Microsoft® Excel. $295. Pro Series: $395.

OPA Software
P.O. Box 90658
Los Angeles, CA 90009
800–321–4100; 213–545–3716
Loren Bellocchio, marketing director
• Options Pricing Analysis
Online software for theoretical pricing, selecting best strategy, and evaluating potential profit or loss. $250. (Also see listing in Custom Programming.)

OptiManagement Resources Inc.
CN 851 701 Mt. Lucas Rd.
Princeton, NJ 08542
609–924–8957
Tom Harding, director of marketing
• The Trading Assistant
Software for online data on more than 1,000 instruments from deal capture through profit/loss statements. Generates intra-day and end-of-day reports. Begins at $19,500.
• Focus
Creates customized end-of-day reports using The Trading Assistant files. Call for price.

The Options Group
50 Broadway
20th Floor
New York, NY 10004
212–785–5555
Mark Veale
• TOG
Online option analytic and portfolio analysis for exchange-

traded and OTC options on non-equities and stock indexes worldwide. Call for price.

- TOG Plus
Similar system to TOG for PCs includes dynamic price updating. Call for price.

TOG Europe

61–64 Bell Court House
11 Bloomfield St.
London, England EC2M 7AY
01–628–1316
Craig Bennett

- Same services as provided by The Options Group, for U.S. and European markets; adheres to Continental conventions for dates. Call for price.

Optionomics Corp.

3191 S. Valley St.
Suite 155
Salt Lake City, UT 84109
800–255–3374; 801–466–2111
David L. Miller, vice president

- Optionomic Systems™
Real-time option valuation, portfolio management, and graphics system available on a leased basis. Base price of $425 per month on a yearly lease.

Option Vue Systems

175 E. Hawthorne Parkway
Suite 180
Vernon Hills, IL 60061
800–447–7734; 312–816–6610
Len Yates, marketing director

- Option Vue Plus
Options trading program provides profit/loss scenarios and identifies

optimal strategies. Fair values, implied volatility, delta, time decay, and other parameters displayed for each option. $695.

Programmed Press

599 Arnold Rd.
West Hempstead, NY 11552
516–599–6527
Sarah Bookbinder, partner

- Fifty statistically oriented programs for stocks, bonds, foreign exchange, and forecasting developed by Dr. Albert I.A. Bookbinder, economics professor at the City University of New York and Fordham Graduate School of Business. $119.95.

Pumpkin Software

P.O. Box 4417
Chicago, IL 60680
312–794–1777
Raymond J. Kaider, owner

- The Option Evaluator
Calculates fair market value, implied and historical volatilities for equity, stock index, and futures options. Two types of delta sheets for single or multiple option strategies. $129 plus shipping.

Quotient Inc.

45 Broadway
22nd Floor
New York, NY 10006
212–943–0171
Joseph Bruno, sales executive
Terry Prall, senior sales executive

- Cmark
Fully integrated front- and back-

office system for listed and over-the-counter interest rate, currency, index, and commodity options. Pricing and portfolio analysis software focuses on global capital markets. Call for price.

Quotron Systems, Inc.
12731 W. Jefferson Blvd.
Los Angeles, CA 90066
213–827–4600
Howard Taylor, vice president, sales
* Programmed Indexes
  User-created dynamic indexes from a vast combination of securities and statistics. Index values calculated in real-time and monitored via Enhanced Monitor Service. Call for price. (Also see listings in Technical Analysis, Databases, and Quote Vendors.)

Telekurs (North America), Inc.
111 W. Jackson Blvd.
Suite 1900
Chicago, IL 60604
312–663–4143
Phil Tufts, regional sales manager
* OMS/PLUS*
  Real-time analytical software that can be used on a stand-alone basis, or with S&P's Ticker III or Ticker IV data stream and PRICE MACHINE database. Call for price.
  * Formerly offered by Standard & Poor's Trading Systems.
  (Also see listing in Quote Vendors.)

Terco Computer Systems
P.O. Box 388206
Chicago, IL 60638
312–495–7123
Bob Grzyb, owner
* Option Master
  Pricing and valuation with customized reports for equity, stock index, bond, and futures options. $195.

Townsend Analytics Ltd.
100 S. Wacker Dr.
Suite 1506
Chicago, IL 60606
312–621–0141
MarrGwen Townsend
* Option Risk Management
  Real-time analytic capabilities and portfolio management for equity and futures options. Calculates risk and return over time and market movement. Call for price.

Track Data Corp.
61 Broadway
New York, NY 10006
800-223-0113
Stan Stern, vice president
* MarkeTrak
  PC-based, real-time quote retrieval and analysis system. $550 per month.
* MX-386
  Advanced quotation service using Intel 386 technology. Includes features of MarkeTrak plus enhanced graphics, real-time spreadsheets, and multiple monitor capability. $600 per month.

- Optrack
  Equity options analytics service offering an array of strategy analyses; can design your own hedged positions. $925 per month for first unit.

Xcaliber Trading Systems Inc.
401 S. LaSalle St.
Suite 403
Chicago, IL 60605
312–786–5353

Steve Balz, sales manager
- The Position Manager
  Theoretical evaluation of options; portfolio evaluation. Based on real-time quotes from North American equity, option, and futures exchanges. $1,250 per month per station.

Portfolio Management

Advent Software Inc.
512 Second St.
San Francisco, CA 94107
Michael Stark, sales manager
415–543–7695
Lisa Church, sales manager
212–481–1188
- The Professional Portfolio™
  Microcomputer program for institutional investors that includes reports for portfolios, management, performance, billing, and mutual funds. Starts at $2,700.

Automated Trading Systems Inc.
40 Exchange Place
New York, NY 10005
212–968–0800
Kenneth Troy, vice president, financial systems group
- TOM
  Options portfolio risk-management system. Begins at

$6,300. (Also see listing in Options Analytics.)

Coherent Software Systems
771 Anthony Rd.
Portsmouth, RI 02871
401–683–5886
Meg Jackson, marketing director
- Rory Tycoon™ Portfolio Analyst
  Portfolio management, charting and electronic quote retrieval for up to 2,500 investments. $150. (Also see listing in Options Analytics.)

The Comhedge Partnership
210 Sylvan Ave.
Englewood Cliffs, NJ 07632
201–569–3522
Lillian Zito, manager
- The Portfolio Manager
  Keeps track of up to 50 positions in options and futures. $4,500. (Also see listings in Options Analytics and Trading Systems.)

Commodity Communications Corp.
250 S. Wacker Dr.
Suite 1150
Chicago, IL 60606
800–621–2628; 312–977–9096
Paul Huske, sales manager
* Option Source
Online quotations and real-time
trading evaluation and simulations
for OEX and options on futures.
Call for price.

Market Vision Corp.
40 Rector St.
19th Floor
New York, NY 10006
212–227–1610
Donna Knief, marketing
* Market Data Spreadsheet
Portfolio management software
using real-time data. Call for
price. (Also see listings under
Technical Analysis and
Databases.)

Maxus Systems International
20 Waterside Plaza
Suite 13G
New York, NY 10010
212–481–3688
Sean Mansfield, president
* Capri
Real-time analytic and portfolio
management system for options
on equities, indexes, bonds,
futures, and currencies. Interfaces
with online data feeds and
Microsoft® Excel. Starts at $995.

Optionomics Corp.
3191 S. Valley St.
Suite 155
Salt Lake City, UT 84109
800–255–3374; 801–466–2111
David L. Miller, vice president
* Optionomic Systems™
Real-time option valuation,
portfolio management and
graphics system available on a
leased basis. Base price of $425
per month on a yearly lease.

Pro Plus Software, Inc.
2150 East Brown Rd.
Mesa, AZ 85203
602–461–3296
Sales representative
* Wall Street Investor™
Technical analysis, fundamental
analysis, and portfolio
management package for stocks,
options, bonds, and mutual funds.
Online trading with major
discount brokerage firms. $695.

Savant Corporation
11211 Katy Freeway
Suite 250
Houston, TX 77079
800–231–9900; 713–973–2400
Mark Randall, sales manager
* The Investor's Portfolio
Portfolio management for equities,
options, and futures. $495. Multi-
currency version: $695. (Also see
listing under Technical Analysis.)

Shaw Data Services Inc.

122 E. 42nd St.
New York, NY 10168
212–682–8877

Scott Magnussen, marketing representative

- Portfolio Management Service
  More than 800 online displays and 150 hard-copy reports for portfolio accounting information on equity, fixed-income, options, futures, mortgage-backed securities, and international securities. Price based on hardware needs and monthly data storage requirements.

Smith Micro Software Inc.

P.O. Box 7137
Huntington Beach, CA 92615
714–964–0412

Bill Smith, president

- Stock Portfolio System
  Portfolio management system for equities, options, and futures on PC or Macintosh.™ $225. (Also see listing in Technical Analysis.)

Vestek Systems

388 Market St.
Suite 700
San Francisco, CA 94111
415–398–6340

Roberta P. Lyon, vice president

- Vestek Online
  Timesharing service for security analysis, portfolio management and index fund management. Call for price.
- Vestek Onsite
  Similar service to Online, but at customer site. Call for price.
- Vestar
  Integrated portfolio management and analysis on microcomputer. Call for price.

Wismer Associates, Inc.

22134 Sherman Way
Canoga Park, CA 91303
818–884–5515

Bruce Vollert, vice president of marketing

- SERIES 2™ Investment Management System
  Advanced securities accounting, portfolio management, operation, and trading support for institutional investors. Incorporates a full range of security types, including options. Call for price.

Risk Management

ATIS Inc.

29 W. Hubbard
Chicago, IL 60610
312–527–2847

Gerald Saweikis, president

- Back-office accounting software for options, futures, and options on futures. PC or mainframe. $75,000 plus $1,500 per mo. for equity and nonequity products; $60,000 plus $1,000 for futures.

Board of Trade Clearing Corp.

141 W. Jackson Blvd.
Suite 1460
Chicago, IL 60604
312–786–5700

Tom Hammond, member services
representative

- Risk-management system for
  OEX, futures, and options on
  futures that figures equivalent
  futures positions for margining
  purposes. Mainframe. Price per
  transaction.

David Bruce & Co.

211 W. Wacker Dr.
Chicago, IL 60606
312–641–2207

Joanne R. Smith, director of
marketing

- Equity Best Hedge System
  PC-based risk-management
  software that hedges portfolio
  exposure by hedging for delta,
  gamma, and omega. From $2,500
  per month.
- Equity Risk Analysis System
  PC-based risk-management
  software that evaluates the
  exposure of portfolios consisting
  of equities, equity indexes, and
  options to changes in price,
  volatility, time to expiration, and
  interest rates. From $2,500 per
  month.
- Futures/Options Best Hedge
  System
  PC-based risk-management
  software hedges portfolio
  exposure by hedging for delta,
  gamma, and omega. From $2,500
  per month.

- Futures/Options Risk Analysis
  System
  PC-based risk-management
  software that evaluates exposure
  of portfolios comprised of futures,
  options (including CBOE bond
  options), cash commodities, and
  OTC options to changes in price,
  volatility, spread, time decay,
  interest rates, and basis. From
  $2,500 per month.

BSI

10 S. Riverside Plaza
Suite 1930
Chicago, IL 60606
312–559–0250

Sam Detina, director of sales and
marketing

- Disaster Recovery Service
  One-hour disaster recovery for
  Chicago and New York clients
  using BSI's hardware and
  peripherals. Call for price.
- RISC
  Back-office accounting and
  margining for exchange-traded
  indexes, currency options,
  futures, and options on futures.
  On-line, real-time, re-margining
  for all accounts. Multi-currency
  capability. Designed for use on
  IBM AS/400 mini computer. Call
  for price.
- Settlement Price Service
  Transmits settlement prices via
  modem daily. $300 per month.
- TRACS
  On-line margining package for
  microcomputer that computes
  margins at day's end. Multi-
  currency capability. Call for price.

- David Bruce & Co. products
  Risk-analysis software that
  interfaces with back-office
  systems and exchanges. (See
  listing for David Bruce & Co.)

GMI Software Inc.
300 W. Adams St.
Chicago, IL 60606
312–726–5298
Jeff Geldermann, president
Robert Murtaugh, executive vice
president
- Real-time back-office and
  accounting software for stocks,
  options, bonds, and commodities
  worldwide. Call for price.

Investment Support Systems
1455 Broad St.
Bloomfield, NJ 07003
201–338–0321
Jeff Arnold, chief operating officer
- FUTRAK Risk Management
  System
  Integrated analytic and back-office
  systems. Option pricing package
  uses real-time data and is tied to
  portfolio analysis package. Back-
  office accounting handles index,
  commodity, interest rate and
  currency options and futures. Call
  for price.

Quotient Inc.
45 Broadway
22nd Floor
New York, NY 10006
212–943–0171
Joseph Bruno, sales executive
Terry Prall, senior sales executive
- Cmark
  Fully integrated front- and back-
  office system for listed and over-
  the-counter interest rate,
  currency, index, and commodity
  options. Pricing and portfolio
  analysis software focuses on
  global capital markets. Call for
  price.

Software Options Inc.
210 Sylvan Ave.
Englewood Cliffs, NJ 07632
201–568–6664
Marketing director
- COTS/FairValue® Interest Rate
  Options Software
  Dealer-support system including
  risk-management and back-office
  functions for institutional trading
  in equity options, cash index
  options, and Treasury options.
  Begins at $25,000.

Software Vendors

Dynacomp, Inc.
Dynacomp Office Building
Webster, NY 14580
716–265–4040

Sales representative
Vendor of wide range of software.
Option products include:
- The Calcugram Stock Option
  System

Analytical program for single, spread and combination option positions. $169.95.
- Covered Options
  Option evaluation program for covered or uncovered positions. $99.95.
- Options Analysis
  Analysis for six strategies, based on Black-Scholes pricing model. $99.95.

Emerging Market Technologies, Inc.
Presidential Commons
Suite 10
3781 Presidential Parkway
Atlanta, GA 30341
404–350–9043
Jeffrey S. Multz, president
- Vendor of 50 investment software programs aimed at the brokerage communities. (Also see listing under Options Analytics.)

National Computer Network Corp.
233 W. Jackson Blvd.
Suite 1202
Chicago, IL 60606
312–427–5125
Tom McDonald, director of marketing

- Library of 100 programs for equity options, featuring position reporting, theoretical values, and volatilities on an end-of-day or real-time basis. Call for prices. (Also see listings under Databases and Custom Programming.)

SCIX Corp./Investment Software
2010 Lacomic St.
P.O. Box 3244
Williamsport, PA 17701
800–228–6655; 717–323–3276
Dealer of 125 software packages for investment purposes. Proprietary programs include:
- Options Strategy Tutor
  Teaching aid for equity options trading. $49.
- OPVAL Advanced
  Options valuation program based on Black-Scholes pricing model. $169.
- Portfolio Tracking System
  Multiple portfolio program for equities, options, bonds and futures. $265.
- Quote Transporter
  Translates historical quote data among software packages. $99.

Technical Analysis

Compu Trac Inc. A Telerate Company
1017 Pleasant St.
New Orleans, LA 70115
504–895–1474; 800–535–7990
Norbert Rudek, marketing manager
- CompuTrac
  Technical analysis charting

program includes studies and profitability testing of trading methods. Private studies can be added by user. Advanced modules and annual updates available. Starts at $695. Program maintenance and phone support: $300 annually.

Commodity Communications Corp.

250 S. Wacker Dr.
Suite 1150
Chicago, IL 60606
800–621–2628; 312–977–9067

Paul Huske, sales manager

* Future Source Technical
  Real-time technical analyses with
  quotes, graphs, analytics on
  domestic futures and indexes,
  including OEX. Call for price.

Cyber-Scan, Inc.

Route 4, Box 247
Buffalo MN 55313
612–682–4150

Harold Hoffmann, president

* Technical analysis software
  applicable to equities or stock
  indexes. $350.

Ensign Software

2641 Shannon Court
Idaho Falls, ID 83404
208–524–0755

Howard Arrington, owner

* Creates real-time and historical
  charts; technical analysis
  capability. $1,195.

Equis International Inc.

P.O. Box 26743
Salt Lake City, UT 84126
800–882–3040; 801–974–5115

Curtis Carman, sales manager

* MetaStock-Professional
  End-of-day charting and technical
  analysis software for 40 studies.
  $295.

Foley Financial Inc.

McCormack Station, P.O. Box 4535
Boston, MA 02101
800–662–7355; 617–237–3001

Mary Lou Halloran, president

* EasyCharter
  Lotus Symphony® or 1–2–3®
  template for generating intra-day
  line charts of stocks, options,
  futures, and options on futures.
  $100.

Gannsoft Publishing Company

11670 Riverbend Dr.
Leavenworth, WA 98826
509–548–5990

Peter Pich, president

* GANNTRADER I
  Market cycle software based on
  W.D. Gann trading methods that
  works with Compu Trac or
  Commodity Systems, Inc.
  Quicktrieve data. $699.

Inmark Development Corp.

139 Fulton St.
New York, NY 10038
212–406–2299

Bard S. Stephens, vice president of
sales

* Market Maker
  Charts for historical data for stock
  options and futures. $495.

**Intermountain Technical Services
Inc.**

10900 N.E. Eighth St.
Suite 900
Bellevue, WA 98004
206–643–3716

Jerry Flynn, president

- Graphics PLUS
Charting software for IBM® PCs.
$195.

Investment Software
P.O. Box 2774
Durango, CO 81302
303–563–9543
Robert E. Jenkinson, partner

- Technical Indicator Program (TIP)
Eighteen technical indicators for
timing stock purchases. $89.50.
- Personal Market Analysis (PMA)
Charting and technical analysis on
daily price data. $149.
- NYSE Data
Daily historical data to use in
conjunction with two previous
programs. For TIP, $10 per year,
with data from 1976. For PMA,
data includes six indexes from
1984 for $10.

Market Vision Corp.
40 Rector St.
19th Floor
New York, NY 10006
212–227–1610
Donna Knief, marketing

- Athena
Real-time and historical charting
service with technical analysis
capabilities. Call for price. (Also
see listings under Portfolio
Management and Databases.)

NewTEK Industries
P.O. Box 46116
Los Angeles, CA 90046
213–874–6669
Jules Brenner, general manager

- Compu/CHART EGA
Technical analysis with high-
resolution graphics including on-
line capability for daily and
historical data. $259.95.
- Compu/CHART Jr
Down-sized version of Compu/
CHART EGA with fewer charts.
$179.95.
- The Retriever Plus
Creates and maintains data files in
Lotus® formats. $79.95. (Also see
listing in Data Bases.)

N-Squared Computing
5318 Forest Ridge Rd.
Silverton, OR 97381
214–680–1445
Greg Morris, director of technical
analysis

- Stock and Futures Analyzer/
Optimizer
Advanced technical analysis of
stocks, stock indexes, options,
and futures. $595.

The Pardo Corp.
950 Skokie Blvd.
Suite 310
Northbrook, IL 60062
708–564–9903
Robert Pardo, President

- Advanced Chartist v4.0
Comprehensive charting/graphics
program features 7 chart types,
spreads, scaling, and formatting
functions, 13 graphic tools, 15
advanced graphic studies, and
more than 30 price, volume, and
open interest indicators. $595.
- Advanced Chartist + Cycle
Two separate programs merged to

provide cyclic, analytic, and forecasting ability for price and indicators. $695.

- Advanced Trader v1.0
  Features of Advanced Chartist + Cycle combined with Script language for user to build, plot, or optimize any type of indicator, filter, or trading model. $1,395.
- Calvin
  Generates signals from models based on volatility channels. $995.
- Cycle
  Finds, analyzes, plots, and projects cyclic components of price action. $295.
- Dataman
  Data base management for CSI and CompuTrac formats. $95.
- Expert Trader v1.0
  Includes features of "Advanced Trader" plus integrated artificial intelligence shell. $1,995.
- Forecast
  Automated numeric and graphics implementation of proprietary cyclic techniques that generates price/time forecasts of price trend changes. $995 and $1,995.
- Max II
  Generates signals from low drawdown models based on price patterns that signal large moves. $895.
- Numbers
  Plots daily and historical Market Profile® charts. Isolates, defines, evaluates short-term Fibonacci support and resistance numbers. $195.
- Profile
  Statistical analysis of market price structure based on price swings of

varying time periods, volatility, support, and resistance; daily price overlap. $195.

- Rank
  Ranks equities or futures portfolio based on greatest return on capital. $195.
- Trend
  Automatable graphics program that analyzes trends and anticipates or identifies major price tops and bottoms. $395.
- Trio
  Generates market entries, exits, reversals from models based on channels, volatility, breakouts, and moving averages. $2,500.

Pro Plus Software, Inc.
2150 East Brown Rd.
Mesa, AZ 85203
602–461–3296
Sales representative

- Wall Street Investor™
  Technical analysis, fundamental analysis, and portfolio management package for stocks, options, bonds, and mutual funds. Online trading with major discount brokerage firms. $695.

Quotron Systems, Inc.
12731 W. Jefferson Blvd.
Los Angeles, CA 90066
213–827–4600
Howard Taylor, vice president, sales

- Intraday Graphs
  Bar charts of price movements, in 15-minute intervals, for selected securities, statistics, and commodities. Call for price.

- QuotChart ™
  Performs comparative analyses using Quotron's real-time price and market data, providing up to eight dynamic, real-time colored charts and trendlines simultaneously. Eleven continuously updated technical studies available. Call for price.
- FAME®
  Interactive software designed to maintain and access a wide range of time-series data, integrated into a single, logical data base accessible for statistical analysis, graphing, and reporting. Call for price.
- Research-Pak™
  Investment analysis application from FAME® Software Corp. integrating various industry-standard data bases (e.g., daily pricing, Compustat® Value Line,® and I/B/E/S®) into a common environment. Call for price.
  (Also see listings under Options Analytics, Databases, and Quote Vendors.)

Roberts-Slade Inc.
750 N. 200 West
Suite 301–B
Provo, UT 84601
800–433–4276; 801–375–6847
Morgan Roberts, vice president of sales and marketing

- Master Chartist
  General-purpose technical analysis for real-time data on stocks, options, and futures. One-time fee of $1,295; $295 annually.

- Chartist P.M.
  End-of-day version of Master Chartist for longer-term analysis. One-time fee of $500; $195 annually.

Savant Corporation
11211 Katy Freeway
Suite 250
Houston, TX 77079
800–231–9900; 713–973–2400
Mark Randall, sales manager

- The Technical Investor
  Historical charting and technical analysis for equities, options, and futures. $395. (Also see listing under Portfolio Management.)

Smith Micro Software Inc.
P.O. Box 7137
Huntington Beach, CA 92615
714–964–0412
Bill Smith, president

- Wall Street Techniques
  Technical analysis and charting system for PC or Macintosh™. $295. (Also see listing in Portfolio Management.)

Technical Analysis, Inc.
9131 California Ave. S.W.
Seattle, WA 98136
800–832–4642; 206–938–0570
Mike H. Takano, financial systems manager

- Technical Analysis Charts
  Data-charting software that allows development of own routine; emulates Macintosh™ on Apple II™. Database Manager within package allows manual input of market data, including updates of purchased data. $129.95.

Subroutines of technical analysis programs printed in *Stocks and Commodities* magazine available on disk.

WarMachine
1912 W. Hood
Chicago, IL 60660
312–262–1318
Richard Batchelor, president

- WarMachine
  Technical analysis software for use with Lotus Signal®. $895 for IBM®; $1,095 for Macintosh™ or Apple II™.

Trading Systems

AIQ Systems, Inc.
916 Southwood Blvd.
Suite 2C
P.O. Drawer 7530
Incline Village, NV 89450
800–332–2999; 702–831–2999
Mike Gross, marketing manager
- AIQ IndexExpert™
  Artificial-intelligence based expert system in combination with Black-Scholes pricing model for trading index options. $1,588.
- AIQ OptionExpert™
  Artificial-intelligence system in combination with Black-Scholes pricing model for trading equity options. $1,588.

AVCO Financial Corp.
8 Grigg St.
Suite 3
Greenwich, CT 06830
203–661–7381
Anthony R. Vartuli, president
- The TTA Day-Trading Method
  Fully disclosed, proprietary day-

trading system for OEX and futures. $695.

Bristol Financial Services Inc.
23 Bristol Place
Wilton, CT 06897
203–834–0040
Ken Martin, director of marketing
- Insight v2.0
  Real-time trading software for stocks, options, and futures. Options valuation and ranking capability available. $1,200 annual license; $500 start-up.

The Comhedge Partnership
210 Sylvan Ave.
Englewood Cliffs, NJ 07632
201–569–3522
Lillian Zito, manager
- On-Line Trading and Accounting System
  Trading system for options and futures; includes back-office accounting system. Price depends on customization. (Also see

listings in Options Analytics and
Portfolio Management.)

William Finnegan Associates, Inc.

21235 Pacific Coast Highway
Malibu, CA 90265
213–456–5741
William Finnegan, president
* The Market Forecaster
  Econometric model that provides
  an 80-day forecast of the stock
  market, with a correlation to
  future market moves of R = .80
  over the last 25 years. $339.
* The Strategy Simulator
  Twenty-five-year database to test
  trading strategies. Can manipulate
  data and construct own variables.
  $249.

Golden Enterprises

2410 Sand Point Court
Byron, CA 94514
415–634–6634
Jack Burow, president
* The Golden Option
  Technical trading system for OEX
  includes trendlines, trading bands,
  and Gann angles. Call for price.

Mendelsohn and Associates

50 Meadow Lane
Zephyrhills, FL 33544
813–973–0496
Lou Mendelsohn, president
* ProfitTaker
  Trading system for stock indexes
  and futures with ability to
  customize. $995.

TLM Inc.

420 Westchester Ave.
Port Chester, NY 10573
800–451–1392
Bob Lesser, president
* Market Timing Software
  Trading system for OEX and XMI
  requiring daily entry of high, low,
  and close. $149.95.

Trend Index Company

Box 5
Altoona, WI 54720
Dave Green, owner
* Dow Jones Market Intelligence
  Trading System
  Proprietary trading system that
  uses Dow Jones Industrial
  Average data to generate signals
  in OEX. Also does charting and
  technical analysis. $1,000.

Databases

Commodity Systems Inc. (CSI)

200 W. Palmetto Park Rd.
Boca Raton, FL 33432
800–327–0175; 407–392–8663
Nassrin Berns, director of
marketing

* Daily or end-of-day historical data
  for equities, stock index options,
  futures, options on futures, and
  mutual funds. $29 per month
  minimum.

CompuServe®

5000 Arlington Centre Blvd.
P.O. Box 20212
Columbus, OH 43220
800–848–8199
Ohio and Canada: 614–457–0802

* Investment Services
  Access to several price and
  information databases in the
  financial industry. $39.95 one-time
  membership fee. Fees vary
  according to online time.

DRI/McGraw-Hill

24 Hartwell Ave.
Lexington, MA 02173
617–863–5100
1–800–345–6374

Bonnie Liggett, marketing manager,
equity and commodities

* DRI Commodities Data Base
  Includes options, indexes, futures,
  and options on futures.
* The Financial Market Indexes
  Data Base
  Nearly 1,000 financial indexes for
  equities and fixed-income
  products on a global basis.
* Morgan Stanley's Capital
  International Data Base
* Standard & Poor's Industry
  Financials Data Base
  Stock fundamentals by industry.
* The Russell Equity Indexes Data
  Base
* DRI U.S. and Canadian Equity
  Data Base
  Includes all publicly traded stocks
  on every major and regional
  exchange.

Prices based on usage.

Dun & Bradstreet Financial Information Services

95 Hayden Ave.
Lexington, MA 02173–9144
617–863–8100

Joel Fink, manager of equity
product management

* Comprehensive historic data base
  of equities, including their
  options. Complete CBOE
  database since 1973. Also real-
  time CBOE quotes. Available on
  Marketplus product. Call for
  price.

Genesis Financial Data Services

P.O. Box 150628
Arlington, TX 76105
214–642–0781

Glen Larsen, president

* Historical and daily data on
  stocks, stock indexes and futures.
  Call for prices.

Information Sources Inc.

1173 Colusa Ave.
Box 7848
Berkeley, CA 94707
800–433–6107; 415–525–6220

Ruth Koolish, president

* Database of investment software
  information available online. Price
  based on online time.

Market Vision Corp.

40 Rector St.
19th Floor
New York, NY 10006
212–227–1610

Donna Knief, marketing

- Market Vision Databank
Online system that collects and
consolidates multiple exchange
feeds; maintains historical
database. Call for price. (Also see
listings for Technical Analysis and
Portfolio Management.)

National Computer Network Corp.
223 W. Jackson Blvd.
Suite 1202
Chicago, IL 60606
312–427–5125
Tom McDonald, director of
marketing
- Database of historical volatilities
and equity and equity option
prices. (Also see listing under
Custom Programming and
Software Vendors.)

NewTEK Industries
P.O. Box 46116
Los Angeles, CA 90046
213–874–6669
Jules Brenner, general manager

- Commission Comparison
Small database of discount
brokerage commissions allows
price shopping. $39.95. (Also see
listing in Technical Analysis.)

Warner Computer Systems Inc.
17-01 Pollitt Drive
Fair Lawn, NJ 07410
201–794–2870
Ronald Perez, manager of market
data products
- End-of-day and historical data
from all U.S. exchanges plus
Toronto and Montreal Stock
Exchanges. Stocks, options,
futures, indexes, and mutual
funds. Call for price.

Quote Vendors

All-Quotes, Inc.
40 Exchange Place
15th Floor
New York, NY 10005
800–888–7559; 212–425–5030
Bronson Conrad, president
- Real-time or delayed quotes for
all North American stock,
options, and over-the-counter
markets. Also futures quotes from
CBOT, CME, and CEC. New
York metropolitan area: 39 cents
per minute to monthly maximum
of $99.99. Other areas: 59 cents
per minute. Exchange fees extra
for real-time.

Audio Response Services Inc.
3030 Clarendon Blvd.
Suite 301
Arlington, VA 22201
800–999–1868; 703–247–3482
Ron Elasik, marketing director

- voiceQuote®
  Real-time quotes via tough-tone telephone from major U.S. stock exchanges, options exchanges, and over-the-counter markets. Also carries mutual fund quotes. Features include portfolio construction, stock volume, highs and lows. Can construct portfolios. Per-minute fee.

Beta Systems

330 E. Kilbourn Ave.
Milwaukee, WI 53202
414–225–3000
Peter Frank, president

- Real-time quotes from North American stock, options, and futures exchanges. Analysis capability, graphics, options montage, time and sales, and news available. Call for price.

Bonneville Telecommunications Co.

19 W. South Temple
Salt Lake City, UT 84101
800–255–7374; 801–532–3400
Marrianne Roberts, director of marketing

- Market Center
  Real-time quotes from U.S. equity, option, and futures exchanges plus London commodity exchanges. Starts at $197 per month.

Broker Services

5950 S. Willow Dr.
Suite 206
Englewood, CO 80111
303–779–8930
Ken Roberts, manager

- Delayed quotes on options and their underlying stocks via Telenet. $395 per month includes access charges.

Cambridge Planning & Analytics Inc.

55 Wheeler St.
P.O. Box 276
Cambridge, MA 02138
617–576–6465
Richard J. Goettle, president

- Series of six databases on U.S. economic and financial data, focusing on credit markets. Also includes data on major U.S. trading partners. Complete system: $3,000 annually.

CMA, Inc.

151 W. 46th St.
11th Floor
New York, NY 10036
800–262–4126; 212–382–1822
Rafael Vila, marketing

- Real-time or delayed quotes from all U.S. stock, options, and commodity exchanges. Also carries South American stock exchanges and Telerate™ service. Call for price.

Commodity Communications Corp.

250 S. Wacker Dr.
Suite 1150
Chicago, IL 60606
800–621–2628; 312–977–9067
Paul Huske, sales manager

• FutureSource Technical
Real-time technical analysis with
quotes, graphs, analytics on
domestic futures and indexes,
including OEX. Call for price.

• Option Source
Online quotations and real-time
trading evaluation and simulations
for OEX and options on futures.
Call for price.

ComStock/McGraw-Hill Financial Services

670 White Plains Rd.
Scarsdale, NY 10583
800–431–5019
New York and Canada: 914–725–
3477
Harry Sachinis, director of sales
and marketing
• ComStock is a real-time quote
service covering 65,000 stocks,
options, and commodities from
dozens of U.S. and international
exchanges via satellite or
dedicated phone line. ComStock
works with a variety of third-
party software packages and also
provides a datafeed that can be
fed into head-end computers for
redistribution throughout large
companies. Call for price.

CQG, Inc.

P.O. Box 758
Glenwood Springs, CO 81602
800–525–7082; 303–945–8686
Marketing representatives

• Decision-support systems for
futures industry over own
broadcast network, including real-
time quotations and enhanced
graphics for OEX and futures.
Starts at $390 per month.

Data Broadcasting Corporation Inc.

8300 Old Court House Rd.
Vienna, VA 22182
703–790–3570
Bernie Gould, vice president of
sales
• FNN: Marketwatch
Real-time and delayed quotes
from major U.S. stock, options,
and futures exchanges via
television feed or satellite. Begins
at $80 per month.

DATALINE
A Subsidiary of Mead Data Central, Inc.

67 Richmond St. West
Suite 700
Toronto, Ontario M5H 1Z5
416–365–1616
David F. Moxam, director of sales
• Real-time quotes from North
American equity, options, and
futures exchanges. Call for price.

Datastream International Inc.

One World Trade Center
Suite 9069
New York, NY 10048
212–524–8400
Drew deGanahl, sales manager
• Online, delayed quotes from the
European Options Exchange and

London Options Exchange. Call for price.

ILX Systems, Inc.
111 Fulton St.
New York, NY 10038
212–964–1199
Anthony Campiformio, vice president of sales
• Real-time quotes on all North American stock, options, and futures exchanges; news service. Also offers office automation systems. Call for price.

Knight-Ridder Financial Information
55 Broadway
New York, NY 10006
212–269–1110
Sales representative
• MoneyCenter
PC-based real-time quote and news service covering all major U.S. and foreign cash, futures, and options markets. Internationally contributed real-time cash prices for U.S. Treasury, money market, and mortgage-backed securities, plus corporate, municipal, and foreign government bonds, foreign exchange, and commodities. Call for price. (Also see listing in Options Analytics.)

Knight-Ridder Unicom
72–78 Fleet St.
London, England EC4Y 1HY
01–353–1020–4861
Sales representative
• Sells Knight-Ridder TradeCenter and MoneyCenter products to all

international clientele. (See Knight-Ridder Financial Information listing in Options Analytics section and previous entry.)

Lotus Information Network Corporation
1900 S. Norfolk St.
Suite 150
San Mateo, CA 94403
800–367–4670
Sales representative
• Quotrek®
Portable FM-based quote service. $399 plus monthly fees.
• Signal®
Real-time quotes on all U.S. stock, options, and futures exchanges via FM airwaves. PC-based. $595 plus monthly fees.

PC Quote Inc.
401 S. LaSalle St.
Suite 1600
Chicago, IL 60605
800–225–5657; 312–786–5400
Susan Barber, director of marketing
• Real-time stock and option quotes via satellite. Option theoretical value page available. $395 per month. Additional terminals $75 per month.

Telekurs (North America), Inc.
111 W. Jackson Blvd.
Suite 1900
Chicago, IL 60604
312–663–4143
Phil Tufts, regional sales manager
• Invest Data[SM]
Real-time prices and quotes for

more than 220,000 securities from exchanges and contributors worldwide. Provides access to back-office data base. Call for price.

* Portfolio Valuation Pricing Service
Daily portfolio valuation prices on a global basis. Provides prices from every exchange for multiple-listed securities. Call for price.

* Ticker III*
Real-time quotes on all North American exchange-traded securities. Call for price.

* Ticker IV*
Real-time quotes on North American and international exchange-traded securities. Call for price.

* Formerly offered by Standard & Poor's Trading Systems
(Also see listing in Options Analytics.)

Telemet America Inc.
325 First St.
Alexandria, VA 22314
800–368–2078; 703–548–2042
James G. Roberts, sales manager
* Real-time quotes from all U.S. stock and commodity exchanges via hand-held FM units or satellite broadcast. Begins at $27.50 per month.

Telerate Systems Incorporated
One World Trade Center
104th Floor
New York, NY 10048
212–938–4298

Rick Snape, vice president, sales and marketing

* Tactician™
Fundamental decision-support system for the fixed-income market. Combines live market data for monitoring current trading positions, analyzes historical trends, searches for arbitrage opportunities, and performs "what-if" analysis. Call for price.

* Telerate Matrix
Advanced PC workstation with custom applications. Subscribers can access Telerate data via satellite, FM sideband, or leased line. Real-time and historical charts and prices available on government and mortgage-backed securities, money markets, foreign exchange, energy, corporate bonds, futures, options, equities, and more. Call for price.

* TeleTrac®
Comprehensive graphics and studies. Captures live pricing information tick-by-tick and transforms it into high-resolution graphic displays. Call for price.

* TIQ™
Telerate International Quotes provides real-time quotes on stocks, options, futures, and listed bonds from North America, major U.K., and Asia/Pacific exchanges. Can be delivered as a data feed or local area network. Call for price.

Trade*Plus
480 California Ave.
Suite 301
Palo Alto, CA 94306
National: 800–952–9900
California: 800–972–9900
Customer service representative
• Last sale and at least 15 minutes
  of prices from all U.S. equity and
  commodity exchanges. $15 per
  month fee includes 60 minutes of
  access.

Wang Financial Information Services Corp.
120 Wall St.
Ninth Floor
New York, NY 10005
800–423–2002; 212–208–7700
Carole Gevlin, marketing assistant
• SHARK
  Real-time quotes for stocks,
  options, and futures. Also
  provides option analysis and news
  services. Call for price.

Databases and Quote Vendors

Automatic Data Processing (ADP) Brokerage Information Services Group
300 W. Adams
Chicago, IL 60606
312–332–7176
Thomas W. Wilbeck, district sales manager
Front-office and back-office services for firms. Market data and database products.
• ADP Financial System One
  Real-time stock, bond, futures,
  and option quotes plus news,
  tickers and databases. Starts at
  $1,300 per month.
• ADP Comtrend Videcom
  Real-time, online price and
  trading data from major financial
  exchanges around the world.

Graphic and numerical displays.
Starts at $1,175 per month for 36-month term.
• Database Services
  Library of electronic databases
  including Dow Jones News
  Retrieval, Standard & Poor's
  MarketScope, and others.
  Monthly fees vary.

Bridge Information Systems Inc.
717 Office Parkway
St. Louis, MO 63141
800–325–3282; 314–567–8100
Real-time and historical prices on options, stocks, stock indexes, futures, bonds, and money market instruments worldwide. Call for price. Includes the following:

- Option Market Ranking
Scans and ranks entire option market according to user criteria.
- Option Summaries
Allows user to rank a class of options for a selected stock.
- Option Strategies
Value calculations based on the Black-Scholes pricing model; 14 strategies.

Dow Jones News Retrieval

P.O. Box 300
Princeton, NJ 08543
800–522–3567; 609–452–1511
Customer service

- Current Quotes
Online, delayed option prices. Priced per minute online.
- Tradeline
Historical quotes through life of contract. Priced per minute online.

Quotron Systems, Inc.

12731 W. Jefferson Blvd.
Los Angeles, CA 90066
213–827–4600
Howard Taylor, vice president of sales

- Financial Database Services
An expanding library of online data includes fundamental data, research, financial analysis, statistical data, and reports, as well as commentary covering equities, fixed-income, and foreign exchange markets. Call for price.
- Market Data Services
Global, real-time information for stocks, bonds, options, mutual funds, financial futures, and commodities, plus market statistics. Call for prices. Products include:

- Dynamic Option Class Display
Theoretical values, hedge ratios, and performance evaluation graph for user reevaluation based on certain variables such as interest rates, projected dividends, and volatility.
- Enhanced Monitor Service
Same information as Monitor Service plus ability to monitor volume, bid, ask, size, open, high, low, contract high/low, open interest, trading limit, opening range, options strike price, and time of last trade for user-specified securities.
- Monitor Service
Last price for listed and inside bid for OTC stocks, tick, net change from close, and status flags for each security to indicate news story or special condition.
- Option Class Display
Strike price and exchange for all option series of an underlying security. Tick-last-net, bid, ask, time, volume.
- Option Trading Information Service (OTIS)
Displays trading activity by volume and current bid and ask of specified option series, displayed in time sequence with last sale first.
- Quoteline
Composite last sale, exchange, tick, net change from previous close, best bid/ask with size,

composite volume (cumulative across exchanges), time of last trade, and flags for special conditions.

- Real-Time Ticker Service
Listed securities, commodities, and options reported in real-time, displayed as raw, selective or block tickers. (Also see listings in Options Analytics and Technical Analysis.)

Reuters Information Services, Inc.
141 W. Jackson Blvd.
Suite 2900
Chicago, IL 60604
312–294–2500
Maureen Cullen, marketing manager central region
Real-time information:

- Equities 2000
Provides real-time quotes of 165,000 instruments including equities, futures, and options from all North American and international exchanges as well as fixed-income and foreign exchange prices on color terminal. Users can program their own portfolios and access Reuters news services and market reports. $950 per month for the first unit; additional units are $250 per month.
- ART 2000
Complete decision support system combining all features of the Equities 2000 with calculation and analytical tools including charts, a portfolio management system, and a real-time spreadsheet (Microsoft® Excel) in a multi-

windows environment. $900 per month for the first unit; additional units are $500 per month.

- Schwarzatron
Provides full option statistics, implied and historical volatilities, position keeping, time and sales, and sophisticated Limit Minding facilities. $900 per month for each unit.
- Reuter SDS2 Futures Service
Provides spot prices and futures/ options quotes from exchanges worldwide. Coverage includes physical markets, contributed data from leading industry sources, news and statistics. $595 per month for the first unit; additional units are $175 per month.
- Reuter SDS2 Futures Marketfeed
Enables users to feed live futures and options prices into a PC for further analysis. With Reuter software packages—Marketview, Reuter Chartist, Spreadsheet Link—data can be turned into color graphics or technical studies. $175 per month per feed.

Historical Information*

- Reuter Pricelink
Provides historical information on 70,000 instruments from different stock, commodities, option, futures, bond, and money markets. Information can be loaded into a PC for financial analysis, to update portfolios or to produce graphical displays.
- S&P Marketscope
Textual and statistical information on over 4,800 U.S. companies. Analysis of stocks and industry

developments, investment and portfolio recommendations, earnings estimates, and forecasts.

• Snapshot
System for updating client portfolios at regular, predefined intervals with Reuter sourced data. Data covers equities, futures, options, indices, foreign exchange, bonds, and mutual funds.

• Corporate Action Line
Provides users with global coverage of corporate dividend and capital change announcements.

* Prices are usage-based.

List of Trademarks

The Professional Portfolio is a trademark of Advent Software, Inc.

AIQ IndexExpert and AIQ OptionExpert are trademarks of AIQ Systems, Inc.

Apple II and Macintosh are trademarks licensed to Apple Computer, Inc. Apple is a registered trademark of Apple Computer, Inc.

voiceQuote is a registered trademark of Audio Response Services Inc.

Market Profile is a registered trademark of the Board of Trade of the City of Chicago.

Rory Tycoon is a trademark of Coherent Software Systems.

CompuServe is a registered trademark of CompuServe Information Services, Inc.

InvestNow! is a registered trademark of Emerging Market Technologies, Inc.

FAME and Research-Pak are registered trademarks of FAME Software Corporation.

IBM is a registered trademark of International Business Machines Corporation.

Lotus, Signal, Quotrek, 1–2–3 and Symphony are registered trademarks of Lotus Development Corporation.

I/B/E/S is a registered trademark of Lynch, Jones & Ryan.

Microsoft is a registered trademark of Microsoft Corporation. Windows is a trademark of Microsoft Corporation.

Optionomic Systems is a trademark of Optionomics Corp.

Wall Street Investor is a trademark of Pro Plus Software, Inc.

QuotChart is a registered trademark of Quotron Systems, Inc.

COTS/Fair Value is a registered trademark of Software Options, Inc.

Compustat is a registered trademark of Standard & Poor, Inc.

S&P 100 is a trademark of Standard & Poor's Corporation.

S&P 500 is a trademark of Standard & Poor's Corporation.

InvestData is a service mark of Telekurs AG.

TeleTrac is a registered trademark of Telerate Systems Incorporated. Tactician, Telerate and TIQ are trademarks of Telerate Systems Incorporated.

Telescan is a trademark of Telescan, Inc.

Value Line is a registered trademark of Value Line, Inc.

SERIES 2 is a trademark of Wismer Associates, Inc.

Index of Appendix Listings

GLOSSARY

adjusting   A dynamic trading process by which a floor trader with a spread position buys or sells options or stock to maintain the delta neutrality of the position. See **delta.**

adjusted strike price   Strike price of an option, created as the result of a special event such as a stock split or a stock dividend. The adjusted strike price can differ from the regular intervals prescribed for strike prices. See **strike price interval.**

aggregate exercise price   The total dollar value transferred in settlement of an exercised option.

American option   An option that can be exercised at any time prior to expiration. See **European option.**

arbitrage   A trading technique that involves the simultaneous purchase and sale of identical assets or of equivalent assets in two different markets with the intent of profiting by the price discrepancy.

ask price   The price at which a seller is offering to sell an option or stock.

assignment   Notification by the Options Clearing Corporation to the writer of an option that a holder of the option has exercised and that the terms of settlement must be met. Assignments are made on a random basis by the Options Clearing Corporation. See **delivery** and **exercise**.

at-the-money   A term that describes an option with an exercise price that is equal to the current market price of the underlying stock.

automatic exercise   Same as **exercise by exception.**

averaging down   Buying more of a stock or an option at a lower price than the original purchase so as to reduce the average cost.

backspread   A delta-neutral spread comprised of more long options than short options on the same underlying stock. This position generally profits from a large movement in either direction in the underlying stock.

bearish   An adjective describing the belief that a stock or the market in general will decline in price.

bear spread   One of a variety of strategies involving two or more options (or options combined with a position in the underlying stock) that will profit from a fall in price in the underlying stock.

bear spread (call)   The simultaneous sale of one call option with a lower strike price and the purchase of another call option with a higher strike price.

bear spread (put)   The simultaneous purchase of one put option with a higher strike price and the sale of another put option with a lower strike price.

beta   A measure of how closely the movement of an individual stock tracks the movement of the entire stock market.

bid price   The price at which a buyer is willing to buy an option or stock.

Black-Scholes model   A mathematical formula used to calculate an option's theoretical value from the following inputs: stock price, strike price, interest rates, dividends, time to expiration, and volatility.

book   Same as **public order book.**

box spread   A four-sided option spread that involves a long call and short put at one strike price as well as a short call and long put at another strike price. In other words, this is a synthetic long stock position at one strike price and a synthetic short stock position at another strike price.

break-even point   A stock price at option expiration at which an option strategy results in neither a profit nor a loss.

broker   A person acting as an agent for making securities transactions. An "account executive" or a "broker" at a brokerage firm deals with customers. A "floor broker" on the trading floor of an exchange actually executes someone else's trading orders.

bullish   An adjective describing the belief that a stock or the market in general will rise in price.

bull spread   One of a variety of strategies involving two or more options (or options combined with a stock position) that will profit from a rise in price in the underlying.

bull spread (call)   The simultaneous purchase of one call option with a lower strike price and the sale of another call option with a higher strike price.

bull spread (put)   The simultaneous sale of one put option with a higher strike price and the purchase of another put option with a lower strike price.

butterfly spread   A strategy involving four options and three strike prices that has both limited risk and limited profit potential. A long call butterfly is established by: buying one call at the lowest strike price, selling two calls at the middle strike price, and buying one call at the highest strike price. A long put butterfly is established by: buying one put at the highest strike price, selling two puts at the middle strike price, and buying one put at the lowest strike price.

buy-write   Same as **covered call.**

CBOE   The Chicago Board Options Exchange. CBOE opened in April 1973, and is the oldest and largest listed options exchange.

CFTC   The Commodity Futures Trading Commission. The CFTC is the agency of the federal government that regulates commodity futures trading.

calendar spread   Same as **time spread.**

call option   A contract which gives the holder the right (but not the obligation) to purchase the underlying stock at some predetermined price. In the case of American call options, this right can be exercised at any time until the expiration date. In the case of European call options, this right can only be exercised on the expiration date. For the writer (or grantor) of a call option, the contract represents an obligation to sell stock to the holder if the option is exercised.

carrying cost   The interest expense on money borrowed to finance a stock or option position.

cash settlement   The process by which the terms of an option contract are fulfilled through the payment or receipt in dollars of the amount at which the option is in-the-money as opposed to delivering or receiving the underlying stock.

Christmas tree spread   A strategy involving six options and four strike prices that has both limited risk and limited profit potential. For example, a long call Christmas tree spread is established by buying one call at the lowest strike, skipping the second strike, selling three calls at the third strike, and buying two calls at the fourth strike.

class of options   A term referring to all options of the same security type— either calls or puts—covering the same underlying security.

closing price   The final price at which a transaction was made, but not necessarily the settlement price. See **settlement price.**

closing transaction   A reduction or an elimination of an open position by the appropriate offsetting purchase or sale. An existing long option position is closed out by a selling transaction. An existing short option position is closed out by a purchase transaction.

closing rotation   See **trading rotation.**

collateral   Securities against which loans are made. If the value of the securities (relative to the loan) declines to an unacceptable level, this triggers a *margin call*. As such, the investor is asked to post additional collateral or the securities are sold to repay the loan.

combination spread   An option technique involving a long call and short put, or a short call and a long put. Such strategies do not fall into clearly defined categories, and the term *combination* is often used very loosely. This tactic is also called a *fence strategy*. See **fence.**

commodities See **futures contract.**

condor spread A strategy involving four options and four strike prices that has both limited risk and limited profit potential. A long call condor spread is established by buying one call at the lowest strike, selling one call at the second strike, selling another call at the third strike, and buying one call at the fourth strike. This spread is also referred to as a *flat-top butterfly* or a *top hat spread.*

consecutive expiration cycle See **cycle.**

contingency order An order to conduct one transaction in one security that depends on the price of another instrument. An example might be, "Sell the XYZ Jan 50 call at 2, contingent upon XYZ being at or below \$49 1/2."

contract size The amount of the underlying asset covered by the option contract. This is 100 shares for one equity option unless adjusted for a special event, such as a stock split or a stock dividend. For index options, the contract size is the index level times the index multiplier.

conversion An investment strategy in which a long put and a short call with the same strike price and expiration are combined with long stock to lock in a nearly riskless profit. The process of executing these three-sided trades is sometimes called *conversion arbitrage.* See **reverse conversion.**

cover To close out an open position. This term is used most frequently to describe the purchase of an option to close out an existing short position for either a profit or loss.

covered option An open short option position that is fully collateralized. If the holder of the option exercises, the writer of the option will not have a problem fulfilling the delivery requirements. See **uncovered option.**

covered call An option strategy in which a call option is written against long stock.

covered combination Same as **covered strangle.**

covered put An option strategy in which a put option is written against a sufficient amount of cash (or T-bills) to pay for the stock purchase if the short option is assigned.

covered straddle An option strategy in which one call and one put with the same strike price and expiration are written against 100 shares of the underlying stock. In actuality, this is not a "covered" strategy because assignment on the short put would require purchase of stock on margin.

covered strangle A strategy in which one call and one put with the same expiration—but different strike prices—are written against 100 shares of the underlying stock. In actuality, this is not a "covered" strategy because assignment on the short put would require purchase of stock on margin. This method is also called a *covered combination.*

credit   Money received in an account either from a deposit or a transaction that results in increasing the account's cash balance.

credit spread   A spread strategy that increases the account's cash balance when it is established. A bull spread with puts and a bear spread with calls are examples of credit spreads.

curvature   Same as **gamma.**

cycle   The expiration dates applicable to the different series of options. Traditionally, there were three cycles: January/April/July/October, February/May/August/November, and March/June/September/December. Today, equity options expire on a sequential cycle which involves a total of four option series: two near-term months and two far-term months. For example, on January 1, a stock traditionally in the January cycle will be trading options expiring in these months: January, February, April, and July. Index options, however, expire on a consecutive cycle which involves the four near-term months. For example, on January 1, index options will be trading options expiring in these months: January, February, March, and April.

day trade   A position that is opened and closed on the same day.

debit   Money paid out from an account either from a withdrawal or a transaction that results in decreasing the cash balance.

debit spread   A spread strategy that decreases the account's cash balance when it is established. A bull spread with calls and a bear spread with puts are examples of debit spreads.

decay   See **time decay.**

delivery   The process of meeting the terms of a written option when notification of assignment has been received. In the case of a short call, the writer must deliver stock and in return receives cash for the stock sold. In the case of a short put, the writer pays cash and in return receives the stock purchased.

delta   A measure of the rate of change in an option's theoretical value for a one-unit change in the price of the underlying security.

delta-neutral spread   A trading strategy, sometimes used by professional market makers, that matches the total long deltas of a position (long stock, long calls, short puts) with the total short deltas (short stock, short calls, long puts).

diagonal spread   A strategy involving the simultaneous purchase and sale of two options of the same type that have different strike prices and different expiration dates. Example: Buy 1 May 45 call and sell 1 March 50 call.

discount   An adjective used to describe an option that is trading below its intrinsic value.

discretion   Freedom given to the floor broker by an investor to use his judgment regarding the execution of an order. Discretion can be limited, as in the case of a limit order which gives the floor broker 1/8 or 1/4 point from the stated limit price to use his judgment in executing the order. Discretion can also be unlimited, as in the case of a market-not-held-order. See **market-not-held-order.**

dynamic hedging A short-term trading strategy generally using index options in which the delta of an index option is taken into consideration so that the total price movement of the index options used will approximate the total dollar value change in an equity portfolio. See **delta.**

early exercise A feature of American options that allows the holder to exercise an option at any time prior to the expiration date.

edge (1) The spread between the bid and ask price. This is called the *trader's edge*. (2) The difference between the market price of an option and its theoretical value using an option pricing model. This is called the *theoretical edge*.

equity option An option on a common stock.

equity In a margin account, this is the difference between the securities owned and the margin loans owed. It is the amount the investor would keep after all positions have closed out and all margin loans paid off.

equivalent positions Same as **synthetic positions.**

European option An option that can be exercised only on the expiration date. See **American option.**

ex-dividend date The day before which an investor must have purchased the stock in order to receive the dividend. On the ex-dividend date, the previous day's closing price is reduced by the amount of the dividend because purchasers of the stock on the ex-dividend date will not receive the dividend payment.

exercise To invoke the rights granted to the holder of an option contract. In the case of a call, the option holder buys the underlying stock from the option writer. In the case of a put, the option holder sells the underlying stock to the option writer.

exercise by exception A procedure used by the Options Clearing Corporation to exercise in-the-money options, unless specifically instructed by the holder of the option not to do so. This procedure protects the holder from losing the intrinsic value of the option because of failure to exercise. Unless instructed not to do so, the Options Clearing Corporation will exercise all equity options of 75 cents or more in-the-money in customer accounts, and 25 cents or more in firm and market maker accounts. For index options subject to cash settlements, the Options Clearing Corporation, unless instructed not to do so, will exercise all index options 25 cents or more in-the-money in customer accounts, and a penny or more in firm and market maker accounts.

exercise limits   The total number of puts and/or calls that a holder is allowed to exercise during any five consecutive trading days.

exercise price   The price at which the holder of an option can purchase (call) or sell (put) the underlying stock from or to the option writer.

exercise cycle   See **cycle.**

expiration date   The date on which an option and the right to exercise cease to exist.

extrinsic value   Same as **time value.**

fair value   A price that favors neither buyer nor seller. In the case of options, this term is often used to describe the theoretical price of an option derived from a mathematical formula.

fence   A strategy involving a long call and a short put, or a short call and long put at different strike prices with the same expiration date. When this strategy is established in conjunction with the underlying stock, the three-sided tactic is called a *risk conversion* (long stock) or a *risk reversal* (short stock). This strategy is also called a *combination.* See **conversion** and **reverse conversion.**

floor broker   A trader on an exchange floor who executes trading orders for other people.

floor trader   An exchange member on the trading floor who buys and sells for his own account and therefore functions as a market maker.

frontrunning   An illegal securities transaction based on prior nonpublic knowledge of a forthcoming transaction that will affect the price of a stock.

fundamental analysis   A method of predicting stock prices based on the study of earnings, sales, dividends, and so on.

fungibility   Interchangeability resulting from standardization. Options listed on national exchanges are fungible, while over-the-counter options generally are not.

futures contract   A contract calling for the delivery of a specific quantity of a physical good or a financial instrument (or the cash value), at some specific date in the future. There are exchange traded futures contracts with standardized terms, and there are over-the-counter futures contracts with negotiated terms.

gamma   A measure of the rate of change in an option's delta for a one-unit change in the price of the underlying security. See **delta.**

good-until-cancelled (GTC) order   A type of limit trading order that remains in effect until it is either executed (filled) or cancelled, as opposed to a day order, which expires if not executed by the end of the trading day.

grantor   Same as **writer.**

guts   The purchase (or sale) of both an in-the-money call and an in-the-money put. A box spread can be viewed as the combination of an in-the-money strangle and an out-of-the-money strangle. To differentiate between these two strangles, the term *guts* refers to the in-the-money strangle. See **box spread** and **strangle.**

haircut   Similar to margin required of public customers, this term refers to the equity required of floor traders on equity option exchanges. Generally, one of the advantages of being a floor trader is that the haircut is less than margin requirements for public customers.

hedge   A position established with the specific intent of protecting an existing position. Example: an owner of common stock buys a put option to hedge against a possible stock price decline.

hedge ratio   Same as **delta.**

holder   The owner of a long stock or option.

horizontal spread   Same as **time spread.**

implied volatility   The volatility percentage that justifies an option's price, as opposed to historical volatility, which is a measure of actual stock price changes over a specific period of time.

index   A compilation of several stock prices into a single number. Example: the S&P 100 Index.

index option   An option whose underlying entity is an index. Generally, index options are cash-settled.

institution   A professional investment management company. Typically, this term is used to describe large money managers such as banks, pension funds, mutual funds, and insurance companies.

intermarket spread   A strategy involving opposing positions in securities related to two different underlying entities. Example: long OEX calls and short SPX calls.

in-the-money   An adjective used to describe an option with intrinsic value. A call option is in-the-money if the stock price is above the strike price. A put option is in-the-money if the stock price is below the strike price.

intrinsic value   The in-the-money portion of an option's price. See **in-the-money.**

iron butterfly   An option strategy with limited risk and limited profit potential that involves both a long (or short) straddle, and a short (or long) strangle.

jelly roll spread   A long call and short put with the same strike price in one month, and a short call and long put with the identical strike in another month. This is the combination of synthetic long and short positions in different months. Generally only floor traders use this spread.

kappa   Same as **vega.**

last trading day   The last business day prior to expiration during which purchases and sales of an option can be made. For equity options, this is generally the third Friday of expiration month. For other types of options, the specification of the last trading day varies greatly.

leg   A term describing one side of a position with two or more sides. When a trader *legs into* a spread, he establishes one side first, hoping for a favorable price movement so the other side can be executed at a better price. This is, of course, a risk-oriented method of establishing a spread position.

leverage   A term describing the greater percentage of profit or loss potential when a given amount of money controls a security with a much larger face value. For example, a call option enables the holder to assume the upside potential of 100 shares of stock by investing a much smaller amount than that required to buy the stock. If the stock increases by 10 percent, for example, the option can double in value. Conversely, a 10 percent stock price decline can result in the total loss of the purchase price of the option.

limit order   A trading order placed with a broker to buy or sell a security at a specific price.

liquid market   A trading environment characterized by high trading volume, a narrow spread between the bid and ask, and the ability to trade larger sized orders without significant price changes.

listed option   A put or call traded on a national option exchange with standardized terms. In contrast, over-the-counter options usually have non-standard or negotiated terms.

local   A floor trader on a futures exchange who buys and sells for his own account, thus fulfilling the same role as a market maker on an options exchange.

long position   A term used to describe either (1) an open position that is expected to benefit from a rise in the price of the underlying stock such as long call, short put, or long stock; or (2) an open position resulting from an opening purchase transaction such as *long call, long put,* or *long stock.*

margin   The minimum equity required to support an investment position. To buy *on margin* refers to borrowing part of the purchase price of a security from a brokerage firm.

market basket   A group of common stocks whose price movement is expected to closely correlate with an index.

market maker   An exchange member on the trading floor who buys and sells for his own account and who has the responsibility of making bids and offers and maintaining a fair and orderly market.

market maker system   A method of supplying liquidity in options markets by having market makers in competition with one another.

mark-to-market   An accounting process by which the price of securities held in an account are valued each day to reflect the last sale price or market quote if the last sale is outside of the market quote. The result of this process is that the equity in an account is updated daily to properly reflect current security prices.

market-not-held-order   A type of market order which allows the investor to give discretion to the floor broker regarding the time and price at which a trade is executed.

market quote   A trading instruction from an investor to a broker to immediately buy or sell a security at the best available price.

married put strategy   The simultaneous purchase of stock and the corresponding number of put options. This is a limited risk strategy during the life of the puts because the stock can be sold at the strike price of the puts.

mixed spread   A term used loosely to describe a trading position that does not fit neatly into a standard spread category.

model   A mathematical formula used to calculate the theoretical value of an option. See **Black-Scholes model.**

naked option   Same as **uncovered option.**

net order   Same as **contingency order.**

net margin requirement   The equity required in a margin account to support an option position after deducting the premium received from sold options.

neutral   An adjective describing the belief that a stock or the market in general will neither rise nor decline significantly.

90/10 strategy   An option strategy in which an investor buys Treasury bills (or other liquid assets) with 90 percent of his funds—and buys call options with the balance.

non-equity option   Any option that does not have common stock as the underlying asset. Nonequity options include options on futures, indexes, interest rate composites, physicals, and so on.

nonsystematic risk   The portion of total risk that can be attributed to the particular firm. See **systematic risk.**

not-held order   A type of order which allows the investor to release the floor broker from the normal obligations implied by the other terms of the order. For example, a limit order designated as ''not-held'' allows the floor broker to use his discretion in filling the order when the market trades at the limit price of the order. In this case, the floor broker is not obligated to provide the customer with an execution if the market trades through the limit price on the order. See **discretion.** See **market-not-held order.**

OTC option   An over-the-counter-option is one which is traded in the over-the-counter market. OTC options are not usually listed on an options exchange and generally do not have standardized terms.

omega   Same as **vega**.

opening rotation   See **trading rotation**.

opening transaction   An addition to or creation of a trading position. An opening purchase transaction adds long options (or long securities) to an investor's total position, and an opening sell transaction adds short options (or short securities).

open interest   The total number of existing option contracts.

open outcry   The trading method by which competing market makers make bids and offers on the trading floor.

option   A contract that gives the buyer the right, but not the obligation, to buy or sell a particular asset (the underlying security) at a fixed price for a specific period of time. The contract also obligates the seller to meet the terms of delivery if the contract right is exercised by the buyer.

option period   The time from when an option contract is created to the expiration date.

option pricing curve   A graphical representation of the estimated theoretical value of an option at one point in time, at various prices of the underlying asset.

optionable stock   A stock on which options are traded.

Options Clearing Corporation (OCC)   A corporation owned by the exchanges that trade listed stock options, OCC is an intermediary between option buyers and sellers. OCC issues and guarantees all option contracts.

option valuation model   See **model**.

option writer   The seller of an option contract who is obligated to meet the terms of delivery if the option holder exercises his right.

order book official   An exchange employee in charge of keeping the public order book and executing the orders therein.

out-of-the-money   An adjective used to describe an option that has no intrinsic value, i.e., all of its value consists of time value. A call option is out-of-the-money if the stock price is below the strike price. A put option is out-of-the-money if the stock price is above the strike price. See **intrinsic value** and **time value.**

overwrite   An option strategy involving the sale of a call option against an existing long stock position. This is different from the covered-write strategy which involves the simultaneous purchase of stock and sale of a call.

over-the-counter-option   Same as **OTC option.**

overvalued   An adjective used to describe an option that is trading at a price higher than its theoretical value. It must be remembered that this is a subjective evaluation, because theoretical value depends on one subjective input—the volatility estimate.

parity An adjective used to describe the difference between the stock price and the strike price of an in-the-money option. When an option is trading at its intrinsic value, it is said to be *trading at parity*.

physical option An option whose underlying entity is a physical good or commodity. For example, currency options traded at the Philadelphia Exchange and many OTC currency options are options on the currency itself, rather than on futures contracts.

pin risk The risk to a floor trader with a conversion or reversal position that the stock price will exactly equal the strike price at option expiration. The trader will not know how many of his long options to exercise because he will not know how many of his short options will be assigned. The risk is that on the following Monday he will have a long or short stock position and thus be subject to the risk of an adverse price move.

pit Same as **trading pit.**

position The combined total of an investor's open option contracts and long or short stock.

position limits The maximum number of open option contracts that an investor can hold in one account or a group of related accounts. Some exchanges express the limit in terms of option contracts on the same side of the market, and others express it in terms of total long or short delta.

position trading An investing strategy in which open positions are held for an extended period of time.

premium (1) Total price of an option: intrinsic value plus time value. (2) Often this word is used to mean the same as **time value.**

primary market (1)For securities that are traded in more than one market, the primary market is usually the exchange where the most volume is traded. (2) The initial sale of securities to public investors. See **secondary market.**

profit graph A graphical presentation of the profit and loss possibilities of an investment strategy at one point in time (usually option expiration), at various stock prices.

profit profile Same as **profit graph.**

public order book The limit buy and limit sell orders from public customers which are away from the current market price and are managed by the order book official or specialist. If the market price moves so that an order in the public order book is the best bid or offer, that order has priority and must be the first one filled at that price.

put option A contract that gives the buyer the right (but not the obligation) to sell the underlying stock at some predetermined price. For the writer (or grantor) of a put option, the contract represents an obligation to buy stock from the buyer if the option is assigned.

ratio calendar combination A term used loosely to describe any variation on an investment strategy that involves both puts and calls in unequal quantities and at least two different strike prices and two different expirations.

ratio calendar spread An investment strategy in which more short-term options are sold than longer-term options are purchased.

ratio spread (1) Most commonly used to describe the purchase of near-the-money options and the sale of a greater number of farther out-of-the-money options, with all options having the same expiration date. (2) Generally used to describe any investment strategy in which options are bought and sold in unequal numbers or on a greater than one-for-one basis with the underlying stock.

ratio write An investment strategy in which stock is purchased and call options are sold on a greater than one-for-one basis.

realized gains and losses The net amount received or paid when a closing transaction is made and matched together with an opening transaction.

repair strategy An investment strategy in which an existing long stock position is supplemented by buying one in-the-money call (or one at-the-money call) and selling two out-of-the-money calls, all calls having the same expiration. The effect of this strategy is to lower the break-even point of stock ownership without significantly increasing the risk of the total position.

resistance A term used in technical analysis to describe a price area at which rising price action is expected to stop or meet increased selling activity. This analysis is based on historic price behavior of the stock.

reversal Same as **reverse conversion.**

reverse conversion An investment strategy used by professional option traders in which a short put and long call with the same strike price and expiration are combined with short stock to lock in a nearly riskless profit. The process of executing these three-sided trades is sometimes called reversal arbitrage.

rho A measure of the expected change in an option's theoretical value for a 1 percent change in interest rates.

risk arbitrage Commonly used term to describe the purchase of a stock subject to takeover rumors with the hope of selling at a significant profit to a company effecting the takeover. The risk is present because there is never any guarantee that a takeover will materialize.

risk conversion/reversal See **fence.**

rolling A trading action in which the trader simultaneously closes an open option position and creates a new option position at a different strike price, different expiration, or both. Variations of this include roll up, roll down and roll out.

rotation   See **trading rotation.**

scalper   A trader on the floor of an exchange who hopes to buy on the bid price, sell on the ask price and profit from moment to moment price movements. Risk is limited by the very short time duration (usually 10 seconds to 3 minutes) of maintaining any one position.

SEC   The Securities and Exchange Commission. The SEC is a federal government agency that regulates the securities industry.

secondary market   A market where securities are bought and sold after their initial purchase by public investors.

sequential expiration cycle   See **cycle.**

series of options   Option contracts on the same underlying stock having the same strike price and expiration month.

settlement price   The official price at the end of a trading session. This price is established by the Options Clearing Corporation and is used to determine changes in account equity, margin requirements and for other purposes. See **mark-to-market.**

short option position   The position of an option writer which represents an obligation to meet the terms of the option if it is assigned.

short position   Any open position that is expected to benefit from a decline in the price of the underlying stock such as long put, short call or short stock.

short stock position   A strategy that profits from a stock price decline. It is initiated by borrowing stock from a broker-dealer and selling it in the open market. This strategy is closed out at a later date by buying back the stock.

specialist   An exchange member whose function is to maintain a "fair and orderly" market. This is accomplished by managing the limit order book and making bids and offers for his own account in the absence of opposite market side orders.

speculator   A trader with an expectation of a particular market price behavior.

spread   A position consisting of two parts, each of which alone, would profit from opposite directional price moves. These opposite parts are entered simultaneously in the hope of (1) limiting risk, or (2) benefiting in a change of price relationship between the two.

spread order   Trading order to simultaneously make two transactions, each of which would benefit from opposite directional price moves.

standard deviation   A statistical measure. One use of the standard deviation is to measure how stock price movements are distributed about the mean.

stock index futures   A futures contract which has as its underlying entity a stock market index. Such futures contracts are generally subject to cash settlement.

stop-limit order   A type of contingency order placed with a broker that becomes a limit order when the security trades, or is bid or offered at a specific price.

stop order   A type of contingency order placed with a broker that becomes a market order when the security trades, or is bid or offered at a specified price.

straddle   A trading position involving puts and calls on a one-to-one basis in which the puts and calls have the same strike price, expiration, and underlying entity. A long straddle is when both options are owned and a short straddle is when both options are written.

strangle   A trading position involving out-of-the-money puts and calls on a one-to-one basis. The puts and calls have different strike prices, but the same expiration and underlying stock. A long strangle is when both options are owned, and a short strangle is when both options are written.

strap   A strategy involving two calls and one put. All options have the same strike price, expiration, and underlying stock.

strike price   Same as **exercise price.**

strike price interval   The normal price difference between option exercise prices. Equity options generally have $2.50 strike price intervals (if the underlying security price ranges from $10 to $25), $5.00 intervals (from $25 to $200), and $10 intervals above $200. Index options generally have $5 strike price intervals at all price levels. See **adjusted strike price.**

strip   A strategy involving two puts and one call. All options have the same strike price, expiration, and underlying stock.

suitability   A requirement that any investing strategy fall within the financial means and investment objectives of an investor.

support   A term used in technical analysis to describe a price area at which falling price action is expected to stop or meet increased buying activity. This analysis is based on previous price behavior of the stock.

synthetic position   A strategy involving two or more instruments that has the same risk-reward profile as a strategy involving only one instrument. The following list summarizes the six primary synthetic positions.

synthetic long call   A long stock position combined with a long put.

synthetic long put   A short stock position combined with a long call.

synthetic long stock   A long call position combined with a short put.

synthetic short call   A short stock position combined with a short put.

synthetic short put   A long stock position combined with a short call.

synthetic short stock   A short call position combined with a long put.

systematic risk   The portion of total risk that can be attributed to the overall market. See **nonsystematic risk.**

technical analysis   A method of predicting future stock price movements based on the study of historical market data such as the prices themselves, trading volume, open interest, the relation of advancing issues to declining issues, and short selling volume.

theoretical value   An estimated fair value of an option derived from a mathematical model.

theta   A measure of the rate of change in an option's theoretical value for a one-unit change in time to the option's expiration date. See **time decay.**

tick   (1) The smallest unit price change allowed in trading a security. For a common stock, this is generally 1/8th point. For an option under $3 in price, this is generally 1/16th point. For an option over $3, this is generally 1/8th point. (2) The net number of stocks upticking or down ticking. For example, if there are 10 stocks total with 7 having traded on upticks and 3 having traded on downticks, then the tick is + 4.

time decay   A term used to describe how the theoretical value of an option "erodes" or reduces with the passage of time. Time decay is specifically quantified by theta. See **theta.**

time spread   An option strategy most commonly used by floor traders which involves options with the same strike price, but different expiration dates.

time value   The part of an option's total price that exceeds intrinsic value. The price of an out-of-the-money option consists entirely of time value. See **intrinsic value** and **out-of-the-money.**

trader   (1) Any investor who makes frequent purchases and sales. (2) A member of an exchange who conducts his buying and selling on the trading floor of the exchange.

trading pit   A specific location on the trading floor of an exchange designated for the trading of a specific security.

trading rotation   A trading procedure on exchange floors in which bids and offers are made on specific options in a sequential order. Opening trading rotations are conducted to guarantee all entitled public orders an execution. At times of extreme market activity, a closing trading rotation can also be conducted.

traditional expiration cycle   See **cycle.**

transaction costs   All of the charges associated with executing a trade and maintaining a position. These include brokerage commissions, exchange fees, and margin interest. The spread between bid and ask is sometimes taken into account as a transaction cost.

Treasury bill option strategy Same as **90/10 strategy.**

type of options The classification of an option contract as either a put or call.

uncovered option A short option position that is not fully collateralized if notification of assignment is received. A short call position is uncovered if the writer does not have a long stock position to deliver. A short put position is uncovered if the writer does not have the financial resources in his account to buy the stock.

underlying security The asset that can be purchased or sold according to the terms of the option contract.

undervalued An adjective used to describe an option that is trading at a price lower than its theoretical value. It must be remembered that this is a subjective evaluation because theoretical value depends on one subjective input—the volatility estimate.

unsystematic risk Same as **nonsystematic risk.**

upstairs trader A professional trader who makes trading decisions away from the exchange floor and communicates his instructions to the floor for execution by the floor broker.

vega A measure of the rate of change in an option's theoretical value for a one-unit change in the volatility assumption.

vertical spread (1) Most commonly used to describe the purchase of one option and sale of another where both are of the same type and same expiration, but have different strike prices. (2) It is also used to describe a delta neutral spread in which more options are sold than are purchased.

volatility A measure of stock price fluctuation. Mathematically, volatility is the annualized standard deviation of daily returns.

volatility test A procedure in which a multisided options position is evaluated, assuming several different volatilities for the purpose of judging the risk of the position.

unit of trading The minimum quantity or amount allowed when trading a security. The normal minimum for common stock is 1 round lot or 100 shares. The normal minimum for options is one contract (which covers 100 shares of stock).

wasting asset An investment with a finite life, the value of which decreases over time if there is no price fluctuation in the underlying asset.

write To sell an option. An investor who sells an option is called the writer, regardless of whether the option is covered or uncovered.

INDEX